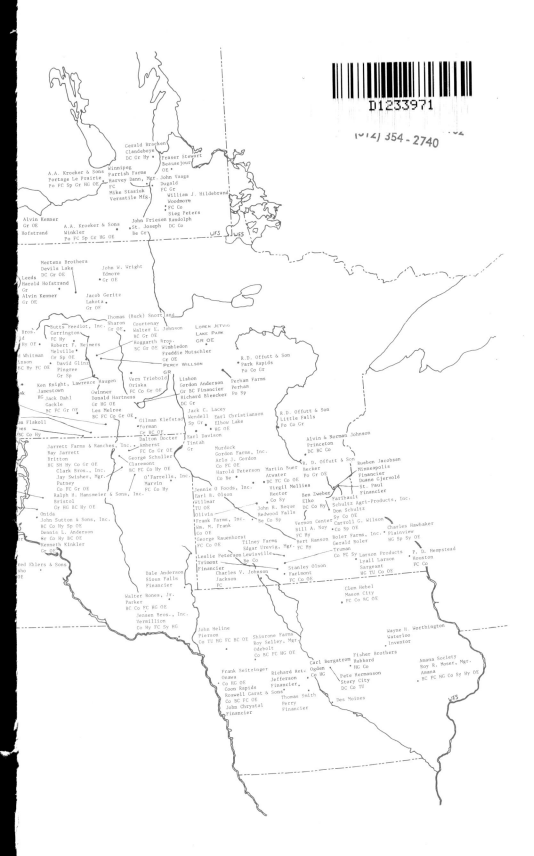

Tomorrow's Harvest

By the same author:

THE DAY OF THE BONANZA

and

THE CHALLENGE OF THE PRAIRIE

Published by
The North Dakota Institute for Regional Studies
Fargo, North Dakota

Also

BEYOND THE FURROW

Published by
The Interstate Printers & Publishers, Inc.
Danville, Illinois

Tomorrow's Harvest

Thoughts and Opinions of Successful Farmers

HIRAM M. DRACHE

Concordia College

THE INTERSTATE PRINTERS & PUBLISHERS, INC.
Danville, Illinois

Dedication

TO THE WIFE OF THE SUCCESSFUL FARMER,

who will continue to be a major key
to progressive farming,
just as she has been in the past

ABOUT THE BOOK

This book is modern farming as experienced by the business-minded, modern, progressive, family-oriented farmer. It is future-shock farming for those whose sentiments are still in another era. It is farming in the twentieth century as it has come about because of constant pressures by the consumer for ever cheaper food.

The social pangs of an overexpanded agriculture are nearly gone. The human suffering that took place because of that phase of our history was not in vain, for it helped to make America the great nation that it is. But there are those who would like to turn back the clock. Today the threat of social legislation against progressive family farming is mounting. This book attempts to portray to the consumers the blessings derived from modern agriculture, for in the end it is they who will pay the bill. What type of agriculture will they be willing to pay for? The choice is theirs.

ABOUT THE COVER

David Behlke, a former student of the author and now Chairman of the Art Department at Valley City (North Dakota) State College, read the manuscript and used his imagination to portray what he thinks the book says. Mr. Behlke used a farmer's wife who is a student in his class for the focal point of his picture. The farmer indicates a man of strength, and the modern house with three generations in the foreground are "what it is all about." The crops and soil depict what was promised in Genesis VIII:22.

Foreword

AMERICAN AGRICULTURE has witnessed a series of events which have influenced the development of a system of food production envied throughout the world. As one reviews American history, it is quite obvious that agriculture has played a vital part in establishing the social and economic system we know today in the United States. In many quarters there is much discussion about the role of the family farm and whether it can survive. The author, Hi Drache, in this his fourth book, once again brings to his reader the drama and excitement that has made American agriculture a great adventure. He compares some of today's modern pioneers with those of the bonanza farms of the late 1800's and early 1900's. He calls attention to the important interrelationships between the man on the farm and the industry that supports modern agriculture.

An often misquoted statistic has to do with the place of American agriculture in the total work force of the United States. Very often the figure of 4 per cent is used for that portion of the work force in agriculture, but that figure makes reference only to persons on the land. The input and output industry, plus production agriculture, makes up the total of agricultural business, which on a national basis accounts for about 28 per cent of the work force. This interesting statistic has changed little over the last 50 years. The labor movement has been away from farm production and into the service aspect of agriculture. Some predict that by the year 2000, instead of 6 or 7 people servicing each individual on the land, as is the case today, there will be 10 or 12. This will be part of tomorrow's harvest.

This book comes at a time when the world is challenged by tremendous population pressure, especially in the developing nations; at a time when those nations are attempting to gain a place under the sun; and at a time when they recognize the need to provide more and better food supplies for their current and future populations. The successes that have been experienced by American agriculture may not be transplanted directly to the developing nations, but certainly adaptation of some of the technology can be and has been extremely useful. The development of new seeds for many crops and the development of cultural practices so essential in bringing together all of the production inputs for a successful harvest need to be at the forefront of research and education, as well as in the mind of the practicing farmer as he looks at his own developing farm business.

The major question lying behind this book is whether tomorrow's harvest can be as successful as the harvests we have known in the recent past. Many constraints external to the farm and industry seem to be impeding agricultural production. It seems that at times we "tilt with windmills," as exemplified by the fact that farm size is a main criterion in preserving American agriculture and the family farm. We must do more than maintain the present system. To do less is a step backward. Many laws have created restrictions and a bureaucratic policy that make it almost impossible for farmers to make the business of agriculture profitable. And yet, as Dr. Drache's three previous books have indicated, throughout American history agriculture has somehow weathered the adversities of flood, drought, pestilence, poor markets, and the many vagaries that make one wonder how this industry survives.

Those individuals in American agriculture today who have developed their farms into businesses have also developed an outstanding way of life. Tomorrow's harvest then provides a major challenge to those of us who are willing to think through carefully the author's message concerning what may lie ahead in agriculture in future years and what role we should assume in seeing that American agriculture prospers in the decades ahead so that it is the shining light for a hungry world.

WILLIAM F. HUEG, JR.
Deputy Vice President and Dean
Agriculture, Forestry, and Home Economics
University of Minnesota
St. Paul, Minnesota

Preface

A PREFACE gives the author an opportunity to inform prospective readers what the book is about. This volume, my fourth on American agriculture, is in some respects a sequel to *Beyond the Furrow*. That book provides the historical setting for this book, which is a look at current and future American and European agricultural potentials based chiefly on interviews with progressive, innovative farmers. This is not a history of agriculture; it is a survey of what leading farmers and their wives think of their business and its future.

It is the opinion of these farmers, just as well as mine, that the goal of agriculture should be to provide an abundant supply of food to American and world consumers at the lowest possible cost. This goal must provide adequate returns to labor, management, and investment for the farmers who operate sound, viable, efficient economic units. These units are those generally found in Class I and Class II Census categories and include only about 500,000 farmers in America. There are about 2,500,000 farmers in the nation, but a major portion of those with smaller units derive the bulk of their income from non-farm sources. If you are in agreement with this basic goal, read on, because the account that follows describes how innovative, progressive, family-oriented farming has fulfilled and will continue to fulfill that goal.

On the other hand, if you believe that our nation, Canada, and Europe should perpetuate the traditional Jeffersonian agrarian myth and maintain small uneconomic units in agriculture in modern times, you will be uneasy as you read the following pages. If you believe that the goal of agriculture should be to serve as a social welfare institution and thereby provide support for the greatest possible number of people, you will be unhappy with this story. But if that is your belief, then you must ask yourself if you are willing to pay out a far greater share of your income for food and if you are willing to deny the hungry people of the world access to what was and still is low-cost American food.

The European society has long paid a great price for maintaining its small-farm peasant-oriented agriculture. But times are changing rapidly; and since World War II, Europe has awakened to the fact that fragmented peasant agriculture is an expensive luxury. Europe has realized that providing high supports to small farmers while restricting larger farmers stagnates agriculture and in the long run increases the cost of food. Even though European politicians have hesitated to admit it publicly, they have come to realize that food costs can be reduced and the farmer's income can be improved best through the process of restructuring agriculture into viable economic farm units. The number of farms and farm workers will continue to be reduced by legislative action. Europe has discovered that total production in agriculture has risen as the remaining more progressive farmers have been able to make better use of technology. Those who have left the farm have been absorbed into industry, and the total society has profited.

North American farmers,* in a sense, have paid dearly for an overexpanded agricultural base, but because we were not as tradition-bound as Europe's farmers, we have let economics determine the direction. The number of farms and farm workers has been reduced greatly since its peak around 1920. But the nation has benefited from that movement through an ever-increasing supply of food at relatively decreasing costs. Our nation has the option of letting this natural economic process continue as technology directs an ever-improving agricultural base. In that case, our agricultural potential is far from reaching its capacity. Surpluses under that free style of agriculture will continue to be the greatest threat to the profitability of the efficient family farm. But, I suspect, in the future, as has been true in the past, the dedicated adaptable family enterprise will make the necessary adjustments for survival.

There is the other socio-economic option that some farm organizations, some politicians, and many people with good intentions but little real understanding of agriculture would like to have us take. That option would restrict farm size through various regulations and laws, including negative taxation processes. Such legislation, which has popular appeal, touches the sentiments of many

---

*When the term "North American" is used, I am referring to both Canada and the United States, because their agricultural patterns have been so similar.

but makes poor economic sense. This writer fears that such unwise legislation may be enacted because the American (and Canadian) populace basically fails to appreciate that an unrestricted agriculture has been a blessing and has been a key to the progress our nation has made. The American public ought to remind itself that the countries of the world that have the least economic and social progress are those where primitive peasant-oriented agriculture predominates.

Dr. Vernon W. Ruttan explains, "The process of growth in agriculture, in a progressive economy with rising real wage rates, is one of education, technology, capital, and shifting surplus workers to other production which enables total social growth." Social progress comes when members of each successive generation are capable of doing more than their fathers. I hope that this volume will shed some light on why we ought not tamper with the phenomenon that has proven to be one of the greatest events of social progress mankind has ever experienced.

HIRAM M. DRACHE
Professor of History
Concordia College
Moorhead, Minnesota

Acknowledgments

A<small>NY</small> <small>BOOK</small> is the result of the joint effort of many individuals. Four students of Concordia College who earned part of their college expenses by gathering data, typing, and cataloguing materials were Barbara Carriere Holmquist, Laurie Nornes, Julie Hanson, and Cindy Williams. They learned about agriculture and lightened the burden by doing many basic jobs. Thanks to you jolly, willing workers.

Farm owner, Assistant Professor of English, Director of the Concentrated Approach Program, and co-author of a series of books on vocabulary teaching methods, Howard Peet again served as grammarian and stylist. Friend Howie has the knack and qualifications to give the added touch necessary to keep the reader interested.

The supportive attitude of the administration of Concordia College and the cooperation of fellow members of the History Department of the college helped to create the excellent atmosphere conducive to writing. Dr. Verlyn Anderson and his efficient staff at the Concordia Library were always able to produce requested documents and sources. The Tri-College Library advantages quickly became apparent when indepth projects called for help.

The late Oswald Daellenbach developed many of the pictures, as he had done for my three previous books. He looked forward to retirement, when he would be able to spend more time on such projects, as well as share his agricultural expertise. We have missed him, but, fortunately, our son David Drache has Ozzie's patience, so necessary in order to develop fine prints.

The maps were developed by graduate student William Shirk under the direction of Dr. Warren Kress of North Dakota State University.

Much advice has been obtained and much insight gained through conversations and correspondence with members of the

xiii

staffs of various agricultural departments of several midwestern and two Canadian universities.

For the fourth time Dr. Leo Hertel has served as editor. His breadth of knowledge and understanding of human nature are great assets. Professor Hertel consistently knew when to replace a harsh word with a more pleasant one without lessening the impact of the sentence. For that, the reader should be grateful. The conversations over tea while editing have taught me much.

Son Paul, who manages the farm, and wife Ada, who does every job that no one else can do, have both lightened the burden. Because they are closest to the writing room they know that writers can be grumpy.

About 250 farm families or individuals in agri-business have contributed directly to this book through the information that they offered in interviews and correspondence. Many of them have since become close friends and have flattered me by acknowledging that their being interviewed has enhanced their farming business because of the insights gained through answering questions about themselves. The experiences of being in the homes and offices of these farmers in Canada, in eight countries of Europe, and in the United States have provided an excellent education in the hows and whys of agriculture. The strength of these people made it clear that the future of agriculture lies with the dedicated family team. Unfortunately, the future will be no less difficult than the past has been, and in some respects, the tensions may be greater.

HIRAM M. DRACHE

Table of Contents

Tomorrow's Harvest

CHAPTER I

An Introduction

W<small>HEN THIS BOOK</small> was originally planned, the proposed theme was to establish to what degree technology had been responsible for the recent dynamic changes in agriculture. Technology is machinery, chemicals, energy, computers, and all that is associated with them. To that must be added land, labor, capital, and management. The result is modern agriculture.

To do this an author must have an open mind. He must be willing to let the facts found in research dictate the theme of the book. Data gathered from interviews, however, led far afield from the pure theory related to technology in action. Surprisingly, research pointed to a single factor controlling the lives of the farmers encountered—personal motivation.

Personal motivation, positive mental attitude, and sheer determination have been strong factors in the success of American agriculture. Much has been written about homesteading on the frontier and its related hardships. One can only surmise as to the real cost of opening the frontier in terms of blood, sweat, toil, and financial ruin.

The farmers of the pre-electrified, pre-mechanized era are generally not as fascinated by the romance of shocking corn or grain, picking potatoes, building straw piles, hand milking cows, or chopping wood as are the poets and artists who delight in portraying those nostalgic days. It is virtually impossible to find a person who has previously performed those tasks who would like to go back to the "good old days." But it is not difficult to find twentieth century Americans who advocate perpetuation of the "homestead-type" farm. The paradox is ironic.*

---

*For an excellent personal touching story of pre-electrified, pre-mechanized agriculture, see Carl Hamilton's *In No Time at All*, Ames, Iowa: Iowa State University Press, 1974.

3

The homesteading era, which produced the opening of the frontier, was responsible for the rapid expansion of American agriculture and ably supported the nation's developing industrial economy. Although Americans are nostalgic about that era, we must ask ourselves: Did the homestead pay a fair return to capital and labor? How many homesteads succeeded, even when the family dug in, denied itself a decent living, and refused to quit? Can we, as a nation, afford that type of agriculture in the future?

Historically, agriculture has been one of the least profitable industries. It is only because of land appreciation that many farmers of the past have been able to afford retirement. At the same time, however, our over-expanded agricultural base with its resultant abundance of cheap food has been a boon to the American society. The irony of this situation is that in our modern, urban society, people are either unaware or uninformed that the cost of food nationally is only 16.8 per cent of their take-home pay. The consumer attitude, together with the traditional cheap food policy of our government, exerts a pressure on the American farmer that will be as great or greater in the future than it has been in the past.

The very nature of the free enterprise system will force continued innovation, mechanization, and consolidation of farms at an ever faster pace. This bodes ill for the progressive farmer as well as for those who persist in perpetuating the myth of the homestead. But the family-oriented and family-managed farm will endure for the foreseeable future. However, it will be far different from the romantic picture of a traditional farm of the past. History does not concern itself with sentiment, and it is but a matter of time before the remnants of that nostalgic era will be found only in books and museums.

The Five *M*'s

Some of the elements that enabled farms of the past to survive and even to prosper depend upon human qualities which are still found in the men and women living on today's farms. Five basic essentials appear to be responsible for the accomplishment of our more prosperous farmers. The formula for successful farming can be exemplified by the Five *M*'s. These Five *M*'s will be a surprise to many; some will disagree with them; some will regard them as out of order; but others will support them. In some respects, the Five *M*'s may be as unrealistic as the distorted image of a conventional farm. But they have evolved from evidence gathered through interviews, research, and a lifetime of contacts with successful farm families. Listed in the order of their importance to a successful, commercialized, industrialized, family-oriented farm, they are: *Mate, Motivation, Management, Money,* and *Mechanization.*

Anyone working and living with farmers fully appreciates the significance of the *Mate's* role in the typical operation. It is true that there are farms that have succeeded without any contribution from a woman, but these farms are a small minority of the total. This does not imply that bachelors, corporations, or even farm families where the female might be a negative factor cannot succeed, for there are exceptions to every rule.

Nevertheless, the history of American agriculture, to a great extent, has centered around the family unit. Women as partners bore a greater burden during the homestead era than did the men. Apparently, they are still extremely essential in modern agriculture, and the wives of nearly all of the farmers interviewed for *Beyond the Furrow* and this book were also participants. Frequently, during these interviews the husband turned to the wife for an answer, and in many cases she had the more profound or the only answer to some of the questions.

The interviewing process clearly demonstrated the important role of the wife on these successful farms. Even on farms that had absentee owners with professional managers, the managers' wives were found to be influential in some of the decision making, and they were totally involved in the mental processes of management.

The second most important *M* is *motivation*, which to a great extent shows up in the teamwork of the farm family. This teamwork is expressed in a strong desire for successful farming. Motivation shows itself in the eagerness to create and produce in partnership with nature. Great satisfaction is derived from knowing that you are providing abundant food for the family and mankind. The concept of building and working for the next generation is often the strongest form of motivation.

A properly motivated family understands the need to reduce spending in adverse times, the need to buy a machine rather than a luxury, the need to work 12 hours or more a day during critical periods, or the need for a vacation. The wife may work off the farm to generate cash flow in the early years of the enterprise, or she may fully immerse herself in the farming operation to eliminate or reduce the need for hiring outside labor. The farm wife who keeps the accounts, writes the checks, runs the errands, does the telephoning, commands the central radio base, and drives a truck during peak-labor loads is commonplace and vital to the team. But as important, if not more important than this, is the motivational contribution of the farm wife toward her husband and her family.

Motivation creates a desire for good *management*, a key element in the capital- and management-oriented agriculture of this industrial age. Some management traits are instinctive; some are learned. However, all can be improved with the proper motivation. Most of the farmers involved in this study agreed that it was during periods of adversity that they learned to do their best managing. An interesting aspect of their management was the fairly extensive use of consultants hired either on a retainer or on a piece-work basis. This factor links directly to the willingness of the more innovative person to accept the knowledge of others and to incorporate it into his management program. There is also much evidence of correlating improved net profits with the use of consultants.

Money is the fourth important element in capital-management-oriented agriculture. Many farmers never have enough money; many others have an adequate or even abundant supply. It is no secret that American agriculture as an industry is in a financially good position, for it has less than 17 cents of liability for each 100 cents of assets. Unfortunately, the surplus funds are not always available to those who need them most, particularly the young farmer who is trying to build a farm.

A common complaint heard in rural areas is that it is impossible for young couples to start farming. But before any couple should give up their efforts, they should ask themselves if it was any easier a century ago. Each year, local, regional, and national contests of outstanding young farmers provide an excellent example of young couples who had the desire to farm and succeeded.

Money, then, is not a problem for agriculture as a whole, but it is a problem for individuals who do not have the records, the cash flow, the profit potential, or the management ability to command and manage the funds that are available. Outstanding farmers are often more concerned with the ease with which funds can be secured than with the lack of money. Many agricultural loan officers recognize the importance of the woman in farm financing. Since she is generally involved in the management, loan officers often insist that the wife participate in major financial ventures. In some operations she may be responsible for much of the financing.

One basic problem related to money is a psychological trait best described as risk aversion. Many farmers and farmers' wives have a great fear of using credit beyond a preconceived limit. They are unable to accept the fact that industrialized, commercialized agriculture has intense demands for capital. Without a source of adequate capital, borrowed or otherwise attained, there is little chance for success in a modern, low-margin, high-volume-oriented farm business. If risk aversion is a problem for the farmer and his wife, they will quite likely find themselves living on a subsistence unit, or accepting full-time off-the-farm work to maintain a living from a substandard farm operation.

Mechanization is the fifth *M* and the one given the lowest priority in the success of any individual, even though it may have the greatest economic impact. Mechanization, in the context of this chapter, implies chemicals, hybrid seeds, fertilizers, computers, radios, teletypes, mechanical and electrical power, automation, large-scale machinery, science, and technology. These inputs are the contributions of the very large agri-business industry and have been a major factor in the dynamism of today's agriculture in America. If the other *M*'s are accepted, this step becomes inevitable because without mechanization a farmer is not competitive, nor can he survive as a commercial farmer. Nevertheless, mechanization can also be the economic death sentence to a farmer if he is not able to fully utilize large equipment even though he is able to buy it. Thus, mechanization becomes the first step in a negative cash flow that leads to eventual failure. A high machinery investment per acre, however, is not necessarily undesirable, for many of the most intensely mechanized farms are also among the most profitable. One reason is that mechanization is the modern farmer's way of substituting capital for labor. He has no alternative, for the cost of labor in relation to its productivity when compared to purchased technology is extremely high.*

---

*An outstanding example of what technology has done for the American farmer—hence, for the consumer, who is always the ultimate benefactor—is found in the case of herbicide application on corn to control weeds. It takes 38,000 kilocalories of energy to manufacture and apply atrazine for weed control on one acre of corn. To cultivate that same acre for weed control would require 56,000 kilocalories of energy. Hand hoeing that acre twice would require only 33,000 kilocalories of energy.

The hand hoeing appears to be the most efficient. However, assuming a 71-million-acre corn crop and 60 hours of labor to hoe an acre twice, a total of 4.468 billion hours of labor would be required in a six-week period. That would mean about 17.7 million workers in agriculture that now has just over 4 million full-time laborers. Or, the 4.468 billion hours can be contrasted to about 9 billion hours total annual input of all agricultural workers.

Dr. Nalewaja, author of the above information, defends the use of non-human energy in agriculture in general and in weed control specifically by putting the facts in proper perspective: "With no energy input the efficiency would be infinite, but the world could only support 10 million people."[1]

A sixth *M*, *marketing*, could very well fit into the theme of *M*'s, for most of the farmers involved in this study were astute marketers. In fact, many of them spent more time in marketing than they did in any other phase of their operation. It was the consensus of these farmers that it was easy to hire management and labor for production because many individuals were trained to excel in production, and a large number of good farmers were doing so. Marketing took great personal effort and apparently was a function not as appealing as producing. A large portion of these farmers were involved in direct marketing and purchasing. Because of their large volume and personal efforts, they received premiums and discounts respectively, which enhanced their profit margins considerably.

The Five *M*'s provide a theme for successful commercialized, industrialized, family-oriented agriculture. Under this system the farm is far different from the traditional family farm, but it is still largely family-oriented.

Closing the Frontier

To provide the reader with information about some of the people who are referred to in this book, the following topics will summarize the content of one of the writer's previous books, *Beyond the Furrow: Some Keys to Successful Farming in the Twentieth Century*.[2] *Beyond the Furrow* contains the histories of a select group of farmers in the states of Iowa, Minnesota, Montana, North Dakota, South Dakota, and the province of Manitoba. These accounts deal with second and third generation farmers, or with homesteaders who were part of the closing of the agricultural frontier. Historically, that was not long ago, for much of Montana, the Dakotas, and Manitoba was not settled until the era just prior to World War I.

M. L. Wilson, noted Montana agriculturalist and later Under Secretary of Agriculture, surveyed Montana in the 1920's to determine why some homesteaders were able to survive drought and low prices while the great majority of their neighbors failed. Wilson's principal finding was that the survivors had farms that were nearly twice the state's average. On the other hand, he determined that a very large portion of those who failed had not been farmers prior to homesteading in the state and were not prepared for the hardships they encountered.

Charles and Jessie Grant are a good example of a farm family who came to Montana, suffered reversals, but never quit. The

Grants simply moved to another location in the state after their first four years of homesteading in the "Big Dry" ended in failure. They moved from farm to farm in northeastern Montana and through persistence and innovation, and by farming on a larger scale than average, eventually succeeded. In retrospect, Grant says that it was his wife, Jessie, plus management and innovation that were the keys to better days.

F. A. Gummer and Fred Romain, two farmers in north central Montana, had experiences not unlike those of the Grants. Both had jobs off the farm to maintain cash flow when the land yielded little or no income. They suffered and they lost, but they never quit. This was not the case with their neighbors, however, for 68 out of 100 gave up and left Gummer's mail route between 1914 and 1945. The evidence of some of the suffering caused by an expanded agricultural base is not often as apparent as in Montana, one of the last farm frontiers. The time between settlement and failure was frequently only two or three years.

Fingal Enger, Tom Thompson, L. B. Garnaas, Percy Willson, and Oscar N. Sabe are all examples of newcomers to North Dakota at the turn of the century who came, endured, survived, and succeeded. Enger built the largest farm of any of the above, amassing nearly a township of land between 1874 and 1913. He knew how to manage people and money and how to survive the obstacles of drought and low prices.

The Sabe farm has passed through three generations. It has survived by careful management of money and land resources plus the diligent work of family members. The original 160-acre homestead has expanded to a total operation of 2,580 acres plus a thirty-fold increase in livestock numbers during these first 67 years.

The Tractor

The closing of the frontier by homesteaders coincided with the advent of the next era in American agriculture—that of the tractor. Mechanical power to pull more efficient machines and to reduce the cost of production proved to be the big innovation for farming in the second, third, and fourth decades of the twentieth century.

The tractor was not an unmixed blessing to American farmers, however. Although it was a far more efficient and less costly source of power than the horse, it compounded existing problems. Each new tractor replaced about four horses. This freed land from producing horse feed to producing cash crops. Increased production came at a time when the market was already suffering from surpluses. This further reduced already low farm prices, which depressed land values that had inflated rapidly during World War I. This caused a serious loss of equity to many farmers. Lower prices for horses because of the adoption of the tractor caused an additional decline in equity.

Agricultural products were among the few anti-inflationary goods or services during the 1920's, a period of otherwise spiraling prices and costs. The resulting economic cost-price squeeze was more than many farmers could withstand. As they went into bankruptcy, they took many rural banks and small town merchants with them, causing the face of rural America to change drastically. The reduction of the over-expanded labor base in the over-capitalized agricultural sector of the nation started in the late 1920's and has continued to the present. It is still uncertain how far the ultimate reduction will go.

Farmers like the Reitans, Pazandaks, Peppels, Youngs, Robinsons, Lunds, Underlees, Pages, Romains, Flaats, all early tractor users, survived the 1920's and '30's. These farmers credited the early adoption of the tractor to their farming business as a major factor in their long-range success. Many farmers refused to adopt the tractor because they claimed they were not mechanically inclined. The farmers mentioned previously agreed that knowledge of mechanics was an asset, but many of them were the first to admit that they had little or no mechanical ability. The greatest handicap many farmers had in shifting to tractors was that they were horse lovers. They simply disregarded economics until they were forced to change.

Probably the acid test for the adoption of the tractor came when finance companies, who were holding large acreages of repossessed land, sought renters and buyers. These commercial land holders realized that the tractor farmer was probably not only the most innovative but also the one most capable of getting his crops in on time and keeping the weeds under control—critical factors in better production.

The full realization of tractor power is not yet at hand, for only a small portion of today's farmers have four-wheel-drive, diesel-powered units. Many farmers are still too small to economically justify the latest in technological progress. On the other hand, there are farmers who are already looking beyond the furrow in anticipation of the two-engine, eight-wheel-drive tractors currently under development.

Some Unique Farmers

The word "unique" has been chosen to describe several farmers whose life stories were not too common in the scope of midwestern agriculture. The fact that they succeeded when others failed was not by itself sufficient to merit distinction. But the magnitude of their success and innovation at a time when agriculture was passing through one of its most prolonged periods of adversity gives them uniqueness.

Frank Kiene assumed full responsibility for the support of his mother and his younger sisters and brothers at age 15. Six years later he purchased the family homestead and at the same time entered the Agricultural College at the University of Minnesota. In 1900, at the age of 24, young Kiene had accumulated $25,000 that he invested in a mercantile company in Kennedy, Minnesota, and in a farm one mile from that village. Kiene was astute in trading, in the handling of people, and in the use of borrowed money, all of which eventually led to great success. But this success was not to come without adversity, for he lost two wives by death and he suffered through a complete financial reversal that nearly wiped out his sizeable fortune before he became what was probably Minnesota's largest private farmer. He had 18,000 acres of land and extensive business holdings, as well as substantial cash investments, at the time of his death.

Few American farmers have received more publicity than Thomas D. Campbell, who lived from 1882 to 1966. Born on his parents' farm near Grand Forks, North Dakota, Campbell, early in life, learned to manage the family farm, which at one time was 4,000 acres. Campbell was very resentful of the fact that farm people, particularly women, had to work so hard attempting to keep the farm successful. It was while attending college that Campbell came to realize that the greatest weakness of agriculture was its lack of mechanical power and its failure to use industrial methods.

World War I and the resulting food shortage presented Tom Campbell with the opportunity to test his theories in a big way. With governmental support he opened a 210,000-acre farm in Montana. Adversity was a by-word in Campbell's career, but he became the acknowledged wheat king and for nearly a half century operated what was probably the world's largest wheat farm. Campbell was one of the pioneers in mechanized, industrialized, and commercialized agriculture.

Critics of Tom Campbell and his concepts were those whose

image of an ideal farm was a small family-owned and family-operated unit. Some of these critics pointed to the bonanza farms of the Red River Valley of the North during the period from the 1870's to the 1920's and felt that Campbell would fail like most of the bonanzas had failed. What most of his critics overlooked was that Campbell's innovations were the primary reason for the success of large farms in the new era. Campbell's major innovations included the complete acceptance of mechanical power, complementary machinery, and industrial techniques.

Campbell knew that there was still another limitation besides that of animal horsepower which did not permit the bonanza farms to survive. The limitations of horsepower could have been overcome by the adoption of mechanical power if there had been sufficient managerial urge on the part of the owners of those farms. Unfortunately, for the bonanza farms, most of them were owned by a fairly large number of individuals, many of whom had other interests in distant places. Of those owners who did reside on the farms, nearly all their children went on to college, and most of them never returned to the land.

Stockholders who did not live on the farm generally preferred to receive dividends on their investment instead of seeing profits reinvested in the farming operation. These absentee owners were generally dissatisfied with on-the-farm money management practices and, whenever possible, disposed of their stock. Many second and third generation descendants lived at a higher standard than the farms could provide, and it was easy for them to dispose of the land whenever they needed additional funds to maintain their life style, or to make non-farm investments.

The giant Dalrymple bonanza farm was completely liquidated on contracts-for-deed in the boom period of World War I, only to revert back to the family in the 1920's and early 1930's. The capital of the Amenia and Sharon Land Company grew from $92,000 in 1876 to a combined total remaining assets of about $7.1 million in 1922, which was after four years of deliberate "milking" of the company assets before final division. That bonanza farm had a history of 34 years of profits out of 42 years of operation. Company assets were divided among second and third generation members of the families and became so fractionalized that within 30 years it was difficult to recognize any sizeable farms remaining from that once "durable" empire.

The history of American agriculture is filled with examples of individuals who have gone up and down the roller coaster of success as dictated by cycles of natural and economic disaster. Otto Engen and Earl Schwartz of North Dakota, along with Ray Jarrett and Eugene Young of South Dakota, are excellent examples of farmers who experienced the drought, insects, wind, dust, low prices, and bank failures of the 1920's and 1930's. They experienced failure once, twice, and even three times before they succeeded. They all worked at other jobs in addition to their farming in an effort to develop cash flow. They went through great sacrifice to make their farms succeed.

Roswell "Bob" Garst and his wife Elizabeth started farming near Coon Rapids, Iowa, in 1922 on land that had been in the family since 1885. For a brief period in the 1920's they were involved in real estate in Des Moines, but it was not to their liking. However, during this time they became acquainted with Henry A. Wallace, who was then working on the development of hybrid seed corn. Bob Garst quickly recognized the value of that seed to American agriculture, returned to farming, and seized the opportunity to become the promoter of what would amount to a virtual explosion in the production of corn. Later, Garst turned to artificial drying, commercial fertilizer, and chemicals to push production of corn to even greater heights. At age 74, Garst, the innovator, was probably the best known farmer in America and was as alert as ever to the dynamics of farming.

Bert and Irene Hanson turned to alfalfa on their way to success in farming. They started farming in 1926 in southern Minnesota. Their livestock inventory consisted of a herd of registered Shorthorn cows, a herd of registered hogs, and a stable of outstanding Percheron horses. It was early in Hanson's farm career that he recognized the value of alfalfa and was a consistent top producer of that crop in one of the most productive counties of Minnesota. He quickly capitalized on the commercial production of alfalfa, and after 1951, on haylage fed from sealed storage for beef cattle. He also reportedly had the first John Deere corn planter in Minnesota that had fertilizer attachments.

The Red River Valley of the North—which geographically consists of northwestern Minnesota, eastern North Dakota, and southern Manitoba—is one of North America's finest pockets of rich soil, ideal for potato and sugar beet production. The treeless, stoneless, fertile prairie, with its large flat fields with prevailing long summer days and cool nights, provides an excellent setting for the production of such crops. It is also ideal for the development of agricultural techniques and equipment.

Commercial potato production commenced in the Valley in the 1890's with Henry Schroeder and George W. Bilsborrow as the recognized pioneers. Potatoes slowly worked their way north into Manitoba as farmers sought diversification to improve their income. The greatest handicap in potato production was its high demand for labor. It was not until the late 1940's that Ole A. Flaat and several associates developed a machine that speeded up the harvest, reduced potato bruises, and cut labor requirements. The high initial cost of this machine caused many small growers to quit raising potatoes, while, at the same time, it enabled other growers to expand into larger, more efficient units of production.

In another attempt for greater diversification in the early 1920's, sugar beets were introduced to the Red River Valley. Carl Wigand, Ferdinand Ross, and R. T. Adams were among pioneer growers near Crookston and Fisher, Minnesota, where the first production occurred. Sugar beets did well in the rich soil, but hand hoeing, hand blocking, hand topping, and hand loading made sugar beets a back-breaking, labor-consuming business that discouraged any significant expansion in acreage.

Mechanization came to the aid of the farmer. It came gradually in the 1930's, but in the early 1940's because of the war-time labor shortage, farmers eagerly sought labor-saving machinery. Production per acre and production per man-hour increased sharply, making beets an attractive crop. By the 1970's the Red River Valley contained seven farmer-owned sugar processing plants that produced nearly one-third of the nation's beet sugar.

In the day of small, subsistent farms, nearly every unit had a flock of poultry. That little flock was a typical aspect of the small farm and it was probably one of the most disliked and poorly managed phases of the farm operation. It is rather strange then that poultry should become one of the first segments of American agriculture to become vertically integrated through all phases of production.

The Earl B. Olson story typifies what one man can do with progressive methods of farming. A creamery manager, Olson used eight months of recuperating from an accident to plan a future in the turkey business. After his recovery in 1941, he started a small turkey venture that he methodically expanded through good years and bad years until he became one of the nation's largest producers of turkeys.

In the early stages of large-scale turkey production, Olson and others in his area who succeeded were criticized. But as time passed, the farmers and the elevators that have found a steady local market for their grains in an area that was once a grain exporter are pleased with the better sales and profit opportunities. The workers on the turkey farms and in the related processing and service industries found new opportunities to remain in their preferred rural setting. The consumer, who benefits from a year-round supply of economically priced processed turkey, has little reason to complain.

The Four-Wheel-Drive Tractor

Mechanical power was a significant step in the development of American farms, especially the adoption of the tractor. There were typical pioneering problems, but basically American tractors were good, and they were improved each year. Farmers not only demanded improvements, but they also sought increasingly larger tractors. There were three basic justifications for the movement to more powerful tractors. Probably the greatest single justification for a bigger tractor with larger implements was that many farmers saw it as the best way to reduce or eliminate expensive labor costs and still keep their expanding farm as a family unit. As more was learned about the value of timing in crop production, this became a strong second motive for using larger tractors. The low margin of profit in agriculture makes timing especially important because generally it is one of the surest methods of improving volume and quality, both of which directly increase gross income. Reducing the unit cost of production through greater economy of operation was an obvious and compelling third reason why farmers sought larger power units.

The sales of the conventional tractor increased each year until 1965. Since that date the total number of commercial farm tractor sales has declined, but total mechanical horsepower has continued to grow as tractors have increased in size. It was only a matter of time before a large, all-wheel-drive tractor would be developed and accepted by the farmer.

The search for a four-wheel-drive tractor commenced as early as 1912. Successive models were tried and abandoned. But in the late 1940's and the early 1950's, farmer inventors in the Midwest and Great Plains began in earnest to develop an all-wheel-powered tractor. Even the agricultural colleges became involved as they experimented with tandem tractor hookups, which quickened the interest in four-wheel power.

The Schmidt brothers of Ohio, the Steiger brothers of Minnesota, and Wagner of the Pacific Northwest are probably the first to produce an original model four-wheel-drive. Somewhat later came Pakosh and Robinson with their Versatile, followed by Big-Bud and MRS. Of the major companies, Wayne Worthington, an engineer for Deere and Company, probably was the pathfinder of this power innovation. Worthington visited the Lang Museum in Germany in 1953 and carefully studied what is believed to be the first fully articulated four-wheel-drive, invented by Hans Huber in the early 1900's.

The time was ripe for the next big revolution in agriculture—the era of four-wheel-drive tractors. With sales increasing from 50 in 1965 to over 10,000 in 1975, there was no doubt that the revolution was well on its way. The farmer, faced with continually rising production costs and (except for brief market spurts) low prices for his products, will, as in the past, strive for greater efficiency. In the 1920's he substituted tractors for horses; in the 1930's and 1940's, electricity for hand labor; and then in the 1970's, four-wheel-drive tractors for the conventional two-wheel models.

Big tractors, big equipment, and continually rising production costs created the opening for the next major phase in the progress of agriculture—the age of capital.

Farming Demands Big Capital

Much has been written about the shortage of capital in agriculture. Farmers of the twentieth century, even in prosperous times, frequently could be heard lamenting the lack of capital for their business. But in reality, agriculture, as an industry, has not suffered from a lack of capital nearly as much as it has from the misplacement of capital. Historically, good managers of capital usually have been able to secure adequate funds, but often they have been handicapped by the inability to secure long-term loans. In the past the problem of agricultural financing was complicated because of the ease with which poor managers could become involved in farming. These farmers generally suffered from undercapitalization. Many of them secured money because of the speculative attitude that much of the nation had toward financing the pioneering and expanding phases of agriculture. Farmers were fortunate that lenders were willing to take risks where land was the collateral.*

---

*For a good account of risk capital on the frontier, see John Kenneth Galbraith's *Money: Whence It Came, Where It Went*, New York: Houghton Mifflin Company, 1975.

The great number of small, undercapitalized, loosely operated frontier banks added to the long-range problem of financing agriculture in the past. These banks, under highly competitive conditions, over-extended themselves and with the slightest weakening of the economy were in difficulty. So were those they financed. But somehow, some of the farmers who had been financed on the proverbial shoestring managed to succeed. They indirectly paid the bill through higher interest rates partially in order to make up for the losses the speculative investors incurred.

Financing agriculture was not left to bankers alone, for nearly every manufacturer, processor, merchant, or laborer who extended credit to the farmer became involved. When farmers failed, the creditors all felt the loss in varying degrees. The high rate of failure among pioneer rural merchants was obviously directly linked to voluntary or involuntary extension of credit to farmers.

Unfortunately, the great burden of financing agriculture up to the era of World War II fell directly upon the shoulders of the men, women, and children of the farms. In good years they lived, but in poor years they only existed. The price paid by human beings who struggled to open the agricultural frontier will never be totally calculated, but the price of the "free homesteads" was extremely high.

An example of what happened on a successful homestead is given by J. L. Rendahl, a lifetime friend of the Pottenger family of Fillmore, North Dakota. Crayton Pottenger homesteaded in 1900, and his son Lloyd retired from that farm in the early 1960's. Lloyd Pottenger remarked on his retirement that the sum total of all the profit made above expenses in those years was approximately equal to the free labor of the 14 children raised on that farm.[3]

American farming is one of history's most dramatic illustrations of a free enterprise society. Despite all the failures and obstacles to progress, there has been a constant series of successes. Innovative, progressive, risk-oriented, and determined farmers have been the basis for that success story. Those individuals have been able to get money for their businesses, and, as Iowa banker Richard Retz commented, they have also brought the bankers into the twentieth century.

Farmers can no longer rely on "free" land and the unpaid labor of their wives and children to generate capital. They realize that they can no longer rely on casual bookkeeping to prove from whence they came and whither they are going. Cash flow and net profits have become a vital part of the farmer's and the banker's thinking. But the twentieth-century banker also knows that the farmer understands correspondent banking and, therefore, he is willing to make large loans to the farmer. Capital has become one of the most important determining elements of the Five *M*'s of successful farming, and bankers are attune to the needs of commercialized, industrialized, family-oriented farming.

Tomorrow's Harvest

Some of the preceding concepts may seem strange when applied to a business as "commonplace" as farming. If that is so, there will be even greater disbelief in the futuristic concepts of the farmers who provide the basis for *Tomorrow's Harvest*. However, the book is futuristic only to the degree that innovators are sometimes decades ahead of the crowd. Many people will oppose much of what is contained in the following chapters because resistance to innovation is an historical fact. But innovators tend to pave the way to progress. George Rauenhorst, an agricultural innovator, pointed out that what the innovators are doing is not futuristic at all—it is only that the masses have not yet awakened to the present![4]

NOTES

[1]John D. Nalewaja, "Energy Requirements of Various Weed Control Practices," *Proceedings of the North-Central Weed Control Conference*, Vol. 29, Agricultural Experiment Station, North Dakota State University (1974). Dr. Nalewaja is a Professor of Agronomy at North Dakota State University.

[2]Hiram M. Drache, *Beyond the Furrow: Some Keys to Successful Farming in the Twentieth Century*, The Interstate Printers & Publishers, Inc., Danville, Illinois (1976). All material in this chapter that is not otherwise cited comes from the pages of *Beyond the Furrow*. This chapter is a summary of that book to provide the reader with a setting if he is not familiar with the earlier volume.

[3]Interview with J. L. Rendahl, Moorhead, Minnesota, July 19, 1977.

[4]Conversation with George Rauenhorst, Olivia, Minnesota, April 10, 1976.

CHAPTER II

Supplying Food for the World

Sᴛᴀᴛɪsᴛɪᴄs show that America's farmers, comprising only ¹/₁₀ of 1 per cent of the world's population, produce food for nearly 25 per cent of the world's people. Or putting this figure in a more specific perspective, if only the top 750,000 of the American farmers who produce over 80 per cent of our food and fiber were used as a basis for calculation, then it could be said that ³/₁₀₀ of 1 per cent of the world's population produces food for nearly 25 per cent of the world's people.*

Many readers will question the above figures, and many more will refuse to believe them. But those figures show that these contributions to the world's food supply since 1830 were made by the American farmers working in free enterprise with the help of significant technological breakthroughs. And there cannot be any doubt that much of the world's technical, economic, and social progress in the last century and a half has taken place because for the first time food became more plentiful for a large portion of the people of the western civilization.

Once similar progress is made in agriculture in other nations of the world, they too will be able to enjoy the higher standard of living now experienced by the leading western nations and Japan. Colin Clark, former head of the Oxford Institute in England, expresses such a belief when he states that if all farmers of the world employed methods now used by the leading farmers, the world would be capable of feeding 10 times its 1974 population at a level of the prevailing American diet. This is rather ironic in light of the occurrence of great starvation that is currently taking place in

---

*In 1977 there were 4 billion people in the world, with most projections indicating an increase to 8 billion by 2012.

many parts of the world. What is more ironic is that even in the United States many people who are aware of what technology is capable of doing in today's food production refuse to take advantage of it. This explains why progress sometimes comes slowly.

But progress will come, for enlightened American farmers are 25 to 75 times more productive than many of the world's less fortunate farmers are. To appreciate what is possible in agriculture in the future, there is no better way than to visit some of the most progressive and innovative farmers of America and the West in order to observe, question, and analyze what they are doing.

To give reliable documentation to the theme of this book, a select group of innovative farmers in the American Midwest, Manitoba, and Western Europe were interviewed on their farms. This selective list resulted from personal contacts, from cooperation with farm organizations, agricultural extension workers, farm magazines, and even from lists of large-scale recipients of government programs. A special attempt was made to get a cross section of enterprise and geographical distribution.

Generally, some details of the family history were requested, going back at least three generations. This was done in an attempt to determine how these farm businesses grew to their present size. After the family history, complete data on the size of the farm, the size of the various enterprises conducted on the farm, on the labor force, on power units, and other pertinent information was secured. Then 11 basic questions were asked of all interviewees, and in every case the farmer was allowed to expand into all facets of the question. This provided the writer with substantial insight into each of the operations. In most cases the farmer's wife also took an active part in the interview.[1]

Can We Compete with Worldwide Agriculture?

So much pro and con has been written about the ability of American farmers to compete with other farmers of the world that it would be virtually impossible to reduce that material into a single book. Because such data is so abundant and readily available to the reading public, no attempt is made to include it in this book. Historically, American midwestern farmers have not been export-minded, probably because of their distance from the oceans. Unfortunately, this attitude is not based on good logic and foresight because exports to foreign countries have always played a significant part in the total agricultural economy. At no time prior to 1930 did agricultural exports produce less than 42 per cent of the total value of all American exports. In the meantime the actual value of food and fiber products has increased greatly and constantly since World War II, reaching an all-time high of $24 billion in 1977. It is only because of the tremendous growth of foreign demand for our industrial products since World War II that the percentage of agricultural products has fallen. In recent years, however, agricultural products have been the most favorable factor in our balance of trade relations with the world.

In light of the above facts, it is regrettable that many farmers and more particularly farm organizations and politicians constantly concern themselves with the threat of foreign agricultural products invading the American market. They ignore the fact that to export you must also import. We have heard many times at farm meetings that "all foreign agricultural products ought to be banned from our shores." The politically oriented Farm Bloc of the 1920's, led by powerful farm-state congressmen, used that approach, and their initiated legislation unfortunately put another nail into the coffin of the already depressed farm economy.

Since World War II, world population has skyrocketed and former surplus agricultural producing countries have become deficient food nations, while the developed nations, particularly Australia, Canada, and the United States, have gained ever increasing attention as being the nations most capable of supplying the world's needs for food. Farm magazines have had a major role in alerting American farmers to these needs of the world. Indeed, the billion-dollar grain purchase by the Russians in 1972, the largest single business transaction in history, made everyone aware of America's importance in the world's food supply. The energy crisis of the 1970's has made the consuming public aware that agriculture is the one industry that has the products foreign countries most want in exchange for oil. The consumers were aware of those facts, but they disliked large agricultural exports, for they felt that this caused higher prices for food and fiber in the United States.

It should be mentioned that most of the farmers who were interviewed prior to the Russian grain purchase and the energy crisis did not anticipate those two recent dramatic events in agricultural history. Their impressions were based on a long-range view that the world will increasingly come to rely on the products of American agriculture. Of the American farmers interviewed, not one doubted his ability to compete with any farmer of the world in a free economy. On the contrary, nearly all of them had reservations about the impact of any governmental policies, either American or foreign, that would handicap American farmers from doing the most efficient job possible in their efforts to provide the nation with an abundance of food as well as a surplus for export.

Vernon W. Ruttan, an international authority on world agricultural resources, wrote:

Throughout most of the world the major agricultural policy problem remains, as in the time of Malthus (1766–1834), how to speed up the rate of growth of agricultural output and relieve the pressure of population on food supplies. In contrast, a major policy problem in American agriculture during the last 3½ decades [since 1935] . . . , has been how to deal with the problem of agricultural abundances. . . .

To be sure, the problem was that the productivity gap in agriculture between the developed and the developing nations was widening. Quite obviously agricultural leaders in the developing countries were at a loss as to how to stimulate agricultural technology in their countries in an effort to narrow the gap. The problem in the underdeveloped countries was even more serious.

All of the farmers interviewed were pointedly asked the question, would they be willing to compete on a completely free world market? Only those living in Manitoba and Europe expressed any doubts about that willingness. The statement of Walter Kroeker was quite typical of the reactions of the farmers from that province: "With the world subsidy situation as it is we cannot be competitive with some specialty crops of various countries. In potatoes and grain, yes. In hogs we are among the world's most economical producers. . . . In a completely free world I would be afraid of being swamped by the farmers of the United States. . . ."

When asked if they would be willing to compete with the world's farmers, farmers from the five American states gave answers that sounded affirmative. Only a few even hesitated before giving their answers and then went on to express fears of problems that would complicate their ability to dominate the world market. Iowa farmer Clem Hebel retorted:

We have the climate and soils in Iowa along with our technology that give us great advantage in corn and beef production. We are still wasting lots of products that could give us profits. As far as I'm concerned, Iowa farmers could live on what they are wasting, that is how far ahead we are.

Richard H. Grotberg of North Dakota agreed about waste, stating that "the very fact that we waste as much as we do on our farms indicates that we have little fear about competition. If there was a real need and incentive for the farmer, we could tighten up on the use of our resources because we waste as much as many people produce."

In South Dakota Charles A. Cannon's concern dealt with the fact that the marketing and transportation systems of both America and the foreign nations would have to improve if the world really wanted to take all the American farmers could produce for the international market. He expressed the opinion that those systems would improve once it was clear that foreigners could and would buy American food and fiber at an ever increasing rate.

Another South Dakotan, John Sutton, Jr., said, "We have really never tested our efficiency. . . . We don't know how efficiently we can really produce because we are so tradition-minded. But in a worldwide market we would wake up and produce better products at less cost."

P. D. Hempstead, Minnesota cattle feeder, verified Sutton's feelings by commenting, "We have everything to gain by opening up the world markets. The farmers should have more freedom to develop these markets. I am willing to compete as a beef producer and am prepared to do so. Worldwide competition would make us even more efficient and this benefits everyone."

"We haven't pushed our production limits," asserts Walter Krueger of North Dakota. "We have just been coasting. I want to be able to produce for the world market."

Donald Jarrett of South Dakota agreed: "We are helping many farmers of the world improve their ability to farm and that is going to make competition rougher, but this just spurs us to do a better job, like competition has done in the past."

Kenneth Kinkler, a native Texan, felt that South Dakotans were not taking advantage of all their opportunities, and he moved to that state to produce wheat. He said:

As a wheat farmer I am geared to the foreign market because for years the foreigners have been taking more than 50 per cent of our production. If we have any hope for larger markets, it has to be from foreign countries. . . . I am prepared to produce wheat for the feed grain market or as a product to be used in making other materials such as paper substitutes. Our potential markets may be along industrial lines, but industry is sometimes slow to adapt.

Floyd Darroll Warren of Montana said:

I think I can compete in wheat and beef with any foreign farmer. I think we have to if we want to stay in business, because the world is getting smaller and will depend upon us more than ever. . . . Our area actually was set back by the sugar beet company because it did not make us really look into all of our possibilities. Things were too easy for us. Now that it is gone, we are doing what we should have done years ago.

Minnesota farmer Donald A. Schulz welcomed the world market with confidence, for he felt that he could outproduce any foreign farmer if he were free to operate and to innovate as he has in the past. Schulz felt that an ever increasing portion of his products will have to be sold in the world market. He is eager for the challenge, particularly since "American agricultural capacity is still far from its peak of production."

Many of these farmers gave several basic reasons as to why they felt they could easily compete on the world market. The Keil brothers, living in Montana where freight rates were 70 to 90 cents a hundredweight on wheat, acknowledged that even though freight costs were high, they were cheap by contrast to using water buffalo, pack animals, or men. Edgar Keil said, "We could beat the foreign farmers just on the strength of our technology, and we are doing it by paying freight to get the wheat out of Montana and moving it to a foreign port. In a totally free economy we could compete even better."

John Romain, cattle and wheat man in Montana who is also involved with a chain of elevators, noted that in 1971 the elevator company paid over $10 million in freight charges for an average of nearly 80 cents per hundredweight of grain. Romain recalled one recent year when freight charges paid by the elevator were just over half the total price farmers received for their wheat.

Prior to the price and cost increases of 1972 and after, Clarence Romain, also of Montana, could produce wheat for just over 60 cents a bushel, including the cost of summer fallow. His transportation costs from the rail siding to the West Coast were 50 cents. Allen C. Kolstad, living in the same part of Montana, expressed hope that a port on the Snake River at Lewistown, Idaho, would greatly reduce freight costs to the west coast. "This would put the Asian markets that much more within the grasp of the Montana wheat producer, " said Kolstad, "but I think it would give us an even greater future for our beef because those people are going to want more meat in years to come."

Sugar beet and corn farmer John H. Reque of Minnesota favors the foreign market because he feels it is necessary to sustain the American economy. He added, "I am not afraid of any foreign competition because leading American farmers have adapted to industrialized agriculture and have accepted the new way of farming which puts us way ahead of most of the world's farmers and we will stay there."

"We have the power to overcome any of the world's farmers," says John Heline, a turkey, hog, and beef feeder. "Besides being the most mechanized nation we are backed by transportation, financial, and agri-business complexes that no land in the rest of the world has. All of our purchased inputs make us even stronger. My indirect labor force in all of these farm-related businesses is far larger than my farm labor force. That's where our strength comes from."

The chief reason given for their belief that they, as progressive American farmers, were way ahead of the great majority of the world's farmers was their personal incentive. These men as a group were highly motivated and very confident about their business of farming. They firmly indicated that they would welcome the challenge of being allowed to compete for the world market. Ex-congressman Don L. Short of North Dakota expressed a feeling often repeated during the interviews. "I am a free enterpriser and would like to see free trade." Short added that the only reservation he had about American farmers being able to compete on the world market was the adverse policy of organized labor. He was not worried about getting quality labor who could do an excellent job, but he was concerned about a philosophical hang-up of labor union leadership. That reservation was on the minds of many farmers because they remembered the damaging effect of the longshoremen's strikes on their exports. Allen C. Kolstad said, "The threat of more strikes at our ports bothers me more than any aspect of foreign trade."

Most of the farmers felt that longshoremen's dock strikes caused prices to drop because of the immediate loss of sales. Their greater concern, however, was the long-range impact that the strikes had on the foreign nations who were relying on American farm products. The farmers felt that repetition of these strikes would cause foreign nations to permanently turn to other areas if they could not depend upon a steady flow of food from the United States.

More than one-third of the farmers interviewed had studied foreign agriculture directly or were in contact with foreign agricultural and trade officials who had come to this country. One Minnesota corn and soybean farmer related that he had contact with farmers from 11 foreign countries and felt that he had a good grasp of their basic problems. Five farmers were actually in the process of shipping products to foreign nations at the time of the interview. During a two-year period Walter J. Bones, Jr., of South Dakota shipped 554 cattle to one foreign nation. Several of the potato farmers in the Red River Valley had been involved in foreign exports for many years. Herman A. Schmitz, president of the Great Plains Wheat Board and a member of the North Dakota Wheat Commission, spent about half of his time selling to foreign grain buyers on visits to their nations. He directly confronted Earl Butz, then Secretary of Agriculture, to oppose any curbs on the export of American agricultural commodities. Schmitz felt that only a few foreign nations have any potential at present of being competitors to the American farmer.

Of those farmers who had visited foreign nations and reported on their observations, Stanley D. Olson had a most perceptive comment. Olson felt that Swedish farmers had attained a high level of technology even though their output per man was not as high as on his Minnesota farm. It was his opinion that the farm cooperatives had achieved a certain amount of success, but the other factions, both political and commercial, had stiffened themselves against the farmers because of their organizations. Some of the more progressive Swedish farmers felt that they were being held back by the bureaucracy of their cooperatives. The co-op leaders were not willing to move with the innovators. Olson added, "I do not want to see anything in this country that will hold back the real innovators for it will hurt us in the long run."

A third rather strong theme expressed by nearly all the farmers interviewed was doubt, anxiety, and distrust about the chance of ever really being able to compete for the international markets on a free basis. John S. Dean, a North Dakota small grain, cattle, and oil seed farmer, said, "The American consumers and our own State Department are our own worst enemies." Dean meant that the consumers want to see food stockpiled in America to keep prices low and that the State Department was more interested in the politics rather than the economics of agricultural exports.

Robert F. Reimers, politician and certified seed producer farming in two states, expressed the suspicion that foreign governments are more of a threat than their farmers. He said, "I would rather tackle any of the world's farmers than I would their governmental policies. The world market would be our baby right now if it were not for the political tampering. Unfortunately, we have no control over the international aspects even if the people want our food."

It is obvious that the American government as well as foreign governments posed threats to the philosophy of the aggressive, innovative farmer, but he felt confident that he could compete with any of the world's farmers on a free market. One Minnesotan summed up that feeling: "There is always room for the man with the best to get his product sold. A completely free market would expose the false values that we have built into our so-called economic system." Jack Dahl, a leader in the beef cattle industry, added, "The more affluent the world gets the better the market will be for our products."

The greatest concern expressed by most of these farmers was the impact that American agricultural competition would have on the broad scope of world agriculture. Ralph Hvidsten, a potato and grain farmer, said, "We could easily compete with the world's farmers, but this thing is complicated and it might interfere with the lives of many. The man with the water buffalo would have to work even cheaper than he does now if he would have to compete with our mechanized farming."

The Underlees, sugar beet and wheat farmers, added, "Those poor people have to live too. They simply cannot compete with us and the technology we have. Our biggest concern should be that we do not disturb their social pattern too rapidly."

Interestingly enough, the farmers' fear of upsetting the society of the underdeveloped nations is also in agreement with some authorities in international agricultural productivity such as Ruttan and Hayami:

In recent years a consensus seems to have emerged to the effect that productivity growth in the agricultural sector is essential if agricultural output is to grow at a sufficiently rapid rate to meet the demands for food and raw materials that typically accompany urbanization and industrialization. Failure to achieve rapid growth in agricultural productivity can result either in the drain of foreign exchange or in shifts in the internal terms of trade against industry, and thus seriously impede the growth of industrial production. Failure to achieve rapid growth in labor productivity in agriculture can also raise the cost of transferring labor and other resources from the agricultural to the nonagricultural sector as development proceeds.

Ruttan and Hayami add that agricultural output per worker in India in 1970 was only $1/50$ of that of the American farm laborer. Very few of the undeveloped countries have labor output as high as one-fifth of that of the American workers, and in recent years the margin has widened. This factor seriously handicaps the growth of the economic sector in those countries. Education to improve the quality of labor is the single most important alternative open to those nations in order to increase their productivity. Even if education were possible, the density of population would probably hinder the foreigner's ability to match the North American agricultural worker's output because of a less favorable man-land ratio than in the United States or Canada. Full agricultural labor efficiency then could not be possible without first draining off part of the labor supply from the land. Historically, when that has occurred, the population growth has also declined. It appears, then, that the food-population balance is far from solved even though the innovative American farmer would and could do more to help if he had the freedom to do so.[2]

NOTES

[1]"Formula for World Famine," *U.S. News & World Report*, 76 (January 28, 1974), p. 52.

[2]"A Chronology of American Agriculture, 1790–1965," Economic Research Service, U.S. Department of Agriculture (1966), a chart; Roe C. Black, "Why You Need to Care About Exports," *Top Op*, IV, No. 5 (May, 1972), p. 42; Yyjiro Hayami and Vernon W. Ruttan, "Resources, Technology and Agricultural Development: An International Perspective," Department of Agricultural Economics, University of Minnesota, St. Paul (January, 1970); interviews with the following farmers, in order of citation in context:

Walter Kroeker, Winkler, Manitoba, February 15, 1973
Clem Hebel, Mason City, Iowa, February 21, 1972
Richard H. Grotberg, Oakes, North Dakota, January 21, 1974
Charles A. Cannon III, Pierre, South Dakota, May 5, 1973
John Sutton, Jr., Agar, South Dakota, April 12, 1972
P. D. Hempstead, Houston, Minnesota, March 28, 1972
Walter Krueger, McKenzie, North Dakota, March 10, 1972
Donald Jarrett, Britton, South Dakota, March 2, 1972
Kenneth Kinkler, Onida, South Dakota, April 11, 1972
Floyd Darroll Warren, Hardin, Montana, May 16, 1972
Donald A. Schulz, Faribault, Minnesota, March 25, 1972
Keil brothers, Ledger, Montana, May 12, 1972
John H. Reque, Redwood Falls, Minnesota, March 15, 1972
John Heline, Pierson, Iowa, February 23, 1972
John Romain, Havre, Montana, May 11, 1972
Clarence Romain, Chester, Montana, May 12, 1972
Allen C. Kolstad, Chester, Montana, May 11 and 12, 1972
Don L. Short, Beach, North Dakota, April 7, 1972
Virgil Mellies, Hector, Minnesota, March 16, 1972
Walter J. Bones, Jr., Parker, South Dakota, February 24, 1972
Herman A. Schmitz, Williston, North Dakota, April 5, 1972
Stanley D. Olson, Fairmont, Minnesota, March 29, 1972
John S. Dean, Hatton, North Dakota, November 15, 1972
Robert F. Reimers, Melville, North Dakota, January 6, 1970
George Rauenhorst, Olivia, Minnesota, March 16, 1972
Jack Dahl, Gackle, North Dakota, February 10, 1973
Ralph Hvidsten, Stephen, Minnesota, January 17, 1972
C. H. Underlee and sons, Hendrum, Minnesota, January 19, 1972

"U.S. Farm Products Exports to Reach $21 Billion," Minnesota Crop and Livestock Reporting Service, No. 319 (June, 1974); "Who Says Cows Can't Fly?" *The Dakota Farmer*, 93, No. 5 (May, 1973), p. 51; *The Forum* (February 3, 1974); Yyjiro Hayami and Vernon W. Ruttan, "Agricultural Productivity Differences Among Countries," *The American Economic Review*, 60, No. 5 (December, 1970), pp. 895, 902, 906–908.

CHAPTER III

Economy of Size

THE DEBATE AMONG FARMERS about what is the most economically sized farm is as old as agriculture. In the past as well as in the present the farmer operating on a smaller scale was sure that the large farm had so many inefficiencies that it could not possibly survive. The large farmer, on the other hand, is at a loss to understand how the small farmer lives from his small volume. The small farmer is convinced that hired labor, hired management, four-wheel-drive tractors, and large machinery, besides heavy borrowing of capital, will surely drive the large farmer to bankruptcy. The large farmer, in contrast, thinks of those inputs as necessary tools for profitable production and sees them as the basis for much of his success.

For most of the nineteenth century the average-sized American farm remained at 130 to 140 acres. The Homestead Act of 1862 provided for grants of 80 to 160 acres, and although farm numbers increased rapidly during the following decades, the acreage remained quite stable. As farmers moved into the more arid western lands, the size of homestead grants increased in an effort to provide them with a unit that would produce a better livelihood. About that time (ca. 1910) the tractor was adopted by farmers in an effort to obtain greater efficiency in production. The farmer's concept of the correct farm size grew as tractors increased in size. Average tractor size has increased 10 horsepower per decade. In the late 1940's "package agricultural practices" encouraged even greater technological innovations. This resulted in a rapid annual growth in average farm size during the 1950's and '60's of about 9 acres per year per farm.

The sudden farm prosperity resulting from the sharp export demands in 1972 did not slow down farm expansion, and larger farmers bid more aggressively than ever for additional acres. In

Minnesota expansion buyers made up 67 per cent of the buyers in the three major agricultural regions. In North Dakota during the seven years ending in 1973, expansion buyers purchased 74 per cent of all farms sold. In South Dakota expansion buyers made up 76 per cent of the buyers during the early 1970's. Nationally, about 53 per cent of all buyers were expansion buyers.*

A farm management study conducted in Minnesota during the years 1912–1913 determined that five factors were most important in obtaining satisfactory farm labor income. These factors were size of farm, crop yields per acre, returns per unit of productive livestock, number of days of productive labor accomplished per man, and number of days of productive labor annually accomplished per horse. The top 26 farms out of the 400 studied had annual labor income averaging $947, while the bottom 47 farms with none of the determining factors had a minus $10 labor income per farm. Since these farms were labor-oriented, as is still true of most farms of this day, labor returns meant direct earnings to the farmer as a worker. Labor income rose as farms increased in size in all of the five determining factors, indicating the value of economy of scale even in the horse age.** The most significant factor in increasing labor return was the amount of capital invested per farm.

As late as 1970 there were 1,444,000 farms that had gross sales of less than $5,000 annually. Net income from farming was $1,238, but average off-the-farm income for those units totaled $7,506. Half of our nation's farmers were getting 83.5 per cent of their income from non-farm sources.*** Of all farms with gross sales of over $10,000 annually, 28.4 per cent of the farmers' income came from off the farm. Historically, net per capita income of farmers has been about half of the national average per capita income. It is only in recent years, primarily because of technology and growing farm size, that the average per capita income of farmers has approached the national average.

A farm magazine editor, irritated by the West Coast longshore-

---

*Full-time industrial workers were intense competition in the urbanized areas for land. Farmers in Iowa, southern Minnesota, and around the larger cities, particularly Winnipeg, Manitoba, all reported that the fully employed urbanite was extremely strong competition for the smaller farms.

**The average volume handled per man on those 400 farms was 53.9 acres of crop and 11 units of productive livestock. There was an average of 20.9 acres of crop for each horse on those farms with 4.3 horses and 1.55 men per farm.

***A farm, by census definition, is any unit grossing more than $1,000 from farm sales.

men's strike of 1972 that not only caused a drop in farm prices but also probably had a long-range negative impact on farm exports, wrote that a farmer would have to gross at least $90,000 a year to have a net income equal to a longshoreman. To gross $90,000 in annual sales a farmer would have to have at least $250,000 in capital investment. This was well within the range of many one- and two-man farm operations, but was too large for the great majority of the American farms of the 1970's. Economy of size, so necessary for a good family income, is still far from a reality for the majority of the farmers. But each year the model size unit grows as technology enhances a man's ability to produce more at less cost per unit. And each year it becomes more obvious that two types of farms are evolving—the large family-operated commercial farm and the small part-time farm where the family relies chiefly on off-the-farm income. The latter are the most numerous and quite socially important, but the commercial farmers are the nation's chief food providers.[1]

What Do the Farmers Say About Size?

Farmers provided the basic data used by a U.S.D.A. study in 1973. This study determined that the technically optimum farms having the lowest production cost per unit of output were the fully mechanized, one-man farms. That research pointed out that one-man, fully mechanized farms far exceeded the average-sized farms of 1973. The study determined that 800 acres was the most efficient one-man midwestern corn farm, but the average of existing corn farms in that area was only 263 acres. Likewise the optimum small-grain farm was 1,950 acres, as contrasted to 694 acres for the average-sized 1973 small-grain farm. In both cases the average was only a third as large as the optimum one-man farm.

Since 1910 farmers themselves have been pointing the way as average farm size increased from 138 to 467 acres by 1976. The disappearance of farms from the census Classes III, IV, and V is accompanied by a growth in the number of census Class I and II farmers with gross farm incomes of over $40,000 and Class VI farmers with under $2,500 in gross sales. The latter group are retired, hobby, residential farmers, or industrial workers who farm after hours.

In 1929 there were 7,875 out of 6,288,648 farms that grossed over $30,000 in annual sales. A study of those farms concluded that the larger farms were "more efficient than the average farms as far as the use of land, labor, and capital." These farms were 12 to 24 times the average farms in given specialties. They amounted to only .1 per cent of all farms, but sold 4.5 per cent of all farm production.

Inflation and technology had their impact on large farms—by 1964 $100,000 became the criterion for a large farm, and 31,401 farms met that goal. They were 1 per cent of all farms, but produced 24.3 per cent of all sales. By 1974 there were 114,000 farms of that size comprising 6 per cent of all farms, but producing 54 per cent of all cash receipts from farming. By their actions the farmers have voiced a strong clear trend for the future.

The question, "How large can my farm enterprise become?," is asked by all farmers at one time or another. There are four alternatives they can take to determine the answer: (1) sell out because they do not desire to grow; (2) maintain the farm as it is and take off-the-farm employment; (3) maintain the farm as is and hang on until retirement; (4) innovate, change, and expand. The fourth alternative offers both the greatest risk and the greatest opportunity, but it is also the road to lowest cost production. Some fail, but most succeed. It is the latter who have made success stories unequaled in world agriculture. They are the true providers of much of the food for 25 per cent of the world's population.

David Garst, an Iowa corn grower, believes that there is not necessarily a point of diminishing return per unit of production when the farm grows in size. Garst is concerned that all inputs—land, labor, and capital—be used to their fullest extent. In 1972 he believed that if a farmer fully used a good Iowa quarter section of land to its maximum, his family could receive a fine living from those 160 acres. Garst added, "Everybody knows the secret of how to raise cash corn and that is why the return is what it is." He insisted that a farming enterprise that required year-round employment is the only way labor could be fully used and adequate income provided. In Iowa, according to Garst, that means raising corn for production of pork, beef, or milk.

Charles A. Cannon III, who thinks of himself as a very tight money manager, believes that money management is the most significant single factor in determining farm size. Cannon stresses, "The unit should be as large as one family can handle along with the financial limits that they can manage. The family farm must maintain a sound capital structure, regardless of how small or large it is." Cannon was under the impression that, if a single farmer could get as large as he wanted, there would have to be something wrong with a community where natural competition would restrict the growth of any one farm. In his area the large farmers provided the greatest competition to each other.

Many farmers expressed the idea that it was probably necessary to be sure that management and net income on the existing operation were at their best before expansion took place. This is assuming, of course, that the farm was large enough for a living to begin with. Earl Glidden, a Red River Valley farmer, was of the opinion that size of equipment and horse power were virtually the sole limits on expansion if management was capable of handling it. Glidden tripled his total farm size from 1952 through 1972, and his volume grew much more. He still felt no restraints because of growth. Glidden had individual enterprise accounting for every crop and livestock phase of his farming and stressed that this was the only way to determine if each operation was actually paying its way. Until each farmer did this, he felt there would be little justification for expansion because possibly profits would be greater through better management than through expansion.

Harvey Dann, farming north of Winnipeg, Manitoba, expressed it as follows:

Our worst enemies are the farmers who don't really keep good production records. We budget every phase of our activities and the total operation stays very close to the projected figures. The bulk of the small farmers refuse to do this, and, because they are having trouble making it, they think it is not possible for us to succeed. They oppose us simply because we are big. The four-wheel-drives that pull 10 bottoms each have not only been our biggest cost cutters but they seem to have made the men more eager to want to do field work, but I know many farmers who insist that no one can justify those $50,000 tractors.

Arden Burbidge, North Dakota potato farmer, gained a national reputation speaking on economies of scale and management techniques on his farm. Burbidge had this to say about economies of size:

There are definite economies to size, even though management cost does not decrease per unit as the farm grows. My farm got beyond the limits of tight control before I decided to employ professional management. This increased top management cost, but it gave us better overall management in all of our enterprises than existed under my personal control. We have found that secondary or tactical management costs increased proportionately with the growth of the farm, so that presented no problem.

Individual farmers can compensate themselves as owner, manager, foreman, and laborer, but they probably do not have as good overall management as they would like to think they have. The small-scale operators tend to make uneconomic investments in machinery to avoid labor decisions. We find that there are many ex-farmers who cannot even stand the tensions of being field foremen. As capital and scientific inputs become increasingly more important, it becomes even more difficult for many to understand the management problems of agriculture. This is further complicated by the fact that inflation, which has been so helpful to the man who owned land in the past, will not be such a positive factor as agriculture becomes more specialized. Confined beef barns, hog houses, and dairy barns, cleaning plants, elevators, and potato warehouses depreciate in value rather than appreciate like land does. But it is the specialized facility that may make the greatest net operating profits, and these must be tied to the land for the greatest overall gain.

Most of the farmers interviewed felt that the growth in average farm size was an inevitable process. "Farms will seek their own size level," said George Rauenhorst, innovative Minnesota farmer. "They will grow because of the very nature of our economic system. The pendulum could reverse . . . but that is not likely under the present price structure [March, 1972] where the consumer demands cheap food." Rauenhorst felt that nearly all institutions from the government programs to the farm magazines stressed maximizing the use of our inputs. He felt that environmental programs would increase cost still more and would tend to work to the disadvantage of the smaller operation.

A North Dakota small-grain farmer, Thomas (Buck) Snortland, was not concerned about competition from foreign farmers, American absentee-owned corporate farms, or the small unmechanized American farmer, because by employing three good men plus his own labor, Snortland could produce over 1,000 tons of grain per worker per year. Snortland pointed out that in 1972 he had between $225,000 and $250,000 invested capital for each full-time worker, including himself. He asked, "Why worry about the unmechanized farmer or the absentee-owned inefficient ones?"

The average farm size in Snortland's home township was 1,600 acres, and he stressed that the well-organized farmer could handle that acreage with no help and produce 1,000 tons of grain per year. But he suggested that more efficiency and profit could be gained if the average farm was increased to 3,200 acres and one year-round employee besides the owner was hired to operate the farm. Snortland contends that a 3,200-acre grain farm was large enough to use the most efficient machinery. The efficiency over 1,600 acres results when labor is less costly than management, and machinery cost does not increase as rapidly as acres and income. "With good equipment it is easier to hire top-notch men," says Snortland, "who prefer to work for someone rather than for themselves."

The late Jacob Geritz, a long-time North Dakota grain farmer in the same basic area as Snortland, said, "As machinery gets bigger, we will expand. My son cannot stand still; he wants to operate more than I have. It's a simple matter of technology competing against labor. Machinery is expensive, but in the long run it is much cheaper than labor."

In the four decades that they have farmed, both Snortland and Geritz have seen the average farm size increase rapidly as farmers have adopted new machines. Both are convinced that the average farm size will continue to increase in direct relation to improvements in technology. Snortland has six first line field tractors that average 150 horsepower each. In addition there are eight older models used for light work and as standbys. He also has five combines and five tandem grain trucks plus three smaller trucks for maintenance. Three grain drills, each 42 feet in width, can seed a total of 630 to 750 acres of grain a day, while three other large tractors pulling 42-foot cultivators work the land in preparation for the drilling.

Donald Jarrett, his brother Ronald, and their late father, Ray, have one of the largest diversified livestock, grain, and hay farms in South Dakota. Jarrett feels that they have some inefficiency problems because of their size, but that they have many advantages not available to smaller one-man operations. The Jarretts agree that because of their size they can more readily secure custom operators than smaller farmers. They feel that using custom operators is very feasible in corn and grain harvesting and in haying. To date custom crews have handled most of their harvesting because it blends in well with the use of their labor force which is needed for the livestock chores that are more demanding in the winter than in the summer when the sheep and cattle are on pasture. Jarrett added, "It is a lot easier to take off for a ballgame when you have a crew to do the job than if you are solely responsible for getting the farming done."

Even though land, labor, and capital are the three basic ingredients of production, most of the farmers felt that the ultimate size of a farm was a decision of individual judgment. Jay C. Swisher, a South Dakota grain and livestock farmer who started managing a 3,200-acre family enterprise in 1945, had more than tripled the acres by 1971. He pointed out that growth is a constant factor until one runs out of management. He added, "I find it easier to manage as we get larger, for as we grow, we get both better equipment and better employees and the farm goes more like a clock than it did at the smaller acreage." The farm that Swisher manages came through the 1920's and 1930's, and it is his opinion that its very size was one of the reasons why his predecessors were able to endure on a profitable basis during those trying times. Diversification was a second factor attributing to the farm's durability. Swisher would not want to specialize because he feels it would be assuming a greater risk than he now has with a diversified unit.

Ed J. Dullea, Jr., who started farming in 1929 first in central North Dakota and later in the Red River Valley, looks upon size as purely an individual problem. Many farmers like Dullea are concerned about continuity of management, realizing that what one man builds may be more than the next generation can maintain or desire to work with. Dullea said, "I can make the farm work, but can my successors do it? As the farm grows, there is a factor of people slippage, but you just have to accept that idea when you hire help. Here is where the big four-wheel-drive tractors and equipment enter the picture, for they give us the opportunity we need to grow indefinitely. I have found that under good management, equipment is the key to my profits."

Robert F. Reimers of North Dakota, who started farming in 1945 with a rented quarter section and 200 sheep, said his dream at that time was some day to own a section of land. By 1970 he was farming and owned farms in two states many times the size of his "dream farm" and was far from quitting. According to Reimers, "Size depends entirely on the constitution of the man. If he has the right makeup, there is no limit to the size of his enterprise, because you learn that you can hire management as good as you are. My managers think like I do. About all I have to do is give the go ahead."

Like the Jarretts and many others who farm extensively, Reimers hires a custom operator with eight combines. "This, he says, "eliminates our biggest labor bottleneck because of the tremendous demand for labor during the short harvest season."

Ole A. Flaat started farming in the Red River Valley in the early 1920's and grew to become one of the nation's largest potato farmers in the 1940's. He is convinced that the "nerves of the number-one man are the major basis as to how large a farm can get." Flaat, who is very profit-oriented, stressed that marketing is a phase that too many managers overlook and unless a product is sold, even the most efficient operator cannot survive. Because of that belief Flaat made a business of contracting his production during most of his farming career.

C. H. Underlee of Minnesota started farming in 1934 with a quarter section of land and by 1972 had grown more than twenty-fold. His sons agreed with their 72-year-old father when he said, "Our net income per acre has grown rapidly as we increased our acreage and it is still growing. We thought that gradually this might slow down, but the new four-wheel-drive tractors surprised us. They can move so fast both on the land and on the road that we can see our way clear to continued growth. We would double our beet acreage if we had the opportunity."

Pete A. Hermanson is general manager of his family's diversified farm in Iowa that has several enterprises, each of which is larger than the total of most of the farms in his state. Hermanson is of the opinion that he has not yet seen a farm thas has passed its peak of efficiency because of size alone. The Hermanson farm, specializing in corn, dairy cows, and turkeys, is large, but its expansion continues. "In spite of our size," says Hermanson, "we always seem to have spare time to do custom work, help out a neighbor who is in a bind, or construct a building or increase an enterprise each year. Yes, we will even buy or rent additional land if it becomes available."

Another diversified farmer who prefers to remain anonymous says, "Maybe our growth is cancerous—or is it uncontrollable? Whatever it is, it has been automatically profitable for us. Sometimes neighbors are a problem, and that is not solved until someone buys them out."

George Sinner, who, with other members of his family, operates one of North Dakota's oldest and largest feedlots, as well as a sizeable sugar beet and soybean farm, cautions that size is not as risky as the rate of growth. The Sinners have proven that production per acre has not been hurt as they have grown in size. Their greatest problem comes in timing of work because of conflict between agricultural enterprises and not because of size. The Sinner family has been involved in a gradual and steady expansion during the past 50 years, and their management has improved with their growth. But in controlling their rate of growth, they are careful that the management grows with it. It is their impression that there is almost no upper limit to the size of a cash crop farm, but they feel that there are possible inefficiencies in larger feedlots. They are uncertain, however, where that upper limit was.

Herman Natwick's family has been feeding cattle for five generations in Norman County, Minnesota, where he is by far the largest cattle feeder. He is probably the first farmer in his county to gross over a million dollars in sales in a single year. An active participant in F.F.A., at the age of 18 he got his start by raising turkeys and had five good years in succession. After nine years of renting, he started buying land and purchased everything in his vicinity that came up for sale during the next decade. He has expanded nearly every year that he has been farming and expects that in the next decade he will double his volume.

Natwick is an extremely good manager, and, in addition to running a constantly expanding business, he has found time to be very active in politics and in farm organizations. For several years he was a member of the Minnesota ASCS Committee. Some years he has spent more than 50 per cent of his time away from the farm. According to Natwick the key to expansion in order to maintain full economy of scale is that it be gradual and controlled. Other than that, he feels that there are no restrictions to the size of corn raising, or to turkey or cattle feeding enterprises.

Starting slowly and building gradually but steadily was the key to success for Iowan John Heline. He started raising corn on a small scale, and whenever he could, he expanded by renting or purchasing land. By 1972 his corn acreage alone was larger than that of six average farms in his state, but that was not enough of a challenge. Over the years he had started in a "small way" with turkeys, feeder pigs, feeder cattle, and beef brood cows, and each grew to be a very sizeable enterprise. Heline built his diversified agricultural operations on a solid foundation, and each year one or two of them were very profitable, enabling him to maintain a good steady cash flow.

Like Natwick, Heline is very active in civic affairs, besides having a direct part in several other farm-related business ventures. He has no urgent intention to expand his farm nor does he intend to stand still when an opportunity presents itself. He is of the opinion that the single most serious problem in agriculture is that there are far too many farms that are simply too small to be sound and economically profitable regardless of the price structure. Each of his enterprises far exceeds the combined volume of several average-sized farms.

Roy R. Moser, who was general farm manager for the Amana Society Homestead Farm in Iowa, had a valid experience that proved the importance of size for his farming operation. The farm that he managed consisted of seven sizeable farms. During the 1960's these farms were consolidated. With each merger net profits increased. In 1968 the Society bought larger equipment to accomplish the work more easily. With bigger farm units and with more efficient equipment, operating profits "really stepped up," Moser said. The Homestead Farm that Moser managed was 2,721 acres and is currently being merged with the other farms into two units of about 7,000 acres each. Moser believes that this will be very practical. Consolidation has become possible and profitable with the adoption of large mobile equipment. Moser thinks the four-wheel-drive tractor instead of the former track-type major power unit is the key to consolidation for the Amana Society.*

The land now owned by the Keil brothers of Montana once belonged to 30 farmers in the 1920's. Those farmers nearly all failed, partially because of dry weather and low prices, but chiefly because their farms were too small to provide a living for their families. Mrs. John Keil and her three married sons and their employees earn a good living on that farm today. They came to appreciate what economy of scale meant after they theoretically split their farm into three separate units and proved to themselves that it would be impossible to make a profit if they were operating as three separate farms. Their figures were calculated on a charge of 8 per cent of the current value of their land which they were using as a capital charge in their farming operation.

The Keils have two four-wheel-drive tractors, a large track-type tractor, and a very large three-wheeled "swamp buggy" with huge flotation tires used for spreading fertilizer. These power units are the key to the economy of their operation, and if their farm were subdivided, it would be hard to justify individual ownership of even one machine. The Keils are of the opinion that even with a farm as large as theirs they could be losing out if they could not expand at the rate of at least 6 per cent a year. That expansion is above the steady increase in volume they are experiencing because of better technology and science used on the farm.

North Dakotan Alvin Kenner said, "The 4,600-acre home farm is a real comfortable size as far as management is concerned. But if

---

* Hilly terrain, gullies, waste land, and small fields are a handicap to operating the largest equipment. Two railroads, a national highway, and a river bisect the land. From one spot a viewer could see eight fields, the largest of which was 24 acres and the two smallest 3.8 acres each, but large rubber-tired hydraulically folded and opened machines can be used to farm such land. Moving the equipment from one field to another, however, consumes about as much time as working the land, but it is still more efficient than the use of former smaller machines, "at least that's what the profit record indicates," says Moser. "We will keep some 6-row equipment," Moser said, "just to handle the smaller fields and will do all the bigger fields with the new 12-row planters."

machinery continues to improve, we will probably be able to handle those acres with half the equipment, so we will have to double our size. Timing is so important for maximum returns per acre. We feel we are at the optimum return per acre now, but we will expand as fast as technology establishes the need for a new optimum size." Mr. Kenner added that each unit beyond the basic 4,600 acres might just as well be operated as a completely separate farm as far as machinery and crop production are concerned. Charles Lysfjord, manager for Mrs. Ell Kiene in Minnesota, feels that once a person has passed his own psychological barrier there is no basic limit to size. Lysfjord says, "After you have made up your mind to grow, it is no sweat. After the first two men and machines, it makes little difference. From that point you just grow."

One of the largest farms in South Dakota belongs to the William J. Asmussen family. Most of the land was acquired in the 1930's and early 1940's when many people were abandoning their farms in that state. Stanley Asmussen, who does some of the managing for his father, feels that their farm, which is in excess of 25,000 acres, does not represent the ultimate in size as far as economy is concerned. Asmussen says, "When you have grown up on the farm like I have, you really are not awed by its size. It seems very natural."[2]

What Do the Farmers Say About the Size of Their Specific Enterprises?

Although much has been written and said about the merits of specialized farming, very few of the farms studied were purely one-enterprise farms. Most of these farms had several diversified enterprises of nearly equal volume and importance to the farm. Geography, always a major determinant as to crops and livestock operations, obviously was generally responsible for the type of farms established, but surprisingly enough, personal preference often was the real reason for the ultimate selection. Eddie Dunn, farm economist at North Dakota State University, has helped many farmers in the state make detailed projections to determine what operation would be most profitable for their particular business. Dunn discovered that after all alternatives were reviewed personal preference caused many farm families to ignore the potentially most profitable operation, selecting the third or fourth one instead.

This factor probably is a cause for the failure of many farms.

Instead of being profit-minded they are more determined to follow a traditional pattern rather than innovation. It is the impression of this writer, however, that this was not the case with most of the successful farmers he interviewed. They readily admitted that they had dropped favorite operations once they found where the greater profits were. These people generally were highly adaptive and innovative, and change was not as hard for them as for the great majority of the more traditionlly minded individuals.

Kenneth R. Krause of the United States Department of Agriculture and Leonard R. Kyle of Michigan State University did extensive research on costs of production and income of large farms vs. small farms. They concluded that the large farm probably was not quite as efficient as the highly mechanized one-man farm, but the large farm had definite advantages in buying as well as selling its production. These advantages amounted to $10 to $13 per acre savings in production costs and $5 to $6 an acre greater income from sales than two- or three-man corn farms of the 500-acre size.

Lindley Finch, vice president and agriculturalist for the Continental Illinois National Bank of Chicago, which is very active in midwestern agricultural financing, points out that farms have become so mechanized and large that production resources of $1.5 million per worker (1974) were common. Finch adds, "Much higher amounts per worker are not rare. And capital requirements are increasing rapidly."

Then Secretary of Agriculture Earl Butz, challenging members of the North Dakota Bankers Association to provide adequate financing for farmers, said, "The capital intensity per worker is $150,000 on a family farm worth $500,000 and that compares to $25,000 per worker in industry." N. R. Lake, a Fergus Falls, Minnesota, agricultural banker, says that he does not set a dollar limit on the amount loaned to an individual farmer. Lake instead works backward from cash flow and family needs. He said, "Unless a family plans and projects a net income from farming of at least $12,000 a year [1974], there isn't much point in encouraging them because they obviously are not setting their goals high enough."

When farmers were asked what they thought the minimum-sized economic farm unit must be to provide a living as well as to be able to amortize indebtedness, several preferred to answer in terms of investment and cash flow rather than in the number of acres or animal units. David Garst and John Chrystal of Iowa expressed the opinion that a $250,000 investment per worker would provide an adequate family income. Whether that was invested in large machinery for cash corn farming and rented land or whether that was invested in a smaller farm with an intensive livestock enterprise, all was immaterial as far as net results were concerned.

Charles A. Cannon III stressed the value of money management more than any other phase of his operation and agreed with Garst and Chrystal. He believed that $250,000 was the minimum initial investment necessary to provide adequate family living. Jameson Larimore III of North Dakota refused to place either an acre or dollar figure on the necessary economic unit because he believed that personal desires of the farm family should more than anything else determine the size of the farm. Larimore noted the wide change of styles of living of farm families in his area and commented that the farm size would have to be several times larger in some cases than in others. Although his area in the Red River Valley is an exceedingly prosperous one, he noted that the average farm size was climbing rapidly as the smaller farms were gradually being absorbed into larger units.

Earl Glidden and R. C. Crockett of Minnesota and the late Jacob Geritz and Thomas (Buck) Snortland of North Dakota all preferred to use cash flow to determine the size of unit. Glidden, whose farm has tripled in acres and whose total volume has increased many fold during his nearly 25 years of farming, felt steady growth was necessary just to maintain a certain standard of living. He added, "Labor needs more to live too, so unless you are big enough to really mechanize, what choice do you have but to grow?" R. C. Crockett and Jacob Geritz agreed that, in 1960, $50,000 gross sales were necessary for each person working full time on a farm to provide an adequate living. By 1970 that figure was $75,000, and by the late 1970's they predicted that they would have to gross $100,000 in sales for each fully employed individual to maintain the desired standard of living.

Thomas (Buck) Snortland preferred to use production per man to determine the size of unit. When he started farming, 500 tons of grain was more than adequate to supply a good living and amortize indebtedness. That volume increased steadily and by 1972 Snortland felt that 1,000 tons of grain was necessary to justify a fully employed person. Snortland, like all the other farmers, pointed out that volume per man had to increase because the margin of profit was steadily declining while the consumers were eating better than ever at a smaller percentage of their income. He said, "Only through mechanization and growth can we keep this up." Jacob Geritz concluded, "Too many farmers in our area failed or could not expand their farms as their sons grew up and that's why the boys went to town to work. I can stand still [not grow] but I don't expect my son to do so."

Herman H. Lee, Red River Valley grower of sugar beets, pinto beans, small grain, and various specialty seed crops, said:

We will continue to expand land-wise. Whenever we can either buy or rent a good piece of land at rates under which we can project a profit, we will take it. Right now we could add another thousand acres to our operation without any additional machinery or manpower. In fact, it would be desirable for us to get more land to balance our work load a bit better. Our seed plant is running at full capacity, and my year-round men are busier in the winter than they are in the summer.

George C. Schuller farms over 4,000 acres in South Dakota of which 1,500 are in crops. In addition, he has a separate brood cow herd and beef fattening lot. The Schuller farm was started as a 160-acre homestead in 1911. Land was bought and lost during the 1920's and early 1930's, but after they purchased their first John Deere "A" tractor in 1937, they started to add land "whenever some that was located right became available." Schuller said:

Now we are using tractors of 135 horsepower and have a comfortable work schedule for our four men. I think the smallest livable unit in our area would be one section of corn and alfalfa combined with one section of intensively managed pasture for an integrated brood cow–feedlot operation. You need at least a section to justify good power units and at that small an acreage you would have to rely on custom operators for harvest. If I had to rely on small grain, I would need at least 2,000 acres and then I'm not sure it would be profitable. The government payments [1971] would probably represent the net income. I would not care for that kind of unit.

The bonanza farms of the Red River Valley of Manitoba, Minnesota, and North Dakota were some of the best examples of large-scale mechanized farms of the horsepower era. The bonanzas, which relied heavily on wheat monoculture, were generally professionally managed and well-capitalized in contrast to the average farms of that period. They operated in units of up to 5,000 acres, realizing that full economy of scale was attained by using a plow, binder, seeder, and five or six horses for each 250 acres. The bonanzas generally were simply multiples of 250 acres, and if they had advantages over independent farms of 250 acres, they were via discount buying and direct selling that were made possible because of their volume.

The Sabe family homesteaded in western North Dakota in 1907.

J. Odell Sabe is the third generation to operate that farm, which during the 67 years of occupancy has increased sixteen-fold in land area and thirty-fold in livestock units. Ironically, today less labor is required than at any time in its 67-year history. Young Sabe maintains that even with such growth the farm is still at an absolute minimum needed to produce a living for his family. Sabe operates primarily a grain farm with a brood cow herd to consume all the chaff and straw salvaged from the crops. The calf crop is backgrounded to yearling weights so that except for the wheat all the crop on the farm is sold through livestock.

Small Grains

For this study no sizeable small-grain farms were investigated in Iowa and southern Minnesota. All the small-grain farms considered were located in northwestern Minnesota, the Dakotas, Manitoba, and Montana. In total, 82 farms had small grain for a major or the largest unit of operation. These farmers were asked what in their estimation the minimum economic small-grain unit was for their area. Specifically, the question was, "What is the smallest practical size unit in this enterprise in this area that is necessary to have full economy of scale, to enjoy the kind of living you want, and, assuming you have 30 years, to amortize your land purchase?"

For these 82 small-grain farm managers the preferences for size of farm ranged from 1,000 acres to 10,000 acres. The average-sized practical small-grain unit calculated by them was 3,097 acres. Thirty-five expressed a preference for more than 3,097 acres, and only 11 farmers mentioned fewer than 2,000 acres. Of those under 2,000 acres, all except two gave answers in the 1,600- to 1,800-acre range. Ironically, it was R. S. O'Day of western Montana who quoted the smallest acreage of 1,000 acres as the minimum unit. O'Day also felt that one-third of this minimum unit would be available for summer fallow. In reality, O'Day farms far in excess of what he stated to be the minimum unit and also has auxiliary enterprises. He also expressed the opinion that quite likely he would have to adjust his standard of living to conform to the net profits of a 1,000-acre farm.

Norman Weckerly, farming in North Dakota, expressed a strong desire to have no farm less than a full two-man operation and stated that 7,500 acres, including summer fallow, was the smallest practical small-grain unit he would want to operate. Weckerly agreed that 2,000 acres could be practical, but it was not his preference. Like O'Day, he was involved in several other farm and non-farm enterprises because he preferred diversification and he liked to be busy.

The largest small-grain farm encountered had in excess of 21,000 acres of grain and an equal amount of summer fallow. Several farms had an excess of 10,000 acres of small grain each year, and with only a few exceptions these farms were operated by young men who had used large equipment and had rented land for rapid expansion. After they had generated adequate cash flow through renting, they purchased land on contracts-for-deed whenever they could. Most of these men were in their late twenties or early thirties and were very excellent managers.

Milton Hertz, an ex-teacher with education beyond his B.A. degree, was one of the nation's four outstanding young farmers of America in 1969 and is a good example of the large, progressive small-grain farmer. Hertz believed that the minimum small-grain farm should be at least 4,000 acres. His grain land exceeded 5,000 acres in crop plus an equal amount in summer fallow. Milt Hertz and his wife Carol were also developing a sizeable brood cow herd and a cattle feeding operation. The cow herd depended heavily on the chaff and straw salvaged from the grain business.

According to Hertz, a small-grain operation could grow to 20,000 acres of crop and 20,000 acres of fallow before there would be any loss in efficiency. He felt that there probably was no upper limit to the size of a small grain farm if the management was available. Like J. O'Dell Sabe, Milt Hertz is a third generation farmer who started his operation on a half section homesteaded by his grandfather in 1904 and farmed by Milt's father until 1959 when it was given to Milt. His father, Gothold Hertz, was farming about 3,500 acres at that time, 11 times the size of the original homestead, and by 1973 the third generation had increased the farm to 50 times the size of the 1904 homestead. That growth is in keeping with a previously quoted saying of G. F. Warren of early twentieth century farm management fame. Warren wrote in 1913, "All progress in civilization depends on having each farmer produce more than his father produced."

John S. Dalrymple III, fourth generation farmer of the famous bonanza farm family, agrees with Hertz that there may be no upper limit to the size of a small-grain farm. But he also points out that in eastern North Dakota small grain has to compete with potatoes, sugar beets, and other intense crops, and probably it would be unwise to concentrate on small grains. Dalrymple would prefer 16,000 to 24,000 acres of small grain, no summer fallow included, and 10 full-time employees.

David and Ivan Miller farm on a very large scale in the tri-state area south of Wahpeton, North Dakota. The two brothers farm completely independent of each other, but for the sake of motivation, they are deliberately competitive. The Millers use wheat and barley in rotation with soybeans and sunflowers, and even though they are in what is considered good corn and sugar beet country, they feel that their profits are as good with their crops as with any other. The Miller brothers are third generation farmers who believe that one of their greatest experiences came when they were 11 and 12 years old and had to operate the farm while their father was incapacitated for a long period because of a serious operation. Dave recalls that the experience gave him the "feel for farming" and the confidence that he could do a job. Using their father as a good example of motivation, Ivan and David each started on his own in 1952 and laid the base for two well-known success stories. David Miller says that he had made a profit farming every year, "even in 1962," when a summer of almost continuous rains nearly innundated the upper Red River Valley. The Millers are known for their excellent management. David feels that, although between them he and his brother operate farms more than the size of a township, they could each grow to about 30,000 acres before their farms would get out of hand.

The Hoggarth brothers, David Glinz, James Walton, Freddie Mutschler, and Loren C. Jetvig farm in northwestern Minnesota and the eastern portion of North Dakota on a scale similar to the Miller brothers. It is the opinion of these men that the peak of efficiency in small-grain farming is somewhere between 3,600 and 4,000 acres. (Some of them do have sunflowers, soybeans, or corn in their rotation.) All of these men farm well in excess of what they considered the optimum-sized farm because they were still able to generate satisfactory profits per acre.

David Glinz said of his experience, "Our net profit per acre increased steadily up to 4,000 acres. Then we experienced little change in net profit per acre up to 14,500 acres. I believe we can feel our way safely to 20,000 acres without experiencing any decline in net income per acre."

Glinz felt that if land could be rented or purchased in a relatively solid block he could manage 30,000 to 40,000 acres without experiencing any difficulty. But he also noted that about one-fifth of the total "tractor time" was spent moving between fields. Freddie Mutschler verified Glinz's feelings about moving the equipment. He commented that, even though he had one solid piece of 2,880 acres, his farm was "scattered over 20 miles end to end." Mutschler said, "I would not want to spread out more than 30 miles, but we did 640 acres with two outfits in one day, which included moving twice over a distance of 10 miles. Maybe I would reconsider that limitation if I could find the land."*

The two outfits that Mutschler referred to were four-wheel-drive tractors pulling 42-foot field cultivators. He carried 400 gallons of fuel on each tractor so that he did not have to stop during the day to refuel. Mutschler is a very particular manager who does not tolerate loose ends, and he feels this has given him a psychological advantage with many landlords who want to see their land operated by a good tenant. In spite of his large farm operation, Mutschler spends a great deal of time doing commercial crop spraying with his two planes. The planes introduced him to using two-way radios, and in a few years he had a unit in each of his tractors, pickups, and trucks and in his car (10 in all), which he says greatly reduces time spent on errands and directing operations.

Loren C. Jetvig started farming 90 acres while he was still in high school. Each year after starting to farm full time he has been able to make some expansion, and each time Jetvig expanded, he reduced his costs. He said:

Our costs because of our size are way down compared to most of my neighbors. I don't know where to quit. We may have a little slippage, but it does not show up in our net per acre. We are spread out 40 miles north to south but we have several blocks of 900 to 1,200 acres, so we are able to stay efficient. Our biggest problem is small fields and narrow bridges that restrict the size of our machinery.

George C. Howe, Jr., of Casselton, North Dakota, a third generation farmer who admits that he has no interest payments to make, believes that 3,600 acres is about the optimum small-grain farm in his area. Mrs. Howe said, "Each time we went over that limit, we seemed to hit a point of diminishing return. From time to time we

---

* G. F. Warren, writing in 1913, felt that 320 acres was about the largest farm for peak efficiency, but an exceptionally well-located farm might be as large as 640 acres. It was his opinion that if the farm were larger than 640 acres, it would probably be better to operate the land in separate units to avoid excessive loss of time with horse travel. Freddie Mutschler's four-wheel-drive tractors with rubber-tired equipment can travel over roads 5 to 10 times faster than the farmer with horses, a major factor in enabling farm size growth.

have operated more, but it compounded the responsibility more than the increased income merited." Howe added, "If we were not living within our social and economic objectives, we would increase our operations because then it would be worth the effort."

Howe admitted that he stepped into a very fine farming operation and that he was able to improve it the way he wanted to. That was his challenge. Howe pointed out that if his son wanted to expand he would go along with his wishes. He said, "After all, if I were my son, the first thing I would want to do is to test the limits of my ability." Those are the feelings of a man who readily admits that he did not have to struggle and that by his very nature is conservative, but he would expect his son to show his worth. Howe is a certified seed producer and readily acknowledges that size has its advantages because "seed companies and farmers buying certified seeds naturally look to the bigger growers first."

These are some of the opinions expressed by small-grain farmers who are farming an average of 4,613 acres of small grain even though as a group they acknowledge that 3,097 acres were necessary for economy of scale if no other enterprise were involved. This is in contrast to 1,920 acres which the 1973 U.S.D.A. study concluded was a fully mechanized one-man farm capable of producing grain at the lowest cost per unit, and considerably larger than the 694-acre average small-grain farm in the area surveyed by the government study.

Of the 82 small-grain farmers in this study only 17 relied exclusively on small grain. Nearly all of them had acreages in excess of what they believed was necessary for an adequate standard of living. None of the 82 expressed any serious dissatisfaction with his income. It might be assumed that this is probably because their acreage is over six times as large as the average small-grain farm in their area, not counting their other enterprises.[3]

Corn and Soybeans

The corn and soybean farmers questioned for this topic were all located in Iowa, southern and western and west central Minnesota, the eastern third of South Dakota, and the southeastern corner of North Dakota. They were asked, "What is the minimum size for a cash corn or cash soybean farm necessary to gain the full economy of scale and provide an adequate family living?" Geography was often the major determinant in the difference of minimum size.

In no case did any farmer feel that less than 640 acres of continuous cash corn cropping could provide the necessary economical return. One farmer, Jack O'Farrell of eastern South Dakota, questioned the wisdom of relying on a continuous cash corn crop in his area. He stated that a better practice would be 500 acres of corn for silage combined with 500 head of cattle for each man-year. The O'Farrells exceeded those figures per man in both acres and cattle numbers. The largest number of acres believed necessary for continuous cash corn was stated by Martin Buer of central Minnesota who farms on the fringe of the commercial Corn Belt. Buer is in an area where corn yields average 70 to 80 bushels per acre, and he did not feel comfortable with producing only corn unless he had a large acreage. Therefore, he felt 2,500 acres was the minimum continuous cash corn farm he would want. Along with his crop production, Buer preferred to milk cows and feed cattle.

The corn farmers as a group felt that 972 acres was the minimum size desired for a continuous cash corn farm. Generally, the lower figures, those under 800 acres, were given by farmers in Iowa and southeastern Minnesota and the higher average figures in western Minnesota and the Dakotas. Most farmers expressed a preference for some form of diversification and practiced it. The desired minimum corn unit of 972 acres was, according to these farmers, 172 acres over the 800-acre model fully mechanized one-man corn farm determined to be the optimum by the U.S.D.A. study in 1973. In actual practice these farmers averaged 1,646 acres of corn ranging from a low of 450 acres to a high of 7,000 acres. Only one farmer producing continuous corn on 2,400 acres was exclusively a corn farmer.

Clem Hebel of Iowa, who started farming on 160 acres of rented land in 1936, relying on "more than 100 per cent borrowed capital," commented that his concepts of size have changed nearly every year. He said, "When I could finally buy 248 acres in 1947, I thought I was pushing the limits. Now I am not sure where the upper limit is. We had been using three sets of 8-row equipment, but now we have gone to two 12-row planters, two 12-row cultivators, and two combines with 4-row heads. Our bottleneck now is in the operation of our drying plant because it can only handle 10,000 bushels a day. I have come from 2-row planters and cultivators to 12-row equipment, which works better and faster than the machinery I used in the 1930's. I cannot see the ultimate."

Virgil Mellies, born in Kansas and too poor to go to high school, worked his way north to Minnesota. He was unable to get a full-time job on a farm until 1940. By 1944 Mellies had saved $728 and was able to rent a farm from "a man who took a liking" to him. This man loaned Mellies $2,000 for operating funds and co-signed a note for $2,600 to buy machinery. Although the average farm in the central Minnesota area was 240 acres, Mellies was able to rent 440 acres in his first year.

In 1946 he had a chance to buy 160 acres in the vicinity on a contract-for-deed, but because he had invested all of his former profits in bigger and better equipment, he was forced to borrow the $1,500 required down payment. Fortunately, by then he had proven his managerial ability and had the strength to borrow money for the down payment. In his travels Mellies observed what other farmers were doing and by the mid-1950's came to the conclusion that he should expand whenever he could.

Mellies, a big, strong man, was not afraid of hard work and long hours, but, contrary to many farmers, he also did a lot of paper-work to project how he could develop a continuous corn growing program. He liked big equipment, and whenever newer and bigger machines came on the market, he bought them. Machines were his answer to working alone as much of the year as possible. Mellies believed that the minimum economic corn farm in his area would probably be 1,000 acres, which could be handled by a single eight-row planter and combine. "The average man," he said, "should be able to handle that and would not need to hire more than 330 hours of labor a season." Mellies farms more than 2,000 acres of corn and has a much lower average of hired labor per 1,000 acres. He thinks if he gets much larger, he might find his net income tapering off, "But," he says, "there will still be a good profit per acre. Just now I don't have too much desire to expand because we like long winter vacations and our family life should get proper attention. However, if my sons decide they want to farm, we will continue expanding."

South Dakotan Walter J. Bones, Jr., has been using eight-row planters and cultivators since 1960, but he uses six two-row pickers to do the harvest. Bones said, "Now [1972] two combines do the same job in less time and with greater ease. I think a cash-corn operation should have at least 800 acres for each full-time man."

In southeastern Minnesota among the hills and between the creeks and ravines is some of the finest corn land of the state. Here P. D. Hempstead produces an average of 450 acres of corn each year and acknowledges that he has one of the largest corn acreages in his county. He thinks that a truly economical cash corn unit should be at least 600 acres. But he also knows that, because of the intense livestock industry present in the area, there is a corn deficit, and expansion for corn acreage is nearly impossible.

Donald A. Schulz of Minnesota and his father and brother operate what they regard to be an economical corn and soybean farm. They have about 1,500 acres in those two crops. In addition, the Schulzes have other crops and are involved in agri-business, besides finding time to do considerable custom work for neighboring farmers who have smaller acreages and cannot justify purchase of larger specialized machines. Schulz admits it would be economical to expand. "But," he adds, "the local dairy farmers are in a solid financial position and they are hard to budge."

Farm manager Roy Selley from Iowa commented:

I used to think 600 acres was the really economical level for cash corn production, but in the last couple of years I have decided that 1,000 acres is closer to the optimum. You have to have at least 800 acres to justify a combine and with a 12-row planter you can get the job done on that acreage in six to eight days and with the 12-row cultivator it takes two or three days to cover the field. An expansion by units of 600 to 800 acres would be possible and profitable after the initial 800 acres. But that's hard to do in our area.

Two young farmers in central Minnesota, Harold T. Petersen and Arlo J. Gordon, and Stanley D. Olson of southern Minnesota, readily agree that 600 to 640 acres of cash corn may be adequate for a good living. However, they were all quick to add that the optimum level of economy is reached at a considerably larger acreage. Even though their average acreage was greater than the 640 acres, they admitted that their efficiency was still climbing.

The soybean farmers questioned were all using beans in rotation with other crops, and few of those interviewed wanted to classify themselves as professional bean farmers. Many of them had 400 to 800 acres and the top grower had 2,700 acres. The soybean growers expressed a preference of 1,183 acres of soybeans as a minimum for a profitable unit if they had to rely on soybeans as their sole income and to gain the most from them economically. The average acreage of the farmers who used soybeans as one of their major crops was 1,100 acres. In many respects beans appeared an easier crop to grow than corn, but for undetermined reasons the preference leaned toward corn. Many farmers had reduced or quit soybeans over the years. Perhaps, they felt that they were better corn managers.

At the age of 20 Charles Hawbaker and his brother won out over 64 competitive bidders to rent 180 acres in northern Iowa. Nine years later the brothers were able to buy that farm. As the two brothers grew older, it became obvious that they were competing with each other for land, so Charles and Donna Hawbaker decided to move to Minnesota. To gain economy of scale and to pool management, financial, and labor resources, Hawbaker joined hands with some farmer neighbors. The concepts and the economics were right, but after two years, personality conflicts caused the group to disband. Hawbaker said of that venture and experience:

We had so many things going for us and I learned where the real economies were, so after we dissolved, I did all I could to get bigger enterprises. As a boy working under Dad, I had been taught to keep excellent records. Today, I cost account everything. From those records I know I could live from the profits of 500 acres of soybeans, but I would prefer 1,500 acres [1972]. But I would really want to rotate that with 1,500 acres of corn.[4]

Non-crop Enterprises

Of the 136 farms that supplied the major portion of data for this survey, 96 had livestock or poultry operations. Of these, 46 had more than one such enterprise and some had as many as four sizeable animal or poultry units. Of the 40 farms that did not have livestock enterprises, the greatest proportion of them was among the potato and sugar beet farms of the Red River Valley of Minnesota and North Dakota. Potato farming demands significant year-round work to keep the basic farm labor force busy so that the need to seek alternative work is not necessary. Traditionally, sugar beets have provided a sufficiently stable and attractive income so that beet farmers have not sought alternative sources of profits.

Beets and potatoes generally require small grain in the rotation process. Grains do very well on land that has been liberally treated with commercial fertilizers for the beets and potatoes. Many of the beet and potato farms produce small-grain certified seed because the land is relatively weed free following the intensively cultivated beet and potato crops. In the eastern portion of North Dakota large grain, soybean, and sunflower farms represent the next highest proportion of straight cash crop farming. In contrast, many farm animal enterprises completely dominate the farms, and every acre of crop land is devoted to producing feed for animals with no cash sales of any crops. This was particularly true of the intense turkey, feeder cattle, dairy, and hog farms of Iowa,

Minnesota, and the eastern portion of South Dakota. The animal-oriented farms tended to be somewhat smaller in acreage, but gross income per acre was much higher than in the cash grain areas. The Red River Valley again was an exception. Ironically, the largest farms in total acreage in each state surveyed also had the largest livestock or poultry operations. In each state they were by far the largest businesses in total dollar volume.

The consensus of the beef feedlot operators was that 1,000 cattle per employee made a satisfactory enterprise based on economy of scale. In every case, a feedlot of that size was presumed to be a totally farmer–feeder-oriented business and not a commercially oriented lot. As earlier stated, Jack O'Farrell's opinion was that in his area 500 acres of crop feeder cattle per employee made a well-balanced program. The O'Farrells exceeded those figures considerably, but this is probably because several members of the family were involved, and they were willing to exert themselves to a greater degree than can be expected of hired labor. O'Farrell felt that it took a feedlot of at least 1,500 head to maximize the use of an adequate line of special equipment needed for such an operation.

Most feedlot operators expressed some fear about how large a feedlot could get before it drew too much criticism from the public because of potential pollution problems. The O'Farrells felt that possibly they would prefer building a totally new and separate facility rather than enlarging their current lot. Stanley D. Olson and P. D. Hempstead in southwestern and southeastern Minnesota, where population density is much greater than in the Dakotas or Montana, were among those who commented about feedlot limitations because of pollution risks. Hempstead said, "Frankly, the restrictions on feedlots threaten present economics in a feedlot. We are sensing public irritations towards the lots in our neighborhood. "Confinement housing and manure injection," commented Olson, "could be the way of the future and they seem to be economically feasible as well as environmentally safe."

For many years Dalton Docter has owned and operated the largest private feedlot in South Dakota. Docter has suffered and overcome some severe setbacks during his feeding career. Docter's father, a small town repairman, let Dalton start farming on 320 acres of land. The land was low and flat and unattractive to the neighboring farmers, but 13-year-old Dalton was unconcerned, for he wanted to be a cattle feeder. His father had used machinery from trade-ins at his garage and let Dalton "go farming." Dalton said:

I knew we were and had always felt poor and I soon learned that farmwise we were behind everyone and thought we could never catch up. I really put in the hours and did all the custom work I could to get a cash flow, but I knew that cattle feeding is what I wanted. It didn't take me long to figure out that the secret to feeding was numbers, and because I was poor and lacked credit, my only solution was to turn to custom feeding to build volume.

It seems ironical that when I started out I just could not borrow money to get a start, but now that I have become established, most of the time there is more money available than I need. I have had big losses from bad winter storms, wet spring weather, a loss from theft of 321 cattle valued at over $112,000, and a setback of $260,000 when American Beef [Packers] went broke. These setbacks always seem to come just when everything has been going well, but even with them we keep moving ahead. In spite of them I have moved away from all custom feeding to feeding more of my own cattle. I don't mind the risk.

Although Docter has a very large acreage under cultivation, feedlot consumption far exceeds the production from his farm. It is his opinion that the size of feedlot is more governed by the availability of feed than by any other factor.

I don't care to have another major feedlot within a hundred miles of me or I lose a competitive advantage. The expense of moving cattle is not bad compared to the cost of moving feed. In the location I am in I would like to feed 20,000 cattle during the good feeding months and then taper off to 5,000 to 8,000 in the most severe months. This is big enough to give me all the advantages of size. Maybe if we go to more confinement, we will be better prepared to keep our numbers up during the bad months.

Not everyone feels that a feedlot the size of Dalton Docter's is necessary, but his has been built on a boyhood dream, with lots of ambition and hard work. He knows and is prepared to take the hard knocks, and more than anything else is motivated by the challenge because he remembers when he felt he was "poor." His one-time feedlot capacity is 12 times the size of what most feeders felt was the smallest size needed to gain full economy of scale for a farmer-feedlot operation. Like all sizeable ventures, Docter's is highly visible and subject to considerable criticism, but Dalton Docter seems immune to it all, satisfied that he has made his mark.

A study by agricultural extension economists in North Dakota indicates that over the years fewer than half the beef brood cow herds made an actual profit based on true cost accounting figures. At the same time, however, many owners of small cow herds claim that they have never lost money on their enterprises. The figures of agricultural economists in the Midwest, based on data of beef brood cow owners in record keeping groups, indicate that it costs in excess of $200 a year to maintain a cow. But Delbert Moore, president of the North Dakota Stockmen's Association, has publicly asserted that it would be difficult for most of the cow raisers of that state to show over $100 cash costs per year. Many farmers do not place a value on their labor nor do they charge the capital cost of their land against the cows. Some farmers, especially those in grain production, feel that the cow herd utilizes only land that cannot be used for crops and would otherwise be wasted; therefore, no charge should be made for it. By-products from grain production are used to carry the cows during much of the winter, and no charge is made for that. Some good grain farmers with cow herds stated that they get by with less than $50 direct out-of-the-pocket costs per year on each cow.

But, in general, the consensus of the brood cow owners interviewed was that a cow herd had to consist of 572 head to gain full economy of scale. The range of opinion varied from 250 head to 1,000 head, with most owners expressing a preference for a 500-head herd because that was large enough to justify the use of two people. The composite average-sized herd of all the owners was 856 head. The smallest actual herd was 250 head, while the largest contained 4,000 animals. In only a few cases did the cow herd represent the sole enterprise of the farm or ranch. Ironically, when it was the sole enterprise, the herd generally was smaller than those of the diversified operations.

The two largest cow herds numbering 3,000 and 4,000 cows were located in Iowa and in both cases were part of a larger diversified farming operation. The manager of one of those herds, Roy Selley, said, "A profitable cow herd is one big enough to utilize all the roughage produced on the farm that the cows can salvage themselves. You want to haul as little as possible to a cow herd." Selley lets his cows graze on intensively developed pastures in the summer time and corn stalks during the winter season.

Jack Dahl, an outstanding North Dakota rancher, gave 250 cows as the smallest practical cow herd, even though his own well-managed herd was over 700 head. In spite of his relatively low estimate for a profitable cow herd, Dahl added, "The size of a well-managed herd depends entirely on the manager's ability. I am a perfectionist, so that limits me to probably 1,000 cows. I do admit that a good manager with proper help could run a cow herd of any size he set his mind to." Dahl has completely computerized performance test records of his cow herd dating to 1959. He was one of the early computerized record keepers in North Dakota, and because of the good performance of his cattle, they consistently sell at a premium to the same buyers over the years.

William A. Stegner also has one of the top performance-tested commercial herds of North Dakota. Stegner, the son of a homesteader who lived in a sod house until 1927, has used artificial insemination on a brood cow herd of 1,200 animals since 1964. Stegner, like Dahl, is a good record keeper and, like Roy Selley, believes that cows should live from a high portion of salvage feeds. He has intense pasture management, but he also purchases straw from neighbors farming up to 8 miles from his ranch. Using good records, Stegner had a cash-cost-per-calf born in 1972 of under $100. Stegner was advised by professional agriculturalists that, based on averages, his ranch could support 260 cows, but by using straw and chaff, he has been able to provide for 1,200 cows. His ranch produces enough beef from the steer calf crop alone to provide the meat needs for nearly 2,200 Americans each year, but before those animals are slaughtered, they represent the meat requirements of 5,500 consumers. This gives no allowance for the female calf crop increase which, if used for beef purposes, would provide the needs for an additional 4,500 people.

Milton Hertz combines a grain, cow herd, and feedlot operation on his farm in his effort to get total integration and to make full use of nearly all he produces on the land. Like the better ranchers, Hertz uses intensive pasture management on both seeded and native pastures for summer grazing. At the end of the pasture season, his cows are fed chiefly from the chaff and straw collected in wagons behind the combines. Hertz was able to increase his brood cow herd by over 100 cows without adding an additional acre simply by salvaging a formerly wasted product. He also uses a straw-grain mix to background as many as 1,200 calves each year in his feedlot operation.

Clem Hebel of Iowa professes that his brood cow herd has been "a real money maker, even better than the feedlot, because they thrive on salvage products." Hebel said, "Our next expansion will be in the size of a cow herd so it will be large enough to use all of the excess stalklage we have from our corn crop."

Walter J. Bones, Jr., has one of South Dakota's best known

Hereford ranches. Bones has relied heavily on the salvage of shucks and stalks from a large corn crop to keep his sizeable cow herd fed. Most of the corn crop is fed to his hogs rather than to beef animals. Bones said, "Many farmers have had a cow herd as a sideline and they have let them graze the corn fields. But as land costs get higher, they will probably have to confine their cows to reduce the waste and will have to haul the stalks to the cows. We save our cobs and leaves [shucklage] as it comes from the combines and leave it in dumps in the fields. The cows thrive on it."

Turning waste into food, keeping good records, and breeding excellent animals are some practices that innovators such as Bones, Dahl, Garst, Hebel, Hertz, and Stegner have adopted that have enabled them to grow and succeed.

The milk cow farmers interviewed expressed the opinion that a milking herd should contain at least 153 cows to be really efficient. Although only two farmers had fewer than 150 milk cows in their herds, the average size of the herds of the interviewed farmers was 197 cows. In all cases other operations were carried on by the dairy cow farmers. Some of them processed and retailed milk, most had feeder cattle sidelines, some had hogs, one had a trucking business, and nearly all sold some cash grain.

Richard C. Bleecker of North Dakota started with 20 milk cows and built his herd to 200 milkers by gradual expansion over 19 years. Bleecker noted that modern milking equipment had improved so much that his management problems were no more difficult with 200 head than with 20. Bleecker saw no need for diminishing returns per cow up to and beyond 1,000 cows. He acknowledged that with a milking herd that large he would want completely confined and environmentally controlled facilities. He said, "I certainly would not want to be reliant on the use of straw." The only reservation Bleecker had with a 1,000-head herd was the obvious need to have to contract with many neighbors for the production of feed because each animal consumed the production from nearly 4½ acres annually.

The Mertens brothers of North Dakota, who have a dairy herd about the same size as Bleecker's, reported that they were once concerned about their cow herd becoming so large that expansion would stop by virtue of the need to farm too much land. The short harvest season for good quality forage appeared to be a bottleneck to top production until the Mertens erected several large Harvestore sealed storage structures. Production for the entire herd based on well-kept records increased 62.5 per cent with no change in total acres farmed. The Mertens found that high moisture barley and low moisture stored haylage increased their production over the traditional dry fed crops. In addition, they saved thousands of dollars each year because of the greatly reduced need for processed feeds. Suddenly, a limited local market rather than the lack of land became the factor that appeared to be the greatest obstacle to expansion. The Mertens agreed that they profited more by "getting better rather than getting bigger."

The composite ideal hog operation in the opinion of the hog farmers interviewed was 2,609 head of hogs marketed each year. In actual practice these farmers, as a group, marketed an average of 5,184 hogs per year. The smallest number of hogs produced annually was 1,900 and the largest was 15,000. In all cases these were family-run operations including the largest unit, which was owned and managed by the Fisher brothers of Iowa, who called themselves "Hawkeye Hogs." The Fishers have a farrow-to-finish business, farrowing about 2,100 litters each year.

David Fisher mentioned that, while it takes about one person to produce 2,000 hogs from farrow-to-finish each year, that same man will be able to handle 3,000 hogs by the 1980's. James Irwin of Iowa, who produced 2,000 hogs farrow-to-finish in 1973, says that his goal for 1984 is 1,000 acres of corn or 4,000 hogs per man farrow-to-finish. Irwin says that his dollar goal, discounting serious inflation, will be $250,000 gross sales per man by that year. Lyall Larson of Minnesota has produced more than 2,000 hogs per man per year. Larson acknowledges that a well-managed, 160-acre corn farm with 2,000 hogs produced per year farrow-to-finish run by a father and two school-aged sons could make an excellent living. Irwin, Fisher, and Larson, however, all prefer the challenge of larger units and would not be satisfied with just producing 160 acres of corn and 2,000 hogs.

With the exception of the Fisher brothers, who raise a large acreage of corn for their hog enterprise, all the farmers involved had at least two other major enterprises in their farming operation. Earl Christianson, a large volume hog producer in Minnesota, admitted that he became involved in the hog business afer he had purchased a farm for the purpose of hunting ducks. After he had the farm, he observed the success of several good, scientific, confined hog breeders in a nearby community. What started as a small sideline soon developed into a sizeable business, but it has been profitable. Christianson admits that he had talked with many other breeders before entering hog raising. He said:

When we started looking for good management, we looked for experienced men, but in our discussions always came to the conclusion that these men were too tradition bound. We decided our idea about hog raising was novel enough. We ought to start with someone who was green to the hog business so he would not be hung up by traditional ideas.

Wayne Roberts, who was working for us, seemed to grasp ideas and adapted as quickly as anyone we knew, so we asked him to be our manager, under the guidance of Dr. Morgan who knew the problems of hog raising. Roberts proved the key to success, and although our costs have exceeded projections, our volume has been far greater than anticipated and the profits are as good as any enterprise I am involved in.

All of the hog farmers, like most of the beef and dairy farmers, felt that because of pollution problems and because of economic feasibility, automated, confined facilities were "the way of the future." Some management problems were more difficult with confinement, but others became much easier and the profit potential became much greater.

Another striking feature of the farmers visited was that 88 per cent of them were involved in one or more off-the-farm businesses. Most of those businesses were related to agriculture, but they were not necessarily directly associated to the main farm enterprise. Nearly all of these businesses were financed from the profits generated on the farm. Grain elevators, farm machinery dealerships, chemicals, seed houses, fertilizer supply houses, automobile agencies, and service stations headed the list of subsidiaries owned by these farmers. Locally owned banks, bowling alleys, retail dairy products firms, commercial feedlots, irrigation companies, crop pelleting plants, and potato processing plants were the second most numerous sideline businesses owned.

The most unusual auxiliary business was the ownership of an oil business and 106 producing oil wells by a farmer who felt so much local resentment against his buying any more land to farm that he turned to oil because, as he said, "I didn't want to stop growing." Another was the sole owner of a large electronics company. Still another had a meat packing plant that he built for slaughtering cattle from his feedlot. This plant was later purchased by the nation's largest packer. One Iowa farmer had a chain of seven fertilizer plants started as a result of direct buying of fertilizer for his farm. Several had part or total interest in liquor and eating establishments. A one-third interest in a Holiday Inn was held by one Dakota farmer; another owned several Country Kitchens; a Minnesota potato and livestock producer owned two liquor and dining facilities, besides having a Ramada Inn under construction.

Several farmers possessed land in Canada. Others had land in distant states, particularly in the Southwest, where they had specialty crops such as citrus fruits that were adapted to the warmer dry climate. One had a large cow herd in Florida. These people generally had their own airplanes, thus enabling them to travel between their widely separated holdings. In several cases the southern farms were started as the result of wintertime vacations, and these alert northern farmers took advantages of good opportunities that were made available to them. In a few cases the ventures proved to be bad financial risks, but the interviewees admitted that this was due to management mistakes—not because of the business itself.

Generally, the auxiliary business made satisfactory returns although, as in the case of all speculators and investors, many had lost money in various non-farm ventures. Nearly all the farmers felt that the risks in their other businesses were as great or greater than in farming. Generally, they felt more secure in their farming ventures. One South Dakotan's reply to a question about the profit potential of his auxiliary enterprise said, "I found out that our banking business is nearly as profitable as farming. In any case I am satisfied with it."

Only 8 farmers among the 136 did not have an auxiliary or subsidiary business. One of these, however, did extensive custom work with his four-wheel-drive tractors. But, as this farmer said, "Custom work is only done to generate extra cash for the boys and to spread the cost of the tractor. I personally do not need or want the income or the work, so I let the boys have all over the actual expenses. As soon as we can expand our farming operation, the custom work will come to an end."

Another farmer preferred to devote a good share of his time to civic activities and, therefore, did not want to become involved in other businesses. Two of the eight were young farmers expanding so rapidly that they needed all their cash flow in the farm account. The remaining four were older farmers who had surplus funds, but preferred to invest in the traditional stocks, funds, and insurance rather than in outright ventures. Two of these four had sons who were much more content than their fathers had been and actually discouraged the fathers from expanding. One of these fathers said, "My boys [both mature family men] are too comfortable and aren't as innovative or as eager to expand as I was at their age." Even though it greatly bothered this father, he controlled his urge to grow and wisely sat back, content to "ride it out" as his family

preferred. Fortunately, he has been able to keep himself involved
in civic activities.

The scope of second and third ranking enterprises in nearly all
cases far exceeded the total volume of the typical average-sized
farm. Yet, these enterprises were well-managed and profitable and
in all cases were managed by the family. They were not the
mythical Wall Street operators so glibly talked about by politicians
and farm organization leaders. They were farm boys who grew up
in farming and who wanted to farm. The non-farm, auxiliary, or
subsidiary activities that they owned and commonly managed
were often the result of their desire to reduce the costs of production by being able to purchase farm provisions cheaper if they
owned businesses on Main Street. Or many times they became
involved in Main Street ventures because the townspeople knew
these farmers had surplus funds and were looking for expansion
that offered diversification. A third factor, and a very powerful
one, was the sheer desire on the part of these successful farmers to
challenge themselves on unknown frontiers. If these men had
started out as merchants in the towns near where they are now
farming, they would not have stopped until they owned all the
businesses in their block and a section or two of land besides. This
is the nature of the man who loves the challenge of being his own
boss and likes the risk of free enterprise.[5]

NOTES

[1]*Gopher State Review*, Minnesota Crop and Livestock Reporting Service Bulle-
tin 329 (April, 1975); Philip M. Raup, "The Minnesota Rural Real Estate Market in
1973," *Minnesota Agricultural Economist*, No. 555 (May, 1974), p. 5; Jerome E.
Johnson, "The 1973 Farmland Market," *North Dakota Farm Research Bulletin*, 31,
No. 4 (March–April, 1974), p. 18; Terry L. Bentley, "Most South Dakota Land Sales
Made for Expansion," *The Dakota Farmer*, No. 13 (December, 1972), p. 9; A. H.
Benton, Andrew Boss, W. L. Cavert, "A Farm Management Study in Southeastern
Minnesota: Factors Influencing Profits," University of Minnesota Agricultural Ex-
periment Station Bulletin 172, St. Paul (October, 1917), pp. 4, 40–43; *Congressional
Record*, 118, No. 101 (June 21, 1972), H5905, H5910; Thomas Huheey, "To Begin
With," *The Farm Quarterly*, 27, No. 3 (March, 1972), p. 4.

[2]"Efficiency Winner: The One-Man Farm," *Agricultural Situation*, ed. Geraldine Schumacher, 58 (March, 1974), pp. 2–4; R. D. Jennings, "Large Scale Farming
in the United States, 1929," U.S. Bureau of the Census, *Fifteenth Census of the
United States: 1930, Census of Agriculture*, pp. 3, 8, 27; *Gopher State Review*,
Minnesota Crop and Livestock Reporting Service Bulletin 322 (September, 1974);
Radoje Nikolitch, *Our 31,000 Largest Farms*, U.S. Department of Agriculture, Agricultural Economic Report No. 175 (1970), pp. 1, 40, 111; interviews with:

David Garst, Coon Rapids, Iowa, June 12, 1972
The Garst Farms staff (David Garst, Stephen Garst, Roswell Garst, John Chrys-
   tal, Bob Henah), Coon Rapids, Iowa, June 13, 1972
Charles A. Cannon III, Pierre, South Dakota, May 5, 1973

Earl Glidden, Hallock, Minnesota, January 17, 1972

Harvey Dann, Winnipeg, Manitoba, February 16, 1973

Arden Burbidge, Park River, North Dakota, January 3, 1970, and March 14, 1973

George Rauenhorst, Olivia, Minnesota, March 16, 1972

Thomas (Buck) Snortland, Sharon, North Dakota, January 8, 1972

Jacob Geritz, Lakota, North Dakota, November 7, 1970

Donald Jarrett, Britton, South Dakota, March 2, 1972

Jay C. Swisher, Groton, South Dakota, March 1, 1972

Ed J. Dullea, Jr., Georgetown, Minnesota, January 5, 1972

Robert F. Reimers, Melville, North Dakota, January 6, 1970

Ole A. Flaat, Fisher, Minnesota, and Grand Forks, North Dakota, January 18 and February 15, 1972, and April 18 and 19, 1974

C. H. Underlee and sons (Nolan and Leslie), Hendrum, Minnesota, January 19, 1972

Pete A. Hermanson, Story City, Iowa, February 22, 1972

William Sinner, Casselton, North Dakota, December 28, 1969, and June 21, 1973

Ellery Bresnahan, Casselton, North Dakota, December 28, 1969, and June 21, 1973

George Sinner, Casselton, North Dakota, December 28, 1969 and June 21, 1973

Herman Natwick, Ada, Minnesota, March 10, 1971, and May 1, 1975

John Heline, Pierson, Iowa, February 23, 1972

Roy R. Moser, Amana, Iowa, February 21, 1972

Edgar, Daniel, and Stephen Keil, Ledger, Montana, May 12, 1972

Alvin Kenner, Leeds, North Dakota, December 12, 1970

Stanley Asmussen, Agar, South Dakota, April 13, 1972

Charles Lysfjord, Kennedy, Minnesota, March 14, 1973

International Conference on Mechanized Dryland Farming, eds. W. C. Burrows, R. E. Reynolds, F. C. Strickler, and G. E. Van Riper, Moline, Illinois (1970), pp. 308–309.

[3]Interview with Eddie Dunn, Agricultural Economics, North Dakota State University, Fargo, North Dakota, February 5, 1974; Kenneth R. Krause and Leonard R. Kyle, *Midwestern Corn Farms: Economic Status and the Potential for Large and Family-Sized Units*, U.S. Department of Agriculture, Agricultural Economic Report No. 216, Washington (1971), III, pp. 13–25; Leonard R. Kyle, "Size Is No Limit," *Farm Quarterly* (Spring/Planning, 1970), pp. 52–54; Leonard R. Kyle, "5000-Acre Farms in the Corn Belt," *Successful Farming* 68, No. 8 (August, 1970), pp. 30–31; Lindley Finch, "Structural Changes in the Agricultural Society," An address delivered to a seminar on Feeding the World's Hungry, A Challenge to Business, and a letter to the author, (August 16, 1974); *The Forum*, Fargo, North Dakota, (May 9, 1975); interviews with:

David Garst, Coon Rapids, Iowa, June 12, 1972

John Chrystal, Coon Rapids, Iowa, June 13, 1972

Charles A. Cannon III, Pierre, South Dakota, May 5, 1973

Jameson Larimore III, Larimore, North Dakota, December 12, 1970

Earl Glidden, Hallock, Minnesota, January 17, 1972

Jacob Geritz, Lakota, North Dakota, November 7, 1970

R. C. Crockett, Pelican Rapids, Minnesota, February 17, 1971

Thomas (Buck) Snortland, Sharon, North Dakota, January 8, 1972

Herman H. Lee, Borup, Minnesota, February 17, 1971

George C. Schuller, Claremont, South Dakota, April 10, 1972

Oscar N. Sabe, Gascoyne, North Dakota, April 8, 1972, and April 14, 1973

R. S. O'Day, Great Falls, Montana, May 14, 1972

James Walton, Breckenbridge, Minnesota, April 20, 1972
Norman Weckerly, Hurdsfield, North Dakota, March 8, 1972
Milton Hertz, Mott, North Dakota, April 7, 1972

"Milt Hertz Wants to Do Better Than His Dad," *The Bismarck Tribune* (April 19, 1969); G. F. Warren, *Farm Management*, New York (1913), p. 31; interviews with:

John S. Dalrymple III, Casselton, North Dakota, March 7, 1973
David Miller, Wahpeton, North Dakota, February 12, 1973
Gerald Hoggarth, Courtenay, North Dakota, March 8, 1972
David Glinz, Pingree, North Dakota, June 24, 1971
Freddie Mutschler, Wimbledon, North Dakota, June 24, 1971
Loren C. Jetvig, Lake Park, Minnesota, January 14, 1972
George C. Howe, Jr., Casselton, North Dakota, December 22, 1969

Gopher State Review for Crop and Livestock Reporters, 308 St. Paul, Minnesota Crop and Livestock Reporting Service (July, 1973); "Efficiency Winner: The One-Man Farm," *Agricultural Situation*, ed. Geraldine Schumacher, 58 (March, 1974), pp. 2–4; G.F. Warren, *Farm Management*, New York (1913), p. 265.

[4]Interviews with:

Jack O'Farrell, Marvin, South Dakota, February 25, 1972
Martin Buer, Atwater, Minnesota, April 1, 1972
Clem Hebel, Mason City, Iowa, February 21, 1972
Virgil Mellies, Hector, Minnesota, March 16, 1972
Walter J. Bones, Jr., Parker, South Dakota, February 24, 1972
P. D. Hempstead, Houston, Minnesota, March 28, 1972
Donald A. Schulz, Faribault, Minnesota, March 25, 1972
Roy Selley, Odebolt, Iowa, February 23, 1972
Harold T. Petersen, Murdock, Minnesota, March 30, 1972
Arlo J. Gordon, Murdock, Minnesota, March 15, 1972
Stanley D. Olson, Fairmont, Minnesota, March 29, 1972
Charles Hawbaker, Plainview, Minnesota, March 2, 1973

[5]Interviews with:

Jack O'Farrell, Marvin, South Dakota, February 25, 1972
Stanley D. Olson, Fairmont, Minnesota, March 29, 1972
P. D. Hempstead, Houston, Minnesota, March 28, 1972
Dalton Docter, Amherst, South Dakota, December 16, 1972, and March 17, 1975
Roy Selley, Odebolt, Iowa, February 23, 1972
Jack Dahl, Gackle, North Dakota, February 10, 1973
William A. Stegner, Rhame, North Dakota, April 8. 1972
Milton Hertz, Mott, North Dakota, April 7, 1972
Clem Hebel, Mason City, Iowa, February 21, 1972
Walter J. Bones, Jr., Parker, South Dakota, February 24, 1972
Richard C. Bleecker, Lisbon, North Dakota, February 11, 1972
Mertens brothers, Devils Lake, North Dakota, March 11, 1974
David Fisher, Hubbard, Iowa, January 26, 1974
James Irwin, Bagley, Iowa, January 26, 1974
Lyall Larson, Sargeant, Minnesota, March 26, 1972
Earl Christianson, Elbow Lake, Minnesota, February 26, 1973
Earl Schwartz, Kenmare, North Dakota, April 4, 1972
George C. Schuller, Claremont, South Dakota, April 10, 1972
Alfred Ehlers, Presho, South Dakota, April 10, 1972
Merl Allen, Moorhead, Minnesota, July 9, 1974

The Britton Journal (May 10, 1972); Conversations with Delbert Moore, Forbes, North Dakota, November 20, 1974; "Computer Record Keeping," *The Dakota Farmer*, 93, No. 9 (August, 1973), pp. 60, 62; "Pasture and Chaff Help Hertz Produce More Beef," *Successful Farming*, 71, No. 6 (April, 1973), p. W4.

CHAPTER IV

The Psychology of Success

Much has been written about the importance of mental attitude and the mental state in determining success or failure in one's career. Most students of history, psychology, or sociology can point to specific events in individual lives that caused a change in attitude. Anyone who lives or has lived in a farming community is well aware of what might be called the depressed farm syndrome attitude so often encountered among farmers. Farmers have long been known as chronic complainers, and it is obvious that politicians and farm organization leaders all too often do all they can to encourage the farmers along these lines.*

Several questions in this survey were used to determine the attitudes of the farmers interviewed, and in most cases, the wives joined in the response. In general, it is the feeling of this writer that most of these respondents do not fit into the category of chronic complainers. But it is also true that a few individuals did complain and frequently their spouses combatted the negative remarks in such a manner that it was obvious that the complaining was habit and not because of any particular issue. Ironically, the most negative attitude of all individuals interviewed was that of a man who had formerly been a very active officer in a farm organization. He became disillusioned with that organization and carried a considerable chip on his shoulder. But most of the interviewed farmers spoke freely and quite objectively about their good and bad experiences in farming. Only a few others, besides the previously mentioned exception, expressed any degree of mental

---

*In the 25 years that this writer has been professionally writing and speaking about agricultural affairs, he has taken special note of chronic complaints. The irony is that so much of the complaining comes from those with more than adequate living and material resources. Country gas stations, beer stops, and pool halls would provide excellent research grounds for anyone who desires to write a book on negative attitudes.

negativism, which was more often caused by the nature of his personality rather than by farm-related experiences.

Liberty Hyde Bailey, in preparation for a book published in 1927, contacted a large number of farmers throughout the nation to determine their attitudes and satisfactions. According to Bailey's findings, "The letters do not reflect the discouragements one would expect from current publicity of the [farm income] situation, and," he continued, "the greatest disaster would be a settled habit of complaint on the part of the farmer. I fear that some of our difficulties are states of mind. Dissatisfactions are hard to cure when they reach the heart."

In a 1901 publication on the profits of farming, Bailey stressed the importance of attitude in farming:

Most men desire to be cogs, or at least they are willing to be. The daily life is a routine which is made and prepared. Having reached a position that insures a comfortable financial return, the struggle for existence is reduced to its lowest terms, and the person is content. Now and then a person longs for a broader view, more dependence on personal initiative, a more perfect individualism. Perhaps such a person may not go on a farm, but he may consider it.

Bailey's article continued by saying that many farmers succeeded but also many failed. The biggest difference between failure in the city and on the farm was that the farm failure was more visible than the city failure which quickly became part of another man's business. Bailey felt that a good farmer could also make a good living "selling buttons." He commented, "They are not clodhoppers. They are not pessimists. . . . They ask more direct and pointed questions than all the experiment stations in the world can answer. They think their own thoughts."

Liberty Hyde Bailey and other farm management authorities have long realized that the best place to study farm management is on the farm of the successful operators. Surveys of national outstanding young farmers in recent years have made us more aware of the great potential for success in farming for a good manager. Bob Moraczewski wrote a series of articles in *The Farmer* about the 1971 national "Outstanding Young Farmer" recipients. In his articles Moraczewski noted several distinctive traits and practices of these young men that separate them from the average of their age group: (1) They built enthusiasm by reading about new ideas and successes of others; (2) They visited with other farmers, research personnel, and extension workers a great deal and they attended farm meetings; (3) They did much brainstorming and experimenting; (4) They prayed and exhibited abundant faith in God; (5) They took vacations that gave them a chance to think and to rest; (6) They borrowed heavily for new and modern equipment; (7) They were never satisfied and were always searching for something better.

These "Outstanding Young Farmers" had learned that by being involved in other activities they extended their experiences beyond their own farm, which gave them a better perspective, enabling them to see the major problems in farming without the clutter of detail that absorbs the thoughts when one is on the farm. Such activities also exposed them to the ideas of others, which enabled them to have a better view of the main problems of their own farming operation and of agriculture in general. Moraczewski quoted one of Minnesota's "Outstanding Young Farmers": "I had a neighbor who had so much trouble with little problems that mine looked insignificant. A few minutes with him would give me a big lift."

Above all, these "Outstanding Young Farmers" were highly motivated men. They were self-starters who were not afraid to tackle any problem. Motivation is a personal trait; it has to be developed, but it is the factor that "turns potential into performance. It takes a challenge to turn yourself on."

Hard work, historically meaning the back-breaking work of farms of the past or the undermechanized farm of the twentieth century, is not revered by the "Outstanding Young Farmers." The hardest and the most profitable work done by them is managing. "Pencil pushing can be as hard as digging postholes—but the pay often is better." Of the 87 "Outstanding Young Farmers" interviewed, only 18 per cent spent less than half of their time managing, 58 per cent spent at least three-fourths of their time managing, and 24 per cent spent more than 90 per cent of their time managing.

The "Outstanding Young Farmers" enjoyed making decisions, solving problems, and accepting responsibility. They liked the challenge of the problems and the risks that went with farming. Characteristically, these young men were aggressive, self-confident men who had a great urge to get the job done. They were innovative, open-minded, and more achievement-oriented than security-oriented.

Contrary to the popular myth that it is virtually impossible to start farming because of the high financial demands, the "Outstanding Young Farmers" were able to do quite well for themselves. Of the 46 national "Outstanding Young Farmers" of 1969, "about half had received only token help—verbal encouragement, an FFA calf, or a co-signer on a note—getting started farming." Yet, after 10 years of farming and at an average age of 32, those 46 had achieved an average net worth of $228,876. Bob Rupp, editor of *The Farmer* and one of the national contestant judges, wrote, "They are proof agriculture is still an expanding industry with a bright future for aggressive, determined, properly trained young men."

Repeated surveys over the years of the "Outstanding Young Farmers" revealed that most of those men started farming with an average of less than $10,000 and by their mid-thirties had net worths ranging from $150,000 to $500,000. H. B. Howell at Iowa State University studied 800 farms in Iowa and determined that the bottom third had average net incomes of $5,611 and had a return of 1.5 per cent on investments. The top one-third of those 800 farms had average net incomes of $22,334 and earned 11.3 per cent on investments. In his judgment management made the total difference in earnings. Howell wrote, "With good management, income [from farming] has become highly competitive with other opportunities." G. F. Warren's study of 1,200 farmers from 1906 to 1910 proved, like Howell's, that management more than any other factor determined profits.

Most people experience a definite turning point in their lives which determines whether they go on to become successful or go in the other direction and become "cogs in the machine." Successful people recognize the point at which their lives turned for the better. The less fortunate ones miss this point and its challenge, and life takes a turn "for the worse," for in the minds of many of them "things were always bad."

All the farmers interviewed were asked if they could identify the "event, factor, or trait in their lives that proved to be their turning point," the key, perhaps to their success. There was not one farmer who did not have an instant response to the question. Many had experienced numerous reverses before their situation improved. In some cases it was a definite adversity that put the farmer through extreme mental, financial, or physical pain, testing him thoroughly. Such tests separate the failures from the successes.

Most of the farmers interviewed were innovators, and some gave innovation credit for their success, while others assumed that innovation was something that everyone naturally had and gave no further thought to it. Ross Parish, in a study of innovative wheat farmers in the early 1950's, came to certain conclusions about innovation that are also valid for the individuals questioned for this survey:

Farmers who have adopted many innovations have, in general, earned higher incomes and had more contact with the agricultural extension services than those who have adopted few innovations.

The propensity to innovate seems to reflect a great capacity for enterprising action in general. Evidence for this view is provided by the fact that all individuals who were outstanding by enterprising in fields other than the adoption of innovations (viz. in local affairs and in business matters) were also innovators.

The article continued to emphasize that innovation reflected skills and attitudes more than economic or technological factors. A state of mind linked with past experiences, combined with certain qualities of leadership, tended to make an individual innovative. Not all innovators were aggressive. In fact, some actually stated in the interview that laziness made them innovative.

According to a Michigan State study in rural sociology, innovation commonly requires more thought, courage, and effort than many people are willing or capable of putting forth, so most of them decide that it is easier and less risky to stay with the traditional methods. It is a matter of a special human trait even stronger than the profit motive. This Michigan State report concluded that, with limited exceptions, farm ownership, the amount of education, the level of income, the size of the farm operation, and the degree of social participation were signs of innovation that were positively associated with the adoption of improved farm practices.

Pete A. Hermanson of Iowa attributed much of the success on his large multiple enterprise farm to "being quick to pick up new innovations. Heavy use of fertilizer at an early date and securing a corn drier as soon as they came out were two of our real profit makers. Fortunately, we have not made a major mistake in adopting new ideas." Hermanson's final statement implies that his family is fully aware of the risks involved in innovating—the very factor that keeps many from adopting new techniques.

George Rauenhorst of Olivia, Minnesota, who was involved in extensive seed corn production from the early 1930's, noticed that when he used his new Farmall tractor to cultivate during a hot day in 1935 the corn started to wilt. On closer examination in order to determine the reason for the wilt, he discovered that deep cultivation, which was the accepted practice at that time, was responsible for cutting the corn roots. This caused him to experiment with a flame thrower, along with numerous fertilizer plots and rates of corn plantings that produced average yields in excess of 60 bushels an acre when the national average yield was about 26 bushels.

Rauenhorst, well-known for his innovative farming procedures, said that his father had been a great innovator, so he was well-indoctrinated along those lines. He added, "My father unfortunately made more misdirected innovations than good ones and that proved costly to him, but profitable to me for I learned from observing his mistakes. I think I developed a more practical economic judgment from those early impressions."

The Clark Farm of South Dakota is still in existence because John Clark showed his innovative spirit by adopting tractors in the World War I era. John Clark was the eldest son and only 15 years old when his father died. He hated horse farming so much that he seriously considered selling the inherited farm. He decided to give tractors a try (ca. 1916) and liked them so well that he not only continued to farm but also actually expanded during the 1920's and 1930's when farming in general was experiencing hard times.

South Dakotan George C. Schuller, farming with his father and brother in the 1930's, attributed much of his success to the purchases of a John Deere "A" in the 1930's. The tractor was purchased with a team of horses and 20 acres of brome grass seed. Schuller said that the tractor was started Monday morning and was not shut off until Saturday evening as he and his brother kept it running around the clock:

We never imagined how much work we could do with that tractor. My brother and I were spurred by new visions of what we could do because of that tractor. We could get our work done on time, which not only enabled us to handle more acres, but we were able to increase our yields at the same time. Timing of crop production is so critical and the tractor made the difference. We realized that the future was in tractor farming, so we unloaded our horses while they were still high priced and bought another tractor.

Donald A. Schulz of Minnesota attributes the good fortune of their father-and-son enterprise to the fact that his father was a mechanically minded innovator who even built a tractor of his own in the 1930's. Even though the tractor was successful, the elder Schulz saw the advantages of the commercially made equipment and became an early adopter of the largest possible piece of equipment. Each time bigger and better machines were produced, the Schulzes adopted them and, as Don said, "We pushed them to their limits. We get a kick out of this new machinery, but we still find ways to improvise on it to make it even better."

"I have the third Steiger made," said Arthur L. Skolness, Red River Valley farmer, when asked what his best break was. "That big power unit gave me a big advantage even though I had been using 'Cats' for many years. My big power units enabled me to ditch land that had brought nothing but failure to other people. We are in a low wet area, but now it pays. Adopting a grass seed specialty was the next break tied to the four-wheel-drive and ditching. We are one of the largest grass seed growers in the nation, and it has been profitable."

Ditching and conservation practices played a prominent part in the success of other farmers. Roswell "Bob" Garst and Bert Hanson, both outstanding farmers, spent a great deal of time discussing the merits of those practices in relation to the economy of their farms. John W. Wright attributes draining and ditching practices as the most important single management move of his farm career. Wright's original farm in northeastern North Dakota was over 40 per cent waste land, but by draining he acquired nearly 400 additional acres of crop land at a very low cost. About the same time, he started heavy applications of commercial fertilizer when "almost no one in our area was using the stuff. I also purchased the biggest tractor I could buy, which sharply reduced my labor bill and gave me better crops at the same time. That was more than 20 years ago, and it has meant considerable profits to us over the years."

Floyd Darroll Warren, who farmed in the shadow of the Campbell farm in Montana for 40 years, attributes his success to "the fun of doing new things. I just love to try out new ideas," said Warren. "I only wish my family was as interested in farming as I am."

The Torske brothers, farming on the other side of the Campbell farm, are two graduates with liberal arts degrees. The Torskes, who enjoy farming, have been very receptive to new ideas and equipment "because that was something we always saw in our dad and grandfather—they had tractors in the early 1920's and anything else that came along," the brothers said. "Many times we have been criticized for our experimenting, but it has paid well." The Torskes added that by completely adapting their grain operation so that chaff and straw could be saved for their brood cattle they doubled the net income from their herd.

Minnesotan Gerald Boler, who also has a liberal arts degree, said:

My grandfather was a banker and a farmer and really loved farming. He was innovative and had what was probably the first completely tiled farm in the area. He switched entirely to tractors in the early 1920's, so my father, who was born in 1913, never worked with a horse. By the time Dad did much field work as a boy, he was using Caterpillers. Both my grandfather and dad were eager to try new ideas, and because of that worked with farm equipment manufacturers testing new machines before they were introduced to the market. This has given us several advantages in adopting new equipment.

One of the most unique responses to why he had become a success came from Minnesotan Stanley D. Olson who attributed being a seed corn salesman as an important part of his farming career. Olson's seed corn selling job is about equal "in time and returns" to 200 acres of additional corn crop. Olson quickly explained, "But there have been greater benefits because we are aided and encouraged to excel in our own corn production, and by better techniques I have really increased my corn profits." He continued that another hidden but important benefit was that he came in contact with many farmers and learned a great deal from their management practices, "both good and poor ones." Olson, who was a Minnesota "Outstanding Young Farmer" in 1964, felt the corn sideline has helped him to broaden his vision and has given him a better perspective of agriculture as a whole.

Innovation is a risky business and most innovators realize this, but they also understand that not to innovate can be even more disastrous. Innovation, combined with solid management techniques, has always proven profitable in the long run. The aggressive, innovative farmer is not willing to wait for final proof, for he knows that the windfall profits from innovation come in the initial stages of any change. We have always had innovators, but it appears that because of better communication and a higher level of education among farmers the rate of innovation is greater than at any time in the past. That pace is sure to quicken, and because of it changes in agriculture will be more rapid and violent than ever.[1]

Timing

Young people have often asked, "When is the best time to start farming?" The standard advice given by most agriculturalists is, "Start farming as soon as you are ready and don't wait for the right time." Anyone involved in agriculture accepts the wisdom of that advice, for probably no better answer could be given, and no one has the necessary insights to know the market trends more than a few weeks in advance.*

John Link, the father of North Dakota's Governor Arthur Link, when interviewed at age 96 pointed out that part of the reason for his success as a farmer was that several of his neighbors failed during the dry seasons and he was able to acquire their abandoned land at relatively low prices even for those years. The Links left the Sudeten area, formerly of Austria and now of Czechoslovakia, where they had worked in textile mills, and after a brief stay in the mills of the American East Coast, they migrated to western Dakota in the early 1900's. The failure rate among homesteaders in that region was exceedingly high, partly because of drought, partly because the homesteads were too small, and partly because many people were simply not prepared to endure the hardships demanded of pioneer farming on the frontier. The Links suffered intensely too, but by making use of the opportunity to enlarge and through sheer determination, they succeeded.

Several of the farmers who were old enough to start farming in the 1930's attribute part of their success to having been "lucky enough" to be farming during that decade. Clarence Carlson of Minnesota said, "We were just getting out of the depression, and we were producing certified seed potatoes which brought premium prices. Our volume was big enough, so we could buy more land without mortgaging what we had. We worked and really stayed on the job and took advantage of every opportunity for more land whenever some became available."

The F. J. Dilse family, who homesteaded in southwestern North Dakota, "never really had hardship" because their farm was tractor-plowed by 1918, was larger than average, and was well-diversified. They also had a custom rig for threshing that provided

---

*An interesting sidelight on knowledge of the future of farm prices was gained in conversations with then Secretary of Agriculture Earl Butz and Jack Jenkins, Dr. Butz's speech writer. The two men expressed the opinion that any well-informed farmer has just as much basis for judgment on future farm prices as the combined staff at U.S.D.A. Jenkins stated, "What we know at 4 P.M. one day can be known by any farmer in the nation by 8 A.M. the next day."

cash flow during the period of declining prices in the early 1920's. By 1926 T. A. Dilse and his brother Clarence started farming using their father's machinery, to which they added a Caterpillar 30 and a Holt combine. Other farmers in the area were eager to reduce their threshing costs and hired the Dilse brothers to custom combine at $1.00 per acre, which they did after they finished their own 3,000 acres. At this time farmers started to leave the area, and the Dilses added land whenever they could.

The Dilses were able to make enough profit from sheep raising during 1937, 1938, 1939, and 1940 to buy the cheap land made available from absentee owners who preferred to sell rather than lose it through non-payment of taxes. Most land had back taxes to be paid, but fate was with them. One quarter section that cost $4.70 an acre in the spring of 1940 produced a $48.00 an acre barley crop that year. T. A. Dilse at the age of 71 said in retrospect, "We budgeted ourselves through the 1930's, and when good times came after 1939, we had the cash to really expand. We were able to roll into expansion without being reckless because we had a big cash flow from a volume operation."

Chris Kolstad homesteaded 320 acres at Chester, Montana, in 1910, and by working on off-the-farm jobs each winter, he made enough money to expand gradually. By 1930 his son, Henry, took over, and though he did not have good crops, he was still able to expand the farm because neighbors abandoned or sold very cheaply. When the first good crop came in 1938, the 3,000 acres of wheat produced sufficient volume and adequate profits to buy large track-type tractors and the biggest combine. Higher prices came with World War II. Then came good weather, which enabled Kolstad to produce wheat crops of up to 47 bushels per acre.

Former North Dakota Congressman Don L. Short saw his father lose his ranch with the decline of farm prices after World War I. Don Short had to quit college and take a job in Chicago, but he disliked city life and in 1931 he returned to ranching:

Things really bottomed out in 1933 and 1934. A lot of people left, but we wanted to ranch and live here, so we made up our minds not to leave, no matter how tough things got. So our success is a combination of luck and timing. We stuck it out when times were tough and were on the spot when the tide turned. In the early 1940's I sold cattle from the ranch at over $200 a head, and with our numbers that put me on my feet. It was simple from then on.

One of the largest and best known ranch and farm enterprises in South Dakota belongs to the Sutton family. The real test for survival came to the Sutton family in the 1930's when they virtually could not borrow any additional money. But in spite of this crisis the Suttons decided to stick it out while many of their neighbors were quitting. "Probably we were eternal optimists," said John Sutton, Sr., who at the time of interview was 74 years old, "but we pushed when everyone else stood still." He qualified his answer:

In 1935 we three brothers and six men drove 1,100 cattle 200 miles for winter pasture and that saved our herd. But Dad put the cards on the table and told us he had no more credit unless we three brothers were willing to mortgage some land we had in our name. Dad had nothing left, but we boys decided on the spot to stick it out and it worked, for in 1937 we got some rain, and cattle prices came up a bit. In 1939 we could afford a $500 bull from WHR [Wyoming Hereford Ranch], and this was a big break, for he was a real producer. About that time ranchers came to us wanting to sell out, and we were in a position to buy. Loan companies virtually dumped land to get cash instead of terms, and we were able to generate the cash because we had the cash flow by then.

In 1961 my brothers and I split our holdings. The big unit had its definite advantages, but with three brothers and their five sons too many people were involved. We probably didn't lose too much efficiency by splitting up because each unit is still large and has some irrigated land to give us good production.

In 1913 Fred Romain homesteaded at Carter, Montana, and held a part-time job until 1926, when he averaged 50 bushels per acre of winter wheat on his farm. At this time he decided to expand by taking over deserted homesteads or by buying land from loan companies. Most land at that time was purchased for about $5.00 an acre. In spite of a financial setback in 1929 when the banker "put the clamps" on him, by 1932 he had expanded to 1,500 acres.

In 1936 Romain let two sons start farming on their own with a gift of a 1926 model "D" John Deere. Clarence Romain recalled, "I bought 160 acres at $8.00 an acre with $1.00 an acre down and had a complete crop failure. I have no knowledge of a single combine moving in our area. I worked in the CCC camps to earn money to buy seed, but did not earn enough to plant the entire farm; maybe that was luck." Neither Clarence Romain nor his brother was dismayed by the crop failure and kept farming. In 1939 they were able to buy 2,000 acres for $7.00 an acre including a good house. They had 10-year contract-for-deed, but they had to borrow the down payment from the bank. In 1940 they started saving chaff to feed their small cow herd, and with the better moisture plus higher prices brought on by wartime demands, the Romain brothers were quick to capitalize on their volume for the necessary cash flow to buy more land. "Looking back," Clarence Romain reminisced, "I guess we never thought of quitting. After starting with a crop failure the first year, the only way to go was up. My brother and I thought that if everyone kept pulling out, we really should have an opportunity to grow."

When George C. Schuller, farming in South Dakota, was asked what his best break in farming was, he replied, "I was born at the right time. I was 28 in 1942, my first year of farming completely on my own, and we clicked, cashing in on the good years. What better times could a person have asked for? Success breeds success, and once we got rolling, it was easy."

Two things enabled Earl Davison to develop a sizeable farming operation:

My father homesteaded in western North Dakota, and we grew up seeing the need for larger acreages and the concept of size stuck with me. I had no money when I started farming in Minnesota, but would not have started with less than a section. But I was lucky and landed a section on contract, which called for 50 per cent of the crop for principal and interest payments. I had the volume to make it go, particularly since I was able to use some of Dad's machinery. In five years I had a chance to refinance and have just rolled since.

Ralph Hvidsten, a Red River Valley potato farmer, had the following experience:

I had never intended to farm, but I did not like the prospects of city life. My break came when I was able to buy a half section on contract in 1940. While in college and the service in World War II, I really conceived that the freedom of farming was what I wanted in life, and this motivated me more than anything I know. By the time I returned home from college and the service, my debt was reduced enough so that I had a lever to finance operating income. It has been no big problem since.

"Like Ralph, I was able to buy a half section with the help of my father in 1940," grinned Earl Hvidsten, also of Stephen, Minnesota. "Half of the gross crop went to principal and interest. By the time I was 20, I had that land paid for and had a living unit so I could start expanding. Timing was fortunate because we paid off fast with good years. I have stayed very close to a cash basis ever since."

John Heline admits that starting to farm in 1940 at the age of 22 made him lucky enough to be doing the right thing at the right time:

I think I had the proper mental attitude that caused me to try anything. Before long my drive and luck gave me all the credit I needed, and long-range financial problems became a thing of the past. As I look back, there was one more trait—that of enjoying working with people. That helped me step ahead. Sure, there is slippage to a degree, but if you have the right makeup you can overlook that.

"Timing was important in my getting off to a good start in farming," acknowledged Harold Hofstrand of Leeds, North Dakota. "Agriculture had bottomed out and was on the upswing when I wanted to start in 1938. Starting at the bottom has its advantages." But he felt there was a second factor just as important as timing:

I had graduated from college and then worked for a seed company. Because of my five years' absence, it was easy for me to pick up the new ideas and start right. This helped me to pass up many who had stayed on the farm but had not kept up with changing times. I learned the importance of using new techniques.

South Dakotan Dennis L. Anderson acknowledged that his father-in-law, Eugene Young, was the kind of man who would succeed because "he never knew the word 'quit.' " "But," Anderson added, "being able to secure several thousand acres of land in one block that had never been properly farmed and was abandoned in the 1930's was important to our eventual growth. This land was waiting to be farmed, and the loan companies wanted to get it off their hands. With new farming techniques this became an extremely profitable block of land for us."

Many farmers admitted that they played "hunches" and because their speculations were correct they profited. Most felt that the "hunches" that paid off best were those that were made contrary to popular thinking at the time. The commentaries of three farmers were particularly significant relative to "running when everyone else was walking."

John W. Scott, Jr., of Gilby, North Dakota, who had the privilege of learning to farm from his very successful father, observed that the ability to out-guess the market has been a decisive factor in their success. John W. Scott, Sr., attributed his success to his planting of hundreds of acres of potatoes in 1937 when everyone else was reducing his acreage as the greatest single stroke in his farming career. The younger Scott admitted that it took tremendous courage to go contrary to what everyone was predicting or doing at that time. "But we are not conformists nor are we concerned with popular public opinion." The fact that the Scotts have a very solid economic base of operation probably gives them the additional bit of courage they need to buck the trends at any given time.

David Garst, like John W. Scott, Jr., had the advantage of growing up under the tutorship of his progressive, innovative father, Roswell Garst. Dave's observation about the success of their farming enterprise was that much of it came because of "priority timing." Dave noted that for his father it was a matter of "doing the right thing at the right time." Dave Garst remembered:

We bought land when you could buy 5 acres of pasture land for the price of one cow—in a short time that same land cost as much per acre as a cow. Then I remembered when Dad said, "Cash grain [also corn] farmers are producing themselves out of business—let's buy cows." Some years fertilizer has been a better buy than others and we bought accordingly.

John S. Dalrymple III made the following observation:

I believe my understanding of agriculture, in the total view of the economy, gained because of my contact with people who are in the know in various phases of the business world. This gives me a better insight on the immediate problems of agriculture. My dad showed me the value of what is to be gained from such contacts—he made many of the right moves when actually farmers nationwide were deciding the other way. I think this ability to withstand popular trends is one of the most important phases of management because quite frequently they lead to the biggest profits.

Walter Kroeker, residing on the Manitoba farm started by his grandfather in 1876, attributes his father's progressive optimism as being the chief factor of success for their multi-enterprise farm. After Abram Kroeker's death, A. A. Kroeker became the mainstay of the family even while getting his education. He learned to adopt new ideas rapidly. During the 1930's he planted corn to stop the wind erosion and quickly discovered that the corn stalks caught enough snow to provide sufficient moisture so that summer fallowing could be eliminated. Soon the Kroekers found themselves in the commercial seed corn business, which enabled them to generate an all-important cash flow.

During the interview Walter Kroeker responded:

Dad was basically an optimist and any dilemma was a challenge to him—somehow he always found his way out. He always said, "Keep your eye on a fixed point just like plowing, when you are going forward; if you look back you are finished." I remember his big test. About 1937 he started to dabble in potato production. Corn had been so profitable that it was hard for him to look at other crops. Then in 1942 we had a frost in August that killed our corn crop which was in the milk stage. Our corn pyramid crumbled, but Dad quickly turned to potatoes and that has become our bread and butter crop. A case of bad luck really became a good fortune.

Most of the farmers interviewed expressed timing of production, timing of marketing, and timing of the start of their farming career as important. They could recall the specifics and credited certain events or turns in the markets, weather, or economy as having been important to them and their eventual success. But also, making judgmental decisions that were contrary to the accepted opinions of others at a given time and making quick shifts in crops, livestock, or mode of operation when chances had to be taken were the things to do. Timing to these men seemed important. But so were other things such as cash flow, volume, or innovation. All were a part of their story.[2]

Financial Management—Another Key to Success

The old saying, "every cloud has a silver lining," apparently had significance for several of the farmers interviewed. When asked to point out the most significant factor or event in their farming career that caused much of their success, they instinctively responded with reference to a financial predicament.

Jacob Geritz, who started farming in 1934, commented about his beginnings:

I think the 1930's was a good time to start farming. Everyone was equal; we were all broke—we had lots of friendships and cooperation in our area, so being broke was no handicap. We did not have a good crop until 1941. Fortunately, by then I was farming two sections, most of which was rented, and the volume from that crop got us started. I must add that my wife really was the big factor, for it took real sacrifice to keep farming during those years and most of the sacrifices came in the home. I was slow to learn how to use credit, and getting elected to the Production Credit Board was probably the biggest external boost I ever received. Sitting on the PCA Board taught me about the basic problems of agriculture that had not been bothered about much before that. I also learned a lot about what makes a good manager, and most important, I learned the real concepts of how to use financial leverage. I applied all of these things to my operation and it made a big difference.

C. H. Underlee was operating a general store in Hendrum, Minnesota, during the 1930's and noted that he was losing business. He found that there were two reasons for it. Many farmers were leaving the area, but more importantly, those who were remaining had cars and they were passing through town to go to the larger shopping centers. Underlee said, "I could see that the day of the small town was past and decided that I had better sell out while I still had a chance. Farming looked like a better alternative."

Like Geritz, C. H. Underlee started farming in 1934 with very limited capital. He remembered that they had to tighten their belts because they needed all their money for a used Fordson tractor, a plow, and other equipment. He did well enough in 1934 to buy a bigger tractor and equipment for the second year.

Ernest C. Hector's dad homesteaded in western North Dakota in 1906 and by World War I he was able to build his farm to 2,240 acres, only to lose 1,000 acres in the 1920's. After World War II, Ernest Hector tried his luck in $500 to $1,000 an acre cotton, vegetable, and citrus land in Texas. After three good years, Hector experienced two years of frost and then declining prices. "Looking back, " Hector said, "I realized that crisis was a great teacher. I learned the limitations of crops, that high quality, skilled labor is cheaper than low class labor, and I learned that the profit is in the finished product."

With those lessons and a depleted bank account, Hector returned to North Dakota to develop some new ideas. By renting rather than buying, Hector could stretch his dollars to get the volume he wanted. Living in traditional cash small-grain country interspersed with livestock, Hector decided that he could improve his income best by using the whole grain crop instead of just the heads and process it into pelleted cattle feed. In this manner he felt he could double or triple the income per acre. In 1971 Hector did not feel that there was enough profit in small grains to make that type of farming attractive. "Because of low grain prices I don't think the small-grain farmer is much removed from the depression days right now." By using the entire grain plant, he greatly increased the feed value per acre. By pelleting it, he put the crop into a compact, easily moveable form that also was less wasteful to feed. Then he transported the pelleted feed to his cattle and hog locations.

Financial losses of the 1950's caused Ernest Hector to analyze the total process of farming, and he concluded that the more integrated he could become, the more "drought protection" he had. "I saw how the people in our area got set back then and I learned about processing from my bad Texas experience," said Hector. "So why not try to avoid the very things that caused the problem?"

The five Mertens brothers, North Dakota dairy farmers who had been in partnership since 1957, were basically satisfied that they had a good crew and, therefore, things should have gone right. Henry Mertens, the eldest brother, said:

We were just not making the profits we wanted. So the five of us analyzed our operation in a five-person session and concluded our crop production was good, but our milk cows were not doing the job. Was it our management or the feed? We decided to really dig into the financial sock and put up a free stall barn to reduce labor and to put up a Harvestore to do a better job storing our feed. In one month our production started to climb and in two years we nearly doubled our production. It was hard to believe, but our records and income are proof. There is no doubt in our minds about the turning point in our farming success.

John S. Dean and Freddie Mutschler had the identical instant response when asked about the biggest single factor in their farming careers. They both stated, "Getting a new banker." Mutschler said, "It seems that too many bankers have a negative attitude toward farming and our former banker was one of them." Dean added, "I was lucky, for I switched bankers early in my career. It is my opinion that too many farmers are held down by traditional thinking bankers."

Dean stated that about the same time that he changed bankers he also got involved with contracting all or part of the production of his various crops. This gave him greater financial stability and a more uniform cash flow. Some of his crops had a limited market making the contracting of production quite essential.

Dalton Docter and Herman H. Lee both remembered the rather Spartan home life of their boyhood and felt that from that they built the attitude that they might as well venture all they could, for they had nothing to lose. Docter started with rented land and cast-off machinery. He had a financial struggle until he was able to secure a contract to feed cattle for Swift and Company:

That contract was a real break because it gave me the volume I needed, and because of my success with Swift, I got recommendations to financial people and that was what I most needed to get going. Our local bank has been good to us because they have faith in us. The cattle business has its ups and downs, but we have had no basic financial problem. Sometimes that surprises me, but maybe it's because of our experience and reputation.

Tremendous drive, caused in part because there was "not much at home," is what Herman H. Lee attributes to be the key factor in his success. Lee started farming on a rented farm with a 16-year-old truck. The truck was necessary because Lee bought and sold used machinery in an effort to generate a cash flow and to get some equipment for himself. Lee recalled his experiences as a young farmer working as a machinery jockey: "I was taken several times by people refusing to pay or with a misrepresented piece of equipment. There were some bad tumbles, but every time I have bounced back and every time I have felt a bit stronger."

Once Lee got a start, he was able to rent some sizeable pieces of land to give him the cash flow he worked so hard for in the machinery business. In that business he learned a great deal about people and decided to hire only the best men for a labor force. In an effort to keep good employees, he started a certified seed business that prospered under good management.

It was a reversal in the certified seed business that gave George Rauenhorst a few sleepless nights before he learned more about the natural phenomenon of weather and rust. From his exposure to foundation seed corn he was able to secure some new Thatcher seed wheat in 1934. Despite a dry year he averaged 14 bushels on 8 acres, but he was unable to sell any of the crop for seed. He was forced to seed 40 acres of that wheat in 1935 and got a bumper yield of 40 bushels an acre when everyone else suffered an almost total crop failure because of rust. In 1936 Rauenhorst had 1,600 bushels of seed wheat that sold for $2.50 a bushel.

Rauenhorst recalled that he sold enough wheat early in the 1936 season to enable him to pay rent on a farm and buy a full line of machinery. But the good start in 1936 was soon to wither away in a summer drought, which prevented his corn from making ears. All the corn had to be put up as silage, and Rauenhorst was forced into a new venture, cattle feeding, an enterprise that he continued for the rest of his career.

In the spring of 1937 he sold half the cattle to pay off the note, and the other half produced return on his crop and time. After expenses he had $2,100, which he used to buy an I.H.C. F-30 tractor with a four-row corn planter, four-row cultivator, and a four-bottom plow. He grinned, "In this respect the rust of 1935 and the drought of 1936 proved to be real profitable for us."[3]

Mind over Matter

When Ray S. Jarrett, a very successful farmer, was asked at the age of 76 if he had ever experienced any losses and if they had taught him a lesson, he instantly replied, "Oh, yes, I have had my share of losses, and I expected them. For there can be no success without some failure."

All the farmers interviewed had at one time or another experienced reversals, but several of them had to give much thought to how serious the reversals had been and what part they had played in their eventual success. Financial losses were assumed by all the farmers as an inevitable part of their business, and they felt that some monetary reversals were so severe that they were a test of character. Many times other losses or reversals outside farming caused financial problems. "But on the other hand," banker Allan M. Severson said, "you'd be surprised how many times people suddenly develop sickness or allergies when their finances are touch and go and the 'squeeze' is on."

Only one farmer, Jack C. Lacey of Minnesota, could not place his finger on a specific factor or event that had enabled him to increase his operation from 960 acres to over 3,000 acres in four years' time. Lacey had been tutored by his very progressive father who, when he retired in 1964, expressed the opinion that "1,200 acres is a big enough farm for anyone." Jack C. Lacey and his two brothers farmed in partnership to get a cash flow and equipment before they wanted to go their separate ways.

From 1968 to 1971, Lacey, now on his own, expanded as rapidly as he could rent or buy land. By 1971 he was confronted with the opportunity to buy more land and realized that at his age of 30 a loan company was willing to loan him just short of a half million dollars for additional expansion. Jack and his wife were stunned at the very thought of being able to borrow that amount in one transaction. At that point Lacey wondered what had been the key to his success up to then. "I guess we would have to say it is Providence that has put us where we are because it seems like each move I have made has worked right." Jack C. Lacey farms with confidence and does his job well.

After traveling around the Midwest looking for a good place to farm, James J. Walton purchased 1,200 acres in the Red River Valley in 1955 and caused a wave of rumors about a farmer with great wealth coming into the area. But the rumors were far from the truth. Jim Walton's father died in 1936 when Jim was eight years old, leaving the mother with seven children and a big mortage on their farm in Ohio. As Walton remembered:

The mortgage was so big that the banker and everyone else pleaded with my mother to get rid of the farm. That made us kids really cry, but on second thought we got mad and decided to dig in and prove to everyone that she didn't have to sell out. After a few years we not only had the farm paid for but were expanding. This made us so confident and it was so challenging that my brothers and I made bets on who would become the first millionaire. Two of my brothers beat me to it.

Jim Walton took over the home farm at the age of 20 and operated it for three years when he was able to buy a farm of his own. In five years his Ohio farm grew to 1,120 acres. It was at that point that he decided that it would be easier to expand into larger scale farming elsewhere than in Ohio, where there was intense competition from other large farmers and industrial workers who were moonlighting at farming. The Red River Valley of the North appealed to Walton because the large flat fields lent themselves well to big machines and the competition for land was less intense.

In spite of pressure and tensions which come from operating several large scattered units, Jim Walton attributes his desire to be a big farmer to the banker who tried to force his widowed mother to sell the homestead. "Bankers are still a challenge," Walton commented. "When one banker found out how much I owed, he did not even let me sit down to discuss my profit record or show my net worth. Every place I have had land, even when I was back in Ohio, I heard everyone was giving us two years to go broke, but our profits just keep adding to our net worth. The people we do business with know we can pay our bills and I guess that's all that counts from an economic standpoint."

Skulason Moe, who farms in Montana, feels that his ability to work with employees and to cope with adversity enables him to overcome crisis. Moe was 16 years old when his father suffered a severe heart attack. "That made me rise to the challenge because I found myself in charge of the farm," recalled Moe. "A second factor, probably as significant as that challenge, was that, while my dad was dying, he told me about all the unfinished things he had wanted to do on the farm. It bothered me and it was not until I had been exposed to some special motivation courses that I was fully prepared for the task that my father and I had set out to accomplish."

Jack E. Lang's father was a barber in northern Montana, but Jack decided during his period of service in World War II that he wanted to farm. He started ranching on a small scale in 1948 and built his herd very rapidly until 1953 when he was able to buy several thousand acres on a contract-for-deed. He disposed of his cow herd to raise money for the down payment and the purchase of machinery. Each time he heard of any land for sale, Jack bought until he tripled the size of his original farm and at the same time he became involved in other non-farm enterprises.

Jack and his wife Rita both agreed that they expanded their farm because they were challenged by their work and because they liked what they were doing. Jack acknowledged that the greatest single change in his career came when he overcame an alcoholic problem. He said, "I had the persistence and determination to get ahead and I liked the challenge of seeing my farm grow, but after my rehabilitation I did a lot better job of thinking of life as a whole and not just about farming." Rita smiled in agreement.

Mr. and Mrs. Darrell Miller were both excited to tell about the special event that changed them from "second-rate underdog farmers" to a progressive farm family. Darrell grew up on a 640-acre Richland County, North Dakota, farm. Prior to his marriage he farmed 160 acres with small used equipment or equipment borrowed from his father whom he worked for to pay machinery rental. When he found a 320-acre farm that he could rent, he decided to get married. Darrell was anxious to get on his own "to see if I could really farm." Two years later the young couple rented another 160 acres and in two more years found another 160 acres that was for sale.

The 160 acres that Darrell wanted to buy at that time had such a poor reputation that "neither the Federal Land Bank nor FHA would look at it." Darrell's father borrowed money to finance that quarter section, and Darrell paid for the land with his first crop. In 1957, just three years after he purchased his first farm, another 240 acres became available, and again there were no buyers because the land was so poor. But because Darrell had paid for his first 160-acre purchase with the initial crop, the Federal Land Bank had confidence in him and financed his second farm. That farm did well too!

Even with this success the Millers felt insecure. They were nervous because his parents constantly reminded them, "Don't get too big." As Darrell recalled those days:

My health was such that I was a nervous wreck. I was running for treatments all the time and one day the doctor told me about a specialist who was offering a course in motivation called Concept Therapy which was really a combination of philosophies. We knew we had to do something and felt this was what we needed, but the course was $100 per person or $150 per couple. I even had to borrow the money to take the course.

After a few sessions we were living in a different world. We got rid of our negative defeatist attitude. My whole mental attitude has changed, and my health has improved with it. Now I know I can do anything I set my mind to because I am convinced the only limits one really has are in his mind.

Darrell Miller went on to explain what happened not long after he had gained a new outlook on life. One day Darrell was offered a chance to buy 7 quarters from a close neighbor. "That purchase doubled my operation to 14 quarters, and this was the break-through I really needed to generate cash flow. After that we were able to continue a steady expansion."

Clem Hebel, who started farming in Iowa in 1936 on rented land, was rather aggressive in his early days. As he expressed his feelings: "There is something new every day and the thing to do is grab on when it comes. It was the impact of new equipment and my eagerness to innovate that always gave me the breaks."

Hebel noted that once those in agricultural businesses found out that he was an innovator they always came to him in an effort to introduce new products and equipment and that proved a decided benefit to him. He had the first rubber-tired tractor in his area and because of that he had access to an experimental 6-foot combine that he was able to use in custom work to generate a cash flow. In 1940 Hebel secured a new hay baler and had to help the dealer figure out how to assemble it. "The cash flow really came in then," said Hebel. "We went day and night and wore out nine balers in six years."

The farm and custom work progressed, but much of it was due to a strenuous day and night schedule kept by Hebel. Then one day it happened. Hebel had finished working in one field and was traveling in his pickup to another farm at the same time he was talking on the two-way radio to a tractor driver at still another. He stopped at a rural crossroad and the next thing he remembered was waking up in a hospital. It was seven months before he left the hospital bed.

Clem Hebel and his wife Myrl agreed that during those months they had lots of time to think and "a whole new outlook on life" opened to them:

More than anything else I learned that it is silly to try to do it all. Why not hire management? I had good men on the farm and in my custom work, and they rose to the challenge when I was laid up. I was absent almost two full years, and everything did quite well during that time. Since then the farm has been operated almost totally by the men—all I do is the very top-level management. My other businesses are pretty much the same. Both Myrl and I have time for more church work. We take lots of time off for vacations just to loaf and to travel around the world to see what other farmers are doing. That has proven as worthwhile and profitable as stay-ing home and trying to do it all myself.

For Thomas (Buck) Snortland a special event proved to be the turning point to his success. Snortland has been reared on a relatively small farm in northeastern North Dakota and was indoctrinated with the idea that the small farm was the right way and the big farm was the wrong way. At first he was content farming about 1,600 acres and working for his farm organization and local community. He said:

I had that small farm complex which kept me from prospering, but as energetic as I was I was not fully challenged and was looking for other activities. I spent from 1947 through 1955 in the state legislature just to keep me active. I spent four years on the Non-partisan League Executive Committee.

Then I got elected to the state board of my farm organization. I almost had the feeling that I had arrived, but sitting on that board really opened my eyes. It was my impression that many things that happened were more for the benefit of certain leaders than they were for the farmer members. I started a campaign to change leadership at the next election. The next thing I knew I had been thrown out.

It was a long drive home from Bismarck after that convention. I had lost my whole world, it seemed, and I wondered what would happen next. That winter I spent a lot of time reading history, economics, and philosophy, and soon I realized that I was developing a new outlook on life. I was determined to carry on as a free enterpriser. It's that simple, and the next thing I knew I had new confidence and was expanding my farming operation. It has been very successful; besides I have also become involved in other businesses.[4]

Family Influence

The importance of the family has been well-recognized in the recorded history of farming. Unfortunately, much of the data dealing with the family discusses the adverse side of farm life: the suffering, hardships, toil, and self-denial. But the farm family as a closely knit unit is of great importance to the whole scene of farm life and its survival. Fortunately, the farm family no longer has to be thought of as being overworked, deprived, and under-privileged. They are still "giants in the earth," but in a different sense, and it was interesting to observe how the spouses and the children followed the interviews of their husbands and fathers. The writer will always have memories of farmers, who operated large farms, turning to their wives and asking, "What do you think?," and often the wife's answer was equal to or better than that of her husband. Yes, the writer remembers one Dakota family where the daughter, a college coed, sat on the counter and intensely pondered every word during a four-hour interview. After supper and late into the night, four more daughters, home from school, joined the audience. It was rather touching how the eldest daughter, Ann, expressed a wish to marry a farmer after graduation from college, for she felt that was the best life. She did.

When Joe Thompson, then 79 years old, was asked what he regarded as the key to his success as a farmer, he answered, "A good wife." Joe Thompson was an aggressive, innovative farmer who was very self-confident, but he felt he needed the backing and prodding of his wife to keep him on "an even keel." Thompson, thinking a bit more, added, "My workers were my friends and we had an aggressive group of neighbors who spurred me on."

Eddie A. Velo of Minnesota, after 40 years of successful farming, said, "My wife and I both had a strong desire to make the farm good, but I really think my wife was the key to our success." Mrs. Velo did all the bookkeeping and most of the desk work in the early decades of their farming, but in later years one of the daughters did that work. The Velos have several grown children who have become full partners in the multi-faceted family farm, and they are known for their great teamwork.

Agricultural economists, rural sociologists, and other students of farm life have long known that in farming, good family and good management go hand in hand. A South Dakota State University study concluded that on some farms the wife was the primary source of management because the husband was totally involved as the chief source of farm labor.

Bob Moraczewski's work with the 1971 nation's "Outstanding Young Farmers" found that 26 per cent of these highly successful farmers stated that their wives were extremely important in management decisions. Another 61 per cent proclaimed the wife to be "important" to "very important" in management. Only 13 per cent professed that the wife was "unimportant" or "slightly important" in the farm management. This writer found that of the farmers interviewed for this study and currently involved in farming the significance of the wife's importance was corroborated. The wife's influence appeared significant even in the case of professional farm managers who were also interviewed.

Another study similar in approach stated, "A good frame of mind is an absolute must for good business management—and a good wife provides it." David Drum put it so nicely when asked about the part that his wife played in his business: "She is a good listener and helps me think through the problems, but more importantly, when I step out of the house in the morning, I know that everything there is right. That way my mind is clear on the really important part of life."

Half of the farms studied were father-son, brother, or brother-in-law partnerships and presented many striking examples of the power of total family involvement in farming enterprises. The O'Farrell family, consisting of a father and seven brothers, each managing a different phase of the farm, illustrated all the evidence of the effectiveness of a family operation. Separate responsibility for various facets of the farm with each family member in charge of one or more employees using the largest possible equipment provides tremendous efficiency for these family partnerships.

The five Hall brothers, known for their large, efficient potato growing and processing enterprise, have a crew of 15 year-round employees in addition to a very large seasonal labor force. The five brothers work very closely, but each handles a definite phase of the operation with full responsibility for men and equipment in that phase. The advantages of economy of scale for the Halls have enabled them to develop a strong cash flow besides creating a strong personally capitalized farm. Five separate farms could not have been nearly as successful as this single five-manager farm. The Halls understand that fact and know it is the key to a good economy as well as to a good life.

Bill and Daryl Spicher of Montana admit that the efficiency of farming on a large scale increases because of the smoothness of a partnership. The partnership enables them to have larger machinery than they could justify individually and that eases the work load. This leaves them time for other business as well as time off for family life and relaxation. Daryl said, "One can be here while the other is gone, and he has nothing to worry about while he is gone."

"The ability of us four brothers to manage together was instilled in us by our father who had very positive ideas about how a big farm could be managed. This is the key to our success," said Gerald Hoggarth of North Dakota. The Hoggarths grew up on a 720-acre farm and as a group started farming independently from their father in 1959. The financial strength of four was better than the strength of each individually. The ability to use the largest equipment, including several four-wheel-drive tractors, plus the management power to handle several enterprises have given the Hoggarth brothers a steady cash flow. They have created sufficient internal income to expand rapidly without relying on excessive external borrowing. Gerry Hoggarth emphasized that four heads working together were better than one. Speaking for his brothers, he expressed the opinion that there was no limiting factor to their continued expansion if they desired to do so.

David Miller does not work in a partnership with his brother, Ivan, but he believes brotherly competition has contributed to his growth in farming, "sort of a ballgame." Dave and his brother Ivan are determined farmers and because of the scope of their operations and their success are the object of both envy and admiration. Dave started farming by himself in 1953, and he gradually increased the acreage he owned twenty-seven-fold in the next 20 years. Dave and wife Valeria through cooperation and good management exemplify the story of a successful farm family.

Up to this point reference has been made to the influence of the brothers and wives in successful farm management. But there is also the strong impact of the parents who have helped to shape the destiny of their sons' and daughters' farming careers.

It was an enlightening experience to interview Edgar, Daniel, and Stephen Keil and their mother, Mrs. John Keil, sitting in the family living room of their Montana farmstead. The four were an alert group, often disagreeing among themselves, but a highly stimulating unit to interview. The power of family and the power of intelligence was conspicuous.

John Keil came to western Montana in 1926 to homestead and to work as a farm laborer. After three years he owned his original farm clear and had his initial investment back. Then he married and started to expand whenever he could. By the mid-1930's the Keils were operating 1,000 acres and by being successful they were able to buy 1,200 acres of abandoned land from loan companies and county governments for $6,000. Keil purchased an RD-6 Caterpillar to break the sod on his new land, but because of dry weather his Holt Model 36 combine was able to save only one wagonload of wheat from the "virgin land."

Keil, however, did not give up, but he did change his techniques. In 1940 he bought a Noble Blade which permitted him to stubble mulch to save moisture. Next, he went to block farming instead of strip farming, which was surprisingly helpful in reducing sawfly and grasshopper infestation. To reduce his dependence on wheat and barley, he turned to planting the short season mustard crop for oil. Mustard paid well in the years when wheat failed.

The Keils lived modestly and within their income "even when

it was zero." Mrs. Keil laughed when she recalled, "My pet economy was saving water because it had to be hauled in. First it was the baby [Edgar], then my hair, then my socks and undergarments, then I scrubbed the floor, and finally I poured it on the flowers."

When Edgar, the oldest boy, was 19, his father offered to "cut him in as a full partner" on the farm that was over 4,000 acres. Edgar grinned, "That was quite a deal for a kid because by then Dad had a D-6 and two D-4 Caterpillars. We were operators." As his other sons grew into their teens, they also were cut in as full partners. The brothers felt that their father was the key to the success of the farm that flourished even after his death. Mrs. Keil attributed this to his innovative ability. The boys acknowledged that as far as they were concerned their mother was also a great motivator.

David Glinz, who has one of the largest grain farms in North Dakota, felt that his father was the key to his large farming operation for a different reason than the Keil brothers. Glinz said, "My father is a speculator—he has the courage and ability to plunge, enabling him to piece large blocks of land together. But watching Dad has made me a cautious farmer, for I realize it is one thing to buy land and another to generate the net profit that it takes to pay for it."

Glinz acknowledged that one of the first things that happened when he took over management of the farm was to hold a big auction and sell all the varied pieces of equipment that had been purchased over the years. He reinvested the money in six large four-wheel-drive tractors and scheduled his labor force to operate around the clock. Labor cost was reduced to just over half of what it had been with the conventional two-wheel-drive tractors and because of the bigger equipment it was easier to get better men.

Raymond Schnell of western North Dakota and his brothers have large brood cow and feedlot enterprises in addition to other interests. The basis of their operation was created by their father, Ray Schnell, who was well-known for his innovations in the livestock industry. Raymond Schnell felt that the key to success was his father's flair for new things. Then he added, "Dad had a role in a country theatre troup, and that experience gave him a feel of how to get along with people. He positively could deal with anyone, and I think we boys picked up a few tips from him. That's the key to success in most businesses."

Anyone familiar with the Red River potato industry has seen the big green semitrailer trucks with a pipe-smoking Irishman painted on their sides. The lettering indicates that the trucks belong to two proud second generation Irish potato farmers, Gerald C. and Thomas W. Ryan. Gerry and Tom were quick to acknowledge that the main factor in their ability to develop, improve, and expand the large farm they took over from their father was their teamwork.

The Ryan brothers are precise and cautious managers who try to operate a first class farm with excellent management. Gerry Ryan is quick to admit that they probably could be farming a lot more than they are at the moment, but their extreme caution has kept them from greater expansion. "The positive aspect," Gerry admitted, "is that although we have had some enterprise losses we have never had a deficit operating year since we started farming." Obviously teamwork and caution are not a bad combination for Tom and Gerry Ryan.[5]

Motivation

Kenneth R. Krause and Leonard R. Kyle, two agricultural economists, in their government-sponsored study of large-scale midwestern corn farms noted that there were several non-economic factors that caused farmers to operate on a big scale. Specifically, these farmers liked the competitive satisfaction of a large unit. They liked the competition with friends who also had large farms, and they liked the challenge and excitement of growth. But it is difficult to separate the various facets of challenge and motivation into neatly defined topics.

Virgil Mellies had worked himself out of the ranks of being a farmer's hired man and in 10 years built a larger than average farm. His decision to develop such a farm came in 1956 when he made a vacation and farm tour into Iowa.

I observed what the Iowa farmers were doing. I got data on their production, their land, labor cost, and taxes, and concluded that if they could make money I ought to expand as fast as I could. About the same time I read a book by Conrad Hilton on his philosophy of life and business concepts and this had a big impact on me. I lost all fear of growth after those two things, and probably even more important, I shed my concern, almost obsession, about debts. Cash flow, net profits, and a good living became more important than having a little farm that was paid for.

Alvin Kenner started farming at the age of 18 in North Dakota in the late 1930's and was apprehensive because of the hardships he had seen on the farms in his area in the previous years. The hardships challenged him and made him determined to avoid going through similar experiences. Kenner, a good listener and a keen observer of what others around him were saying and doing, soon spotted those who in his estimation were the best farmers he knew and became friends with them. He observed:

I learned much from these pals and learned more from traveling around just picking up ideas. You know a good idea as quickly as you see it. It just hits you. I did custom work in my early years to generate cash flow, and this really enlarged my concepts. I saw the value of big equipment and bought it much sooner than I might have if it hadn't been for my combining on these larger farms.

I saw the pitfalls of being overmechanized as happened to so many farmers right after World War II when they had more money than land but wanted the big machines. Custom work made me very cost conscious because I wanted to be sure I was making money when I was out working for someone else. I studied every farm I worked on or visited to find their weaknesses as well as their strengths.

The challenge of putting your neck down and really bucking was fun. When I look back at the nearly 40 years that I have been farming, I really don't think the loss of so many farmers is as sad a story as many would like to have us believe. Look back at the reasons—many passed up good chances to expand when it was practically in their laps. Many just did not want to manage the way they should. This old joke about farmers not farming as well as they know how is more truth than fiction. And I remember many farmers who spent their rainy days playing pinochle and pool and complaining instead of getting the equipment in shape so they could go when the rain stopped. What comes first, fun or work?

For those who know fun-loving Al Kenner the answer was clear—there was plenty of time for fun once the money was in the bank or, as some might say, when the grain was in the bin. "Timing," he said, "was the key to quality and yield and that means getting the job done as early and as quickly as possible. In 37 years of farming I have always had a net profit even though I did experience two years in a row when my small-grain operation had operating losses. But I haven't been carried away by my good fortune because I have not forgotten the 1930's."

Kenner recalled, "When I started in the late 1930's I was at the bottom but felt eager and reasoned, why not push for all I could. By 1942 we were farming 2,720 acres."

Walter Krueger farmed in the same area as Al Kenner. Krueger started farming with his father in 1933, but soon realized there was little chance for expanding the farm, so in 1937 he decided to "go it alone" on two sections of rented land. Krueger learned in shopping for power to run his farm so that he could buy a 32-

horsepower F-20 for $800 when horses were $125 each. He reasoned that he could drive the tractor 24 hours a day (which he did), but horses could only work about 8 hours. With that reasoning the tractor was only about $1/14$ as costly as horses, so he bought a new F-20 "on rubber." Krueger said, "Dad told me I was crazy and especially so because it had rubber tires. That was O.K. because in 1940 I bought two I.H.C. 'M's' for $1,325 each. Then we had three tractors that we worked around the clock."

Like Kenner, Walter Krueger bought a combine and did custom work to generate cash flow. He too figured cost very closely and proved to himself that the total cost of harvest with the combine was $.03 a bushel.*

When asked to point out the key to his success, Krueger could give more than one reason. He said, "Being challenged about that tractor I bought made me want to prove to Dad he was wrong. When I went on my own, I had a goal and I have passed that a few times. The tougher things were, the more we dug in. But the big thing was that I soon learned that you don't have to do all the work yourself. When I learned that, I had time to think and that was the biggest break."

Several other father-son teams had similar experiences to that of the Kruegers. Lloyd Butts, who reputedly has the largest feedlot in North Dakota, said, "I was hungry when I was a kid and this gave me the determination to grow. I had a goal to build a big feedlot and that goal was aided by the mere challenge of creating it." His son, Alan, has never known what being hungry is, but he and his wife, Linda, are determined to use their college education to build on Lloyd Butts' dream. "Really," Alan said, "the only difference is that we are at a higher jumping off point." Alan knew that at that higher point he and Linda could climb higher or fail, but they laughed at the thought of the latter. Father and son both agreed that "you are getting nowhere when you are standing still."   ·

Having grown up in the 1930's in drought-stricken central South Dakota, Alfred Ehlers and his brother traveled in search of better opportunities, but learned from the trip that maybe the best was to return to the home place. Ehlers' father had come from Germany and in 1908 had homesteaded in South Dakota. After purchasing a Hart Parr in 1919, Ehlers expanded his farm rapidly. In 1928 he

---

*Walter Krueger harvested and delivered 692 bushels of wheat to the elevator in his best day in 1939. This shows the capacity and low cost of a combine, in contrast to a threshing machine.

wanted to buy a combine, but the banker refused to loan him the money. So he told the banker to "go to hell" and walked out. The banker followed him out. After getting his loan, Ehlers was able to expand his farm with the cash earned from custom combining. Unfortunately, the bank went bankrupt just after Ehlers had deposited a large check from the Federal Land Bank that was to be used to purchase more land.

His son, Alfred Ehlers, learned from all that, but when he started farming on 12 acres rented on a one-fourth share, he was determined that he was going to make it. Ehlers said, "Like the 1930's I am convinced if we had another depression, the strong would stay and I'm prepared to be among them." He added to his farm profits by trucking and repairing machinery in the 1930's, and the next thing he realized, people wanted him to name a price and terms for their land. "That's when I realized it was time to dig in," he said, and Mrs. Ehlers nodded in approval.

John Bogestad of northwestern Minnesota worked on the "home farm" for a number of years and annually received 5 acres of potatoes as wages. In 1934 at the age of 29 Bogestad decided he had to "set out on his own." He rented 160 acres for one-fourth of the crop. Two years later he was able to buy that farm on a 20-year contract. Next, he purchased a rubber-tired Model "J" Minneapolis. "It pulled three bottoms and rode so smoothly. The dealer carried me because I couldn't get money from the bank."

The tractor proved to be an asset because it enabled him to buy a farm that had quack grass as high as the tractor and no horse farmer could keep it under control. He got a good crop in the first year. "In four years, starting in 1936, I paid for 480 acres," Bogestad said, "but that made little difference because when I started I had my mind made up that I was going to succeed and I never thought about the possibility of defeat." At age 70 Bogestad was still looking ahead.

John H. Reque of south central Minnesota, whose father was a salesman, started farming as soon as he graduated from high school and failed completely in his first year. "In retrospect that was my first good break and I had three years in the service during World War II to think about it." After the war Reque became a field man in agriculture for a sugar beet company and cautiously started farming again on a moonlight basis. He increased his farming activities gradually so that by 1963 he was farming "full time and holding down a full-time job with the company." He was hiring men to help with the farm. After the farm was developing a steady cash flow and he had a solid working base, Reque quit his job.

"When I look back," Reque said, "I think my first year's failure in farming motivated me to look for a different approach. Working as a field man for the beet company, I began to dream about growing sugar beets on a big acreage. So many people challenged my idea and I became so frustrated that I decided to raise a big acreage of beets just to prove my theory."

Ofttimes men tempered by adversity steel themselves for the challenges that lie ahead.[6]

NOTES

[1]Liberty Hyde Bailey, *The Harvest of the Year to the Tiller of the Soil*, Macmillan, New York (1927); Liberty Hyde Bailey, "Can I Make a Farm Pay?: Yes, If You Like It," *World's Work*, 1, No. 4, pp. 548–549; Bob Moraczewski, "Roy Keppy—A Study in Motivation," *The Farmer*, 89, No. 20 (October 16, 1971), pp. 11 and 15; Bob Moraczewski, "How to Turn Yourself On," *The Farmer*, 89, No. 22 (November 20, 1971), pp. 13, 14; H. B. Howell, "Present and Future: Changes in Agriculture," *Iowa Farm Science*, 25, No. 4 (January, 1971), pp. 3, 4; Ross Parish, "Innovation and Enterprise in Wheat Farming," *Review of Marketing and Agricultural Economics*, 22 (1954), pp. 191, 214; Charles R. Hoffer and Dale Stangeland, "Farmers' Reactions to New Practices: Corn Growing in Michigan," *Michigan State University Agricultural Exp. Sta. Tech. Bull.*, 264 (February, 1958), pp. 4, 5; interviews with:

Pete A. Hermanson, Story City, Iowa, February 22, 1972
George Rauenhorst, Olivia, Minnesota, March 16, 1972
Jay C. Swisher, Groton, South Dakota, March 1, 1972
George C. Schuller, Claremont, South Dakota, April 10, 1972
Donald A. Schulz, Faribault, Minnesota, March 25, 1972
Arthur L. Skolness, Glyndon, Minnesota, February 17, 1971
John W. Wright, Edmore, North Dakota, November 7, 1970
Floyd Darroll Warren, Hardin, Montana, May 16, 1972
Larry and Eric Torske, Hardin, Montana, May 17, 1972
Gerald Boler, Truman, Minnesota, March 29, 1972
Stanley D. Olson, Fairmont, Minnesota, March 29, 1972

[2]Interviews with:

John Link, Bismarck, North Dakota, October 20, 1974
Clarence Carlson, Argyle, Minnesota, February 20, 1971
T. A. Dilse, Scranton, North Dakota, April 8, 1972
Allen C. Kolstad, Chester, Montana, May 11, 1972
Don L. Short, Beach, North Dakota, April 7, 1972
John Sutton, Jr., Agar, South Dakota, April 12, 1972
John Sutton, Sr., Onida, South Dakota, April 11, 1972
Clarence Romain, Chester, Montana, May 12, 1972
George C. Schuller, Claremont, South Dakota, April 10, 1972
Earl Davison, Tintah, Minnesota, December 8, 1970
Ralph Hvidsten, Stephen, Minnesota, January 17, 1972
Earl Hvidsten, Stephen, Minnesota, January 17, 1972
John Heline, Pierson, Iowa, February 23, 1972
Harold Hofstrand, Leeds, North Dakota, December 12, 1970
Dennis L. Anderson, Rapid City, South Dakota, April 9, 1972

John W. Scott, Jr., Gilby, North Dakota, March 7, 1973
David Garst, Coon Rapids, Iowa, June 12, 1972
John S. Dalrymple III, Casselton, North Dakota, March 7, 1973
Walter Kroeker, Winkler, Manitoba, February 15, 1973

[3]Interviews with:

Jacob Geritz, Lakota, North Dakota, November 7, 1970
C. H. Underlee, Hendrum, Minnesota, January 19, 1972
Ernest C. Hector, Crosby, North Dakota, April 5, 1972
Mertens brothers, Devils Lake, North Dakota, March 11, 1974
John S. Dean, Hatton, North Dakota, November 15, 1972
Freddie Mutschler, Wimbledon, North Dakota, June 24, 1971
Dalton Docter, Amherst, South Dakota, December 16, 1972
Herman H. Lee, Borup, Minnesota, February 17, 1971
George Rauenhorst, Olivia, Minnesota, March 16, 1972

[4]Interviews with:

Ray S. Jarrett, Britton, South Dakota, March 2, 1972, and December 14 through 16, 1972
Allan M. Severson, Owatonna, Minnesota, June 20, 1974
Jack C. Lacey, Wendell, Minnesota, April 1, 1972
James J. Walton, Breckenridge, Minnesota, April 20, 1972
Skulason Moe, Poplar, Montana, May 9, 1972
Jack E. Lang, Malta, Montana, May 9, 1972
Darrell Miller, Wahpeton, North Dakota, April 20, 1972
Clem Hebel, Mason City, Iowa, February 21, 1972, and June 4, 1975
Thomas (Buck) Snortland, Sharon, North Dakota, January 8, 1972

[5]Interviews with:

Joe Thompson, Grafton, North Dakota, March 13, 1973
Eddie A. Velo, Rothsay, Minnesota, February 26, 1973

Bob Moraczewski, "She Is More Than a Wife," *The Farmer*, 89, No. 22 (November 20, 1971), p. 13; interviews with:

David Drum, Billings, Montana, May 16, 1972, and March 19, 1973
O'Farrells, Inc., Marvin, South Dakota, February 25, 1972
J. G. Hall and sons, Hoople, North Dakota, February 14, 1973
Bill and Daryl Spicher, Hingham, Montana, May 10, 1972
Hoggarth brothers, Courtenay, North Dakota, March 8, 1972
David Miller, Wahpeton, North Dakota, February 12, 1973
Edgar, Daniel, Stephen, and Mrs. John Keil, Ledger, Montana, May 12, 1972
David Glinz, Pingree, North Dakota, June 24, 1971
Raymond Schnell, Dickinson, North Dakota, May 18, 1972
Gerald C. and Thomas W. Ryan, East Grand Forks, Minnesota, February 14, 1973

[6]Kenneth R. Krause and Leonard R. Kyle, *Midwestern Corn Farms* . . ., U.S. Department of Agriculture, Agricultural Economic Report No. 216, Washington (1971), III, pp. 42–44; interviews with:

Virgil Mellies, Hector, Minnesota, March 16, 1972
Alvin Kenner, Leeds, North Dakota, December 12, 1970
Walter Krueger, McKenzie, North Dakota, March 10, 1972
Lloyd and Alan Butts, Carrington, North Dakota, March 7, 1972
Alfred Ehlers, Presho, South Dakota, April 10, 1972
John Bogestad, Karlstad, Minnesota, March 22, 1972
John H. Reque, Redwood Falls, Minnesota, March 15, 1972

CHAPTER V

The Psychology of Growth

AN IMPORTANT FACTOR contributing to the development of any business or institution is the psychology and/or mental attitude of its leaders. Farmers interviewed were asked these questions: Is growth a psychological factor? Specifically, what are the reasons for the growth of your farm? Most of those interviewed had a quick answer and definite ideas as to the cause of their growth. But, strangely enough, the wives frequently had an even better answer than their husbands because they understood what motivated them. Their husbands had never bothered to think about it.* Although many of them had never really thought about the reasons behind their growth, others, in contrast, had given much thought to the question and expressed their personal opinions about the reasons for progress. From the answers it is also evident that this question was generally candidly answered because it was a personal thought question and those interviewed really were interested in the cause of their growth. Some of the true reasons for growth also appeared in disguise—in answers to other questions—and were not apparent until the entire interview had been re-evaluated.

Basically, there appeared to be five definite factors contributing to the basis for the expansion of their farm operations: economics, opportunity, technology, love of adventure, and a combination of challenge and strong ego. Probably at one time all these farmers expanded solely because of economics. Some of the smaller ones still have reason for expanding purely along economic lines, but most are beyond that point and are growing because of other elements. For this group of farmers, farming is profitable, a great way to make a living, "a ballgame," satisfying, exciting, and challeng-

---

*To keep the answers in proper perspective, the reader should be reminded that those interviewed represent a select group of successful midwestern farmers.

ing. That's why they are in it. But in spite of this, one should not underestimate certain psychological factors contributing to a successful operation.

Economics, Not Psychology

Ralph Hvidsten of Minnesota said that he has no motive for expanding his farm other than improving its efficiency. He is not concerned about whether he is larger or smaller than his neighbors. Hvidsten, by inner conviction and sentiment, is interested in the broad distribution of individual and independent farms: "Here is where social and economic ends are in conflict, because we can't have a nation of small farmers and still have an abundance of cheap food."

Earl Hvidsten, living only a few blocks from Ralph Hvidsten, emphasizes that economics is the basis for his expansion. Earl said, "I have expanded because I think it is good business to do so. Fortunately, I have done well enough so that I have not had to buy land until I have had the cash. I am adverse to owing money. All of my machinery is paid for when it is purchased."

Iowan Pete A. Hermanson feels that there are no factors other than economics involved in the growth of his two generation farm. Pete said, "Economic pressures are the reasons why we have grown. The rapid inflation since World War II has made it inevitable to expand. You have to go into debt to expand just to defend yourself."

South Dakotan Kenneth Kinkler agrees with Hermanson and adds, "There is no psychology involved with us, because it is sheer economics that forces us to grow. People are demanding low-priced food and they are getting it. I see no hope for any great increase in the prices we are getting, but our operating costs keep climbing. Only through the economic advantages of bigger equipment and more acres under operation can we combat the declining margins." Kinkler also admits his love of running a large operation. His profits not needed for continued expansion of the farm are being invested in off-the-farm agri-businesses.

"There are many factors that cause growth," said Walter J. Bones, Jr. "Most seem to come by necessity. We grew internally at first because it was the practical thing to do, putting cattle and hogs on the land we had. When our livestock enterprises got larger, they demanded more land, so we bought more land. Then we needed more livestock—so the cycle goes." Bones felt that psychology or emotion had no effect upon the growth of his business. "We were particularly on guard when expanding," he said, "because there is so much opposition to farm growth. When we built our new house there was real heat—people were very critical about it."

Donald Jarrett, who with his father and brother has a sizeable diversified crop and livestock farm and ranch, is not worried about keeping up with the neighbors because the Jarretts are ahead of them. Don was quite moved as he said, "All this talk about the small family farm gets me. Why stay small when you can live better and have the economic advantages of growth? We grew up on a large farm and just take it for granted. Growth is almost like a habit. I visit with other large farmers and all of us think that there ought to be certain peaks to efficiency, but there always seem to be new opportunities."

The Jarretts' operation far exceeds the size of farm that governmental studies have considered to be optimum. In fact, their diversified enterprises would each surpass the optimum-sized complete farm unit as determined by the 1973 U.S.D.A. study, yet the Jarretts keep growing and streamlining. And according to their records and calculations, they have not yet found the upper limit.

"I started at 20 cows and now I am at 200 and I am still improving my efficiency," said Richard C. Bleecker. "Expansion is not a psycho push for me; it is a matter of economics. Besides, I have observed that growth has enabled me to afford help, so that I can spend my time managing instead of doing the daily routine."

Ward Whitman, a North Dakota small-grain farmer and rancher, feels that his drive is determined by the thought of how well he and his family want to live. Whitman feels that if families want vacations and other time away from home, they must farm at a large enough scale to justify a labor force to do the job while they are gone. "I remember too many years," Whitman recalled, "when we could not leave the place because there were chores to do, but we weren't big enough to afford the kind of help we wanted."

Charles V. Johnson, Minnesota cattle feeder and corn producer, enlarged his farm because, even though it provided a comfortable living, it was too small to keep him fully employed. Johnson increased the size of his farm to justify the hiring of a year-round employee of good caliber "who likes to keep busy." The farm now provides a good living for two families and because of large equipment and a mechanized feedlot, they can even take time off for vacations and travel.

The Keogh Ranch of western North Dakota was established in

1905 and endured dry years, erratic cattle prices, and two bank closings. Brooks J. Keogh, after graduating from college, spent seven years in the business world before he took over his father's ranch. Besides ranching, he is very active in non-farm business interests and in many civic affairs. Keogh "philosophically" said that he would like to think that his ranch expansion was chiefly a matter of economics, but he is quick to point out that economics is determined by the style of living one desires for oneself and the family. Keogh, a past president of the American National Cattlemen's Association, commented on business philosophy:

What one wants to do in his business or occupation is determined by a combination of motives, ambitions, and drives as much as by economics. Some people are motivated to do a job for the sake of family comfort. We like that, but we really enjoy traveling, which takes money too. The time we spend working for many causes would not be available if we didn't have a good economic operation to support our being away from the ranch. In my opinion too many farms and ranches are handicapped because cash reserves are never accumulated for family needs, so these needs take too much of the cash flow.

Like the Keoghs, Freddie and Marlys Mutschler want to do more than just farm. They like to enjoy vacations and relax at their Arizona winter home, which they reach by the use of their own airplane. The Mutschlers are active in "Flying Farmers," where they meet and communicate with farmers from throughout the nation and keep abreast of what other innovative farmers are doing. When asked the reasons for expanding their farm, Freddie hesitated for a minute and then said:

I don't exactly know why our farm has grown to this size except that I like to try new things and we like to do things first class. [Marlys agreed.] Marlys and I saw how many farm families live, and we decided that if we had to live that way, we might as well be broke. We agreed that we had to take a chance and expand the farm to do the things we wanted and had to take a risk. We noticed that as soon as we started to step ahead of the rest that resentment popped up, but we decided if we could take the risk of debts, we could also endure resentment. That seems to be dying down gradually.

I think it was the decision to get the big equipment that really turned the tide for us. I only have an eighth grade education, but I don't know any job or profession where we could have done as well. We think we are living the best life and would not trade with anyone we know.*

---

*Few homesteaders could have visualized that a 19-year-old farm boy could have expanded his farm operation to a total of 60 average homesteads by the time he was 40.

Dalton Docter, a South Dakota cattle feeder, felt that way of life was a more important motive than economics in his decision to build a large feedlot. Docter remembers reading what former Secretary of Agriculture Orville Freeman had to say about small-scale farming: "Lots of people are on farms that are too small and can't grow. Perhaps the people are old and uneducated. Some are frozen in because they aren't suited to city jobs. Others can be 'trained out' and ought to be. . . . No price-support program will do any good for a guy on 40 acres with a mule."

Docter took this advice seriously and decided to change his methods of farming. He said with a smile on his face, "I like to make money so I can live the way I want. But basically I am lazy, and I want to make money so I don't have to work. I grew up in a small town surrounded by small farms and I have seen too many old people who are working and I don't like the thought of it." Even though he and his wife Bernice say they want to retire early because they would like to enjoy more leisure, they probably never will because they like the excitement of the feedlot and its rewards.

Two other farmers interviewed expressed the opinion that the federal government, exclusive of the commercial production farm programs, played an important part in their expansion plans. A farmer who prefers to remain anonymous stated that a big factor in his expansion was the "tax structure which virtually forced expansion, especially in buying rundown farms which needed heavy capital inputs to improve them. This helps a farmer with high equity to avoid the high income tax. It is my opinion that this has been as important a factor in enlarging as any governmental interference in agriculture."*

Montana rancher Robert L. Cox agrees with the opinion expressed above. In his early years Cox expanded rapidly to obtain an economical level of operation, as well as to get the cash flow needed to achieve the standard of living he and his wife wanted. To him the move was also good business from the tax standpoint. With a high equity position, Cox realized that expansion would relieve his income tax problem for a few years, but he also knew that sometime later he would be on a higher tax level than ever. Cox said, "This means there is no sense in my expanding too much. We are living at the peak of our desire. If we expanded, we

---

*The research of Krause and Kyle on midwestern corn farms sponsored by the U.S.D.A. bore out similar conclusions.

would only be assuming more responsibility and the only benefactor would be the U.S. Government—so why bother." Estate sales are proof of the wisdom of those words.

J. Budd Tibert, a North Dakota potato and beet farmer, felt that another program of the federal government was partially responsible for expanding his farm. Tibert pointed out that the high welfare payments reduced the available labor supply and hence forced wages to rise. To combat rising labor cost, Tibert and many of his fellow farmers purchased larger equipment. This, in turn, made it possible to handle more acres and indirectly led to farm expansion. The Tibert farm has increased thirty-two-fold since it was first homesteaded in the 1880's, and there are no plans to halt growth unless "income taxes cause too many problems." J. Budd Tibert, looking to the future, said, "As we get bigger and better equipment, we will employ fewer but better people, so we will be ahead and those on welfare will stay there."

Those are the opinions of farmers who gave economics as the reason for their expansion even though in each case additional motives clearly emerged.[1]

Technology and Growth

Farmers, like many other people, are fascinated by big equipment and large power units. Industry in its long history has used a tremendous amount of labor-saving mechanical devices, but probably no other industry in recent years has been so completely revolutionized by power-oriented machinery as agriculture.

Alvin Kenner of North Dakota has never used horses on his own farm, but he grew up as a farm boy working with them. Kenner, who applies strict cost accounting to his business, has used the largest possible equipment feasible for his field work during his nearly four decades of farming. He says:

Technical changes more than psychological have tempted me to expand. It has been easy to grow when you have big equipment because each time a new machine has been introduced it is possible to do more acres with less effort. I have traded machinery regularly, so the increase in cost of larger equipment has not been as noticeable for me as for the man who trades every 10 or 15 years.

If psychology has had any impact on the size of my farm, I suppose it is the negative kind. I know the neighbors resent our growth, and in spite of the technological improvements, I have passed up several good deals close to home because of the neighbors' feelings.

Richard Spicher of Montana recalled that when he was in his

twenties and thirties he could do a great share of field work and still do a proper job of management. Spicher said:

When you are young, you have got to keep busy, but conditions change. Tractor riding is a luxury I can no longer afford. I have more valuable things to do with my time. My wife could not understand the psychology of borrowing money to buy bigger equipment to farm more land until she suddenly realized that I had time to relax. It didn't take her long to catch on to the value of bigger equipment. Women really are a strong force in implementing new ideas.

We have the technology to lead the farmers of the world. There still is a lot to be done in this country. We bought a farm from a neighbor who averaged less than 9 bushels of wheat per acre and in a short time we were averaging 27 bushels an acre. Our equipment, management, and some fertilizer made the difference. Now we would rather enjoy ourselves and not work just to pay more taxes.

P. D. Hempstead also found technology to be the basis for his success:

Using technology as soon as it becomes proven is a matter of economic efficiency. You have to have volume to make mechanical equipment pay, but that is the way you earn the cash flow to hire help. If I devoted full time to farming, there is no doubt we could triple our size, but we like the challenge of the civic work. Emotionally, one cannot stand still. I must confess our standard of living has not changed one bit, even though we have gone through farm expansions, but the challenge was there.

The Hempstead farm has been in the family since 1852. When Dillon and Mary Hempstead took over the farm, it had kept dairy production records continuously from 1912. After farming for a few years, they had the opportunity to more than double their farm in one purchase. Once the land was purchased and improved, they diversified to increase the business volume.

"Technology has made it easier to grow, and the bigger you get, the easier it is," was Ronald D. Shepherd's answer about his motives for farm growth. Shepherd's grandparents were homesteaders in Montana. His parents ran a small farm, did trucking, and had an elevator. Ron started farming at the age of 15 with help from his father. At the age of 19 drought nearly ended his farming business, but he learned from the experience. Returning from service after World War II, he started farming again. This time he had a sideline business to generate cash flow until his farm became large enough to support a family and sustain itself. But they have not stopped thinking of expansion, for, as Ron said, "The bigger you get, the easier it seems to be. Bigger equipment eases the labor problem and increases efficiency at the same time."

Bill Hall and his brothers are known for the excellent management of a quality potato business in the Red River Valley. Hall pointed out that machinery does a better job handling potatoes than human pickers ever could do. He recalled that after the introduction of mechanical harvesters they were not only able to expand production but improved their quality at the same time. The Halls believe that by using the latest in technology and producing in volume they have made their marketing easier. "Besides," said Bill Hall, "we like the challenge of growth—but doesn't everybody?" He concluded, "We get more work done cheaper, quicker, and easier than at any time in the history of this farm [since the 1880's]. Land is higher priced than ever, but still cheaper than what it was in the 1930's if you know what it will do. If it isn't, why is there so little for sale? Equipment, warehouses, and communication make this possible."

The Sinner brothers and brother-in-law Ellery Bresnahan, each with a large family, have experienced significant growth in their cattle feedlot and sugar beet production. Their business dates back to pre-World War I days and has had a slow, steady growth. The business is large enough so that one brother, George Sinner, is able to devote a considerable portion of his time to political and educational activities. William Sinner has been active in livestock groups. Because there are three managers and several children working on the farm, the farm business goes on without interruption. Without both sufficient volume for income and backup management, extra curricular activities would be difficult to indulge in.

The Sinner-Bresnahan farm, although long recognized as one of the major feedlots of North Dakota, did not grow without careful, methodical planning. Although they have the necessary cash flow, they have no compulsion to expand unless growth increases their profit. The family operation is known for its tight conservative management, with excellent records to prove their progress.*

The three families are a tightly knit unit, are very civic minded, and have no compulsion to have the biggest farm, but are concerned that it rank as the best. They are extremely competitive, and the many visitors to their farm signify that other feeders and farmers respect the job they are doing. The Sinner-Bresnahan farm

---

*The late Albert Sinner, father of George and Bill, once said that in over 30 years [since 1929] of his farming career, he had never had a year in which he did not operate at a profit for the year, although he had experienced enterprise losses at various times.

has endured over a half century because of good management and the adoption of innovative methods in farming. George Sinner says, "We don't buy big equipment just because it is the biggest, but because we need it. We are big enough to have the advantages of buying and selling, and we are competitive with the biggest and best. If we felt we needed to expand, capital would be the least of our concerns, but the right use of it would be a problem."

Bill and Daryl Spicher do not feel any great urge to expand purely for the sake of getting large. They feel that technology has made change possible and for their own protection they have to grow. Daryl said, "It appears that growth has been partly economically motivated and partly to have something large enough for the next generation. Also, we don't want to be left behind." To which Bill added, "If land came for sale now, we would buy. We could handle two sections without having to buy any additional equipment—that's where the economy comes in. With extra manpower we could double the hours on our tractors and still have a safety margin if there was some adverse weather."

The Spicher brothers feel that over the years their farm has increased vertically as rapidly as it has horizontally. Their grandfather averaged fewer than 10 bushels an acre after he started farming in 1910. In the period that their father farmed from 1930 to 1964 he averaged fewer than 20 bushels an acre. Daryl and Bill have a proven yield of just over 30 bushels per acre. The brothers agreed that their "salvation has come from increased production because of greater yields and technology, and we expect both to continue to help us, plus we still have some corners to cut."

Walter Krueger, who farms with two sons, said, "When I was young I expanded whenever there was an opportunity because my wife and I both liked farming. As we grew older, we had boys and we expanded so they would have an opportunity. As machinery gets larger, we buy it and can handle more land with the help we have, so we grow. It has never occurred to me that I am larger or smaller than the farmers around me. We just do what is economical."

From the above quotations it is evident that large-scale farming depends on the use of big machinery which contributes directly to the success of the farm operation.[2]

Opportunity Causes Expansion

One frequently hears the expression, "I surely missed a golden opportunity," or "He got all the breaks." Unfortunately, most of the people who make such remarks are those who have passed up the opportunities instead of having taken them. A great portion of the farmers visited and interviewed for this book are second, third, or fourth generation farmers. Some have expanded beyond the success of their ancestors, and others have prospered out of the failure of their ancestors. All, sometime in their lives, had opportunities, took them, and succeeded. Sometimes opportunity appeared because of another's failure, and other times it might have been because of the help of others. The important thing was that the opportunity was recognized and seized.

In 1927 George Gray went to Montana with $35.00 in his pocket. He got a job in the construction business to "keep alive" and then looked for land to rent. He discovered that there were several attorneys in the Carter area who had received land instead of cash for legal services rendered. Gray rented this land on a one-sixth and one-fifth share basis, which meant he had no rent to pay until he harvested a crop. On the strength of his rent contracts, he was able to finance the purchase of a used tractor for $200. By this time he had earned enough money to pay for some machinery and managed to buy the rest on contracts.

An opportunity presented itself when a farmer in desperation sold Gray a section of land for the price of 10 bushels of wheat per acre and gave him seven years to deliver. George Gray would not have purchased the farm any other way because, once he got started, he never bought machinery or land for which he could not pay cash. He preferred to rent land in an effort to build a cash flow and said:

Land was easy to rent because everybody was quitting. I thought about doing the same but never seriously considered it. When I came to Montana, I had set a goal of 1,000 acres of crop each year [50 per cent fallow]. But growth came very naturally and easily. Anyone with land was looking for a good farmer and I was easy to deal with. My first rented land was good so I managed to make steady progress. My best year ever was 1942 when I got 43 bushels an acre. In the early days it took several years to get that many bushels.

When George Gray retired from farming in 1964 he had 5,000 acres of land paid for. With the exception of 640 acres purchased in 1934 on a contract-for-deed, he never owed a mortgage on any land. Gray remembered the resentment against him when he succeeded in the 1930's while others failed. He added, "But I now own the land which was formerly in 22 hands and ironically even though the previous owners resented me when they wanted to

quit, they came to me to sell it. If they had not offered it, I probably would never have taken the opportunity because surely there
must have been other prospective buyers."

The late John Sutton, Sr., of South Dakota reported many opportunities that had come to him during 50 years of farming:

We owed as much money as anyone, but never thought about quitting
because Dad and we three brothers all liked the ranch. When I look back,
our first big opportunity came when Dad's banker persuaded him to buy
tractors and get rid of horses in the 1920's. A horse takes so much more
grass than a critter, you know. Dad just loved horses, but he listened. That
move enabled us to keep a larger number of cows. I think we had about
2,000 head of cattle on hand when the rain started to come in 1937. We
kept the calf crop for two years, and the market jumped about $2.00 a
hundred from the $5.00 and $6.00 level of the previous years. We had
cash then and started to buy land for as little as a dollar an acre from
absentee owners, and there were no back taxes. Right after that I bought
800 acres for $1,500 to the owner and $1,500 back taxes.

The opportunity was there, and it was easy once we generated a little
cash. Our big break came because, when we started our registered bull
sale in 1942, timing couldn't have been better. If we had not "hung
tough" during the bad years, it would never have been possible.

John Sutton, Sr., reminisced about his and his father's careers in
farming and the times when the failures of other farmers presented opportunities for them.

Eddie A. Velo grew up in the rolling country of Otter Tail
County, which is Minnesota's largest agricultural county and is in
an area where small-scale intense livestock farming is the tradition. When asked why his farm grew, he and Mrs. Velo were both
at a loss. After a moment of reflection Velo said, "When we
started, neither of us ever thought that some day we would attain a
farm the size we now have. Land became available when people
quit, and we were able to buy it. We had livestock, chickens, and
turkeys, and our farm operation was intensified. Then we got to
thinking it might be less risky to increase our crop acres and
spread that way as well as vertically."

Mrs. Velo, who was also intensely active in the farming enterprise, added, "We grew so gradually that it never occurred to us
that we had a large farm." She laughed, "It's like having a big
family."

Two young farmers, Larry and Eric Torske of Montana, started
"working into" the business at the ages of 16 and 25, respectively.
They had some definite ideas on why they expanded their farm.
Larry said, "In some respects our growth was accidental. A

neighbor decided to sell out, and one night at the supper table it occurred to us that this was a good chance for us and we took it."

Eric added his comments: "The pride of adding to the farm gives you a feeling that you are going some place. It seems as soon as we accomplish one goal, we look to another one."

John W. Scott, Sr., a North Dakota potato farmer, saw his pioneer father rise and decline in farming, but that experience did not interfere with his progressive attitude. John W. Scott, Sr., started with 80 acres in 1924 and purchased more land in 1926. He had a struggle until the mid-1930's, when he admits to having been lucky enough to outguess the market and cash in on a good potato price. Scott said, "I was just at the right age [mid-thirties] when other farmers were pulling back or walking away from their farms. I couldn't resist the challenge, and when I hit that good potato price with a big acreage, I bought as fast as I could."

John W. Scott, Jr., is a much more conservative man economically than his father and frankly admits that he will not expand purely for the sake of expansion. He said, "If the farm in any way is expanded, it will be purely a matter of net profits."

Ervin Bourgois is on the farm homesteaded by his father in Burleigh County, North Dakota, in 1883. Ervin has seen the size of the farm increase fourteen-fold from the date he started working in partnership with his father in 1928. Now his sons are involved and even though their farm is large in acreage, including nearly 1,000 acres of irrigated land and several separate enterprises, Bourgois expects his sons to continue expansion. In his words: "You grow to survive; there is no middle ground where you can stand still. It never occurred to us that we were big farmers because we grew slowly and steadily. In adverse times we just dug in harder and when things improved, we bounced back twice as fast. Right now the same thing could happen because if things got tough, there is no limit to the corners we could cut. That means internal expansion, doesn't it? Opportunity is where you find it and sometimes that is found within your own operation or in your neighborhood."[3]

The Romance of Growth

It was obvious throughout the months of interviewing that these farmers and their families were excited about their lives. Farming was a romance and big farming was almost a love affair. Like little boys, men often love big machines and big machines justified big farming. They and their families were happy with what they were doing. The all too typical portrayal of a farmer being depressed, underprivileged, and impoverished was not evident among them. At least, they did not feel this way and that probably was one key to their success.

Loren C. Jetvig, a Minnesotan in his thirties, when asked why his farm had grown, said, "I just love the idea of a big operation; it grows on me. We like to live well, but that is not the real reason. Our particular motive is the fun we are having." Mrs. Jetvig, seated by her husband at the kitchen table, smiled in complete accord.

Harold T. Petersen, also in his thirties, had a similar answer:

I love big machinery, and the only way I can afford it is to operate big. My boyhood dream was to become a big farmer. My grandfather started here in central Minnesota in 1895 with 160 acres and got up to 560 acres. Dad started in 1925 with 220 acres and got up to 560 acres. Right after high school I went into partnership with Dad, and when he retired, I was 27. At that time I had already passed him in total acres in my own farm, besides taking over his farm [on contract]. I have added two other farms since. I started farming on totally borrowed money.

Gerald Hoggarth, spokesman for himself and three brothers, all in their thirties, smiled and replied, "Naturally, we all like to make a good living, but really it's an inner drive that makes us grow. There is a lot of excitement in expansion." They had expanded their father's farm twenty-four-fold in their first 12 years chiefly for that reason.

David and Valeria Miller were old-timers in comparison to the younger Jetvigs, Petersens, and Hoggarths, for they were in their forties. Dave and Valeria's beautiful home is on the site of the North Dakota homestead of his grandfather dating back to the 1880's. Dave's father enlarged the homestead, and Dave now has increased it many times. His brother, Ivan, has kept pace with him, which has added to the fun.

When Dave was asked why his farm grew, he answered without hesitation, "There is great satisfaction in growing because I enjoy every minute of farming. There may be many who are critical of me, but I believe I do as good or a better job of farming than any of them."

Norman Weckerly, who grew up on a fairly large North Dakota grain and cattle farm, said with great optimism: "I have the confidence. I want to grow to satisfy a need. Not to grow would be boring. One needs new challenges. I have even added non-farm enterprises just to find out where my limitations are. My only hang-up is the ability to inspire those who work with me. I believe that if one has self-confidence and adaptability and likes the excitement of challenge, there is no reason why he should not push ahead."

Skulason Moe, a Montana wheat farmer, when asked about the motives behind the growth of his farm, readily answered, "We just have the urge to grow. At first we thought it was a matter of economics and that we should have a farm big enough for the future. But once we stopped acreage expansion, we had to turn in another direction, and then we realized it was the love of challenge. Dad was the same way."

Three other farmers, all past middle age but still young at heart, took time to look back at their successful careers in farming and expressed strong feelings about their growth. Ernest Hector, the youngest of the three, said, "I gained tremendous courage surviving the depression and some tough knocks in my early days right after World War II. It's been fun to overcome the gamble." Mrs. Hector laughed at her husband's efforts to avoid giving a more explicit answer and replied, "He is very aggressive and he loves every minute of risk."

Alfred Ehlers of South Dakota started in 1934 on a small rented farm. He said, "I like farming. It's my business and I have grown beyond my needs because of the joy of doing it. Of course, you'd like to leave a start for the kids. Considering everything, it has been a good life—I know a lot of my neighbors will not agree on that." Ehlers also was asked if he still thought about future expansion and replied, "You feel your way and if conditions are right, go. If not, sit back. We certainly are not stopping expansion, at least we are not thinking about stopping."

T. A. Dilse started farming in 1928. He and his wife, Ida, hung wet sheets in the house during the North Dakota dust storms to make breathing easier. When neighbors left during the drought, the Dilses became more determined. They budgeted rigidly during the 1930's so that when good prices came with World War II expansion was easy for them. "We didn't expand because we needed the money. I guess it was the urge to piece a big farm together—the fun of doing it. A good start and education for the family were also an incentive."

Few men enjoy farming more thoroughly than Vernon G. Hagen. Vern had to quit school in the first weeks of the ninth grade to take the place of his father who became ill. At age 29 he had enough resources to live comfortably on the income from interest. After a few months of traveling and observing other farmers and their innovations in farming, Vern Hagen became restless and couldn't wait to get back to his own farm. In the next 17 years he amassed a large farm. His reason: "I have no explanation unless it was the desire to prove that I could do it. I often thought of a lot of other jobs I would like to have tried; but really, all I ever wanted to do was to be a big farmer."

Probably the classic answer to the question, "Why did you continue to expand when you were already making a living?," was received at Vernon Center, Minnesota. When Bill A. Noy was asked the question, "Why did you buy the million-dollar Bert Hanson farm when you were already making a good living?," at first he was unable to answer. There was a long pause. Finally, Shirley Noy, with a big smile, answered, "Bill was bored, and he needed a challenge."

Dennis L. Anderson, with his father-in-law, Eugene Young, as his partner, has one of the largest farms in South Dakota. He is also involved in a farm management firm which gives him a better understanding about farm growth: "It is the man. Many people have had the same opportunity, but do not have the faith in themselves or the farm. I think the preference for bigness evolves from the creative spirit—the pioneering spirit to be the first, the best, and the biggest. These men have the feeling—there is nothing I can't do."

One farmer, who is also very involved in public activity and has great exposure to a cross section of thinking, pointed out the psychology that opposed the growth of farms in this way: "A good operator looks at profit and opportunity, but in our state [North Dakota] we have a negative psychology toward expansion caused by the belief in the small family farm. Utter confusion is caused by this belief. There is a regular cult against farm growth, and because of that, many capable farmers fail to expand when they have a chance. These are the people who look to the farm programs to solve their problems but have failed to recognize that technology and their own psychology have been the basis for agriculture's success."

We have seen that economics, technology, opportunity, and the romance of growth are in general the reasons for farm expansion. As chicken farmer Dean Myhro said, "I guess we need a hill to climb." That says basically all that has to be said about why some farms grow while others remain stagnant or decline.[4]

NOTES

[1]Interviews with:

Ralph Hvidsten, Stephen, Minnesota, January 17, 1972
Earl Hvidsten, Stephen, Minnesota, January 17, 1972
Pete A. Hermanson, Story City, Iowa, February 22, 1972
Kenneth Kinkler, Onida, South Dakota, April 11, 1972
Walter J. Bones, Jr., Parker, South Dakota, February 24, 1972
Donald Jarrett, Britton, South Dakota, March 2, 1972
Richard C. Bleecker, Lisbon, North Dakota, February 11, 1972
Ward Whitman, Robinson, North Dakota, March 7, 1972
Charles V. Johnson, Jackson, Minnesota, March 28, 1972
Brooks J. Keogh, Keene, North Dakota, April 6, 1972
Freddie Mutschler, Wimbledon, North Dakota, June 24, 1971, and June 13, 1975
Dalton Docter, Amherst, South Dakota, December 16, 1972
Robert L. Cox, Baker, Montana, May 18, 1972
J. Budd Tibert, Voss, North Dakota, March 13, 1973

John Bird, "Farewell to Farmer Tuttle," *Saturday Evening Post*, 238, No. 4 (December 4, 1965), pp. 44–46.

[2]Interviews with:

Alvin Kenner, Leeds, North Dakota, December 12, 1970
George and Richard Spicher, Hingham, Montana, May 10, 1972
P. D. Hempstead, Houston, Minnesota, March 28, 1972
Ronald D. Shepherd, Baker, Montana, May 17, 1972
Hall brothers, Hoople, North Dakota, February 14, 1973
Sinner brothers and Ellery Bresnahan, Casselton, North Dakota, December 28, 1969
Bill and Daryl Spicher, Hingham, Montana, May 10, 1972
Walter Krueger, McKenzie, North Dakota, March 10, 1972

[3]Interviews with:

Donald and George Gray, Carter, Montana, May 14, 1972
John Sutton, Sr., Onida, South Dakota, April 11, 1972
Eddie A. Velo, Rothsay, Minnesota, February 26, 1973
Larry and Eric Torske, Hardin, Montana, May 17, 1972
John W. Scott, Sr., Gilby, North Dakota, January 3, 1970
John W. Scott, Jr., Gilby, North Dakota, November 15, 1972
Ervin Bourgois, Bismarck, North Dakota, March 10, 1972

[4]Interviews with:

Loren C. Jetvig, Lake Park, Minnesota, April 14, 1972
Harold T. Petersen, Murdock, Minnesota, March 30, 1972
Gerald Hoggarth, Courtenay, North Dakota, March 8, 1972
David Miller, Wahpeton, North Dakota, February 12, 1973
Norman Weckerly, Hurdsfield, North Dakota, March 8, 1972
Skulason Moe, Poplar, Montana, May 9, 1972
Ernest Hector, Crosby, North Dakota, April 5, 1972
Alfred Ehlers, Presho, South Dakota, April 10, 1972
T. A. Dilse, Scranton, North Dakota, April 8, 1972
Vernon G. Hagen, East Grand Forks, Minnesota, March 29, 1974
Bill A. Noy, Vernon Center, Minnesota, February 28, 1973
Dennis L. Anderson, Rapid City, South Dakota, April 9, 1972
Dean Myhro, Moorhead, Minnesota, June 11, 1975

Henry F. Hansmeier, *This Is My Life*, privately printed (1959); Bob Moraczewski, "How to Turn Yourself On," *The Farmer*, 89, No. 22 (November 20, 1971), pp. 99–100.

CHAPTER VI

Obstacles or Opportunities?

In SPITE of the many positive reasons previously mentioned for large-scale farming, it would be negligent to overlook some of the obstacles, real or imagined, that occasionally hinder making such ventures successful. In every case, the farmers interviewed knew what the obstacles were, and in many cases, they were regarded only as limiting factors. If they existed, they were mostly psychologically negative.

These farmers, and on occasion their wives, arranged these limiting factors in the following categories: lack of desire and motivation, lack of management, lack of courage to finance, lack of land, and lack of willingness to work with hired help.

Lack of Desire and Motivation

Lack of desire was the chief limiting factor most frequently given by the farmers interviewed. This seems to be in direct contradiction to statements in the preceding chapters dealing with desire and motivation in relation to farm growth, but personal inclinations, age, and accomplishments change with time.

Jack Dahl, who has been ranching for over 20 years, emphatically said: "There is *nothing*, absolutely nothing, that prevents my operation from growing. I have not had a setback of any major proportion. Blizzards, drought, disease, poor cattle prices are all part of the game. We expect such setbacks—that's part of the price of success."

The Dahl ranch, although not exceedingly large, is one of the most innovative ranch operations in North Dakota. When the son finishes college and returns home, the incentive of teamwork and building for the future will be all that is necessary to "get the ball rolling." The positive outlook of Jack and Dottie Dahl is contagious, and their children feel as positive about ranching and farm-

114

ing as their parents do. This, as much as any other factor, has established a tradition of generations of successful family enterprises.

Two of the older farmers interviewed, with a farming experience of 80 years between them, were no longer concerned about future expansion. It had been many years since either of them had last faced a limiting factor, but both had words of advice for young farmers. George C. Schuller said:

I had a lot of drive and liked the challenge until I realized my children were not too interested in farming. I became much more conservative after that, and my desire to enlarge slackened. I would like to comment about what my biggest drawback was when I was younger. I always felt a farm should pay for itself in a few years because I hated the idea of a long-term debt. But I would recommend to the young farmer starting today to shut his eyes and push.

After 45 years of farming, George Rauenhorst, mentally alert and active, scratched his head in restlessness and said:

The most limiting factor a young farmer has today is his personal attitude. There has never been a time in the last 50 years when there have been so many farms waiting to be taken over by a young man [1972]. Financing in many cases would come right with the farm. There are good farms waiting for young managers that would give them some real plateaus to strive for.

John W. Swenson of Fergus Falls, Minnesota, acknowledged that he found no limitations relative to land, labor, or capital. Swenson implied that expansion was simply a matter of how involved a person wanted to become.

"I have the time, the capital, the management, and the manpower," said Earl Hvidsten, "so expansion would be a simple matter. Every year I have passed up several opportunities, but we are living well now, and one must take time to live. I suppose if there was no conflict with the family and personal obligations, I would expand again purely for the challenge."

When Keith and Ray Driscoll started farming, they decided to do it on a large scale so that they could give their families the comforts of life. The families grew, but so did their farm. It is their opinion that "many people who had the same opportunities in farming as we had refused to seize them because they were too tradition bound."

In an office only a few miles from the Driscolls, Gerald C. Ryan, speaking for himself and brother Tom, said, "Tom and I really don't care to work any harder, but it seems we keep expanding almost automatically. We feel we should be spending more time with our families, but in some respects the larger you get, the easier it is."

Iowan Frank Seitzinger is involved in several off-the-farm enterprises besides his own extensive corn and cow operations. Seitzinger said, "I simply cannot foresee expanding my farm because I no longer have the desire. In addition to my own farm, I managed 13,500 acres for three years, and I know it can be done. I met the challenge and conquered it. Now I would prefer going into other ventures."

In 1933 Walter E. Johnson left the dry Dakota prairie in search of opportunity for a new career elsewhere. After traveling to several areas, he returned to the home farm with a new approach that motivated him to enlarge the farm and succeed. He started by grazing sheep "on weeds," and 45 years later, Walter Johnson is satisfied that he made the right decision. But because of his age he has no desire to expand further, even though all his life his philosophy has been "grow or die."

The three Keil brothers were always making extensive plans for more expansion. Nevertheless, they recognized a limitation to their plans, which was best expressed by Edgar Keil, speaking for the three: "Probably our most limiting factor is courage. We are in a very solvent position and are concerned about risking our resources. We have so much to lose. One has to constantly challenge his ability, and then there is another generation coming up."

Raymond Schnell, spokesman for himself and his brothers, Bob and Willard, reacted much like the Keil brothers. Raymond said:

We would expand if we could get exactly the kind of land, the lay and quality, we want. We like the cow operation. We have our biggest mental problem over expanding our feedlot. We have done well with it, and our biggest problem is guts. We don't want to lose what we have, so we become cautious. We still have the desire; we have dreamed these dreams; and it thrills us to see them come true.

Robert F. Reimers, North Dakota grain farmer, was temporarily stumped when asked what he regarded as his most limiting factor to future growth. After a pause he said, "Not capital—we have all we need. Not labor—we get the best. Not land—it's there. When we think of expansion, our first concern is how does it complement our existing operation. If it does, we go. There is no limiting factor. Personal desire is the only limitation I see."[1]

Lack of Management

Professional management, the key to success in daily life or business, has not made a major impact on much of American agriculture. In the past it was not difficult to enter farming, which is probably the major reason for the neglect of using good management. There was also a fallacious opinion in the past that if one was not capable of doing anything else, one could always farm. Anyone who has a broad acquaintance in rural areas can recite cases in which the parents bought a farm for a problem child to "get him out of town" and out of trouble.

With only a few exceptions, all the farms involved in this research were family-owned and family-managed. The total family, whether one, two, or even three generations, was fully immersed in the management of those operations. The Hermanson farm of Iowa was typical of a two generation family enterprise. Pete A. Hermanson stated that even though a father and three brothers were involved they were worried about a lack of management. Pete said, "Management limitation is our first problem. We do not like to get away from complete family ownership, and we find it difficult to get the type of management help we need without cutting them in on the action."

For each of the four major enterprises on the Hermanson farm, one of the family acts as an independent manager. Anyone trained in observing farm operations can quickly recognize excellent management by viewing the farm. In addition, excellent records that the Hermansons have are another obvious characteristic of good management.

Richard C. Bleecker, a dairyman, likes the management aspects of farming and has built one of the largest milking herds in North Dakota, generating most of his expansion from cash flow. Bleecker is not concerned about borrowing, but he said, "I get questioned so much by my banker that I am beginning to question my confidence in my management ability. Sometimes I think the banker is afraid because we have one of the biggest herds in the state and the size scares him; and that worries me. I have the confidence, or at least had it, to build and manage a herd of a thousand cows."

Labor management specifically was stressed by several farmers as being a limiting factor as far as future developments were concerned. Herman A. Natwick asserted that his biggest hang-up was labor management. He said:

I have never been able to handle two good full-time men. I can handle one good man who can supervise five or six part-time men. This is important to me because I am gone from the farm at least two days a week on civic activities.

Natwick probably overstresses his problem, because those who are familiar with his business, and there are many, are always amazed at how well his farm is managed, considering his almost constant stream of outside activities.

Donald Jarrett thinks that the greatest problem he and his brother Ron face is labor management. Like Natwick, the Jarretts are not too concerned about the supply or the quality of labor, but they are concerned about the management of labor. The Jarretts have a payroll of 35 employees. Some have been with them for as long as 30 years and many for 10 years. This includes former industrial workers who prefer farm work and rural life.

The Jarretts find that giving definite assignments to each employee works the best, but the seven-day work week in cattle and sheep feeding and the variability of the weather often upset the best schedules. The Jarretts are not sure if a different type of employee is necessary or whether they should hire supervisors who can manage. Don said, "If we did that, it might relieve us of some of the little emotional problems that pop up almost daily."

Anyone who has watched the many employees on the Jarrett farms and ranches at work soon realizes that the men have their particular jobs, and they lose little motion in getting them accomplished. A network of two-way radios is a major factor in that smooth work flow. In spite of this good system, labor management still remains a problem for the Jarretts, possibly because it is the greatest variable in their entire operation. Not even weather is as unpredictable as labor, because the Jarretts have geography and equipment to cope with nature.

Charles V. Johnson, a hog and cattle feeder, operates on a scope far smaller than the Jarretts, but labor is still a limiting factor. Johnson, like 90 per cent of the farmers surveyed in Iowa, did not want to grow too much because of the labor problem. Johnson is pleased with the quality of help that he hires, but he frankly admits that he does not want to be bothered too much with the problem. His farm will expand as equipment is manufactured that will handle more acres in the same amount of time.

Farm machinery manufacturers are well aware that the greatest pressure for increased size of equipment originates with farmers who want to operate as large as possible without having to hire more part-time help.

The Garst farms have five people involved in what they consider top-level management, but they are not completely satisfied that even with five they are doing the best job. In spite of their self-criticism, their records show that they are doing a management job equal to or better than the best. When this was pointed out to David Garst, he admitted that probably their greatest limitation was the inability to motivate secondary management. When reminded that maybe they were searching for the impossible man, Garst laughed and admitted as much. As Bob Reimers said, "Land, labor, and capital are there; if management desires, there are no limits."[2]

Financial Limitations

Some of the farmers questioned for this survey found financial limitations as the greatest restriction to future growth. These limitations appeared frequently as a problem of personal attitude, although it was obvious that a few individuals among them did have serious enough financial commitments to cause them sleepless nights. John Hicks, a noted economic historian, said that the sleepless nights of the enterpreneur are what enable him to get ahead of the hired manager. If that is true, then loss of sleep is not in vain.

Carroll G. Wilson of southern Minnesota complained that farmers are at a disadvantage with other elements of the business community because they do not get the same interest rate on operating capital as the merchants on Main Street. He also feels that livestock and poultry farmers have a better rate of interest than cash-grain farmers because bankers in his area favor those enterprises. Wilson has been very active politically in an attempt to change banking regulations so that they will prove more beneficial to the cash–crop-oriented farmer. He thinks that personal property needed for farm business should be given the same type of treatment that is granted to long-term real estate loans. His idea does not appeal to bankers, but since capital needs for farm operations are increasing, significant changes will have to be made to accommodate the farmers' financial requirements.

Wilson rents a substantial portion of the land he farms. He believes that too many farmers are too concerned about securing land in their name and are paying a premium to get it. He is more concerned about net profit than ownership.

Arlo J. Gordon farms in partnership with his father, Art, and admits that they have a financial problem that is caused by their conservative attitude toward borrowing money. The Gordons use no borrowed capital to operate and have very little indebtedness against their real estate. Arlo thinks this is a limitation because it prevents him from expanding. He likes farming, but he believes it would be a challenge to become involved in some agri-business ventures. After graduating from college, Arlo was involved in the farm machinery business as a block man and saw opportunities that were "nearly as attractive as farming."

John Bogestad started farming in the 1930's and admits that his experience during those years, plus the constant reminder coming from his cautious father, has made him "overly conservative toward financing." Bogestad recalled that his father was very diversified in the troublesome 1920's and '30's and was one of a few men who did not go broke. John added, "After my first land purchases, which were on contracts, I never bought additional land until I had all I owned paid for. I was too cautious, but once I was operating on my own, I never had trouble financing."

John Bogestad, in his late sixties, and son, Roger, were looking at an opportunity for expansion. Their big debate centered around how much they dared to deplete their cash reserves for expansion purposes. John Bogestad knew that finances were his limiting factor to expansion, but he also realized the problem was more his mental attitude than reality.*

"Money" was the simple answer Earl Davison gave when asked what his most limiting factor to farming was. But then he paused and said, "No, it is not really money. I think it is my psychological hang-up because I still remember the depression, and that makes me conservative. Sometimes I have passed up good opportunities, even when I knew the money was available, because I had that fear."

Davison admitted that when his son, Brent, graduated from college, his attitude changed. Earl Davison was pleased at the thought that after 25 years of farming he had some new goals; for

---

*One-hundred thousand farmers like John and Roger Bogestad could operate all the tilled land in America, and they could do it with their own funds. But it would take over 2 million farmers of the 160-acre size to farm all of America's tilled land, and not many would be satisfied to live from the meager earnings of such a small farm.

when his son recently left the teaching profession to join him, they doubled their farm size with one purchase. Money management was crucial, but he readily admitted that personal ambition was the key. His last words about limitations were, "I surely would like to get some of that rolling land to the east or south of us, because it would help reduce the risk."

Ellis Jensen, who farmed with his brother in South Dakota, admitted that a restricted form of financing handicapped the successful expansion of their farm. The Jensen brothers, like far too many young farmers, were tempted to purchase too much land early in their career. Interest, taxes, and principal amounted to far more than cash rent. This shortened their cash flow. Their financiers had extended full credit on land purchases, but then declined to advance credit for operating expenses. This forced the brothers to rely for several years on operating profits of the farm and additional income from outside work. Sometimes they had to rely on suppliers for credit at a higher cost than normally charged by lending institutions. Fortunately, the Jensen brothers withstood the pressure. When the increased prices of 1973 and 1974 came, they took advantage of their large volume to generate the profits necessary to free them from their self-inflicted plight of the previous years.

Minor financial problems were freely discussed in all interviews and generally these farmers were businessmen who looked at long-term borrowing positively.[3]

Taxes—A Brake on Growth

Many American farmers have paid little or no income taxes during their years of farming. Much of this results from the nature of farming as a business which shows a small cash profit after depreciation of the capital investments. On many of the smaller farms, the family income tax exemption is sufficient to absorb any net profit from farming, enabling the farmer to avoid any income tax payment.

The ability to avoid income taxes is directly related to the small farmer's inability to build a cash reserve either for adverse years or expansion. He appears hopelessly locked in. Only by off-the-farm employment or by risking a heavy debt can he hope to improve his position. In the past most farmers have sought off-the-farm employment or liquidated. The number who have sought to expand as evidenced by the census figures has been limited, but they are the efficient commercial farmers as typified by those interviewed for this study. The proven managers with a profit record have had the borrowing ability to expand.

Ernest C. Hector, who is challenged by expansion, says that his enthusiasm to do so is greatly reduced because of income taxes. Hector explained that, unless one continues to expand indefinitely, income taxes take too large a portion of the profits. He added, "If one continues to expand each year for the purpose of minimizing income taxes, all he does is compound his estate tax problem. Expansion then is purely a way of delaying, not avoiding, getting socked by taxes."

The O'Farrells, Inc., a father and seven sons, are involved in a farm-based cattle-feeding business in South Dakota. Jack O'Farrell, speaking for his family, readily admitted that they had sufficient land, labor, and capital, so there was basically no reason why they could not expand if they desired to do so. When pressed to give an economic reason why they might not expand, Jack acknowledged that continuously increasing income taxes and the threat of exorbitant estate taxes were the greatest economic obstacles to be considered.

Milton Hertz, confident and still in his thirties, had expanded his farm to sizeable proportions after 14 years in the business. When asked what his most limiting factor to expansion was he hesitated for a few minutes, then replied, "There is no limiting factor that handicaps my growth other than income tax." A very candid and personal response, but he also knew that the alternative was more painful, because he and Carol had experienced some poor years in farming.

Several farmers mentioned the possibility of future real estate taxes becoming a possible adverse factor to potential farm expansion. John W. Wright summed up the feelings of these farmers by saying:

I am very concerned about real estate taxes; they hit us whether we make a profit or not. We farmers are rapidly becoming a smaller and smaller political minority, so the odds are against us if the legislatures of the various states decide to tax us more. Too many people think that just because you own lots of land that you are always making money.

Each time I see another school bond issue, I get one step farther away from cashing in any liquid investments to buy land. I can visualize the possibility that land could become a poor investment for one who might want to live from its proceeds in retirement.

John Wright's fears were not unfounded, for many state legislators have expressed similar feelings about taxes on farm property. The debate over property taxation is as old as government itself.[4]

Shortage of Land?

It is not uncommon in rural America to hear the remark that a young man cannot start farming because there is a shortage of labor, capital, or land. It is especially the shortage of capital or land that concerns him. Even farmers who are already farming say they cannot expand because there is so little land available, and what is available is too highly priced. On the other hand, it is an historical fact that land is always too high-priced for the average manager, but not for the good manager.

Not one of the farmers interviewed for this book said that there was no land available. Some, especially older farmers or those exceedingly well off, expressed a doubt about the desire to buy more land at the existing prices, but they did not question the availability of land. Several of the older farmers recalled the days when they had purchased land at a relatively low price and longed for such prices again. Those who were in an exceedingly liquid financial position expressed the feeling that they could do nearly as well with other non-farm investments, without adding the responsibility for the care of new land. And interestingly enough, a few elderly farmers were not stopped from enlarging their operations by rising land prices. To be sure, three of them, all in their seventies, were aggressively bidding for land whenever some became available.

Harold Hofstrand was initially hard pressed to name the most limiting factor to his future expansion, but after some delay answered: "I suppose the lack of really good land is a limiting factor. There was much good land available as late as the early 1960's, but now it is in such strong hands. It is harder today to compete against those men for the good land than 15 years ago. Maybe my desire to expand was stronger then than it is now."

Ralph Hvidsten and John H. Reque, both of whom had been farming in Minnesota for about 30 years at the time of interview, expressed a feeling that there was an intense pressure for land in their areas. Reque said, "If really good land became available, either for rent or to buy, I would take it under any reasonable terms. I know I can compete with the best."

Ralph Hvidsten said:

I want only the best land. High interest rates and high cash rent cause one to question the economics of taking on any land but the very best. We have four soil types in our area and each one of them affects the quality of my crop differently, and I am very fussy about the product I sell. The pressure for good land is great, and I don't have quite the desire to compete for it like I did 10 or 20 years ago.

Harold T. Petersen's children were still too young to know whether or not they would be farming, even though Harold and his wife, Sharon, were hoping they would. But Harold expressed the feeling that availability of land was probably his greatest obstacle to future expansion. The chief reason was that there were many good young farmers in his region, and they were all aggressively competing for land. The only chance Petersen saw for more land was when some of the smaller farmers decided that they would rent or sell. Petersen added, "The many small farms initially in our area, plus the terrain problems, make it difficult to put a really economical piece of land together."

These farmers readily admitted that land shortage was a relatively minor factor. If one had the desire and was equipped mentally, financially, and mechanically to do the job, land was available. As the statistics indicate, farm size has increased steadily since 1910 because farmers have always found land that belonged to farmers who felt that they could not make it and sold out.[5]

Weather—An Obstacle to Successful Farming?

Anyone who has grown up on a farm or has lived amongst farmers soon becomes aware of the great concern many of them have about the weather. There is a common saying that goes, "Everyone talks about the weather, but no one does anything about it." So it is imperative that such a topic and the farmers' attitude toward it should be included in any volume attempting to cover general aspects of farming. And who has not heard the sarcastic remark about some larger-than-average farmer in any rural community, "Wait until that big ——— gets hung up with the weather, and then he'll change his mind about big farming."

All farmers interviewed were asked the question, "Does a large farmer have more or less difficulty with the weather than a small farmer? Justify your answer." Contrary to what many people might believe, not one large-scale farmer expressed the belief that a big farmer had more trouble than a small farmer in coping with the weather. On the contrary, every big farmer expressed the opinion that he had a decided advantage over the small farmer in relation to the weather. To back up the farmers' opinions, every banker interviewed expressed strong feelings about the advantages of the larger farmer weather-wise over his smaller counterpart.

Adverse weather, then, appears to be an almost hoped for crisis wished by some upon others. The larger farmer apparently has a much greater risk exposure in relation to the weather, but the danger of a total loss is minimized. Earl Hvidsten had been farming 30 years when he made the following statement: "I can't remember a year when we lost a crop because of the weather. There are always enough days to get the crop done and we don't work on Sundays either. There is a proper time to get the job done and you have to be geared to do it under the most adverse circumstances. I don't think a man should be a farmer if he worries about the weather."

What Hvidsten said was verified by Earl Osterkamp of South Dakota:

Be on the ball and go when it's time, and you will get the job done. We have never been caught in 20 years getting a crop in or out. Good, big equipment is the difference. Even if one unit does break down, things don't come to a standstill because there are several units still going. It's not like the man who has one tractor and tries to do it all alone.

Several farmers pointed out that the key to coping with the weather was adaptability and better long-range planning. Peter A. Nygaard of North Dakota noted that over the years he has consistently completed planting or harvesting his crop ahead of his neighbors with fewer acres. Nygaard added, "I think I plan better and I know I have easier access to custom combine crews than the man with fewer acres. I think the small farmer is often too stubborn to seek help, when I will hire extra crews as soon as I see that I cannot get the job done on time. In my books, lost time means lost income."

Jack O'Farrell of South Dakota sized up his view about the weather in this manner: "I don't think the small operator is as conscious of the damage that adverse weather causes as the larger operator is. We have more at stake and do a better job to guard against it."

Harold Hofstrand, a grain farmer, pointed out that he had little difficulty with weather, and if adverse conditions prevailed, he was quick to rent extra equipment or hire custom crews to get the job done on time. "Timing is profits," according to Hofstrand. "Too many farmers think they have to do all the work themselves because they see only the cost of getting extra crews in, but what they do not see is the loss of profits because of decreased yields and quality."

A Minnesota corn, beet, and beef farmer said, "We got our work done last fall when a neighbor with one-sixth as many acres couldn't get his job finished. It seems that many of them are just not well-organized. We just bought out a man who could never get his work done on time." An Iowan added, "We always plan on bad weather, then we really don't get caught when it comes. We plant and harvest on time and then go out and help our neighbors who just do not have the equipment that we do."

"It depends upon how you are geared for it," said David Glinz. "It takes volume to support a grain drier, and we have two of them. Our big equipment can really roll from one end of the farm to the other. We park our rigs in the driveways so if it rains they are not caught in the field. By working men in shifts, we work full crews around the clock. That way we have much less down time proportionately than any of our neighbors. We have a full repair truck with the tools to do most repairs right in the fields; that greatly reduces down time."

Cautious Dave Glinz has minimized the weather problem by placing his six big four-wheel-drive tractors and their equipment so he can move almost every day once the crop season starts. Glinz's 108-foot drills are nearly matched by Allen C. Kolstad's 99-foot drill. Kolstad's drill holds 150 bushels at a filling and will seed well over 500 acres per day. That has been Kolstad's answer to weather problems for many years. Kolstad has one field with a six-mile furrow and his smallest field is 640 acres, so little time is lost in traveling between fields. Clem Hebel of Iowa thinks that a farmer with a larger volume can take the jolt of bad weather better than one with a small acreage. He said, "Most small farmers are under-financed and their living takes too large a fraction of the total farm income. Family living takes such a large portion of a small farmer's volume that there is no margin left for loss of crop because of adverse weather."*

Paul Horn, Jr., Minnesota potato grower, asserts:

We have records of each field each day of the production season. We know how many days we have to put the crop in the ground in each field. Our records have not only told us how many rain-free days we will have on the average to get a crop in and out, but they also tell us the increased

---

*A U.S.D.A. study of 1973 farm families showing annual living costs of $10,786.19 bears out Hebel's contentions.

cost of production because of bad timing and loss of income for the same season.

The Horns irrigate a considerable portion of their land, which has made them very conscious of the value of precise records, both in regard to rainfall and the costs. Horn's records are used to select the size of equipment they need to get their production accomplished in the rain-free days their charts have proven for each field.

"We have different soil structures and rain belts on our land and have been able to chart our anticipated progress in planting and harvesting across the farm," said Vernon Triebold. Triebold added that he did not think he would have the nerve to gamble with the weather as the small farmer has to with a single piece of land.

Fellow North Dakotan Robert F. Reimers agreed: "I'd rather be a big farmer in any season, because you always have some place where you can work. We charted our crop-loss records very closely as we expanded, and quickly discovered that there was no point in carrying crop insurance. There is no way the small farmer can compete from a weather standpoint."[6]

Equipment, Weather, and Area

In regard to weather, variety of soils, and the distribution of land, Charles Lysfjord, who manages the Kiene farms in northern Minnesota, had this comment:

We are spread out 34 miles. This gives us a variation in soil type and rainfall. We have more flexibility with our labor force; power units are bigger and can cope with much worse conditions. Besides, our radio communication helps us shift around with very little wasted effort. We find that we don't get as emotionally involved with the weather as the small farmer does, probably because we don't have all of our eggs in one basket.

Alfred Ehlers agrees with Lysfjord, although his basic problem in South Dakota is drought, while for Lysfjord in northern Minnesota, it is excess precipitation. Ehlers said, "When your land is scattered, you have the breaks on your side. Crop insurance is not nearly the concern as it is with the smaller farmer when you are spread out 35 miles as we are. Those big four-wheelers give you a big advantage."

"We are spread out 30 miles," Darrell Miller said, "and there is seldom a day we cannot work. The men get disgusted because there is never a rainy day for rest, as they remember them on smaller operations. The only crop insurance I carry is on some high risk quarters."

Virgil Mellies of central Minnesota has his land spread out over 30 miles because he deliberately purchased or rented scattered land. "I didn't want to concentrate in one area because of the weather hazard. We have a shorter corn season on the north end of our farm than on the south end. Besides, we have not carried hail insurance for years."

The Spicher brothers, along the "highline" of northern Montana, have two units that are 31 miles apart. Richard Spicher said, "We feel lucky to have two sizeable blocks that far apart. It really divides our risk. Besides, we have the power to move when the weather is right."

Kenneth Kinkler of South Dakota agreed with the Spichers and Ehlers on the value of the big power units. Kinkler said, "Give me the larger spread. You may have trouble with it, but when we have a quarter section ready, we can turn it in five hours with one big rig."

Herman A. Natwick, a cattle feeder, has 3½ sections in virtually a solid block and considers it a handicap from a weather standpoint. Natwick felt that if he could find land distant from his present operation, he would secure it in order to divide his risk, even though it would present an extra hauling cost for his feed.

Arden Burbidge, a potato farmer, admits that it costs extra to move his potatoes. His farm is 50 miles from north to south, but the advantages of variation in weather and even growing season more than offset the additional cost.

Dennis L. Anderson, farm owner and professional farm manager, said:

We have two separate units, each spread out about 16 miles long and at right angles to each other. This gives us a definite advantage. We carry no form of crop insurance. We have irrigation units down near the water [Oahe] where we have our longest growing season. On the west part of our land we have more snow, that's where we plant our winter wheat. With the four-wheeler it doesn't take long to move the soil, once things are fit.

"Naturally, large farmers are less concerned with weather than small farmers. They wouldn't be large farmers if the weather upset them that much," said Arthur L. Skolness. "We have very little down time because of the weather. It's more like working in a factory. Our men like to know that they are going to be busy every day. We think it is part of good labor relations."

A 760-H.P., 1,472 cubic-inch engine "Big Bud" made by Northern Manufacturing Co., Havre, Montana. Weighs 100,000 pounds without ballast. Thirty-five-inch wide, 8-foot high tires. An 850-gallon fuel capacity. Retail price about $300,000. Capable of pulling a 28-foot wide sub-soiler with 15 3-inch shanks, 30 inches or deeper.

Big Roy, an experimental Versatile four-wheel-drive, 600 H.P. with 1,150 cubic-inch engine pulling a 60-foot chisel plow with sweeps 12 inches deep at 6 mph in third gear. Operating weight 58,000 pounds. Has 30.5- by 32-inch tires. Fuel capacity 500 gallons. Has T.V. monitor at drawbar and viewer for operator.

Three Versatile 700's, each with 167 H.P., pulling a combined total of 117 feet of field cultivators and harrows. Capable of jointly doing 90 acres per hour. Kiene Farms, Kennedy, Minnesota, 1975. Charles Lysfjord (with hat), farm manager. (Photo, Vernon Lee)

A Versatile 900, 325 H.P., with a 43-foot folding cultivator and rod weeder and three 14-foot drills moving to the field on the Bill and Daryl Spicher farm, Hingham, Montana. This rig is capable of preparing, fertilizing, and seeding 200 acres every 10 hours.

A 310-H.P. four-wheel-drive, 42-foot tandem disk, and three 14-foot drills with fertilizer boxes on the Peter A. Nygaard, Sr./Jr., farm, Williston, North Dakota. The three operations are done at the rate of 20 acres per hour. Electronic monitors on control panel alert driver of drill malfunctions. Holds enough fertilizer for about 38 acres and enough grain for 75 acres. About 40 minutes are required for augers to load the unit with grain and fertilizer. This total rig sells for about $100,000.

Three 14-foot drills folded for road travel. Capable of seeding and fertilizing 20 acres an hour. Hydraulic folding from the cab enables one man to put in position for road or field. (Photo, *Dakota Farmer*)

A Versatile 900, 300-H.P. four-wheel-drive, pulling two 14-foot duplexes, an 18-foot disker grain drill, and a fertilizer tank holding 850 imperial gallons. Total load is more than 25,000 pounds, including fertilizer and 70 gallons of wheat. Field speed varies from 6.1 to 7.4 mph or 30 to 40 acres per hour. Ernie Karlowsky, Brunkhild, Manitoba.

A 120-foot folding harrow with liquid fertilizer attachment on the David Glinz farm, Pingree, North Dakota. One of six four-wheel-drive tractors on this small grain and sunflower operation. (Photo, Tom Kiss)

Massey-Ferguson's first self-propelled combine, developed by Australian Tom Carroll in 1939. The first practical commercial model, pictured here with Carroll as the operator, was introduced in 1940. (Photo, Massey-Ferguson)

Six Massey-Ferguson No. 90 combines on the Don and Jean Gray farm, Carter, Montana. This farm was started in 1934 on 640 acres purchased at a cost of 10 bushels of wheat per acre for a seven-year term. In 1928, 640 acres were rented at $1/16$ crop share. These strips, for wind erosion protection, are 40 rods by 2 miles and contain 160 acres. Wheat is seeded in 14-inch rows. These combines are each capable of doing 7 to 10 acres an hour.

A 36-row Kinze corn planter bar on the Carl Hamilton farm, Hampton, Iowa. Folds backward to 18.5 feet in five minutes for transport. Note four tires on each tractor wheel to give floatation. At 20-inch rows the planting width is 60 feet. Capable of planting up to 40 acres per hour. Planter cost is about $32,000; one fill of seed corn costs $1,400 to $1,800; herbicides, etc., another $3,000 to $4,000. (Photo, *Farm Show*)

Typical method of drying home-grown seed corn in the days before hybrid seed became available commercially (1926–1930). Note wallpaper design and two pictures on the right. Most seed was dried in the upstairs or attics of farm homes. (Photo, University of Minnesota, St. Paul)

Single-row corn cultivator steered by handles and foot pedals. Corn was not in straight rows like today for it was seeded by hand planters, or early mechanical planters were hand-tripped and not always uniformly done. About 9 to 11 acres could be cultivated in a 10-hour day. Introduced in 1870's. (Photo, University of Minnesota, St. Paul)

A Case 300-H.P. four-wheel-drive tractor cultivating 12 rows of soybeans. This rig can do 120 to 180 acres a day depending on the height of the crop, which dictates ground speed. (Photo, University of Minnesota, St. Paul)

A single-row pull-type corn picker, capable of 800 to 1,000 bushels in 60- to 80-bushel corn, alongside a "corn husker" who could pick 60 to 110 bushels, depending on corn yield and the ability of the man. Ca. 1938–1940. (Photo, University of Minnesota, St. Paul)

A cornstalk chopper, loader, and baler requiring a three-man crew, central Iowa, March 13, 1930. The modern combine-chopper-blower combines the corn and blows the total residue into a trailing wagon, requiring only one man. (Photo, Iowa State University)

Dr. Andrew Boss, prominent agricultural economist and researcher at the University of Minnesota, hand spreading fertilizer for 1905 test plots at the research station. (Photo, University of Minnesota Archives)

Eight-foot lime or fertilizer spreader capable of spreading about 2 acres per hour. Fall application prior to plowing, ca. 1920–1930. (Photo, *The Farmer*)

High floatation fertilizer spreader on the John Keil and Sons farm, Ledger, Montana. This machine cost $30,000 to $35,000 and was capable of spreading 40 to 50 acres per hour in 1972. On good going it can travel 15 mph with higher speeds on the road. When tank is installed for liquid fertilizer, 60 acres can be covered per hour. (Photo, Mrs. John Keil)

Bob Boles and his Stearman Boeing after 25 years of agricultural flying in the Big Sky Country, Hardin, Montana. Mr. Boles was a pioneer aerial sprayer, starting with canning company crops in 1947, then moving to Montana in 1948 to establish a commercial crop-spraying firm. (Photo, Mrs. Robert Boles)

A 1959 Hiller 12D, 250 H.P., capable of 70 mph. The 1978 price $55,000. Used on Keith and Ray Driscoll farm, East Grand Forks, Minnesota, for field observation after rains or after strong winds to spot weed growth or to check fence lines for livestock. Some farmers use these machines for emergency parts trips, others for fertilizing, seed, and chemical applications.

A four-man baling crew. Man on top had to control hay flow to avoid slugging the baler. The other two men had to feed wire to the baler and tie the bales of 100 to 200 pounds each. Ca. 1932. (Photo, Iowa State University)

Stack moving on the farm of Ellis Jensen, a commercial alfalfa producer who normally gets four crops per year. A load of three stacks, 2 to 3 tons each, being hauled from field to alfalfa pelleting plant. The pellets are sold basically to southern feedlots. Farm is located at Vermillion, South Dakota.

Herman A. Natwick, Twin Valley, Minnesota, 1974, with variable speed that works with density of the crop. A 250-H.P. engine capable of chopping 1 ton of haylage in 3 to 5 minutes or, with a three-row corn head, 1 ton of silage in 2 to 4 minutes. The operator in the air-conditioned cab is a 68-year-old retired farmer "enjoying hay making." Cost about $55,000.

A 24-row beet planter (22-inch rows) folded hydraulically from the tractor cab for road travel. Dan Skolness, operator, plants 160 acres each day after the field is first worked for seeding by three four-wheel-drive powered equipment. One fill of seed is $1,000 to $1,100; herbicide, $700 to $1,400. Fertilizer is pre-broadcast. This planter, first used in 1977, is owned by Skolness, Inc., Glyndon, Minnesota. There are no other known units of this size. (Photo, Don Lilleboe and Jim Conn)

Young girl beet worker near Fisher, Minnesota, October 1937. An expert topper could do about ¼ to ½ acre of 7 to 10 tons of beets per day. (Photo, Minnesota Historical Society)

In 1956, Merle S. Allen had Walter Quandt of Stewart, Minnesota, build a four-row self-propelled beet harvester-lifter using a road maintenance chassis. Quandt had made a machine for personal use in 1954. Steering was the mechanical problem that handicapped full development of this idea. It also proved to be expensive in relation to a pull-type machine. Cost was $22,000. Could easily lift a ton a minute on good going. The pull-type harvesters have an electronic row finder.

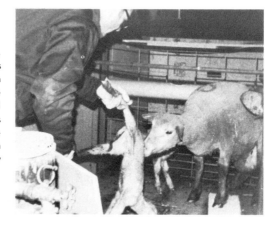

Jarrett Farms and Ranches, Britton, South Dakota, have about 7,500 ewes which lamb February to May each year. Lambing is done inside three large barns with single-ewe elevated lambing pens where mother and lambs are kept for one to two days so the mother and lambs "identify each other." Don Jarrett, holding a new lamb to its mother.

Turkey loaders used for loading 1,000 turkeys into a semi. This method requires 11 men, 30 minutes to fill the truck. Total man-hours per load is only 22 percent of handloading. Earl B. Olson farms, Willmar, Minnesota.

Hog facilities on Don Hartness farm, Gwinner, North Dakota, managed by Donna Hois, who holds a degree in animal husbandry. The farm also has a climate-controlled farrowing and finishing facility.

A climate-controlled hog farrowing unit owned by Peter Pankratz and sons Marlin, Robert, and Loren, who operate as Con-Fed, Inc., Mountain Lake, Minnesota. Employees must shower on entering and leaving for disease control. This 120- by 325-foot unit holds 3,500 hogs at all times and is divided into 12 isolated units. Holds 600 to 700 sows, 25 boars, 850 nursing pigs, 1,100 pigs up to 120 pounds, and as many finishing pigs as room allows. The sows are never removed from the building. Note hog trailer at right.

Covered feed bunk where silage was carried in a litter carrier on a track and then ground corn and protein from the wagon was spread on the silage. This was the next step beyond the scoop shovel and bushel basket. (Photo, University of Minnesota, St. Paul)

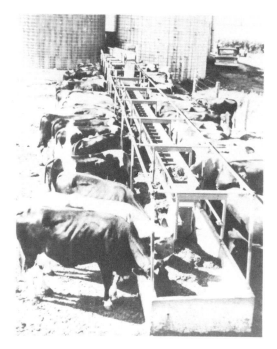

Current single-chain feeder and single-chain conveyor carrying feed to dairy cow herd. A bunk up to 300 feet could be efficiently operated in this manner. Grass and corn silage could be blended from the silos, and grain and concentrates fed into the conveyor at the same time. Hand labor was virtually eliminated. About 25 cattle could be fed every five minutes. (Photo, Van Dale, Inc.)

P. D. Hempstead of the "Hempstead Homestead," Houston, Minnesota. Cattle are fed at the bunk line from a feeder-mixer wagon, which contains a completely blended ration of haylage, silage, grain, and minerals. All work is done by tractors or push buttons.

A Clay liquid manure "Honey Wagon" with a vacuum pump to remove manure from the pit below slatted floors of livestock facilities. A 3,000-gallon load weighs 12 tons without tank weight and can be loaded and hauled to the field in less than 10 minutes. Liquid manure tends to have higher fertilizer value than normal barnyard manures. The tractor is a 300-H.P., 2470 Case four-wheel-drive. (Photo, University of Minnesota, St. Paul)

Feedlot of George and William Sinner and Ellery Bresnahan, Casselton, North Dakota. Homes of Bill Sinner and Bresnahan visible, upper left; seed-cleaning plant in center; full-service shop, upper right; feed mixing and storage, center right. Semi-housed feed yards hold 1,500 cattle. This lot has been in operation since the 1920's. Several third generation members provide the labor force which also handles extensive sugar beet, sunflower, and specialty crop production.

Lakeview Dairy, Devils Lake, North Dakota, owned by five brothers, who milk 190 to 220 cows and supply milk to the city of Devils Lake. Each brother has a definite part of the management. Milking cows are kept in total confinement. Sealed storage structures hold high moisture barley and low moisture grainlage, sweet clover, or alfalfa. Milk production has more than doubled since their adoption.

Dick and Arlene O'Day, Prairie Nest Ranch, Great Falls, Montana. Five employee houses in foreground. Office is small white building in center. Capacity storage is 350,000 bushels. The O'Day house is in the tree area next to the man-made lake.

Aerial view of the 5,000-acre Don and Jean Gray farm, Carter, Montana. This farm is under 50 percent summer fallow. Has a fully equipped winterized farm shop (center) and 200,000 bushels of grain storage (right). The Grays operate this farm with the aid of their son Robert. The 40-rod-wide alternate strips are necessary to control erosion. The view on left up to the wider grain field is 3½ miles.

Fisher brothers' hog-feeding operation at Hubbard, Iowa. About 21,000 hogs are farrowed and fed each year. The brothers raise corn, alfalfa, and hogs on what is believed to be the largest family hog operation in Iowa. Many hogs are farrowed in old-style "A-frames" on pasture in adverse weather. A climate-controlled farrowing house (pictured) is used. Starting and finishing barns are also confined.

Dairy cow barn with straw roof (not a loft). Note wooden stanchions. Horse stalls not visible, but note harness at left. This was a typical pre-electric era barn. (Photo, University of Minnesota, St. Paul)

Farmer's Co-op Creamery, Sauk Center, Minnesota, area, ca. 1900. Farmers delivered their cream in 10-gallon cans on alternate days or every day, depending on the season. It was made into butter and the buttermilk was sold or dumped into the sewage system. Milk was skimmed by hand-powered separators at the farm. The skim milk was fed to poultry, calves, and hogs. (Photo, Minnesota Historical Society)

First use of electricity furnished by R.E.A. for this milking herd in central Iowa, November 15, 1937. Mechanized milking dates to the late 1800's, but most farmers hand-milked until electric power. It took a very good man to milk 20 cows twice a day. (Photo, Iowa State University)

Interior of the milk cooling room in the "open side" of a basement barn, late 1930's. Rapid-Flo is a brand of milk strainer pads. Note water heater at right. (Photo, University of Minnesota, St. Paul)

Blue Tower Farm of Ben and Mary Zweber, Elko, Minnesota, a family operation of 165 milk cows on 400 acres of land. Climate-controlled milk cow barn. Herd is divided and fed according to production. Dry cows and replacement cattle kept in buildings in background. Sealed storage structures contain high moisture corn, haylage, cornlage, and stalklage.

Manuel Jerger's milking parlour, Barnesville, Minnesota. Two people milk six cows every six minutes. White plastic hoses are milk lines leading directly from the cows to a cooling tank. Black hoses are vacuum lines. Normally, 115 cows are in production. Summer, 1977.

Manuel Jerger's milkroom, Barnesville, Minnesota. This is completely isolated from the cow barn. Glass bulb on right has milk flowing through it on the way to a 3,000-gallon cooling and holding tank. The milk is never exposed to the air from the cow to the tank. Summer, 1977.

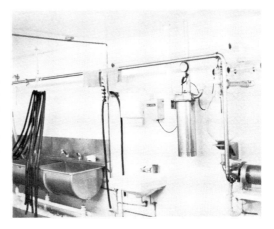

James Hough milk truck, Fergus Falls, Minnesota. This truck hauls nearly 7,000 gallons from bulk tanks on the farm, where the milk is picked up every other day. This is an aluminum covered and stainless steel inner tank with heavy insulation so that milk gains only 1° temperature on normal delivery. Summer, 1977.

Insulated and electrically heated (floor) farm shop of Delmer and Ardell Schultz, Davenport, North Dakota, where complete overhauls are done in off seasons to keep full employment. Both doors can be opened and center post removed so that the largest piece of equipment can be driven into the 60- by 60-foot building, which contains a full washroom, employee lounge, and office. Summer, 1977.

Machinery storage and overflow building on the R. D. Offutt and Son farm, Glyndon, Minnesota. Potato harvester chains on right. Note size of semitrailer in background. Fertilizer boxes and spreader on left. A fully electrically heated shop adjoins on right where five trucks, tractors, or harvesters may be repaired at one time. This storage warehouse can store 40 semitrailer rigs. Summer, 1977.

Corncrib made of one 50-foot long fence to "air dry" corn. Capable of storing about 900 to 950 bushels. (Photo, University of Minnesota, St. Paul)

Farmers unloading grain from a typical double-wagon box. This was standard procedure for getting grain into storage prior to the advent of grain elevators about 1902. The test of a "good man" was that he was supposed to be able to unload a 60-bushel load non-stop. (Photo, "Pioneer Ackley," Iowa)

Grain storage facilities on the Orten and Sandra Brodshaug farm, Hickson, North Dakota. Grain is weighed and dried to proper storage moisture at harvest. Most drying is done by a very advanced minimum or no fuel requirement drier for this 1.2 million bushel storage. Summer, 1977.

Feeders Supply Corp. constructed two metal grain storage buildings in 1972, each with a capacity of 1 million bushels. Located east of Huntley, Montana, the buildings measure 400 by 100 feet and 420 by 100 feet and have 26-foot walls. The auger system is designed to handle 7,000 bushels of grain an hour. An electronic hopper scale is installed. (Photo, Yellowstone Valley Electric Co-op, Inc.)

Oahe Grain Corp., Onida, South Dakota, the state's largest independently owned elevator, held by 33 farmer stockholders. Built in 1955, with 500,000-bushel capacity and enlarged to 1,100,000-bushel capacity in 1972.

Farmers marketing livestock at what is believed to be the cooperative sale barn at Litchfield, Minnesota, ca. 1915. (Photo, University of Minnesota Archives)

One of the O'Farrell feedlot trucks of Marvin, South Dakota, being prepared to haul 45,000 pounds of cattle to market. Alvin O'Farrell and seven sons are involved in the integrated farm-feedlot operation. They buy and haul all their cattle from ranches and auction barns, as well as transport all fat cattle to market.

The livestock portion of the Daggett Truckline, Frazee, Minnesota, one of the nation's oldest and largest livestock hauling companies, which includes a refrigerated fleet. The business was started in August, 1930, by Vern Daggett, who in 1978, with sons Marvin, Delta, and David, was operating the 75-livestock and 60-refrigerated semitrailer units. The average livestock load is 45,000 pounds.

Tandem drive truck and "pup" used for hauling 800 to 1,000 bushels from Virgil Mellies farm, Hector, Minnesota, to terminal market or farmer feeders. Direct sold by Mellies, who specializes in corn and soybeans.

Hydraulically raised scale unloading grain at General Mills Flour Mill, Minneapolis, Minnesota, July, 1976. Truck loaded at a farm in Dakota with 800 bushels of wheat is unloaded in about two to four minutes. (Photo, Minnesota Historical Society)

Eight grain barges going south from Twin Cities, Minnesota, terminals on the Mississippi River. Each barge holds about 60,000 to 70,000 bushels. (Photo, University of Minnesota, St. Paul)

Ocean freighter at Superior, Wisconsin, elevator terminal, 1968. St. Lawrence Seaway has made mid-American grain more easily available to world markets which must buy 25 to 35 percent of our crop production if agriculture is to remain successful. This vessel can leave Duluth-Superior harbor with 1 million bushels of wheat and quite likely will take on 500,000 to 600,000 more bushels beyond the straits, which are only 27 feet deep. (Photo, University of Minnesota, St. Paul)

Leslie W. Peterson, Farmers State Bank, Trimont, Minnesota. Peterson, who is also involved in farming, is a very active spokesman for progressive financing methods required in southwest Minnesota. He speaks throughout the nation.

Richard Retz, agricultural banker, Home State Bank, Jefferson, Iowa. Retz is a former farmer with a full knowledge of the high capital needs of modern agriculture. His bank conducts seminars on modern agriculture for its major borrowers.

A historic event, as two Iowa extension agents witness one of the first farmers to sign for the "Corn Hog" program, January 4, 1934, at the Henry A. Wallace (then Secretary of Agriculture) farm, Grimes, Iowa. (Photo, Iowa State University)

Bert Hanson and his third plane, which cost him $5,000 in 1947. He was the first secretary of the National Flying Farmers. Hanson said of his experience, "It was costly in time and cash, but invaluable in education."

Donna Hois, hog operations manager of Don Hartness farm, Gwinner, North Dakota. Donna has a degree in animal husbandry.

Left to right: Edgar, Mrs. John, Steve, and Dan Keil, who operate a large-grain farm, cow herd, and feedlot, including some irrigated land at Conrad, Montana. This farm was started in the 1920's by the late John Keil, who added to his holdings as smaller farmers lost their land. Family partnerships such as this, in the author's opinion, are the epitome of strength, dedication, economy of scale, and efficiency.

Left to right: Alan and Lloyd Butts of Butts Feedlot, Inc., Carrington, North Dakota, with Lloyd's other sons, have one of the largest lots in the state, with a 12,000-head capacity. Butts operates 4,000 acres of land, much of it irrigated, for forage. The office contains a ticker-tape system which provides constant market information.

"Bruce's Angels" was the title of an article about these three ladies who operate three combines for Bruce and Dewel Viker, who farm along the Red River in Traill County, North Dakota. The combines, with air-conditioned cabs, are "gleaners," each capable of handling more than 4,000 bushels of wheat per day. Left to right: Mrs. Bruce (JoAnn) Viker, Bruce, Tammy Habeck, Mrs. Mary Lundstrum. About 2,500 acres of grain are combined by the trio. (Photo, Allis Chalmers)

"First cake" from a combination wood burning and electric stove after installation of R.E.A. service near Ames, Iowa, November 15, 1937. Note wall telephone. (Photo, Iowa State University)

Mrs. David (Valeria) Miller in her all-electric kitchen, including a microwave oven. Mrs. Miller does book work and considerable driving on the farm to keep things going smoothly. She is a key factor in the success of this extensive, well-managed, small-grain, soybean, and sunflower operation near Wahpeton, North Dakota, May 11, 1978.

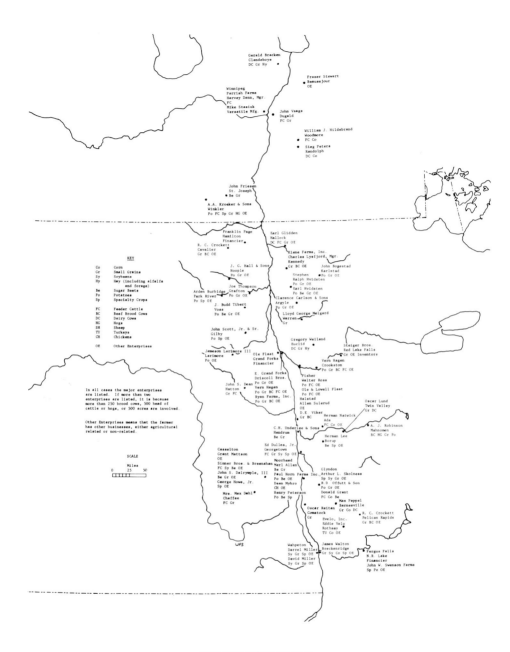

In all cases the major enterprises
are listed. If more than two
enterprises are listed, it is because
more than 250 brood cows, 500 head of
cattle or hogs, or 500 acres are involved.

Other Enterprises means that the farmer
has other businesses, either agricultural
related or non-related.

KEY

Co	Corn
Gr	Small Grains
Sy	Soybeans
Hy	Hay (including alfalfa and forage)
Be	Sugar Beets
Po	Potatoes
Sp	Specialty Crops
FC	Feeder Cattle
BC	Beef Brood Cows
DC	Dairy Cows
HG	Hogs
SH	Sheep
TU	Turkeys
CH	Chickens
OE	Other Enterprises

SCALE

Miles
0   25   50

THE RED RIVER VALLEY

Containing parts of Manitoba, Minnesota, and North Dakota

Map No. 1

Note: Symbols for all maps are on this page.

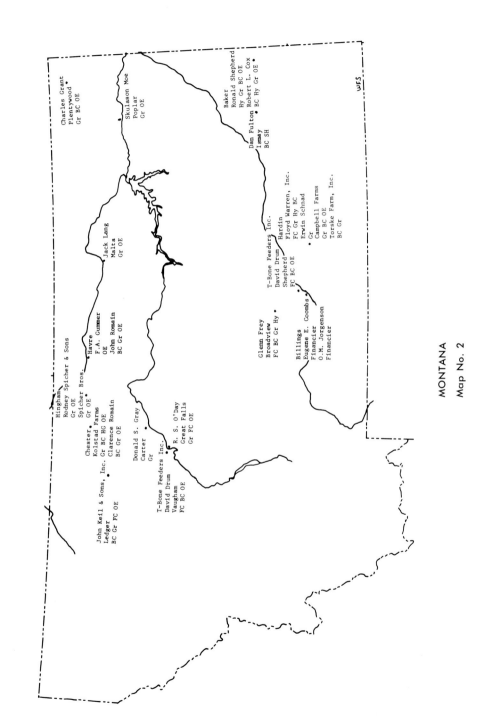

MONTANA

Map No. 2

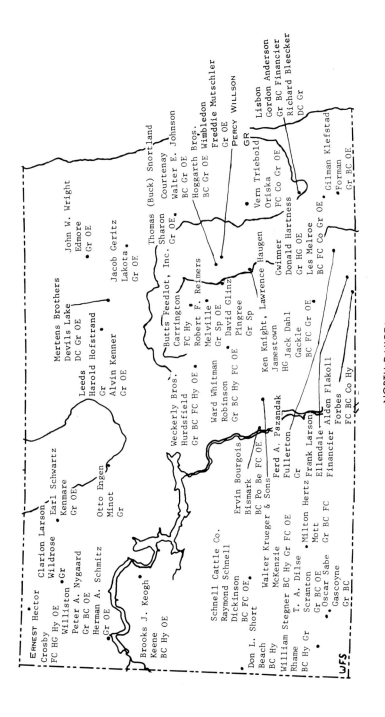

NORTH DAKOTA

Map No. 3

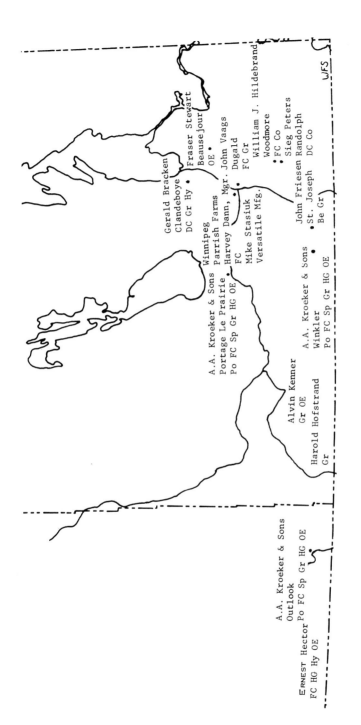

SOUTHERN CANADA

Map No. 4

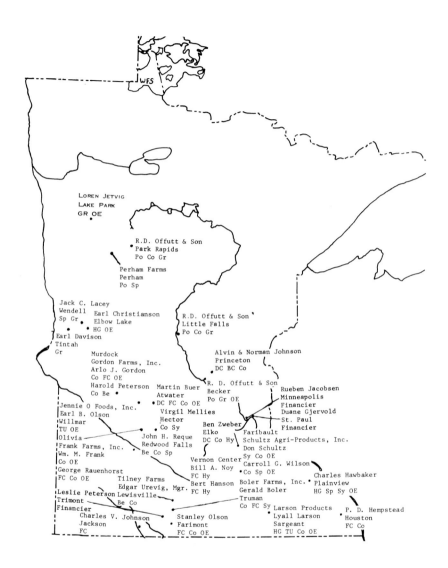

Loren Jetvig
Lake Park
GR OE

R.D. Offutt & Son
Park Rapids
Po Co Gr

Perham Farms
Perham
Po Sp

Jack C. Lacey
Wendell   Earl Christianson
Sp Gr   Elbow Lake   R.D. Offutt & Son
              HG OE   Little Falls
Earl Davison   Po Co Gr
Tintah
Gr   Alvin & Norman Johnson
        Murdock   Princeton
        Gordon Farms, Inc.   DC BC Co
        Arlo J. Gordon
        Co FC OE
        Harold Peterson   Martin Buer   R. D. Offutt & Son
        Co Be   Atwater   Becker   Rueben Jacobsen
Jennie O Foods, Inc.   DC FC Co OE   Po Gr OE   Minneapolis
Earl B. Olson   Virgil Mellies   Financier
Willmar   Hector   Duane Gjervold
TU OE   Co Sy   Ben Zweber   St. Paul
Olivia   John H. Reque   Elko   Financier
Frank Farms, Inc. Redwood Falls   DC Co Hy Faribault
Wm. M. Frank   Be Co Sp   Schultz Agri-Products, Inc.
Co OE   Don Schultz
George Rauenhorst   Vernon Center   Sy Co OE
FC Co OE   Bill A. Noy   Carroll G. Wilson
                          FC Hy   Co Sp OE   Charles Hawbaker
        Tilney Farms   Bert Hanson Boler Farms, Inc. Plainview
        Edgar Urevig, Mgr. FC Hy   Gerald Boler   HG Sp Sy OE
Leslie Peterson Lewisville   Truman
Trimont   Be Co   Co FC Sy   P. D. Hempstead
Financier   Larson Products   Houston
        Charles V. Johnson Stanley Olson   Lyall Larson   FC Co
        Jackson   Farimont   Sargeant
        FC   FC Co OE   HG TU Co OE

MINNESOTA

Map No. 5

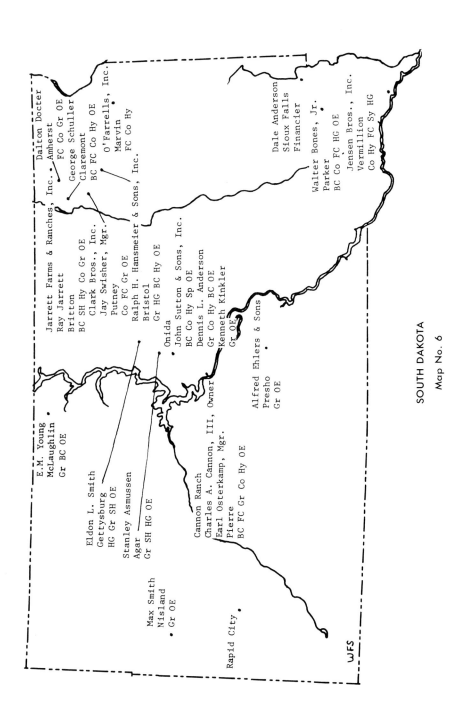

E.M. Young
McLaughlin
Gr BC OE

Dalton Docter

Jarrett Farms & Ranches, Inc.
Ray Jarrett
Britton
BC SH Hy Co Gr OE

Amherst
FC Co Gr OE

George Schuller
Claremont
BC FC Co Hy OE

O'Farrells, Inc.
Marvin
FC Co Hy

Clark Bros., Inc.
Jay Swisher, Mgr.
Putney
Co FC Gr OE

Ralph H. Hansmeier & Sons, Inc.
Bristol
Gr HG BC Hy OE

Eldon L. Smith
Gettysburg
HG Gr SH OE

Stanley Asmussen
Agar
Gr SH HG OE

Onida
John Sutton & Sons, Inc.
BC Co Hy Sp OE
Dennis L. Anderson
Gr Co Hy BC OE
Kenneth Kinkler
Gr OE

Dale Anderson
Sioux Falls
Financier

Walter Bones, Jr.
Parker
BC Co FC HG OE

Jensen Bros., Inc.
Vermillion
Co Hy FC Sy HG

Max Smith
Nisland
Gr OE

Cannon Ranch
Charles A. Cannon, III, Owner
Earl Osterkamp, Mgr.
Pierre
BC FC Gr Co Hy OE

Alfred Ehlers & Sons
Presho
Gr OE

Rapid City

WFS

SOUTH DAKOTA

Map No. 6

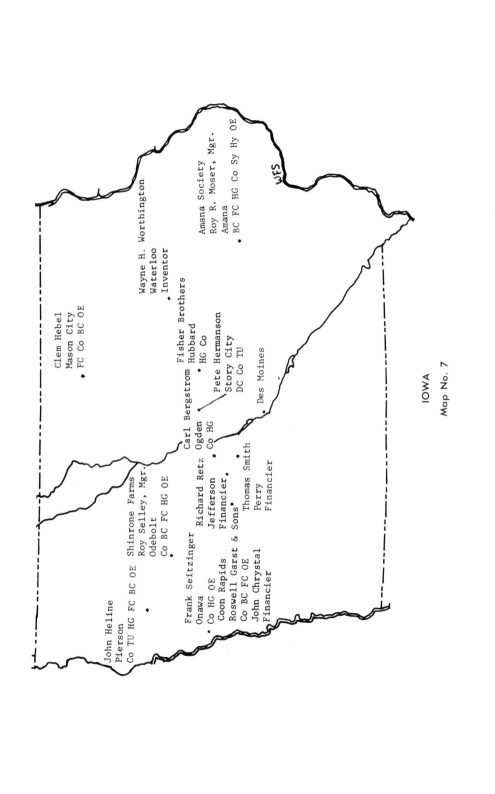

IOWA

Map No. 7

The 1,400-horsepower Skolness tractor units are able to finish the fall tillage only a few hours after the self-propelled combines move out of each field. "Our big four-wheel-drive tractors with 26-inch duals on each wheel give us a big advantage. Much of the land we own would not be in production if it were not for those big four-wheelers, plus our shop, where we have made many adaptations to our machinery to better handle the job."

The Sinner brothers and Bresnahan responded instantly when asked what was their greatest advantage in combatting weather. They recalled that on several occasions they had to modify equipment in order to cope with the weather. It was their well-equipped shop that enabled them to do their jobs and keep going when others, who were not large enough to justify owning a shop, had to wait for ideal conditions.

Donald A. Schulz, who produces corn and soybeans, recalled seeing a 160-acre-farm neighbor wiped out in one storm. "Our history tells us that we have less trouble than the smaller operators. We beat them in and out nearly every year. It is organization, planning, equipment, and being spread out. It seems as if every year we help a few of them to get their work done," said Don. Then he went into detail about the precautions he once had taken in anticipating bad weather. He purchased a second combine with a cab, a heater, and lights. "We started on 160 acres with two combines at 11 P.M. one night, as soon as the ground was frozen. One combine broke down at 2 A.M., but our mobile shop fixed it on the spot. No small operator could afford either the extra combine or a mobile shop. We did the entire quarter that night while a neighbor, whose entire farm was smaller than 160 acres, slept. It took him over two weeks to get his crop out."

Robert L. Cox, a Montana cowman, contends that the large operator has it easier because he can economically justify equipment and labor-saving devices in order to cope with the weather. "Our road patrol [large self-propelled road grader and snow plow] is a good example. We can get to the cows in winter storms and also get ourselves out to the main highway. I'd rather operate with volume because it only takes a small per cent of your gross income to live, and when the weather breaks in our favor it is not so hard to catch up."

C. H. Underlee, who has harvested more than 40 crops, was very emphatic in explaining that it took volume to justify the use of a D-7 Caterpillar with a blade and a scraper to do their drainage. In the flat Red River Valley, drainage is critical and requires constant attention. He added, "The boys can almost float with their dual-wheeled, four-wheel-drive tractors. It just whips the little rigs."

Several of the farmers interviewed did have their farms in solid blocks of land. Contrary to what the majority expressed, those farmers were satisfied that the land was not divided into individual parcels.

Roy Selley, a professional farm manager, said: "We have a solid block of 10 sections, and I do not remember any period in which there has been rain on the entire farm. We can almost always work some place on the farm. But even if we can't we have enough work in construction, fencing, and repair of yards or machinery so that those rainy-day breaks prove profitable. At least, we don't worry about weather like a lot of people I know."

E. J. Dullea, Jr., who has farmed in a relatively dry area of central Dakota as well as in the flat and wetter Red River Valley, said:

We have to learn to live with the weather as a part of the business. Timing is the key. Loss of crops has caused me to have operating losses for some fiscal years. But I believe weather is part of management and the larger operator has lots of advantages, particularly from an equipment standpoint. The manufacturers are learning to make equipment that adapts itself to moving. Out in Dakota I was spread out 15 miles; here I am in nearly a solid block, and I prefer it because there is still a variance in conditions and the cost of travel is so much less. We are getting the largest combine made and have a 30-foot swather. This eliminates the need for two men, but also lets us get the work done faster. That's how to beat the weather.

"Even though our farm is nearly a solid block, it is still spread out five miles," said Jay C. Swisher, "and we go from heavy to light soil fron north to south on our farm. This gives us natural advantages with different crops, plus a difference in when the land gets ready to be worked."

Swisher commented that a large continuous-flow drier, capable of drying 1,000 bushels of wheat an hour, enabled them to start combining wheat at the 16 per cent moisture level. This stretched the combining day by hours and shortened the harvest season, thereby reducing the risk of weather loss. The drier gave them the same advantage in harvesting their 3,000 acres of corn after the wheat harvest was over. Swisher noted that weather was a "real hang-up" for many farmers he knew, and it was the major reason why some of them did not expand.

Walter Kroeker, who farms in Manitoba, disagrees fervently

with some farmers' fears of expanding. Kroeker contends that he would rather be large because being spread out is one of the best hedges against failure. Kroeker noted, "Sometimes we have a quarter on our farm that is completely wiped out, but a few miles down the road we have a bumper crop. Besides, we have several animal enterprises large enough to carry us through if a great portion of our specialty crops is lost. This makes it possible to have regular year-round work for everyone."

Kroeker also mentioned that there were nine mobile radio units on their farm in addition to their airplane which, he said, "were invaluable to speeding up work." The radios were used to tell the potato-cutting crew to start and stop cutting; to direct seed, fertilizer, and fuel deliveries; to direct the harvest crew; to call for repairs; or to call for help in emergencies. He felt that large-scale farming would be much more difficult and expensive without good radio communication. It is his impression that much more can be gained from such equipment if the farm is large enough to justify the initial expense.

Lauren Carlson, a Minnesota livestock feeder, agrees that confinement is a partial solution to the weather for the cattleman. Carlson has had a confined barn in operation since 1967, and his records indicate that the barn has been a profitable investment each year in comparison to outdoor feeding. The investment required for a confined cattle-feeding operation might frighten many except the larger feeders from taking the risk.

As has been found true with many agricultural innovations, sound capital investment reduces the per unit cost of production. Carlson's experience proves that point with his system of confined feeding. Carlson estimates that he has had less than $20.00 feed loss in the feed bunks during eight years of feeding in his 600-head building. One group of cattle, taken from a muddy outside lot and placed in a building, reduced their consumption by 30 per cent and improved gains. Manure tests in 1968 indicated $7,500 worth of fertilizer from 600 cattle, based on the relatively low price of commercial fertilizer at that time. Carlson calls that the "hidden value," which he said was enough to pay for the barn, exclusive of the other benefits. Since the value of confined feeding has so proven itself, he uses his outside lots primarily to take advantage of good buys and to supply his building with a steady supply of cattle.

Hail and crop insurance is a major concern of many farmers because it is virtually the best income protection against a natural disaster. David Miller felt that distance gave him a good hedge on the weather; therefore, after he passed the 4,000-acre level, he quit taking out crop insurance.

Probably the best comment on the advantage of size came from Stanley Asmussen:

> We are spread out 80 miles northwest to southeast, but like all larger farmers, we look to size as a safety factor. That's why we have not carried crop insurance since the 1940's. I believe we have had some weather loss every year we have farmed, but a good crop on another part of the land. In 1966 we had our worst loss, about $150,000, but the rest of the land had close to a bumper crop, so our returns were almost normal for that year.

As in so many previous facets, it appears that the predominant factor is one's own mental attitude toward weather—one of the major variables in agriculture. Successful farmers accept it as part of the business, even though they neither like it nor are they immune from losses that adverse weather brings.[7]

NOTES

[1]Interviews with:

Jack Dahl, Gackle, North Dakota, February 10, 1973
George C. Schuller, Claremont, South Dakota, March 3, 1972
George Rauenhorst, Olivia, Minnesota, March 16, 1972
John W. Swenson, Fergus Falls, Minnesota, January 11, 1970
Ralph H. Hansmeier, Bristol, South Dakota, March 3, 1972
Earl Hvidsten, Stephen, Minnesota, January 17, 1972
Keith and Ray Driscoll, East Grand Forks, Minnesota, January 17, 1972
Gerald C. Ryan, East Grand Forks, Minnesota, February 14, 1973
Frank Seitzinger, Onawa, Iowa, June 16, 1972
Walter E. Johnson, Courtenay, North Dakota, March 8, 1972
Keil brothers and Mrs. John Keil, Ledger, Montana, May 12, 1972
Raymond Schnell, Dickinson, North Dakota, May 18, 1972
Robert F. Reimers, Melville, North Dakota, January 6, 1970

[2]Interviews with:

Pete A. Hermanson, Story City, Iowa, February 22, 1972
Richard C. Bleecker, Lisbon, North Dakota, February 11, 1972
Herman A. Natwick, Ada, Minnesota, March 10, 1971, and May 1, 1975
Donald Jarrett, Britton, South Dakota, March 2, 1972
Charles V. Johnson, Jackson, Minnesota, March 28, 1972
David Garst, Coon Rapids, Iowa, June 13, 1972

[3]Interviews with:

Carroll G. Wilson, Fairbault, Minnesota, February 20, 1972
Arlo J. Gordon, Murdock, Minnesota, March 15, 1972
John Bogestad, Karlstad, Minnesota, March 22, 1972
Earl Davison, Tintah, Minnesota, December 8, 1970
Ellis Jensen, Vermillion, South Dakota, February 24, 1972

[4]Interviews with:

Ernest C. Hector, Crosby, North Dakota, April 5, 1972
O'Farrells, Inc., Marvin, South Dakota, February 25, 1972

Milton Hertz, Mott, North Dakota, April 7, 1972
John W. Wright, Edmore, North Dakota, November 7, 1970

[5]Interviews with:

Harold Hofstrand, Leeds, North Dakota, December 12, 1970
John H. Reque, Redwood Falls, Minnesota, March 15, 1972
Ralph Hvidsten, Stephen, Minnesota, January 17, 1972
Harold T. Petersen, Murdock, Minnesota, March 30, 1972

[6]Interviews with:

Earl Hvidsten, Stephen, Minnesota, January 17, 1972
Earl Osterkamp, Pierre, South Dakota, October 19, 1972
Peter A. Nygaard, Williston, North Dakota, April 4, 1972
O'Farrells, Inc., Marvin, South Dakota, February 25, 1972
Harold Hofstrand, Leeds, North Dakota, December 12, 1970
Arlo J. Gordon, Murdock, Minnesota, March 15, 1972
Pete A. Hermanson, Story City, Iowa, February 22, 1972
David Glinz, Pingree, North Dakota, June 24, 1971
Allen C. Kolstad, Chester, Montana, May 11 and 12, 1972, and letter of January 26, 1973
Clem Hebel, Mason City, Iowa, February 21, 1972, and June 4, 1975
Paul Horn, Jr., Moorhead, Minnesota, December 23, 1969
Vernon Triebold, Oriska, North Dakota, February 13, 1973
Robert F. Reimers, Melville, North Dakota, January 6, 1970

Gopher State Review, No. 330 (May, 1975).

[7]Interviews with:

Charles Lysfjord, Kennedy, Minnesota, March 14, 1973
Alfred Ehlers, Presho, South Dakota, April 10, 1972
Darrell Miller, Wahpeton, North Dakota, April 20, 1972
Virgil Mellies, Hector, Minnesota, March 16, 1972
George and Richard Spicher, Hingham, Montana, May 10, 1972
Kenneth Kinkler, Onida, South Dakota, April 11, 1972
Herman A. Natwick, Ada, Minnesota, March 10, 1971, and May 1, 1975
Arden Burbidge, Park River, North Dakota, January 3, 1970 and March 14, 1973
Dennis L. Anderson, Rapid City, South Dakota, April 9, 1972
Arthur L. Skolness, Glyndon, Minnesota, February 17, 1971
Sinner brothers and Ellery Bresnahan, Casselton, North Dakota, December 28, 1969
Donald A. Schulz, Faribault, Minnesota, March 25, 1972
Robert L. Cox, Baker, Montana, May 18, 1972
C. H. Underlee, Hendrum, Minnesota, January 19, 1972
Roy Selley, Odebolt, Iowa, February 23, 1972
E. J. Dullea, Jr., Georgetown, Minnesota, January 5, 1972
Jay C. Swisher, Groton, South Dakota, March 1, 1972
Walter Kroeker, Winkler, Manitoba, February 15, 1973
David Fisher, Hubbard, Iowa, January 26, 1974
Lauren Carlson, Chokio, Minnesota, June 17, 1975
Jack E. Lang, Malta, Montana, May 9, 1972
David Miller, Wahpeton, North Dakota, February 12, 1973
Stanley Asmussen, Agar, South Dakota, April 13, 1972

CHAPTER VII

The Changing Labor Scene*

ONE OF THE MAJOR FACTORS in the improved level of living for farmers since 1910 has been the great increase in the productivity of farm labor. This has been accompanied by an enormous reduction in the number of workers required to produce the nation's food and fiber. In 1910, 10.4 million male workers were engaged in agriculture; by 1972, that figure had been reduced to 2.8 million full-time farm workers. By the mid-1960's only Australia and Canada had more acres cultivated per worker than the 351-acre average for the American farm worker and only New Zealand and Australia had a higher wheat output per worker than America.

Since 1910, farm output per man-hour has risen just over 3 per cent per year, and by the 1970's American farmers were raising nearly four times more crops per hour of labor.** The adoption of mechanical power, large machinery, electricity, fertilizer, and chemicals was the major cause for the increased production per man-hour. Each time the American farmer increased his capital inputs by purchasing labor-saving machinery, total production rose. Because of this trend, agriculture was rapidly becoming one of America's most capital-demanding industries.

Many farmers have not thoroughly comprehended the obvious change from a family–labor-oriented enterprise to a capital-intensive business requiring a degree of management far beyond the standards of the past. Capital, machinery, and management have been used to replace labor wherever possible, because in the

---

*Because of the sensitive nature of the material in this chapter, the names of farmers, their wives, or employees are not used. This was the agreement with these individuals at the time of interview. However, all documentation is on file with the author.

**Man-hours of labor on farms can imply the hours worked by the owner, members of his family, or employed individuals.

thinking of many farmers, those three inputs have been more available than either land or labor. From 1880 to 1960 the price of machinery in relation to the cost of labor dropped in ratio from 100 to 4, encouraging farmers to substitute machinery for labor as rapidly as machines became available. As late as 1940, half of all the rural-employed were farm operators, managers, or laborers, but by 1960 less than one-fifth of the rural workers were so employed. Total agricultural employment was not reduced, because many former farm workers became involved in agricultural-related industries. Manufacturing far exceeded farming as a rural employer by the later date, and the trend has continued in that direction since.*

Dramatic as the shift of labor from the farm to manufacturing or other industries has been, it has not been sufficient to take care of surplus farm laborers. Consequently, under-employment still plagues many rural areas. Many consider this drain of workers from the land as a national calamity. Data to prove such beliefs is popular, but not conclusive. The farm laborer of the past experienced a substandard living because through much of the period since 1910 his wages were only about 30 to 50 per cent of those of the urban factory worker. As a result he has not hesitated to move away from the land when the opportunity presented itself.

A U.S.D.A. study during the 1930's predicted what would happen to a changing agriculture as soon as farmers comprehended the new agriculture:

Tradition and inertia are . . . part of the farmer's heritage, and a change in method often requires a genuine mental effort. More important, a subtle change in which the farmer regards his farm has come about. More and more it becomes simply a place to earn a living and is regarded in a colder, more commercial light. . . . A considerable degree of inertia, however, still remains and provides a limit to the rate at which farm technology can improve.

World War II caused an increased demand for industrial workers, which provided the necessary impetus for many farmers to leave the land. At the same time it enabled those who remained on the land to adopt the new technologies that provided the basis for a profitable commercialized agriculture unlike any experienced in the past. The 23 billion man-hours required in agricul-

---

*See Fred A. Shannon, "The Homestead Act and the Labor Surplus," *American Historical Review*, XLI, No. 4 (July, 1936), pp. 637–651, for excellent data on the impact of the Homestead Act on the labor supply.

ture in 1920 to provide the food and fiber for the nation decreased to about 14 billion man-hours in 1940 and to 6.5 billion in 1971. Even a larger population and larger anticipated export demands will not affect manpower requirements, and only 4 billion manpower hours will be needed for the future.

North Dakota, as an example, had its number of farm workers reduced from 153,000 in 1947 to 44,775 in 1975. The projection for 1985 is 28,775 workers, yet total crop production has increased steadily during the past years and is predicted to continue to increase.

Historically, a farmer's "hired man" has not been held in much esteem in the American scene. One farmer interviewed, who employed more than 30 men, said that the biggest handicap he had in hiring good labor was the tendency of local, small, independent farmers to look down on those who worked for another farmer. He felt that this caused the more sensitive people to seek industrial work rather than work on a farm.

Probably one of the reasons farm labor has not been looked upon in a favorable light is the way farmers have treated their hired help in the past. The plight of the farm laborer, especially the seasonal laborer, has not been a bright spot in the history of American and world agriculture. Usually this was because underdeveloped agriculture offered sparse returns for the small farmer-owner and even less for his laborers. To this day many independent small farmers want as little as possible to do with hiring labor on the competing industrial wage scale.

Farmers Look at Labor

The modern commercialized farmer differs. The 1959 agricultural census revealed that 76 per cent of the largest farms (Class 1 census definition) hired some workers in contrast to 20 per cent of all commercial farms. Over 44 per cent of the Class 1 farms had more than one full-time laborer compared to 4 per cent for all commercial farms. The size of the Class 1 farm (by census definition this means over $40,000 in gross sales) has grown considerably. Similarily, all the large farmers interviewed for this work and in the same farm census category (over $100,000 in gross sales) showed that the percentage of farms with several full-time employees is far beyond the average for all agriculture. These farms employed an average of 8.85 full-time and 8.78 part-time workers.

The most striking trait of these farmers was their recognition of the need for good quality labor and management help and their willingness to hire such employees. These farmers appeared much more tolerant than the average farmer in their expectations of what labor was capable of doing. Few of them had an upper limit as to the number of laborers they were willing to employ. Although they admitted that labor, next to marketing, was their greatest problem, they generally accepted it with a practical attitude.*

One farmer interviewed said, "Labor is a function of management. It is the most used and most abused factor of poor management. We pay well, but just as important is that you have to make conditions of work as pleasant as possible. Consider the job you are asking him to do, and then look at the facilities and equipment he has to do it with. Provide the best. Our labor cost is considerably less than our interest bill."

"You cannot afford a cheap man. We hire several men, some of whom have worked in industry. But labor is not a problem, because we pay well, have a retirement program, and furnish good houses with the job. They are capable, so when there is no field or cattle work, we can do any construction or overhaul work that needs to be done," stated another farmer.

A third farmer agreed: "A poor man is expensive at any wage he asks. I look for only good men. But it is not much of a problem because we have several small farmers nearby who rely on me for cash income. They do excellent work, do not need supervision, and really enjoy working with my big tractors with air-conditioned cabs. Their tractors are small and old, and probably they will never buy anything better."

Another farmer, who was thinking about expanding, wanted to find out the availability of labor, so he placed a single help-wanted ad in a large city newspaper and had 35 applicants who expressed a desire to leave their big-city jobs. "I got a real cross section of people and skills—some outstanding men. One was a department manager in a feed mill with 25 men under him. He expressed the desire for work in the country and to get away from the responsibility of managing others. I have no concern about competing with the industrial pay scale as long as I can use the men on big power units and they will follow my management. The future looks good."

A farmer with several enterprises and a half dozen permanent

---

*This is in contrast to previously mentioned studies that have indicated that hired labor is the major limitation most farmers placed on their expansion potential.

employees just had an employee of 31 years to retire. His most recently employed worker had been with him for five years. This farmer felt that his men were capable of doing almost any job without supervision, and at least two of them could manage the farm, although neither expressed the desire to do so. His men were not clock conscious; but, on the other hand, they were not docked for sickness and were permitted time off in addition to specific vacations.

It was the impression of this farmer that good housing and regular hours, regardless of season or problems, plus occasional day or half-day breaks were extremely important in keeping the wives happy. He added, "We have turned strictly to quality labor. They seem to have fewer domestic problems and have much less of an operating problem with the big machines or the technical work." All construction and repair work is done by the permanent labor crew of that farm.

A diversified farmer, who employs 26 full-time people, still has the first man he hired on his staff. He balances the work schedule so that everyone has to work only every fourth weekend to do the necessary feeding chores. He seeks only the best men for the job and has engaged only professionally trained men or former farmers. It is his opinion that this has greatly reduced his management problem and improved his overall operation.

Another farmer expressed a similar feeling by noting that he had many very good former farmers who had been with him for over 30 years. But he was concerned that the top quality youth tended to leave the farm and go to the larger urban centers or to school instead of seeking farm work. The only turnover among their 18 employees was among the people under 30. But he saw no long-term problem in securing good quality help.

All farmers interviewed expressed a concern to be able to retain good men. One of them commented that when he had a good solid staff of five men, he set up a certified seed plant to keep them busy the year round. Another noted that the morale of his men improved once they were assured of steady work, and he has had no turnover in 10 years. The men have regular hours and are on their own most of the time.

A farmer with many off-the-farm interests said, "I could really get by with very little hired labor, but I discovered that there are so many good people available on a part-time basis that I hire them. This way I can spend about half of my time away from the farm. It relieves the boredom and is also profitable."

Another said, "I have to make many scheduled meetings with committees that take me away from the farm for several days at a time. My men have extreme freedom, but they are of the finest quality so the job gets done. There have been emergencies when I have been called out of meetings to give directions by phone, and, generally, what that amounted to was assuring them they were doing the right thing. It helps to relieve their tension."

Referring to a very similar situation, another farmer pointed out that he had very good men, who not only had great freedom, but also frequently had to operate the business for months at a time while he was operating another farm in a distant state. "There is no point in having men if you have to watch them all the time. The telephone helps me keep tab on what's getting done."

A farmer with three full-time and three part-time employees pointed out that his full-time men were capable of management, but did not want the responsibility. Some had been in management positions on other farms and quit those jobs because that was not what they wanted to do. His farm does all of its own construction and mechanical work because all the full-time men are capable of doing such work.

An owner of a livestock, grain, and specialty crop farm with nine year-round men insists that agriculture requires a more qualified man than most other industries. He bases his judgment on the fact that his men must be able to work with livestock, in addition to being able to do technical field work, machinery repair, and building construction. "Because of that," he said, "we can and must pay wages equal to industry. We feel both a moral and an economic need to pay top-notch wages. Even if we have a slack season, we guarantee our men an annual wage because the men we have are the kind we want to keep."

This farmer also noted that most farmers should spend as much time with their employees as they do with their family, for the personal relationship is a critical factor. The men all work on fixed time schedules, and if there is a problem requiring overtime work the hired management people do that. Even in the most rushed seasons the full-time employees are not expected to work beyond their established hours. He affirmed that the established work schedule has done more to improve the morale of his labor force than anything he had observed in the 55 years of the farm's operation. "More than anything, it seems to have removed the farmer's 'hired-man' stigma. Our men are proud of being farm employees, just as I am proud of being a farmer."

A cash-crop farmer whose labor requirements cover seven months of the year was very comfortable with an improved outlook for labor. He recalled that when he changed to four-wheel-drive tractors with weather-proof cabs and a fully equipped shop, he was able to attract a much higher quality of men. It was his policy to buy the largest possible equipment and hire the very best men to operate it. "As we get the men we want, we put them on a guaranteed annual income, and we will expand the shop to keep them partially occupied in the other five months working over the machinery. We notice that since we have started this system, we have nearly eliminated field breakdowns."[1]

Farm Labor and Its Compensation

A farmer with a large diversified operation said that he switched from track-type tractors to four-wheel-drive tractors and from single-axle to tandem-axle trucks to be able to reduce his permanent labor force from 24 to 16 and his seasonal crew from 36 to 24. He noted that by doing this he was able to upgrade his labor force considerably and also increase wages substantially. This did not surprise him, for in the past the quality of labor had improved each time he had upgraded his equipment. Summing up his attitude toward wages he said, "Agriculture can pay as much as any other industry. If you can't afford to pay labor, why bother to farm?"

A farmer, living near a large industrial city and having multiple enterprises, has paid industrial rates for labor for years, even though his neighbors maintain that a farmer cannot afford to pay such rates. He said, "If a farmer cannot pay the established rate, he isn't a very good farmer. With good management you can pay labor well. Don't worry about labor rate if you can get quality labor."

A potato farmer commented that in the past he frequently lost men to highly paid road construction jobs, but in spite of the high pay some of those men returned to him. One reason was that he purchased four-wheel-drive tractors and he offered to pay those men the same rate they could get on construction jobs, but on the same basis—"no work, no pay." His other proposition to the worker was a year-round income with a bonus system based on quality and quantity of work. His reasoning for such a bonus system was that some men did excellent work, but were slow. Others did much work, but were sloppy. Quality and yield were also figured into the bonus, because both sharply affected profits. He now has several ex-construction workers on his permanent force.

A neighboring farmer had the same trouble with people who left for high-paying industrial jobs. "After a few years, most of them have returned to us and are very happy, because they realized we were paying well and they preferred rural living." His permanent work force is made up of 15 laborers; 4 of them have been with him for over 30 years. In addition to the permanent crew, he hires many seasonal employees, most of whom have small farms of their own. This farmer feels that the quality of available labor has been steadily improving.

A large livestock farmer, operating next to one of the largest industrial sites in his state, has experienced no labor difficulties. He placed one ad in his church paper and had 26 replies, all from industrial workers who wanted to live in the country. He found that good housing and fixed hours were the best innovations he has made in his labor program: "I like hiring couples and make them responsible for a definite period of time each day. They have great flexibility in getting their work done, and I do not interfere unless they ask me." He pays basically the same wages as they do in the local industrial plant. He was not as much concerned about labor cost as he was about labor quality. Overall, he was satisfied that he was getting a good job done with his permanent labor force, made up entirely of ex-farmers.

A rancher–grain farmer, located 70 miles from the nearest sizeable town, was having just the opposite experience with his labor force. During his 40 years of farming, he felt that the quality of labor had declined because the alternative opportunities offered by that town's industries had been so much greater that all the "best had left." He said, "Our aggressive, capable people leave, and the remainder look to welfare benefits rather than jobs. Welfare has become our greatest competitor. The matter of personal incentive makes the difference. The good workers who have stayed are ex-farmers who really like country life. They are all furnished with family houses. They make up our full-time crew, but there are also seasonal men who get room and board in a bunk house."

A cash-grain farmer with extensive non-farm interests said that his permanent men were their own bosses because he was absent much of the time. All his seven permanent employees had been with him since the 1930's and 1940's. Several had never worked for anyone else. These people are paid on an annual basis and have a very light work schedule during five months of the year. His men do all the machinery repair, and he markets all his grain in his own trucks. He has found that assigning a definite truck and four-wheel-drive tractor to each man has greatly reduced maintenance cost and removed an irritant among the men. Besides, they take much pride in their equipment. He stated: "My regular crew is extremely loyal and is responsible for the large number of seasonal workers needed on the place. I have very little contact with them. My regular men know where to get their seasonal help, many of whom have come to us for years."

A farmer with a permanent work force of 100 and with a "long list of people" who would like to work for him gave as the reason for his successful labor relations—a bonus based on each person's performance and not on the net income of the farm. But the loyalty among the workers came because they felt a sense of personal recognition. "They knew they had the best equipment and facilities in the country to work with." About half of the employees' families live in houses on farms acquired by this farmer. Both parties like this arrangement, and employees eagerly seek to live in the country residences.

As previous interviews indicate, farmers who realized that their farms were too small to make a living have been one of the best sources of labor for the successful farmer. One of the reasons why these ex-farmers had quit was their inability to stand the tensions of management. The successful farmer, however, has discovered that these men are excellent workers and can do a good job as long as someone else is responsible for providing the money and making the management decisions.

One farmer, specializing only in cash grain, said:

I have had an excellent man working for me for 15 years. Previous to that he farmed three-quarters of his own land and never could get a good crop on it. He was always behind. He saw that my crops were always better. One day he came to me and suggested that I operate his farm on shares and he would work for me. Now we get good crops on his place, and he makes money by renting it to me, besides the income he gets by working for me. His wife told me that they were really doing well now, and their financial position just keeps improving. The rest of my help in peak season are all retired farmers. They are reliable and easy to work with.

Another farmer has only three full-time employees besides himself, but he operates with large equipment. He has a real rush for 30 days in the spring, 3 weeks at harvest, and 4 weeks for fall work, and needs seasonal help at those times. The four-wheel-drive tractors reduce his labor and fuel bill, and he uses the savings to pay for good quality men: "My regular men have 2 months a year when they are paid, but free to do what they want. Each owns some land (one has 320 acres), and we use my equipment to farm their land at no cost to them except for the seed, chemicals, fuel, and fertilizer. They also get all transportation expenses. That avoids lots of problems."

One farmer with much experience has learned that if he gives his seven employees definite assignments and then lets them alone to do the job all of them will do quite well. Nearly all his labor force have worked at other jobs, but prefer farming. He has his own shop, markets his grain to the terminals in his own trucks, and constructs his own buildings when field work is finished. The family of one of his men live on a second farm where they are permitted to keep a specific number of hogs and chickens and feed them from the farmer's crop. He does not feel that any of his men have management ability, nor do any of them desire to assume the responsibility. "None of them can stand any kind of pressure." It is his opinion that the available supply of good farm labor is improving, but he readily admits that being near to a fairly large town gives him an advantage which farmers in less populated areas might not have.

Livestock farmers often use incentive programs and separate farm housing to keep good employees. One livestock farmer has a man who does nothing but care for hogs and sheep. Besides his wages, a house with all utilities, and all the meat his family can eat, he gets 25 cents bonus for every pig and sheep sold. The hog operation is a farrow-to-finish business, so this gives the man an incentive to save every pig and then to keep them healthy to the end. The farmer acknowledged that the incentive was responsible for improved sanitation that leads to saving more pigs. An ad in a moderate-sized town newspaper recently drew responses from several industrial workers from metropolitan centers. Because of his success in securing good quality laborers, he has expanded in the past and is scheduling additional growth.

A beef farmer who uses an incentive system said: "Besides our family labor we have four full-time employees and two seasonal helpers. All the men are responsible in the calving program for the beef–brood-cow herd. They share 4 per cent of the total calf crop which are fed to butcher market at no cost to the employees. This gives a double incentive to see that the calves are born alive and then stay alive until they are fattened." He felt that providing separate houses on individual farmsteads, which include total utilities, was one of the best labor relations moves he could have made. The families are allowed hogs or milk cows and free feed for their animals. The permanent men arrange among themselves when they want to take their vacations so that only one is gone at a time. They are not docked for sickness or occasional days off. He was very pleased with his labor, and it was obvious that the families working for him felt the same way toward him. Everyone seemed directly interested in what was going on.

A rancher and feedlot owner has two men responsible for just the beef–brood-cow herd of 800 animals. These men each receive $100 for every 1 per cent of the calf crop saved over 85 per cent. This is based on the per cent of calves actually delivered to the feedlot in relation to the cow herd on April 1. He provides good housing for his help, all utilities and transportation, as well as allowing each family to have five milk cows—all expenses paid—for personal use. "Keeping the families independent from us and providing a good environment to live in has proved very important in making everyone happy. We always have a waiting list and are proud to say that many start for themselves if and when they leave us."

One farmer, after having some rather poor experiences in calving, decided that his three men taking care of 2,000 cows should be given an incentive to encourage a better calf crop. He offered a $10 bonus for each calf over 75 per cent of the calf crop. This was split among the three men. The impact of the bonus was immediate and gratifying and has remained very effective over the years. An additional benefit has been a more intensive cow culling program that has helped to improve profits.

This farmer also has several other enterprises on his farm with 40 full-time employees and over 100 for seasonal work. Each enterprise has a grievance committee that meets regularly and generally solves most problems before he finds out about them. Many employees have been with him since he started farming, and he has had almost no turnover in his permanent crew.

Among livestock farmers it is common to let permanent employees run beef-brood cows, beef cattle, or hogs in the facilities at no labor, feed, rental, or medical costs to the employees. As many as 35 cows and their calf crop were allowed in one operation. As an incentive, the permanent employees were often given an opportunity to expand their "free enterprise venture" gradually over the years of employment.

One of the farmers who permitted such a livestock bonus enterprise had some definite feelings about why he used that system. He said, "I am a demanding employer who expects aggressiveness, thoroughness, and neatness. I want only positive thinkers, and if he is not willing to risk a variable bonus that is in the same business as the one that pays his salary, he's not the right man for me. All he has to risk is his investment; I stand all other costs. If he wins big, so do I, but if he loses some, I have lost much more. We have a waiting list."

Farmers in the dairy business all used some variation of a per cent of gross income as an incentive program for the employees. The dairy farmers generally furnished housing, utilities, and dairy products besides a minimum base wage. The major incentive for the employee was a pre-determined per cent, up to 14 per cent, of the gross milk sales as the basis of his income. With one exception, all the dairy farms were close to relatively large centers of population, and they were in direct competition with industry for labor. Many of the dairymen's helpers were ex-industrial workers, and all the rest were dairy farmers who formerly operated farms on too small a scale to make a living.

A number of farmers with dairy herds commented that the employees who had responsibility for milk cows and who were on a percentage wage basis commonly had their entire family involved in the work. Through that system herds were expanded and the employees were able to earn a larger income. In all cases dairy employees worked on a tightly established time schedule. Some of the dairy farms had 24-hour work shifts, which excluded the need for overtime work. Weekends and holidays were rotated by schedule, thus removing one of the most undesirable aspects of the 365-days-a-year work in the dairy business.

Labor was not considered a serious management problem by any of the dairy farmers with a large volume of business. Contrary to the traditional belief that the work schedule is never ending on a dairy farm, these dairymen have proven that with a large enough volume to justify good working conditions, good facilities, and a scheduled working assignment, very dependable people can be hired.

Most of these dairy farmers made it a point to emphasize that the dairying crew was given as much freedom as any of the field workers. One dairyman specifically stated that he never entered his dairy barn when milking was in progress unless he was called by the employees. That factor, probably more than any other, explains some of the psychology behind a large successful dairy operation.

A feedlot operator and beef–brood-cow farmer in an area of a high concentration of small farmers had an almost ideal labor-management situation. For years this farmer has been employing farmer neighbors and their sons on a straight hourly basis. Because the neighbors had small farms of their own, they did not desire a full-time job, but they needed the extra income. He paid time and a half for any day in which the employees worked under three hours or over eight hours, regardless of how many hours they worked during the week. Some days all that was necessary was doing the chores. In this particular case the owner spent a great deal of time away from the farm, and it was imperative that he have several backup laborers. They were readily available in his area. Some of his part-time farmer employees were hinting very strongly to him that they hoped he would expand so that they could have full-time jobs. One of the part-time farmer employees had been with him for nearly 20 years. Many industrial employees in this area were also eager for moonlighting on the farm.

Moonlighting industrial employees are often used, and it was the consensus of the farmers that they were very satisfied with their job performance. A multi-enterprise farm, only 35 miles from the largest town in the state, had an established practice of hiring moonlighting industrial workers. This farm, with a year-round staff of 9, employs as many as 12 moonlighters during spring planting season and again during harvest season. These men work about four hours each weekday and all day Saturday. They earn $400 to $600 moonlighting and prove to be very satisfactory.

Nearly all the farmers interviewed emphasized the need for supplying adequate housing for their workers if there were no sizeable communities nearby. Some farmers lived in town and had their laborers' families living on the farm, while others lived on the farm and their workers lived in town or on purchased farms. One farmer with nine full-time employees had a housing development a short distance from the main building site for the employees. This farmer encouraged the employees to purchase the houses and, if needed, he helped them with the financing. He was pleased with this arrangement, and the employees had a greater feeling of security and esprit' de corps than they had had in previous times. Each full-time employee was also assigned to a four-wheel-drive tractor.

In most cases employees and employers felt that living facilities furnished by the farmer and separate from the owner's home served a definite advantage for a long-term good relationship. In some cases in which the farms were very distant from any town, employee housing was sometimes on the main farm site. From observation it was obvious that virtually no family contact took place between employer and employees during non-working hours. Everyone involved expressed that such was necessary for long-term working relationships.

Off-the-farm living facilities generally proved most satisfactory when the farmer furnished a pickup for traveling to and from the farm. In that manner employees were free to go directly to their field work without stopping at farm headquarters. In some instances employees lived at opposite ends of the farm, while the headquarters were centrally located.

One grain–brood-cow farmer had 41 applicants for a job from a single newspaper want ad. He offered a good modern house as part of the job's compensation, and many of the applicants expressed the view that the house was one of the appealing factors about the job. This was especially true of the replies coming from the industrial workers in larger cities.

Perhaps the expression of one farm employee best illustrates the significance of worker income problems: "I could not keep up with family expenses and housing working on an industrial job in Minneapolis, but after I took charge of a dairy herd, I not only paid up all back bills but was able to provide support for my children attending college."

Distance also is a factor in hiring labor. A farmer who has two units that are 200 miles apart and lives in a town between his two units had this comment: "We have an elderly sheepherder on one place and he loves the isolation, but it's different for a family man. I have to employ single men and then really watch that they don't get to town, or they are no good for a few days." He hires custom crews for harvesting and for fencing, contracts building erection, and does no machinery repairing because it is his best way of avoiding more involvement with labor. He acknowledges that being closer to a town would be an advantage. Otherwise, the only solution would be to enlarge into a livestock operation to justify having several families on the place and avoid the problem of isolation.

Another farmer also admitted that isolation was an important factor in labor relations. Years ago he had made a firm hiring policy that all employees had to live either in the very small town or on the farm. The small town was 40 miles from the nearest town with a shopping center. He found some people preferred the isolation and became long-time employees. A cook and trailer housing is provided for single men, who must live in the trailers. "We have reduced our seasonal crew from 13 to 6 with new big equipment. This reduces, but does not eliminate, the need for seasonal labor; however, as long as we have bars, we will have seasonal workers. Some of these men have showed up at the farm each spring since the '30's."[2]

Quality of Agricultural Labor

In spite of comments about the lack of motivation and qualification of agricultural workers, most of the farmers interviewed were not worried about the labor supply. In any industry, employers would probably have similar comments about the good and the bad aspects of labor. Labor-management problems date back to the beginning of the history of mankind and even today they are the greatest headache to any form of planned society. The problem is as perpetual as human nature, and it is to the benefit of the successful farmer that he recognize it.

One hard-working farmer, who spent several years as a farmer's "hired man" before be began farming on his own, frankly admitted that he had trouble being an employer. He said, "I am a very fast, hard worker and there are few who can keep up with me. If I could have one top man who could keep pace with me, he and I could do more than I can with three poor men."

This farmer found it to his advantage not to have full-time men. He discovered that he could hire all the part-time help he wanted from neighboring small farms and among retired farmers. He prefers them to any other type of labor because he does not have to tell them how to do a job, and they appreciate working with big new equipment. They do a "first class job." He is not concerned about the quality of supply for agricultural labor. He said, "As we get more mechanized, we will need better labor, but we will be able to afford better people and they will be there. Good wages and good living draw better people."

Another farmer with much concern about labor hires 40 permanent employees and well over 100 seasonal workers. At one point he felt that the supply of good labor might diminish because of industrial competition, but on the contrary, supply has remained steady and has also improved in quality. He is only disturbed by the number of people who would rather draw unemployment relief than work. This tendency has reduced the supply of seasonal workers. "As we demand more skills, our quality of workers improves. There are people who definitely prefer farm work. What disturbs me most is that there are so many talented people who certainly are not well-motivated. They don't seem to care about improving themselves. We think that soon we will be going to two shifts because this will give us the advantage of using our machinery more, and it will be more attractive to the workers. Especially since so many are more concerned about hours than income."

A farmer who employs eight people has similar opinions about motivation. He is satisfied that most of his employees are more motivated by a "good time" than anything else. His men can run the farm one day at a time, but they do not have the ability to change the schedule in case of bad weather. There is one exception—one man who never has to be told what to do. "He is different. He has over $100,000 in cash investments and he has made it all working here. But he, like the others, does not want to change his role in life."

A farmer with a corn and hog operation employing three full-time workers expressed a similar view. He has one "20-year" man who is capable of doing everything on the farm and exhibits good judgment in routine jobs. But this man does not want responsibility to lead others and he does not want to think independently.

A professional farm manager who is responsible for 25 full-time employees and 10 full–crop-season workers has his biggest problem with secondary-management personnel. The top-management people are good and have tenure, but the field foremen, in his opinion, stay only long enough to get the experience and then go on to management positions because there are so many good opportunities in agriculture or in agri-business. He has no concern about the available supply of farm workers, but he thinks there is and will continue to be a shortage of top-notch management. This is caused by the fact that top-management people often start farming on their own.

A potato farmer has had two employees who have been with him from the day he started farming. They receive very little direction. During potato harvesting and processing season he has as many as 23 part-time employees. The one most recently recruited has been with him for 6 years and the oldest, 40 years. Nearly all those men are smaller farmers from the neighborhood and are in need of additional income. This farmer is a very precise manager and expects quality work from his employees. He said, "Cost of labor is not the important factor—it is the quality that counts."

A young farmer has as one of his employees a young man brought up in town whose life's ambition is to be a farm worker. "He likes to be outdoors. He likes being left alone. He does not like indoor work, but he is a trained mechanic and all winter long he gets the equipment in order. He is an excellent worker and is really dedicated to his job." This is important to this farmer because he has to leave his farm several days each month to take care of organizational and civic activities. His foreman has a separate place to live and gets a liberal bonus besides the usual fringe benefits. This farmer feels that although in the past being a farm worker carried a social stigma he now has noticed a decided improvement in that respect. He thinks better wages and the demand for greater skills have contributed to that change.

A grain farmer uses one full-time man for each 6,000 acres of land, but employs some day labor at planting and harvesting. His full-time employees are ex-farmers who quit farming for themselves because their farms were too small to make a living for the family. They earn more money by working for this farmer than they ever made on their own farms. In addition, they receive a bonus based on a formula of price times yield. This bonus has always been more than $1,200 a year.

This farmer, looking into the future, made the following comment: "We have gone to quality labor. We have had plenty of low-grade labor in the past and see our neighbors still hiring cheap labor, but that gets too expensive. People are coming back from California, and with our big equipment that requires intelligence to operate, we can get them to work for us. You can communicate easier with people like that, and they can work independently. We like top-quality men and like to pay them well."

Another farmer who is in a cash-grain and a beef-cow business hired a college graduate with a major in electrical engineering and considerable mechanical experience. He had been employed in California as an aircraft worker and had answered an ad because he wanted to get a job on a farm. This farm is over 60 miles from the nearest large town, and the farmer was concerned about the adjustment that the worker's family would have to make by living so far out in the country. But he noted that the family was determined. The engineer offered to go to work on an hourly basis. In his first year he spent 900 hours in the shop and 500 hours in the field. That year this farmer did not have a single case of downtime because of mechanical failure. He decided that hiring this man trained in engineering had been a good move; therefore, he put him on an annual pay basis. He thinks the quality and the supply of agricultural labor will get better. "The four-wheel-drive tractor attracts good men, and by using such tractors and keeping them in shape, we can pay well, but still keep our total labor bill low."

A farmer with diversified enterprises employs 35 men on a year-round basis. All are family men and most of them live in houses on the farms that this employer has purchased. In order to facilitate communication with the workers living in separate and scattered houses, he has 35 direct-line phones besides two-way radio units. "Even though we have easy communication, we make it a policy not to contact the men unless we need them. They know their responsibilities, and sometimes we may not see some of them for three or four weeks at a time." An old school bus is used on the farm to pick up the men who have to come to headquarters daily to do their work. Work schedules are such that the men all start and stop at the same time so that the bus can run efficiently.

This farmer spent 19 years living in a bunk house and those memories compel him to see to it that his employees live better. He is well aware that good living keeps the family happy and that helps keep a satisfied employee. "We have no trouble getting help. Our current employees are always getting their relatives or friends to apply for jobs, so they must think we are O.K."

He had only one complaint about his total labor-management situation. There was too much breakage, and he could not pinpoint who was responsible because the men blamed each other or no one knew how it happened. However, to his surprise, he has found that his employees are constantly coming up with good ideas about how to reduce cost and feels it definitely pays to take those suggestions.

A hog, beef, and corn producer has several men who work for him on a permanent basis, but none of them are full-time employees. One man specializes in corn production, another in the beef enterprise, and a third in the hog enterprise. The heaviest work load on this farm comes during the winter when four men are busy nearly full time. During the summer the employees alternate their shifts so that they can take turns helping other farmers or working for a canning factory in harvest work. "The men suggested this because it gives them variety and they all dislike a scheduled routine. I would put them on a full-time annual salary, but they want to do it this way, and I don't object as long as the work gets done on time."

A few successful large-scale farmers have sidestepped some labor-management problems by hiring custom operators to do part of the farm work. A large custom operator, who has made a business of operating entire farms or doing just specialized work, hires 8 year-round men and up to 17 seasonal men. He has a firm policy of not hiring any man who drinks. His motto is "patience," and apparently it works, for he has fired only 2 men in 15 years. This operator also makes it a practice of paying good bonuses based on performance and length of employment. Some years the bonuses have equalled 30 per cent of the established wages.

Another farm operator has 12 full-time men and 6 additional men during the seven-month crop year. Summer fallowing for moisture preservation and weed control is one of his biggest jobs in the summertime. He hires a custom operator to do the summer fallow work. The custom operator uses two of the farmer's four-wheel-drive tractors and cultivators, but he takes care of all the labor, fuel, and getting the job done at a fixed amount per acre. In this manner the farmer can concentrate on crop production and livestock, and two of his big tractors operate economically around the clock during much of the summer without distracting him. He finds this far more efficient than trying to dovetail critical work on summer fallow in with the haying and the grain harvesting.

A rancher, who needs only three full-time men for his cow operation, but who is so far from any town that he does not care to become involved with hiring seasonal workers who must be given room and board, hires a custom hay-making operator who uses the very largest equipment and does the job quickly and efficiently. This rancher realizes that by contracting with someone with large equipment, he can not only get his hay made more cheaply than he could with smaller, owned machinery, but he can also avoid any seasonal labor problems.

One reservation that many of the farmers interviewed had relative to the future of labor was the possibility of organized labor becoming a reality in farming. One diversified farmer who employs 9 full-time men and 30 seasonal workers had some definite ideas about that potential development. He said, "The development of mechanization, science, and technology is the farmers' key to labor costs. I am concerned about the power of organized labor limiting the productivity of our farm labor and lowering the incentive of the employees to perform well. This could also seriously inhibit the function of good management."

Most of the farmers who made comments about the possibility of organized labor entering the agricultural labor market were pragmatic, pointing out that in the long-run added costs are passed on to the consumer as they are in all other industries. They generally acknowledged that they would mechanize and automate more intensely to eliminate as much labor as possible. But none of them said that such a change would cause them to stop expansion. That point is highly significant because much evidence indicated that a major reason why many farmers do not expand is their reluctance to become involved with full-time labor.

It is apparent that in the future there will continue to be many small-scale farmers who will look to their neighboring large-scale farmers as an additional source of income. This will give the small-scale farmer the income he needs to support his family while his small farm enables him to lead the life style he wants. This pattern is so clearly established that even the most devoted disciple of "small-scale farming" cannot deny its existence. As quoted earlier in this chapter, a U.S.D.A. study of the 1930's showed that this trend was well-defined by then and has increased in scale. By 1971 over 80 per cent of all farmers holding an off-the-farm job besides running their own small farm considered their own farm as the secondary occupation. It is the acceptance of full-time, off-the-farm jobs by small farmers entering the labor market that has changed the socio-economic profile of the rural scene as much as the expanding commercial farmer who has merely assumed the land made available in the process.[3]

NOTES

[1]Yyjiro Hayami and Vernon W. Ruttan, "An International Comparison," *Technical Bull*. 227, University of Minnesota (1971), pp. 9, 16, 35; Ruben W. Hecht and Eugene G. McKibben, "Efficiency of Labor," *Yearbook of Agriculture, 1960: Power to Produce*, ed. Alfred Stefferud, Washington (1960), pp. 317, 319–326; Louis J. Ducoff, "Occupations and Levels of Living," *Yearbook of Agriculture, 1963: A Place to Live*, ed. Alfred Stefferud, Washington (1963), p. 20; Yyjiro Hayami and Vernon W. Ruttan, "Factor Prices and Technical Change in Agricultural Development: The United States and Japan, 1880–1960," *Journal of Political Economy*, 79, No. 5 (September–October, 1970), p. 1124; Conrad Taeuber, "Rural-Urban Migration," *Agricultural History*, XV, No. 3 (July, 1941), p. 159; John A. Hopkins, "Changing Technology and Employment in Agriculture," U.S.D.A. Bureau of Agricultural Economics (May, 1941), pp. 3, 33–34; "Farmers' Efficiency: The Sky's No Limit," *Agricultural Situation*, ed. Geraldine Schumacher, 56, No. 8 (September, 1972), p. 4; L. W. Schafner and Richard Arntson, "North Dakota Farm Labor Projections, 1975 ... 1980 ... 1985 ... ," *North Dakota Agri. Exp. Sta. Bull. Reprint*

720, Farm Research, 28, No. 3 (January–February, 1971), p. 38; *U.S. News & World Report*, LXX, No. 5 (July 31, 1972), p. 81; "Economic Class of Farm," *United States Census of Agriculture*, A3, Vol. II (1959), p. 1200; A. Gordon Ball, "How Much Do Farmers Want to Expand?" *Iowa Farm Science*, 25 (November–December, 1970), 3-687 to 4-6888; "The Daylighters," *Agricultural Situation*, ed. Geraldine Schumacher, 57, No. 6 (July, 1973), p. 12; anonymous interviews (see footnote on first page of chapter).

²Anonymous interviews (see footnote on first page of chapter).

³Anonymous interviews (see footnote on first page of chapter).

CHAPTER VIII

Some Rewards of Farming*

A 1973 U.S.D.A. STUDY concluded that the average farm family needed $10,786 for living expenditures. At a time when the census figures reveal that about 1,400,000 farmers gross less than $10,000 a year, it is quite obvious that the small farmer is either living in poverty or has a second source of income. Fortunately, most small farmers have worked themselves into the latter category, as was evident from the facts presented in the chapter on farm labor. Unless a farm is operated by the family alone, the gross agricultural receipts would have to be at least $40,000 to yield approximately $10,000 a year net income at above-average prices. This means even fewer farms are actually large enough to produce a good family income unless subsidized by non-farm earnings.

Each year, the gross income required to support a family must necessarily increase because the long-term trend has been for decreasing operating margins in farming. In the 1940's operating costs were less than 50 per cent of gross income, but by the 1970's they had climbed to nearly 85 per cent of gross income.** Increased volume has been the farmer's basic way of meeting rising costs; therefore, he has had to expand either in acres or in yields each year to maintain his standard of living. From 1944 to 1959, farmers had to double their cash sales to maintain their net, and the rate of growth required after 1959 is even greater. Farm size has not increased fast enough since 1944 to give the farmer the

---

*Inflation increased the farm operating costs, but by contrast at the same time the abundance of farm goods tended to keep farm product prices down. This contributes to a cost–price squeeze.

**Because of the sensitive nature of the material in this chapter, the names of farmers, their wives, or employees are not used. This was the agreement with these individuals at the time of interview. However, all documentation is on file with the author.

necessary volume, so this has been compensated by off-the-farm jobs. Labor income increased most rapidly on the farms with the greatest amount of mechanization because machines were the major cause for labor productivity.

A study of South Dakota farms in the late 1960's indicated that the total costs per acre on a 1,280-acre farm were only two-thirds as much as on a 320-acre farm. Although per-acre costs did not drop much after that level, total net profits continued to get larger because of the greater number of acres involved. More recent studies have determined that volume buying and selling gave increased margins up to $20.00 per acre for 5,000-acre corn farms. Russell L. Berry of South Dakota State University concluded that if all South Dakota farms in 1970 had been organized along the lines of the most efficient farms of 1959, the number of farms could drop to one-third or less of their 1959 number and there would be no loss in production. The study assumed that under the realignment, 20 per cent less labor would be needed.

A constant complaint throughout the history of agriculture has been that farmers have not been able to make a living. Lack of productivity and volume have generally been the culprits. Unfortunately, too many farmers, aided by some politicians and farm organization leaders, have overlooked basic economic facts in attempting to find other reasons for those problems. The dialogue has been endless, but the important fact is that the American agricultural base has been overexpanded with too many small units and the cost of readjustment has presented a major social problem. The process is not yet complete, although many have suffered the personal and social pains of readjustment.*

All the farmers interviewed for this study were asked: "Have you had a fair return on your investment and time in your farming career?" Not one farmer encountered answered this question in a negative manner. Some admitted that maybe they were not well paid for both their investment and their time, but they found many other compensations which gave them satisfactions that could not be found elsewhere. A very large portion of these farmers gave precise financial figures of their progress and, in general, the results were exceedingly satisfactory. Some had experienced rever-

---

*Because it was easy to acquire title to land in the past, many supposed home-steaders were really land speculators. In addition, there were many who desired to be farmers, but they also realized that considerable profits might accrue through land ownership.

sals that made their progress less dramatic; but not one farmer indicated any sense of regret, for financial reasons or otherwise, that he had chosen farming as his profession.

These comments are quite different from other inquiries or discussions about impoverished or embattled farmers. However, this study made no effort to seek information from the average farmers in general, but only from the most successful operators, for these are the people who lead the way to a better future. That does not mean to imply that the farmers in this study have had a steady history of success. Most of them realized that frequently their greatest adversities provided them with challenges that had to be overcome, and this, in turn, led to eventual success.

Most of these farmers, obviously interested in a profit and in a high standard of living, also had many other compensations from farming that they felt added to the total rewards they received.

A farmer of the fourth generation, living in the house his great-grandfather had built nearly a century earlier, had made a thorough study of his family farm. Explaining those records he said:

The farm's long-run returns are an interesting contradiction, for the land is not supposed to be a growth investment, but our farm has had nearly a steady growth value, plus has paid profits in all but a few years. Looking back in our 100 years of farming, the technological revolution of the immediate past has given returns far beyond the fondest dreams. I believe the future is even brighter because of what technology is doing for us.

A third generation farmer, with children ready to step into farming, assessed what farming had done for his family in this manner:

It has paid well, but at the same time, it has been so enjoyable. It's rewarding because it is so basic. Banking and the stock market have also been profitable, but not nearly as much fun as farming. Our real profit comes from the cost accounting which flushes out the less profitable enterprises. Farming is such an effective background and opens so many opportunities.

This concept represents the kind of thinking so necessary in the new era of industrialized agriculture. A positive point of view toward farming as a business, as well as viewing it as a real preparation for a great variety of other activities, is a complete reversal from the historic position of many farmers, who believed that if a person couldn't succeed at anything else, he could always make it in farming.

Nearly all the farmers involved in this study were sons of farmers, some from financially successful families, but many of them from families who were making a marginal living or less from the farm.

One ambitious farmer grew up on a small, family farm, and by the time he was 18, he wanted to start farming on his own. He had almost no help from his family to get started. He said:

There isn't anything I can think of that I could have done as well as farming, even though I started on my own in 1929. In the 1930's we didn't pay taxes for six years although we did keep most of our bills current. We just had to ignore taxes and long-term debts. Saving our assets was all we could be concerned about. What helped me was the courage to build inventory during those times; so when the tremendous improvement in prices came, we were able to capitalize on that. By 1946 I was able to pay cash for 3,300 acres because we "hung tough" during the lean years, and when World War II came, everything was ripe to boom. We have not stopped since. Today we split our income four ways and are able to generate all the expansion capital we need right from the farm.

Another very innovative farmer started farming at the age of 21 with $1,000, a rented farm, and the loan of some of his father's machinery. After 13 seasons, he had $24,000 in certificates of deposit and an excellent new house completely paid for. He said, "We associate with many professional people, and I know we not only live as well as any of them, but we also have a better net worth. Neither of us knows of anyone we went to school with [including college] who is doing any better financially." At the time of interview, this couple had been farming 20 years and were widely known in their community because both were active in many church and civic functions.

A very determined farmer, who had done odd jobs before becoming a farmer's hired man, realized at age 31 that he would never get ahead if he didn't break the ice and start farming on his own. "I didn't have enough money to live on that first year I farmed in 1959. I had to keep a full-time job to put bread on the table for the family. Now, I look back at those 13 years and wonder how it was possible to generate the capital so rapidly."

One farmer, who grew up under the guidance of an innovative father, enjoyed farming because he could experiment with everything from cattle and irrigation to flowers and raising potatoes and wheat. He was an associate in the development of several strains of new seeds, and for many years was a foundation seed producer. He said, "I doubt that I could have made a million dollars easier in any other business. But more important, I am sure there is nothing I would have preferred to do but farm. I could not have been happier."

With more than 40 years of farming as part of his history, another farmer, who started with no funds and no family help, was still in love with farming. When he was asked about his profits, he laughed, because he thought of those who called him a fool for wanting to farm. "Today, none of those people are around, but I know of no one at my age with a limited education who has done as well. Farming was a love to me, and I never have regretted being a farmer. My only regret is that I did not have a college education. It would not have changed anything, but it is one thing I wanted to do that I did not do."

This farmer started with nothing but his love of farming and operated on a very conservative basis throughout his 40 active years. He has suffered losses, but in his last 25 years he has always had enough cash reserve for two full years of operating expenses.

An active community leader who is involved in a diversified farm and in some agri-businesses made the following assessment of 35 years of farming: "I don't think anything could have done more for us than farming. After farming a few years, I decided to go to college. I was in my late twenties and was really serious about trying something else. One year in college made it clear to me that all I really wanted to do was to farm. From that point on, nothing stopped me. We have never had a year with an operating loss, although I have operated too conservatively."

Both the husband and wife laughed at that comment because they had lived well, educated a family, and had built a "very fine estate." He remembered that earlier he had said that growth was a "condition of attitude because some people are less content and just push harder."

An energetic young farm couple in their sixth year of the business had some very definite feelings about the rewards of farming. She said, "In farming you are forced to conserve in order to generate capital for the business. I think this has been a major factor in our getting ahead. We don't know anyone of our age who has progressed as much as we have. We know that some of them are living right up to their earnings."

A fourth generation farmer in his early thirties had used the computer to determine whether or not he should buy more land. The land he was operating had been in the family for 90 years. He was drawing $20,000 from the farm for personal living expenses besides enjoying several attractive fringe benefits. He had computed back 5 years' net operating income and had projected that at 5 per cent interest it would take 72 years to pay for any additional land purchased. But he still thought land was a good investment because he could buy and operate a considerable additional amount without having to purchase more machinery or hire extra labor. He was well aware that his cost would not increase in direct relation to the increase in acres. What disturbed him most was the fact that land like what his great-grandfather had purchased for $1.25 to $2.00 an acre was now commanding $800 or more.

A farmer of the second generation, only a few years from retirement, felt much more positively about the rewards of farming and was encouraging his sons to go ahead. He remembered his father's struggles and his own during their years of partnership in the late 1930's and early 1940's. He is now well aware of what technology has done for their family farm. His records showed him that after drawing all the money they wanted for living, education, travel, and personal investments in the form of management payments, the farm was returning 3.5 per cent on current market values. The 3.5 per cent return in dollars was four times what the land had cost his father.

He was amazed at what had happened to land values in the years that he had farmed, and he felt that the price of land could possibly be an obstacle to future expansion for his sons. "But whenever a quarter section comes for sale, if it's what we can use, we will buy it at any price. Farming has been good to us. Besides, it's what I wanted to do."

A third generation farmer with a college degree, who had farmed for 11 years in partnership with his father, felt that a farmer carried considerably more responsibility per dollar of net income than most people in administration in industry. While in college he had considered going to medical school, but after graduation he started farming and decided he preferred that life. His reason— "Challenge is the secret."

Another farmer who did not mind challenge started on $300 of borrowed money. He shared machinery with his father and used credit to operate during his first year. Thirty years later he was farming 13 sections of land, owned a large industrial firm in another state, and was a major stockholder in a bank that he had helped to establish. Looking back over those 30 years and assessing his position, he was not sure he could have done as well financially in any other business. For a real challenge he would have liked to have gained a management position in a large firm, but that probably would not have left him enough time for political and farm organizational activities. His parting thought—"Farming has definitely been good to me."

Eighteen years after starting to farm with the use of machinery from home, a farmer with precise records could prove a 13 per cent return on his investment, after deducting substantial management income for himself. He qualified his answer about the rewards from farming by adding that the 13 per cent figure was not his but that of the Production Credit Association, where he received his financing. It was his opinion that he would have to draw a $50,000 salary in industry to match the financial rewards he received from farming. His parting comment on that was "But then I would not have the freedom or life style that we are enjoying out here."

A former school teacher agreed with the above comment. He and his wife both had taught school, but after a few years decided that although teaching was a life relatively free from worry with pleasant social benefits it was not for them. Their first few years of farming were hard, and the days were never long enough. "Then it seemed like we were over the hump, and it has been an endless joy ever since. There is no comparison."[1]

Rewards That Fit the Personality

When asked if they had received a fair return on their time and investment, it became clear that these individuals had strong personalities, for they had definite ideas about what they wanted from life and what they were prepared to put into life. Few of them had the type of personality that would have made them good followers. They wanted to lead, and they wanted the freedom to act.

A Minnesota farmer with a college degree and with 16 years of farming experience answered the questions on returns for time and investment as follows:

The cash return is not as important as many outsiders might think. The satisfaction received from what you are doing is really the big reward. We have run up and down the profit ladder. Every time after we have expanded, we have hit new lows. This seems to be a continual problem of management.

There may be better dollar returns in other industries, but, frankly, I do not know which ones they are. We started with almost nothing, have suffered some real losses, but still we have lived well and have built a good net worth at the same time. The real satisfaction is creating a large portion of your own expansion capital from operating profits.

But that is all incidental to the fact that neither my wife nor I would want to be doing anything else. Besides making an excellent living, we can see that we are doing a lot of good in our community.

Most farmers acknowledged that the appreciation of land value helped to create a larger net worth than could be obtained from operating profits alone. Generally, operating profits made up one-half to two-thirds of the total increase in net gain. However, many of them, as has been historically true, were generating a great deal of their expansion capital from within the business. Some of the farmers of this study with the best net operating profits were very large renters.

One such farmer, who is widely known for his precise management techniques, rents three-fourths of the land that he farms. After 30 years of farming in this manner, he had doubled his net worth every 6 years. When he had completed 35 years of farming, he said the rate of growth had slowed, but the actual growth in net worth was larger each year than in previous years. "Very little of my net worth comes from appreciation. Most of my increase comes directly from management returns. I am not at all unhappy with farming. Besides, I know that with my temperament it is unlikely that I could have done this well elsewhere."

Thirty years after starting to farm on a rented 160 acres, an innovative farmer owned 5,400 out of 7,900 acres that he farmed. He had definite ideas about the profits derived from farming. In his third year of farming he asked his father to join him in a partnership livestock operation. His father declined because he did not want to risk a loss. This young farmer went ahead on his own and "hit the market just right." From that point on he would not slow down. He said of his overall returns:

I have made some money by appreciation and much from management. So far my management profits have been taxed as income, and the appreciation profits are there to be taxed in my estate distribution.

For today the big thing is operating profits. My banker knows that ours have increased steadily over the years. That's what he is interested in, and I keep expanding because we both know too many farmers are fooling themselves by relying on appreciation profits only.

The really important concern is that a man has to do his thing. Sometimes I have thought that road construction would have been as exciting, risky, and profitable, but farming has been very rewarding to me.

I could not do near the civic and political work I am doing if I did not have the freedom that comes from having a large farm that functions even if I am gone weeks at a time.

A former teacher, who started farming in 1960 because he was looking for a greater challenge, gave a good view of what he had sought and had found in farming.

When I use cold figures, it sometimes seems that we have really not had a good return. But when I compare with college classmates of mine who are in the professions, I'm sure we have done as well as any. The family life, the freedom, and the personal satisfaction are the greatest rewards I can name.

Maybe I have been lucky, but from what I can see, I would not care to trade places with anyone I know—except maybe a few fellow farmers.

This farmer was a very thoughtful individual who had a broad understanding of the values in life. Maybe that is part of what makes him such an outstanding farmer. He has the ability to look beyond the furrow.

A farmer, who farms in more than one state, expresses his feelings about the rewards of farming in a very precise way. With his wife in full agreement, he answered:

Definitely! I have the best occupation there is. I have never considered another occupation. In 1946 when I graduated from high school, I took a warehouse job in Minneapolis, and I got my belly full of city life. That lasted three months and I believe that was a major turning point in my life. I know I could have been successful in other things, but I doubt that I could have done as well financially or lived as well as we have.

A cash-grain farmer explains his opinion as follows:

I am better off than any of the people in the nearby towns. I don't care who they are. Besides, I have complete freedom and a life in the country. The big satisfaction is seeing the family completely involved in the operation—that is rewarding. The only person I could even imagine trading positions with is the man right across the road.

What I can't understand is how these little operators think they are supposed to make it. We have seen our efficiencies continue to improve as we expand, and I feel we have to be this size for sound economics. That just makes business sense.

This farmer lives 65 miles from quite a large town and has only a few small service towns closer. His business contacts, developed through his farming operation, are spread out over 1,000 miles. At his chief business center, 400 miles from his farm, he is involved with an agri-business firm that furnishes him with most of his machinery.

Because of their educational backgrounds, economic ability, and natural aggressiveness, a large portion of the farmers interviewed had regular business and social contacts with big business executives and professional people. It is only natural that this should happen, but it is interesting that several farmers made direct references comparing their life style and financial rewards with those of their acquaintances.

A farmer with a multiple of enterprises had some very positive feelings about such comparisons in regard to life style. He said:

There is nothing that I could have undertaken after graduation from college [1949] that could have put me into the position I am now. It is my feeling that the executives I know in town who live in big fancy houses never get much farther than making house payments and country club dues. We have a better life than most of the professional and executive people we know of. I think that many of us large farmers are doing much better than a big share of rural bankers like to think we are doing. They don't seem to want to believe that farmers can make and build the net assets we have.

Another farmer backed the sentiments expressed above:

We have not only had excellent financial rewards, but a great life. I had never given farming much consideration until I got out of service after World War II, because I had always wanted to go into medicine or finance, but I decided to go farming. There are few people I know who are as well off financially and have had as much fun as we. My farming interests bring me in contact with a large number of executives for big corporations, and I know our life is freer and more pleasant than theirs.

This farmer also sits on several business boards, including the board for one of the nation's largest banking chains. He travels extensively for business purposes and has regular meetings on both coasts.

A farmer, who has many professional friends, thinks that the biggest trouble many of them have is "when it comes to business, they get lost in some little tangent." Maybe what he was trying to say is that some people have good business judgment (often called "seat of the pants"), while others get hung up in theory or detail. Most of the farmers involved in this study had the desire and the ability to make big decisions within short time periods. The details were worked out by them later.

Farming under the free enterprise system was never intended to be a risk-free business. In fact, it became quite evident in this research that many of the men involved were just as challenged by the risk aspect as they were by any of the potential rewards.

A farmer, who was inclined to be a speculator, noted that on paper it was sometimes difficult to show that there were adequate monetary rewards in farming. But he admitted that he had started with nothing, and after 30 years had net assets in the seven-digit bracket. He also admitted that there were times when he almost lost his nerve and thought he had overextended himself. He freely admitted that he liked the speculative nature of farming and that farming itself lost some of its appeal when he reached his boyhood goal of 35,000 acres. He thinks maybe road or dam construction would have been as exciting.

A farmer with a diversified operation, who does not consider himself a speculator, but who has encountered heavy losses that have hurt his net returns over 27 years of farming, said, "I have had four sizeable losses: one in turkeys, one in sheep, and two in cattle. It seems that the losses compound themselves, and it takes about three good years to repay a bad one. That means I have spent half of my time in the farming career recovering at the banks."

He also acknowledged that he had started with only minor help from home and that he did not know another person of his high school era who was as well off as he. He is highly respected by his peers, who have all suffered the pangs of adversity, but he knows there can be no success without some failure.

A farmer with cash-grain, hog, and beef–brood-cow operations has done well, but not without a few reversals. "We have had some tough years, but this is what makes it fun. We have even been forced to sell calves in early summer to save our feed for the cow herd. That same year our wheat averaged 3 bushels an acre. Those are the chances you take in any business. We like the challenge of it."

It appears to this writer that most of the farmers involved in this study felt that something would be wrong if all went well, for they are psychologically prepared for reversals. This sentiment was especially true of the farmers of the Dakotas and Montana, where weather is somewhat more variable. This does not mean to imply that they have the typical drought or depression syndrome, for they do not. They are more realistic.

Not one farmer was able to say that every year had been a profitable one. Most of them had experienced at least two serious losses, either because of crop failure or a price disaster. The interesting aspect which evolved from the interviews was that every farmer and/or his wife could enumerate the years of calamity, and with no little pride was able to relate how they had been put to the test and had bounced back. Farmers in their mid-forties and older, who had a good equity position, were very philosophical about setbacks of one kind or another. Most of them had learned their lessons well and knew how to soften the blows.

An interesting sidelight to the profit potential in agriculture came from farmers who said they were well pleased with their returns from farming, but that they had experienced serious losses in non-farm businesses. One farmer, who had suffered more than one such loss, grinned and said, "I guess you can't blame farming for that." Most of these non-farm enterprises were tried because these farmers had risk funds available and they were willing to take a chance.

Another farmer with very precise records said that he had never made an expansion on his farm that did not bring a 10 per cent return on investment. He was able to prove that in the 30 years prior to interview in 1972 his farm operating income produced an average 18 per cent return on total investments. No appreciation was figured in the total, and no interest was involved because there was no indebtedness. Similar statements were made by other farmers.

One young farmer, who owned a third of all the land he farmed, had operated three years with only moderate success, but when he was able to rent a large block of land, his situation improved. "That did the trick and I really made profits. My net assets increased from $35,000 to $430,000 in the next five years." The irony was that the block of land he rented belonged to a young farmer who quit because he decided farming didn't have enough to offer.

One concern of many farmers was that they were not using their equity to the fullest advantage, but they understood that heavy borrowing was no good unless it could produce operating profits. A farmer, who knew how to use financial leverage and who created three diverse enterprises to reduce his risk, gave this account of his success:

My initial goal was to be an accountant, but I got sidetracked into farming and that was a lucky break. In 1950 I had a net farm income of $2,600, which had to cover family living and have something left over for going into the next year. Just a little over 20 years later, by the use of equity and good financial planning, my net worth is figured in seven digits. The whole family is wrapped up in what we are doing, and that is a big thrill.

It has not been all easy because I have had 4 years of almost total crop loss on my home farm. But there have been other years when we have paid well over $100,000 in income taxes. It's just the way the breaks go, but we have faith that this is what we are supposed to be doing.

The previous comments about rewards of farming are from highly successful farmers. What they have to say about it is certainly not what a large majority of farmers might have to say. The remarks of successful farmers have stressed financial returns. This points out that well-managed farming can be a profitable business. It also clearly points out that although profitable, farming is risky, but so are all other businesses in the free enterprise system. The risk is one of the very obvious challenges that one has to take to be successful, and every year the "Outstanding Young Farmer" contests and awards are proof that young people can start farming and make it a success.[2]

NOTES

[1]"Farm Living Expenditures Averaged Nearly $11,000 in 1973," *Gopher State Review*, Minnesota Crop and Livestock Reporting Service, Bulletin 330 (May, 1975); Jackson W. McElveen, "Farm Numbers, Farm Size, and Farm Income," *American Journal of Agricultural Economics*, XLV (February, 1963), pp. 4–9; Russell L. Berry, "Family Farms: Will They Be Replaced by Large-Scale or Factory Farms?," Manuscript, South Dakota State University, Brookings (October 2, 1970); Russell L. Berry, "Factory Farms in the Corn Belt: Are They Feasible Today?," Manuscript, South Dakota University, Brookings (December 16, 1970); Russell L. Berry, "Economics of Size of Farm Plants and Firms," South Dakota Agricultural Experiment Station, Brookings (December 28, 1970).

[2]Anonymous interviews (see footnote on first page of chapter).

CHAPTER IX

Buying and Marketing Practices
of Successful Farmers*

In a previous chapter on labor relations and conditions it was pointed out that the actual employment on agricultural land has been reduced to less than 4 per cent of the total American labor force. However, when agriculture is considered from the aspect of the total national food and fiber production and processing system, it still employs 16.5 million persons, or nearly 20 per cent of the total work force. This is exclusive of those persons involved in implement and facility manufacturing and distribution for agriculture.

Agriculture is no longer totally farm-oriented. The modern farmer relies on the technical, commercial, input, and market sectors to help him get the job done. Sixty-five to 85 per cent of the farmer's cost of production ($64.5 billion in 1973) is spent for purchases from suppliers and the marketing sector. The farmer generally receives about 30 to 40 per cent of the consumer's cost of food. Labor, marketing, processing, and transportation account for the rest of the food dollar. The farmer's actual contribution, after the value of input and marketing has been deducted, is a small fraction of the total food and fiber cost. The total output value of the combined industry in 1973 was $230 billion.

The massive and rapidly growing complex of agri-business is the farmer's backup force in the food and fiber production system. Presently, we have 1,500 firms manufacturing farm machinery and equipment in the nation. In addition, we have 5,000 retail fertilizer outlets, 13,000 feed manufacturing firms, and 32,000 small

---

*Because of the sensitive nature of the material in this chapter, the names of farmers, their wives, or employees are not used. This was the agreement with these individuals at the time of interview. However, all documentation is on file with the author.

management and technical firms; and huge segments of the transportation, petroleum, chemical, finance, milling, packing, canning, clothing, and other industries depend upon agriculture for a large portion of their business. Accordingly, farmers are only a portion of the large food and fiber industry.

It is no secret that a great many American farmers have been excellent producers, but poor purchasers, and even worse as marketers. Farm magazines, farm management people, and agricultural extension people have constantly reminded farmers not to overlook favorable opportunities in purchasing and marketing. Farm organizations have made many attempts to awaken the farmer to this aspect. Popular pressure has even been strong enough to get legislation favorable to this phase of farming. But it appears that the majority of the farmers have tended to avoid innovative buying and marketing techniques as if they were a plague. It is not all their fault, for in the past most farms were so small that their volume of business could not expect any special consideration.

In the competitive free enterprise system, the volume account usually has a distinct advantage in both buying and selling, for it takes no more effort to deal with a large volume operator than it does with the smallest producer. Everybody from the feed merchant to the machinery dealer, the fuel and seed supplier, the banker, the miller, the packer, and others acts accordingly.

In 1884 a college professor traveling through the Red River Valley with its bonanza farms wrote: "There is [much] complaint about the great farms because they buy altogether at wholesale. . . ." People of that time lamented the bonanza farms, because if the land had been subdivided, there would have been justification for the existence of more towns. In other words, it was popularly believed that farms should exist in order to support town businesses. Since then, much of rural America has paid the price for such thinking. The author of the previous article did acknowledge that people were drawn to the Valley from all over the world to see the drama and efficiency of the factory farms.

The bonanza farms had machinery, horses, lumber, twine, and other supplies shipped in by the carloads. Local dealers were bypassed in both the buying and the selling process, and wholesale discounts and smaller marketing costs were often the margin of profit.*

---

*See *The Day of the Bonanza* for a detailed account of the buying and marketing practices of large bonanzas of the 1870's through the 1920's.

David Askegaard of Comstock, Minnesota, like most bonanza farmers, had his own store, machinery agency, elevator, and bank. The bonanza farm of the Amenia and Sharon Land Company of North Dakota had 33 non-farm subsidiary agencies created to bypass normal retail channels and to serve the farm. Direct buying and discount buying by individual farmers doing a large volume of business are not entirely new in the picture of agriculture.

Buying

The following responses give a good account of the "what's" and "why's" in large-farming buying practices.

A very innovative farmer, who has been volume buying most inputs since the late 1950's and early '60's, initially met with a great deal of resistance because many companies did not want to break up their normal marketing channels. But he persisted, and once he got some companies to sell to him at wholesale, others followed. Today, he calls for bids directly from the distributors and gets nearly all his materials at wholesale in semi or carload lots. The only exception is machinery. He has his own shop and does all his overhauling, but he has found that he still needs help from dealers occasionally and prefers not to bypass them.

All interviewees were asked, "Are you involved in any form of group buying or marketing? If not, how do you buy and market?" Only a limited number of farmers involved were actually in some form of a buying pool. It is understandable that in nearly all cases those interviewees who were involved in such pools and their associates were among the larger farmers in the area, so that when they pooled, they had real buying clout.

A farmer, who has been involved in test plots for fertilizer and seeds on his farm since the year he graduated from college, commented on the value of those plots. Because his farm plots received much publicity, chemical and fertilizer companies suggested that he become involved in group purchasing. He pooled with six of his fellow farmers, who were already associated with him in a processing facility, and they became direct buyers from the producing companies. The arrangement, which had been in existence for nearly 20 years at the time of interview, proved to be very satisfactory.

Another farmer teamed up with several of his larger farm neighbors for purchases of fertilizer and chemicals. He also tried to get several small farmers to join with him, but they all felt that the amount they purchased was too small to make much difference in price. Others just did not want to join them because they thought it would be extra work, or they needed their retailer to supply them with credit.

This farmer also found out that if the members of his group bought their own chemical sprayer, bulk handling and fertilizer spreading equipment, they could pay for their equipment out of their savings. The total volume of their purchases exceeded that of a retail cooperative from whom they formerly had purchased their supplies. It took some additional management to operate the spraying and spreading equipment, but the arragement was profitable and satisfactory. In this particular case the farmer was actually managing the pool at no return to himself other than the savings on his purchase price of chemicals and fertilizer. All the farmers in the pool produced the same crops, which made buying and bookkeeping a rather simple procedure.

An interesting experience in regard to buying on a large scale was reported by a farmer who needed a better feed storage and processing unit on his place to take care of his livestock enterprise. He decided to build an elevator where he could buy and store the extra feed he needed from cash-grain farmers. That elevator would also help him get better discounts on commercial feed, seed, fertilizer, and even short-line machinery. As an excellent farm manager, using those abilities in his elevator business, he soon had the neighbors coming to him, and he found himself with a far larger business venture than he had intended to develop.

The U.S.D.A. study of the early 1970's by Kenneth R. Krause and Leonard R. Kyle established that although larger farms tend to pay higher labor and management rates, their operating costs are lower because they use larger equipment and have substantial discounts on their purchased inputs. They determined that buying discounts are a major factor in the economy of large farm operations. The large, corn farms received discounts that averaged from 12 to 42 per cent less than the retail price for all inputs such as seed, chemicals, fuels, and equipment. The study indicated that many of the larger farms had their own dealerships, but it also noted that full buying leverage was not always used "if such efforts might contribute to an adverse local image."

Of the large farmers interviewed for this study, 189 farmers, or 88 per cent, had some non-farm enterprise in addition to their farming business. In most cases these enterprises were directly complementary to farming, although some were purely investments. Several farms had more than one such enterprise; some had as many as four, such as elevators, fertilizer plants, gasoline service dealerships, banks, specialty crops, processing plants, truck lines, and even a packing plant. One such farm had the largest farm machinery dealership for a major line in a five-state area. Just as in the U.S.D.A. study, our study showed that many farmers do not take full advantage of their buying power because they are often concerned about local resentment.

Ironically, many farmers did not bother to establish agencies for buying their inputs because they discovered that they had enough buying power to get the discounts they wanted without having the headaches that go with owning retail businesses. One farm placed a single order of $735,530 for trucks for use in its multi-enterprise operation. A few of these trucks were over-the-road vehicles, but most were tandem axle trucks for field work.

Another farmer with a payroll of about $750,000 was able to purchase tires for less cost than the largest dealer in his city as long as he stocked a minimum of 460 truck and tractor tires. By bidding for total coverage insurance on all of his enterprises, he saved $23,000 from his previous year's payment. He had a one-time storage capacity of 70,000 gallons, and he purchased all his fuel, fertilizer, chemicals, and tires directly from the processor. In early 1974, when the fuel crisis was very much on everyone's mind, he received bids that varied as much as six cents a gallon on diesel fuel.

A farmer made direct contact with the main offices of large agri-business firms and then called for bids on all his inputs. There was some initial resistance from a few companies, but when they realized how large the total volume to be purchased was, they submitted bids. As a result, he was buying at dealer cost or less. Because of some unique contacts, he was even able to purchase machinery at 10 per cent under dealer cost.*

One farmer had a policy not to receive salesmen unless they had been called or had made a specific appointment. He realized that there could be resentment to his buying practices in his neighborhood, but he responded to this resentment by declaring, "What they forget is that we give full-time employment to 25 family men and hire another 20 seasonal workers who are chiefly small farm operators. Besides, we are producing food cheaper than the small

---

*The U.S.D.A. study determined this to be the case among several of the farmers they investigated.

farmers who do not have enough income to support their families nor any type of business."

A farmer who kept precise records became involved in auxiliary enterprises when he realized that one of the biggest disadvantages he had as a large-scale farmer was the size of the burden of his income taxes. His farm was debt-free and his profit margin was good, so the government received more of his net income than he did. He determined that he should set up auxiliary enterprises and charge the farm full price for everything it purchased from those enterprises. His elevator, which is jointly owned by five farmers, works the same way, and these farmers receive no more for their products than any other farmer who sells to it. The auxiliaries operate independently of each other and are separately much smaller than the farm. This makes the tax rate considerably lower than the rate for his farm.

This farmer realizes that taxes cannot be avoided, but by postponement of the payment of taxes, he can use this money for expansion. On the other hand, it creates an even larger estate, which compounds his estate tax problem. His final comment was "It proves that there are three things we can count on—change, death, and taxes. Because I am an innovator, I am being taxed for it; taxed for making more money than the one who refuses to change and is not making a profit."*

Another farmer remembers that his father never paid the retail price for most of his purchased inputs. So when he started farming, he adhered to a similar policy with his auxiliary enterprises. He has a spraying service, several elevators, a hardware store, a lumber yard, trucking auxiliaries, and a full-service shop, all of which service the farm at cost. A distributor truck makes two stops weekly to deliver parts for his farm shop, in which all machinery is "gone over" each winter.

When he wants to purchase new machinery, he calls for written bids. "Low bidder gets the business because I will not bargain; that is not my nature." He operates 12 tractors, 7 pickups, 4 large farm trucks, 2 airplanes, as well as personal vehicles, and he pays cash for them the day the purchase is made.

A young farmer had the volume to buy most of his inputs at discount from wholesalers, but the manager of a combined imple-

---

*Krause and Kyle stated that as the farmer's equity increases, income taxes tend to work against the larger farmer. To minimize the high tax payment, some farmers compensate by continuing to expand.

ment, service station, and garage did not want to lose his account. So the manager offered to sell all products that this farmer needed on a very small markup over invoice price. In return, the farmer could depend upon this firm for complete service work on his equipment. This farmer felt that this deal enabled him to avoid the cost of building, furnishing, and stocking a shop, plus the cost of at least one full-time mechanic. He felt he could profit more by using his cash flow to rent additional land and to expand his crop operation. He profited by that method and found other work to keep his permanent men busy during the non-crop season.

A farmer with two widely separated farms avoids building a shop because he would need two complete shops to make himself independent of local servicemen. To solve the problem, he has a complete mobile field unit for on-the-spot repairs and a garage that does all of his major overhaul work. He buys gas, fertilizers, and chemicals for less than what the local dealer has to pay. "I buy my fuel six-tenths of a cent less than the local dealer does. I always get full transport loads at each place. I pay cash and the dealer gets 30 days credit. That must account for the difference in price."

A farmer, who purchased an elevator so he could both buy and sell direct, handles seeds, chemicals, fertilizers, fuel, feeds, and machinery short lines. He discovered that about the only benefit coming to him from owning the business was the convenience of having trackside storage and screenings from a larger volume of grain for his feedlot. "We are not selling our grain any better nor buying our supplies any cheaper with the elevator than we were before. We were getting all the discounts without the extra investment." He told us that the government storage program had made the elevator very profitable, so he had no regrets. He neither encouraged nor discouraged business with the public, because the chief function of his elevator was to serve the farm.

A farmer with land in three states questioned the wisdom of getting too involved with retail enterprises because their operation means additional costs as well as greater demands on management. He owns an elevator, but he found that he could neither buy nor sell through it any better than he could through his farm office. Although he has 675,000 bushels of storage on his land, he found that there is a definite advantage in having trackside storage. He was not interested in promoting his elevator business because doing business with the public forced the cost of the elevator up more than it returned.

He also trades all major equipment before the warranty expires. His policy is to buy and trade four units at a time. This is all done by bids, with the understanding that he expects full service from the dealers. He has a farm shop, but he is not entirely comfortable in relying on it for all servicing. "I am in an area of large farms, so dealers are not overly impressed by our volume, but they promote the sale of good big used equipment to small farmers in other areas. This makes it possible to do a good job of trading."

Another farmer has had his own elevators and stockyard on trackside for about 30 years. He buys and sells by carload lots. At times, he has actually sold in trainload shipments. He does not buy fuel direct because he gets a "very good" price from his local dealer who delivers to several storage locations and to his pickup supply tanks and equipment in the field. If it were not for that service, he would need his own fuel truck as well as one full-time man to deliver fuel from his central location. The savings derived would not offset the cost of the service he gets now. They use over 100,000 gallons of fuel each year.

This farmer has a machinery cost of $2.80 per acre per year (1969–1971 figures). He owns 39 tractors and could buy direct from the dealer at the dealer's cost. The farm has a four-stall shop, but he does not want to lose contact with dealer service and the good will of the dealer, so most of the machinery is bought on bids. "You have to pay the piper sometime because nothing is free, and this has worked the best for me in the last 30 years."

A farmer always looking for challenges started a commercial fertilizer business and then became involved in farming. When he proved to himself that he not only liked farming better, but also that it was more profitable, he sold his fertilizer business. However, he retained the right to buy at wholesale in his contract of sale. As his farm grew in size, he discovered he could buy fertilizer just as cheaply as the local dealer could, so now the farm has its own liquid fertilizer semitrailer.

A large-scale, diversified farmer buys his gasoline and diesel fuel by the semitrailer tankerload direct from the pipeline outlet. The same is true of liquid and dry commercial fertilizers.

He has owned a large machinery dealership for over 35 years, which initially was important to the farm because it helped to secure machinery for the farm at a standard dealer discount. As the farm grew, he found it was possible to get discounts on all purchases. "In recent years the dealership has not been that valuable to us. We prefer to buy the machines that we think do the best job rather than the ones our agency handles, but that would not look good for the dealership."

A young farmer owns an elevator, several over-the-road trucks, a hardware store, an implement agency, and a complete feed processing center in addition to his multi-enterprise farm. He has access to fuel, fertilizer, vehicles, and all other farm needs through direct deals or at dealer invoice. He discovered that for public relations in his community and also for the benefit of his own dealerships, it is better to avoid buying direct. He has to accommodate other businessmen in his town, and they, in turn, patronize his businesses.

Because other retailers realize that he can buy at his price, most of them give full discount on his purchases. He finds this to be a satisfactory arrangement and, in addition, has more cordial relations in the community. He is satisfied that his feed mill is his greatest single savings because his premix and concentrate costs were reduced by 50 per cent. The mill paid for itself in one year. His farm uses as much protein feed as several nearby country elevators. "How can businesses that have less volume than comes from one farm be justified?"

A farmer of many years, who once operated several dealerships but later discontinued them, explained: "We trade our most critical equipment, like tractors, before warranty expires. We like to trade in and buy from 6 to 10 tractors on one deal. Bidding gets good, for the dealers seem to have a way of moving big used machines that are in good condition. Competition naturally drives the price way down, and we don't have to squeeze too much."

A farmer with a business larger than most of the businessmen in his town is not interested in setting up his own retail outlets to get discount prices. He is quite civic-minded and has found that the competition between local dealers to get his business is so intense that he has been able to buy at invoice price without any effort. He has been following that practice for 19 years and feels that he has kept the good will of the community and that he has purchased reasonably without having the additional management problems associated with retail businesses.

Another, who has been in business since the 1930's, agrees with the conclusions of this farmer. He noticed even then that as his farm grew in size, the local retailers sought his account:

We have found it good socially and economically to let the local people handle our accounts. The business community is very loyal to us, and they show it in so many ways. They know we can buy as cheaply as they do, and because of our volume they are eager to trade with us. We never bargain with the dealer; we just let them compete against each other, and we end up with a rock-bottom price. It is kind of interesting to watch some of our 160-acre neighbors try to bargain to get the price down. They waste a lot of time and get nowhere. We buy a lot of corn (over 500,000 bushels a year) for the feedlot. By having our own scales, moisture tester, and storage, we save seven cents a bushel. The small farmers who are always critical of us are the first in line to sell to us because we pay a cent a bushel over the local elevator and we can handle the unloading faster than the elevator.

A farmer, who had helped to organize local co-operatives, had some serious concern about his buying practices. But in spite of his deep co-operative philosophy, he has become disillusioned because the service at the co-operatives is not as good as at the independent merchants and the products do not seem to be of a uniform high quality. He also noticed that the local independents are much more aggressive about bidding on sales than the co-operatives, which he sentimentally favored. All this is upsetting to him because he "wanted to stay loyal to the co-operatives" he had helped to organize. Finally, he said, "Unfortunately, I don't think our co-operatives are entirely 'grass roots, farmer-oriented' any more. The very top-management is not much different from that of any corporation. The co-operatives have lost their significance to me."

Another pro-co-operative farmer admitted that he could bypass the service of his local co-operatives, including the elevator, and realize considerable savings. But he felt that the co-operative did a great amount of service for his farm, which was a cost factor that could not be overlooked. He lives in a small remote community, and the extra transportation expense of buying elsewhere tends to force him and other local farmers to stay with the co-operative.

The co-operative had not been making any great profits, and he had suggested to some of his fellow co-op members that possibly they should "kick in some cash" so that the co-operative could have more working capital. This capital would be used to buy better equipment and to offer more services. He was disturbed greatly when his proposal fell on deaf ears.

A local businessman, who started farming with very little money, had to rely heavily on credit from local merchants. He has had good success in farming, and his operation has grown so that after 25 years it has a larger dollar volume than most of the merchants who helped him get started. He said, "I used them in the past. They knew it and were good to me. Now I owe them my loyalty."

A mechanically inclined farmer takes a great deal of pride in the way his farm looks and in how his equipment performs. He has excellent relations with his chief machinery dealer and works directly with the factory through him. He has his own shop that is equipped to do factory overhauls. "Our men have all graduated from the factory training school. They are better qualified to do major overhauls on equipment than most men who work for our local dealer. Our dealer is good, but he knows that our shop is just as good. We have only had to take one piece of equipment to town in the last 10 years."

The total labor bill of his operation is 16 per cent of his gross expenses. The shop's labor bill is 3 to 4 per cent of his gross expense, or a fourth of his total labor cost. However, he thinks it is a small price to pay, for he puts such a value on the timing of his field work that he cannot tolerate breakdowns.

The value of a good shop also means much to another farmer with four full-time mechanics who do nothing but overhauling. He also has several men who are fully employed fixing and repairing his 76 trucks and 39 tractors. He declared that cost-cutting is not the most important reason for a farm shop and a mobile field shop. On-the-spot repairs during lunch periods to keep the machines from breaking down rate first in importance after emergency work. His mechanical facilities also enable him to adapt new innovations to his machinery. He emphasizes good maintenance and periodic overhauls of major equipment after a set number of hours or acres. For example, each of the 10 potato harvesters is completely reworked after 350 acres and a part that shows any wear is replaced. "We don't kid ourselves about service. We buy the machinery we want at rock-bottom price and expect to take care of it ourselves. We feel this is more reliable."

A farmer who leases farm machinery also prefers not to have his own shop because he likes to keep his labor force at a minimum. He has observed that changes in equipment are introduced so fast that what he purchases one year is outdated the next year. He produces much roughage and tries to reduce his labor cost with bigger and better machinery. He leases his biggest tractor, all his roughage harvest equipment, and a four-wheel-drive pickup each year. This has proven highly rewarding because he has not had to tie up capital. He has virtually eliminated repair expenses, and he always operates with the newest equipment. He has a machinery cost equal to 10 per cent of his total cost of production, which may not be cheaper than owning it, but he is satisfied with the arrangement. "Having the latest equipment each year is tremendous. Today [1973], we put up the same amount of hay with two men that required eight men 15 years ago. This really cuts cost, and even more important, makes the wife happy, because they have to room and board with us because we are so far from town."

The experiences of most of the farmers previously quoted substantiate the conclusion of the U.S.D.A. study by Krause and Kyle that large-scale farmers have a decided financial advantage in buying their inputs. The ability to buy cheaper could be a major factor in obtaining a margin of profit. The savings through discount buying for these successful farmers could easily be more than what is needed to cover family living expenses.

Good retailers know that if they do not want to give volume discounts, they will lose customers. However, occasionally for political, social, or practical business reasons, the volume buyer often will not press the issue of buying at discount. Direct volume buying has become but another step in the reduction of the cost of the marketing system. That also gives large-scale commercial farmers an advantage over the small, less efficient operators. In the end it gives the ultimate consumer the lowest prices for his food and fiber.[1]

Marketing

The U.S.D.A. study of the early 1970's of large midwestern corn farmers by Krause and Kyle revealed that these farmers had about a $5.00-an-acre selling advantage after expenses over the average- and the smaller-sized operators. Many of these larger farmers sold their production on contract, guaranteeing time of delivery, quality, and quantity, and gained an additional advantage by that method. Because planned marketing was coordinated into their total farming operation, these farmers saved the cost paid to the middleman and were able to do the job more rapidly and efficiently than by selling through the country elevators. In most cases, the farmer already possessed scales, storage, testing equipment, and trucks, so that little or no additional investment was necessary for direct marketing. In addition, off-season marketing made use of the available labor on the farm in slack periods. Doing their own marketing made these farmers more quality conscious in their production process, resulting in better quality crops.

The study pointed out that volume buyers soon attracted volume producers, who were willing to sell over a period of time, increasing the chances of a better average price. This also gave the large producer a better opportunity to keep his trucks busy over a longer season, thus reducing their overhead per unit of work performed.

Direct marketing is not new to American agriculture. One farmer interviewed said, "We have had elevators on tracksiding since the 1870's. I am the fourth generation to market in that manner. We needed additional storage, so we built it on the tracks. We have the volume, and the elevators are no big thing to us. We profit at least a nickel a bushel over all costs of storage and marketing. In addition, we have felt at times that the country elevators have not always given us the fair breaks."

After such a statement it is easy to ask, what is new in grain marketing that has not already been tried? But there are other implications and complications that must be considered. Most farmers do not have the volume necessary to merit direct marketing. Not all farmers have the knowledge needed to do direct marketing, nor desire to do so. Not all farmers, even if they have the volume and the knowledge, consider direct marketing because of personal or public relations reasons.

According to a University of Minnesota study, about 89 per cent of all grain sold by farmers in 1971 in Minnesota went through country elevators. The other states included in this study had similar percentages, except Montana, where a greater portion of the grain was sold directly. Manitoba, of course, has its unique marketing setup that does not fit into the composite picture as well as that of the five states. The Minnesota study indicated that about 7 per cent of the farmers were selling in large volume to either terminal, processor, or feedlot operators. About 5 per cent of all farm trucks in the state were of 13-ton capacity or greater, and it is probably safe to assume that the large-volume grain producers had those trucks. Price premium was the major reason given by the farmers for direct selling.

An old homesteader with many years of direct marketing had the following experience:

I started shipping grain direct to Minneapolis or Duluth in 1921. My neighbor had been doing it for several years by then. From 1921 to 1937 I sold direct, but went through our local elevators, which charged two cents a bushel for handling. During those years I averaged about eight cents a bushel over the local market. In 1938 I purchased an elevator that held 23,000 bushels for $500 at Daleview [no longer in existence]. That elevator paid for itself three times the first year. I only handled my own grain. From 1938 until 1967, when I retired, I sold my grain through that elevator.

From 1921 through 1967 I sold all my grain to one brokerage house and also secured several other large farm accounts for them. I never had a bond or license and only handled my own grain. In those 46 years there were only 3 years that I did not have No. 1 Hard Dark Northern Spring— 14 to 17 per cent protein. All my grain sold cash on arrival.

He was not an exceptionally large farmer. He owned 4,300 acres of land during his last 30 years in farming. But he was an innovative man in his crop practices, an early adapter of machinery, and a pioneer in direct buying and selling.

Another farmer operated for about 20 years before he started direct selling his grain and specialty seed. By that time he was operating over 3,000 acres. After one year of direct selling, he decided that the additional price margin justified building his own elevator. A cleaning facility was installed, and the screenings fed to his cattle paid for the cost of cleaning. It is his opinion that by cleaning he has eliminated the dockage factor and has helped increase the overall price of his grain, because dockage was the "variable lever" that the buyer used to adjust the price.

Although this man has owned his own elevator since 1953, he has always run his account through the local elevator. The elevator takes less than one cent a bushel and this enables him to avoid bonding, licensing, and some of the problems of direct marketing. He has averaged 6 to 7½ cents a bushel over the local price throughout his 23 years of direct selling. For his farming operation he needs several large trucks which are used for delivery of the grain to the terminals. His concluding comments on direct marketing and owning his own elevator are:

The elevator has paid for itself a few times with increased income. The screenings are a valuable side benefit. We use our labor for a greater portion of the year. From my experience in direct buying and marketing, it seems that too many farmers have thrown much money down the drain building local elevators, fertilizer plants, and service stations in an attempt to keep up with the changing times. At the same time, it has been clear to others for a few decades that the country terminals are going to be the next era in marketing for those who are not large enough to go direct.

A farmer with an integrated operation has not only built a large farm, but he also has his own processing facility. His product is ready for consumption, but he has avoided any attempt to go direct selling because of what he considers excessive capital requirements. His product is for sale by the semitrailer or carload so that he can appeal to the very largest retailers. He sells directly to the retailer to save brokerage fees. "At times," he said, "the brokerage fee has been our profit margin."

A farmer with good business judgment had strong feelings about marketing because it was through doing an excellent job in that phase that he built his large operation. His first comment on the importance of marketing was different from that of the great majority of farmers because of his stress on its value. He said, "Marketing is a business in itself. The chance for real profits comes in marketing."

He processes commodities that could be used directly by other farmers, but he has avoided going the retail route. He retails to only a few very large select retail customers and the largest portion of his sales goes to jobbers. By doing so he avoids having to hire a larger labor force and owning a larger truck fleet than he needs in his regular farming operation. He has also discovered that collection risks increase greatly through retail sales. He avoids contracting ahead on his sales because he is "quite liquid financially" and prefers to take the risk. It is his feeling, gained from careful study, that the contract price, in general, has been the floor price.

A man with farms in four states, after purchasing complete truckloads of seed corn and several carloads of fertilizer in one order, discovered that he was also able to change his marketing practices. He said, "The larger you are, the greater the ease with which you can market, especially specialty products."

He produces a specialty product in such a large quantity that he has been able to secure a direct sale agreement with a large discount chain. To make that sale he had to agree to process, package, and deliver in full truckloads to the chain's warehouses. The nature of the crop enables him to "dovetail" the packaging and storing labor with his farm work force. After he has paid the expense of packaging, storing, and delivering, his increased price has consistently been double the normal market price. It is also his opinion that market development has given him the expansion capital he would not have had otherwise. He believes that it is in marketing that he still has the "greatest potential profit margins." During the last few years he has spent the greatest portion of his time working on markets.

A farmer who concentrates on two crops started selling direct to a river terminal and realized that he could keep a semitrailer busy during the slack season. He netted four to eight cents a bushel of corn after charging full freight rates for operating his truck. After that, he became involved with the Farm Bureau Marketing Corporation, and they have handled the marketing. He delivers his corn to whatever terminal is specified and consistently gets five cents above the local market after trucking costs. His corn is screened on his farm, and he sells all screenings to a local cattle feeder.

He has a specialty that he markets direct to the consumer through his own markets. Although marketing season conflicts with some of his farm work, his net after all direct marketing costs averages from 30 to 50 per cent more than if he sold through regular channels. It has taken him many years to build his retail market. He is adept at handling the public, which is probably the basis for much of his success.

A farmer with several enterprises did a considerable amount of custom farming as he was building his farm operation. Through that work he developed many contacts and learned that if he had volume, he could buy and sell with greater advantage. As his farm expanded, he also developed other farm-related enterprises for volume discount buying and premium selling. A livestock marketing enterprise involving several farmers who thought alike soon became a meat packing plant. These farmers found that the plant could be successful, but as soon as they were making a success of it, they ran into labor problems. Not expecting this or wishing to cope with labor, they decided to dispose of the packing plant. This farmer's conclusion was that although there were some profits in the packing enterprise, there were more problems in it than in farming.

The agricultural marketing system has experienced rapidly rising costs in recent years and only through increased volume have many country elevators been able to maintain their margin of profits. Cost of elevator storage and handling for 1975 was projected to be 9.7 cents per bushel. The cost of receiving, storing, and shipping one bushel of grain for one year at country elevators is 23.6 cents, and at inland terminals it is 22.2 cents.

Some country elevators have been alert to the changing situation. In an attempt to increase their business and to improve the price they can pay to the customers, the more progressive elevators have greatly increased their volume and rate of handling and/or have gone to uni-train service. By 1975 Minnesota had 29 large elevators capable of handling 25- or 50-car uni-trains. The use of the uni-train reduces freight costs to the Gulf of Mexico ports by 20 to 25 per cent. Since most of those firms are co-operatives, it must be assumed that the savings are passed directly to the customer member. The private firms no doubt increased their payments too. Such shipping facilities are necessary if the Midwest intends to hold its competitive position in world trade.

To meet the changing marketing situation, some of the more progressive country elevators have formed sub-terminals to give them a combined volume great enough to be competitive and to handle the multi-car shipments necessary to get reduced rates. As many as six or seven traditional country elevators have joined together to establish a single sub-terminal function in the corn and bean region of Minnesota and Iowa. For years the talk in North Dakota has been that there will be 10 to 12 sub-terminals in the state capable of volume shipments.*

The uni-train loading concept was introduced into North Dakota by the Garvey Elevator Company at Jamestown. It was quickly followed by the Colfax (N.D.) Grain Company, the Horace (N.D.) Farmers Elevator Company, and the Finley (N.D.) Farmers Elevator Company. The Finley elevator owned a large fleet of trucks prior to uni-train car leasing. Such systems will tend to cause many country elevators to either merge or sell out because they will be unable to compete. This trend was very pronounced from the 1950's into the 1970's, thus enabling many farmers to become elevator owners with low cost, trackside storage. Some, like Gordon Bartelt and Charles Sonnek of Waseca County, Minnesota, were able to purchase complete operations and storage facilities for 30 cents a bushel or less.

Nearly all the farmers interviewed for this study were direct marketers of grain. Many had specific opinions about the existing country elevator system. A farmer who had several country elevators in his area discovered that the three elevators closest to his farm were not doing well, and he seized the opportunity to buy all three with 150,000 bushels of storage, cleaning plants, fuel tanks for bulk storage, and other services for exactly 16 cents a bushel storage cost. Others purchased functioning elevators at a cost of 10 to 30 cents a bushel holding capacity. Most of them were already marketing directly, but the purchase of trackside storage

---

*Every community opposes such a move although eventually it would mean improved income for the farmers.

made disposing of the grain at harvest time quicker, enabled cleaning of grain during the slack season, and gave flexibility to either truck or rail shipment.

An innovative farmer was a short-term member of the local farmers' co-operative board because the elevator hoped to get this man's business by putting him on the board. This farmer soon had his eyes opened to the advantages of direct buying and selling. He could not get volume breaks in either buying or selling from the co-operative, and he became disgusted with what he thought was an outdated system. He purchased his own cleaning and moisture testing equipment. "It didn't take me long to learn how dockage and moisture nicking could be as important as pricing." He has over 300,000 bushels of storage capacity that holds a large portion of his crop. He contracts some and sells the balance during up-turns in the market. He has daily contact with marketing centers.

An elderly farmer had 400,000 bushels of storage on his farm and an additional 200,000 bushels of storage capacity in a stage of development. He had been a former co-operative board member and had also worked at an elevator. "I soon learned after farming on my own that moisture, dockage, and cracked kernel nicking were more serious ways of price reducing than the three- to five-cent margin you knew they had to take."

As his farm expanded, he became impatient with having his harvest held up by having to wait in the unloading line. One day when four of his trucks were caught in the line at once, he made his decision to build his own elevator storage complex and to sell directly.*

This gentleman built a storage and drying setup so that one man could handle and ship grain faster than the local elevator. It was his opinion that one man could handle more grain than six men could handle at the elevator where he had been a board member. Since he has completed his own plant, none of his six tandem trucks has to stand in line to unload and the combines run stead-ily. He thinks that is worth as much as the added price he gets from direct selling. He has no trouble getting trucks to haul from his facility because he can load them out in eight minutes. "The truckers always complain how long it takes them to get loaded out at the local elevator, and the drivers tell me they prefer to come to us because they can get going in a hurry."

---

*He had been active in the National Farmers Organization and had learned how to direct market. He could not afford the cost of idle trucks and combines.

A farmer purchased an elevator to do direct discount buying. His elevator was set up as a separate business, and he paid himself the same price as any farmer would receive. This was done to split income. He soon realized an additional unexpected benefit. He found that a considerable amount of very poor quality grain arrived at his elevator that could not be sold to the terminal except with extreme dockage. Because he had a feedlot, he found that he could effectively use the poor quality feed to good advantage there. He also found that he was able to do a better job of marketing his farm grain, because daily contact "with the trade" broadened his insights on price activity.

An excellent manager had long made it a business to sell his grain directly to southern feedlots. Feedlot company trucks came to his 250,000-bushel farm storage, saving him the cost of trucking. He also became involved with several other farmers and organized a large stockholder-owned elevator. That well-capitalized elevator soon dominated the business over a large area and has yielded a constant 12 per cent return on investment. The farmer-owners feel that they profited two ways by joining hands to build a large single elevator for their personal use. One advantage was that large volume has made their direct selling easier, and the other was that the profits from management have been better than expected.

A farm manager, who is responsible for a large, diversified operation that includes 6,000 acres of corn, has an unusual situation. The farm has its own elevator complex. That complex is set up in such a way that it is a separate entity and must pay the market price for corn. This manager often bypasses his elevator because it pays less for his corn than he can get by delivering directly to a major food manufacturer or to river terminals. The farm elevator manager becomes provoked with this because he assumes he should have the option to buy the farm's corn production at the same price he pays the smaller farmers in the area. There are times when the elevator mill pays as much or better than the terminal because the farm is located in a grain deficit community and there are no local reserves.

Another farmer, who never paid much attention to marketing because his business produced for the government storage and loan program instead of using the open market, had over a million bushels of on-the-farm storage and delivered from that whenever the government called for grain. With the reduction in scope of the programs and the increased profits on the open market he had to revise his selling habits. Other farmers in the community who were dissatisfied with the local co-operative elevator invited him to join them in putting up an independent stockholder-owned elevator. He said, "I hope the day of market-oriented production is here, and I think we should do a better job of selling to the world than we have, maybe it is time to get involved."

Several farmers in one area, who specialize in the production of malting barley, own elevators on trackside and have pooled their sales directly to malters. These farmers clean and grade their barley and send samples to the malter for a price quotation. Some of their production is sold with a price-advantage clause on contract, but the remainder is contracted for sale. However, the price is left open until delivery. One of the barley pool farmers kept very close records for "a couple of years" to see how that arrangement compared to local sales. His net was 12 cents a bushel after all additional expenses were paid. The farmers in the pools each provided 40,000 to 100,000 bushels as their contribution toward building volume sales.

One farmer with a long history in direct marketing had some ideas that merit mentioning. He lived 30 miles from his nearest country elevator and 60 miles from the second. He felt neither of them was competitive from a price standpoint. It cost him 10 cents a bushel to load and haul his products to the first elevator, and he had to take the price they offered. In search of a better way, he contacted a broker in Minneapolis, 700 miles distant from his farm, and after the first sale, he realized how much he could net by shipping directly. He had 140,000 bushels of storage on the farm, so he could hold most of one year's crop. After trucking expenses and less the 10 cents savings by not having to haul the crop to the local market, he netted 17 cents a bushel over the local price in the first year of direct marketing.

Now, he is trying to make contact with a firm that can fill and seal containers on his farm. These containers would be hauled either to river or ocean ports and would go directly to an international buyer. "I deliver a pure product with no dockage at the river market, so I know I could satisfy any standard of the foreign buyer. Why do we have to risk foreign sales because of questionable blending that frequently takes place between us and the foreign consumer?"

He also has semitrailer grain trucks of his own, but he uses them only when he has a return load because he does not make a profit under existing rates for one-way hauls alone. After hauling wheat to Minneapolis, his trucks bring back fertilizer and mill feeds for himself and his neighbors.

Changing times caused one farmer to alter his marketing program. He used the government programs to the maximum in order to keep expanding his farm. He sealed all the corn he could and took storage until he could redeem it at a profit. To do this effectively, he had to dry his corn and erect storage for a million bushels. When the corn market improved with export trade and the energy shortage increased the cost of drying corn, he sought to produce for the market rather than for the government.

He went to large livestock feeders in his area who were interested in high moisture corn for their cattle and hogs. These feeders preferred the high moisture product to the dry grain and were interested in having it delivered to their storage at harvest. They paid better prices than the local elevator. In this way the grain farmer did not have the expense of drying his crop nor did he have to slow down his harvest while waiting for it to be dried. "I know this will break a couple of the local elevators, but it represents about $60,000 more to me each year on my corn crop alone, so I think it's a good deal for me."

A farmer, who had farmed for four decades, was always disturbed by the high transportation rate that he had to pay before his grain reached the export market. He decided that the best thing to do was to work with neighboring ranchers and to set up a calf pre-conditioning and backgrounding program to export feed through yearling instead of grass-fed calves. He altered his crop production to fit the needs of the feedlot and greatly increased the net return from his land. Everything is produced to be processed through the feedlot and is all contracted before the crop year starts.

Another farmer has been marketing his cattle directly to packers for several years. He sells either live weight or on a grade and yield basis, and neither he nor the packers have had a complaint about the cattle for several years. He showed us documentation which proved that his direct marketing cost was $8.00 to $11.00 per head less than that at either auction or terminal markets. "I can no longer afford the luxury of the terminal market. I know I am doing better than I ever did going that way because I feed quality cattle, and they have proven themselves to the direct buyers."

He also felt that selling direct was a great timesaver, for he could use the phone to sell cattle. The buyers stopped in from time to time to look at his cattle and knew when they were ready for sale.

A farmer with a feedlot observed that he or one of his managers was spending so much time with cattle buyers that the work wasn't getting done. After a great deal of thought, he came up with the idea of having a bid sheet. A notice was posted on a board indicating which pens of cattle were for sale. A buyer could look at all the cattle, submit written bids on the sheet for any or all cattle he wanted to buy, put the bid sheet into a locked box, and leave. Cattle were available for inspection on Mondays and Thursdays, and the buyers were free to come and go as they pleased on those days. No other communication was necessary. The top bidders were notified according to the time printed on the bid sheet.

He has six packer–buyers making regular stops at his feedlot. Everyone has the same opportunity, and it takes a minimum of time. He admits that sometimes he "visits a bit" with the buyers. "Many of the smaller feeders in our area think I'm a bit touched because they think it is a big deal when the buyer comes around, and they like to visit with him. I would rather get the job done and take a vacation."

One problem mentioned by all the large-scale cattle and hog feeders was their basic inability to buy animals directly from the cow-calf man or the hog farrower. All the large feeders would have preferred to buy directly from the farm to enable them to get fresher animals at less marketing costs, but only a few were succeeding. They expressed several reasons for this. First was the dislike of the small producer having to sell to someone with a larger business than he had; second was the fear of the seller that he was not getting full price, even if a broker entered the transaction by setting the price; third was the heavy pressure that local bankers and auction market people put on these producers to be careful about direct selling; fourth was overcoming the tradition of taking the cattle to market and spending the day there.

Some ranchers and feeder-pig producers have gone to direct selling to feeders and like the practice. These people have frequently been offered the opportunity to contract sell but have declined because they preferred the "risk of the market."

A third generation rancher well remembers the problems his grandfather and father had in selling their cattle. He decided to avoid the trouble. He searched for reliable cattle feeders who would purchase his cattle as he sold them from the ranch. The feeder bought the cattle, which were weighed and priced on the place. He paid for a broker who was called in only to set the price, and the feeder also hauled them away at his expense. As time passed, one buyer wanted his total production and for 23 years has purchased all of his cattle. Only one phone call is made each year, so no time is wasted. Each year he finds out how his cattle performed in the feedlot, so he knows how his breeding program is succeeding.

A pork producer found that as soon as he got his volume to the point where he had three or four truckloads of hogs to sell each week, the packers became very competitive for his business. Because of his volume, he was eventually able to work with one packer and did not have to spend time with the marketing process. He has daily contact with his packer, and he has a teletype service available so he can follow the markets. He likes to sell his hogs at exactly 220 pounds, which means he has to sell a load at least every two days.

The packer, well aware of this producer's volume, uses this farmer's available supply as a buffer to fill slack periods in marketing. Should a big run occur at the plant, he is told not to sell, and as soon as it appears that there will not be enough hogs to keep the men busy, he is asked to send in more hogs. This producer sorts all his hogs, and loads are sold straight as priced over the phone. If he has to hold hogs beyond the 220-pound weight by request of the packer, he is not docked for having overweight hogs. Such an arrangement is beneficial to both the packer and the farmer. By working with the packer, he learns the quality of his final product and is able to determine his breeding program.

There is always considerable discussion taking place about contracting and hedging of agricultural production and how the farmer can protect himself against possible loss. Farmers have been in the business of contracting and futures for many decades. The only reason more farmers have not been involved in it is that they do not understand the system. Others operated at such small volume that even good, sound marketing practices could not have made the difference between profit or loss.

David Askegaard, a bonanza farmer, held a seat on the Minneapolis Exchange in the early 1900's and traded in futures regularly. Members of his family say he boasted of his winnings, but never spoke of his losses. The bonanza farms of Oliver Dalrymple and the Amenia and Sharon Land Company were also active in the contract and futures markets at earlier dates. When Askegaard died in 1919, his seat on the exchange was sold for $5,000.

Charles Grant was active in the futures market starting in the early 1920's. Grant admitted that he felt the decline in the market in 1929 at once because he had hedged "the wrong direction" and lost $14,000. His optimism caused him additional hardships because it came just prior to a period of low prices and drought.

The business of contracting and hedging will become more crucial to farmers each year as they become involved in a more intensely capitalized industry. Those operating on a larger-than-average volume are well aware of this type of marketing. Unless they are financially so liquid that they can afford the risk, most of these larger farmers will become active traders or contractors.

One farmer looks at the 100,000 bushels of storage on his place as a headache. He would prefer to contract his crop the winter before he has to plant and to adjust his production to those contracts. By doing this he feels that he is free to concentrate on doing a good job at production because he does not have to worry about what price he is going to get. He has made a business of contracting, and most years all his crops are sold before he has started to plant.

One farmer, quite positive in attitude, sells potatoes, sugar beets, and sunflowers on a contract basis. Potatoes and sugar beets are his high volume and highest potential income crops. Beets cannot be sold unless they are contracted, and he prefers not to produce any more potatoes than he can contract. He has nearly 5,000 acres in wheat and barley, but he feels so certain about their reliability to "come through" that he likes to wait until he has the crop in the bin before he thinks about selling. After harvest he contracts to sell directly to river terminals over a period of several months.

A young farmer with only a limited amount of cash available has found that he is able to expand because by contracting his crops he is able to get stability of income. He has also been able to borrow more operating capital because his banker recognizes the significance of a contracted price. By contracting about three-fourths of his production each year, he has been able to protect himself against any severe setback and has been able to develop sufficient volume for the necessary cash flow. When the good prices of 1973 and 1974 came, he was able to capitalize on the fourth and his production that was not contracted so greatly that it improved his financial position.

Just the opposite view is held by a farmer with a good supply of cash. He is not interested in risking what he has to any great degree so he has gone to contracting both quantity and price. He reasons that the only risk he takes is nature. His farm's production history dates back to the late 1800's, and by contracting a fixed percentage of production, he feels protected. But for security purposes he has more than a full year's production safely stored in bins. He makes steady progress and has virtually eliminated the risks.

One farmer is somewhat indifferent about direct marketing because he thinks it is not much more efficient than the 30-bushel grain wagon was in its day. He did direct marketing in the late 1940's and early 1950's and then became too involved with other activities to continue doing a good job of marketing. This caused him to go back to the local elevators. He said:

I really don't get excited about direct selling because the big independents and co-ops have too much invested in country elevators today to really encourage us to go direct. These country elevators need from four to eight cents a bushel to come out. If they can't get it on price, they take it on dockage or moisture. When the big firms have their country elevator investments depreciated, they will be sold off and direct marketing will come.

I think our state could support 10 good-sized terminals for loading unitrains. Then, they will go to buying on area average. They will make it more possible for us to compete with the world market where the real opportunity for the American farmer exists.

I believe this will happen because whatever becomes physically possible soon becomes economically feasible.

A farmer, who is an excellent manager, has avoided going the direct marketing route to keep down local resentment, and he "did not want to get involved in trucking." He was not interested in becoming a grain merchant because he considered himself a farmer. He felt that the entire marketing process was in a state of transition. The American marketing and transportation system, in his opinion, has to become geared to massive foreign export business. He is sure of the farmer's ability to produce for the foreign market as well as to provide the American consumers with all they need.

This farmer is a well-informed and involved individual who

looks at the total agricultural picture from a much broader view than most farmers and citizens do. He offers probably the best summation of what most of these successful farmers were trying to say. Most were satisfied that they were buying and selling at much more favorable terms than the great portion of American farmers. They were constantly searching for innovations while remaining conscious of the fact that volume buying and selling is the key to better business. Better business has been the doorway to progress.

All these changes take time, and as one well-versed cash-grain farmer said, "I don't think either the country co-operatives or the farmer-owned elevator is a good investment. Both are too small by today's farm standards to be really efficient. But as the present structures burn or rot away, they will gradually be replaced by the big terminals. But sentiment for the country elevator and resistance to the terminal is still great, so it will take time to eliminate them."[2]

NOTES

[1]"Farm Suppliers: A Mighty Link in the Marketing Chain," *Gopher State Review*, Minnesota Crop and Livestock Reporting Service Bulletin 316 (March, 1974); "A Letter Written by Horace Goodhue, Jr.," *North Dakota History*, XVII, No. 1 (January, 1950), p. 60; interview with Mrs. Hugh Trowbridge, Barnesville, Minnesota, April 19, 1967 (she is a daughter of David Askegaard); Kenneth R. Krause and Leonard R. Kyle, "Midwestern Corn Farms . . .," U.S. Department of Agriculture, Agricultural Economic Report No. 216, Washington (1971), III, pp. 11–15.

[2]Dick Seim, "They Bought a Local Elevator," *Farm Journal*, XCVI, No. 6 (June, 1972), pp. 22A and B; *The Forum* (March 27, 1974); "Market Style of the Future," *Big Farmer Cattle Guide*, II, No. 8 (September, 1972), pp. 12–13; Kenneth R. Krause and Leonard R. Kyle, U.S. Department of Agriculture, Agricultural Economic Report No. 216, Washington (1971), III, pp. 16–17; Reynold Dahl and Maggi Liu, "How Minnesota Farmers Market Their Grain," *Minnesota Agricultural Economist*, No. 549 (September, 1973), pp. 1–4; "Birth to Beef Steak," *Gold Label News Nuggets*, XI, No. 5 (May 1974), pp. 1, 3; "Grain Elevator Costs Climb," *Gopher State Review*, Minnesota Crop and Livestock Reporting Service Bulletin 318 (May, 1974); Reynold Dahl and Michael Martin, "Multiple-Car Rail Rates— Their Impact on Grain Transport," *Minnesota Agricultural Economist*, No. 563 (January, 1975), pp. 1–4; Jim Baccus, "Elevators Buying, Leasing Railroad Cars and Trucks," *The Farmers Forum*, Fargo-Moorhead, North Dakota (June 7, 1974); anonymous interviews (see footnote on first page of chapter).

CHAPTER X

Farm Organizations as Viewed by Successful Farmers*

F ARM ORGANIZATIONS play an important role in today's picture of agriculture. Therefore, all farmers involved in this study were asked the following question in regard to farm organizations: What specific benefits has this farm received from any farm organization? This refers to any of the general farm organizations or to a specific commodity organization.

Because of the ideological and emotional implications involved in this question, the interviewees were asked to speak openly and freely about the subject. In many cases the answers to this question were cynical and not always complimentary to the farm organizations. These men and their wives knew they were not talking to a representative of any special interest group or to a leader of a farm organization. They were asked to speak exactly as they felt.

These people were not rank-and-file farmers. They were selected because they are the innovators of today's agriculture, the pace setters and not the followers. The purpose of the interviews was to attempt to determine what is possible in agriculture as the innovators forecast, not what has happened. Innovators are always a small minority, but they do show the way, and seldom do they think as the masses do. The cynicism expressed in the answers by the farmers interviewed appears closer to the norm than on any of the other questions asked. If farmers could have their wish, or-

---

*Because of the sensitive nature of the material in this chapter, the names of farmers, their wives, or employees are not used. This was the agreement with these individuals at the time of interview. However, all documentation is on file with the author.

194

ganizations would have less input. Historically, that reflects the basic independence of those who farm.

The independence of the farmer is not an unknown characteristic. Some American farmers of the past pulled up stakes, sold out, and went West to get away from the crowd. Probably some aspects of life that we credit as independence may simply have been a cover for stubbornness or resistance to change. Farmers have long used that trait to avoid getting too involved in change or having a closer association with other segments of society. This has tended to hurt their image and weaken their effectiveness. In the past they were clearly the dominant power in the American scene by virtue of sheer numbers. Commencing in the late nineteenth century, they gradually lost in numbers and economic power, and by the mid-twentieth century they lost much of their political power.

Farm organizations have been formed by farmers in an attempt to regain some of their former power by striving to build a unified farmer movement. The outcome was the creation of several farm groups which differed from each other and were involved in a perpetual struggle to win and maintain members. *The Dakota Farmer*, which has its greatest reader concentration in the two Dakotas, polled its readers in 1972. Among the questions asked were those about farm organizations. Of the respondents to this poll, about 18 per cent belonged to the Farm Bureau, 62 per cent to the Farmers Union, and 26 per cent to the National Farmers Organization (NFO)—the three major organizations in the area.* When asked which organization helped most in solving economic problems related to agriculture, 38 per cent gave credit to the Farmers Union, and 33 per cent gave credit to the NFO. Nearly 91 per cent of the respondents wished for more cooperation between the major farm organizations, and, in general, they were unhappy with the leadership of the three organizations.

William Kuhfuss, past president of the American Farm Bureau Federation, said in reply to a question on farmer unity: "I neither expect nor hope to see a single unified farm organization." Mr. Kuhfuss felt that the total problem of agriculture had more to gain through the expression of diverse ideas than through a structured single organization. Louis B. Schmidt, a noted agricultural histo-

---

*The clear leadership of the Farmers Union is due to the large number of service enterprises in the area. Individuals who trade with them are automatically made check-off members of the Farmers Union. Neither of the other two organizations has the widespread service organization in the Dakotas that the Farmers Union has.

rian, wrote in the 1930's that the farm organizations had helped
the farmer through the dissemination of new ideas and methods of
farming. By breaking down his individualism, they have helped
him in the cooperative effort. At the same time, organizations had
created a feeling of class consciousness that has not always produced the most favorable benefits. At that time (1933) Schmidt felt
farmers and their organizations were too concerned with "short-
run solutions rather than long-term objectives." He warned that in
the changing social structure farmers could no longer stand alone
to cope with the problems, but needed to work through their organizations. He believed that before this could happen, farmers
had to give up their attitude of economic fatalism.*

The task of the farm organization has been a difficult one. Oscar
M. Sabe, who grew up on the western North Dakota frontier, recalled an interesting incident that occurred in the early years of
organizing a farmer's group. The "Holiday movement" imported a
tough Chicago man as an organizer in Bowman County, North
Dakota. Sabe remembered seeing the Holiday men stationed on
roads near his farm in order to stop all grain shipments. A
neighbor to Sabe, driving an old Reo truck loaded with 80 bushels
of wheat, could not stop when hailed by the Holiday sentinel. The
sentinel had to jump from a bridge into the creek to avoid being
hit. On a nearby road another farmer with a team and a grain
wagon was also stopped by the Holiday sentinel. The farmer dis-
mounted and "thoroughly beat up" the Holiday man, who quit his
job promptly. Sabe said, with considerable satisfaction, "That was
the end of the Holiday movement in Bowman County."

Many of the farmers interviewed were or had been very active
in various farm organizations. Several actually were involved in
initiating county and state units of their chosen organization. Some
have remained loyal to the organization they helped found, while
others have quit all activity or joined another group. The most frequent immediate response of these farmers, when asked about the
value of farm organizations to their farming, was a pause and then
laughter. Although no numerical count was taken by the inter-
viewer, that reply was probably given more than 60 per cent of the
time.

Those who appeared most antagonistic toward farm organiza-

---

*It is the opinion of this writer that the attitude of economic fatalism was not
prevalent among the farmers he interviewed. In general, they were aggressively
optimistic about a new era for agriculture.

tions gave some quite interesting reasons. One farmer said, "I do not belong to any farm organization. They are all leeches as far as I am concerned. Even the wheat commission is not any real help. I would prefer to be left alone."

Another farmer was virtually stunned when asked about the worth of farm organizations, and then he replied: "Their impact on our farm has been zero. My dad avoided the organizations like a plague. I will probably be a member for good will only. Nation-wide, their impact has been slight, probably because of too little political arm twisting."

A farmer with a broader outlook did not belong to any farm or-ganization because he felt that the large commercial farmers' interests were ignored in favor of the small undersized units where the greater political power was located. It was his opinion that the oratory and the literature of the organizations generally had a negative impact on the public. His reasoning was that too often they implied that farming might not be a viable industry. "You get the impression that only a misfit would want to farm." He was a very active member in two farm commodity organiza-tions, which he felt gave him much good information and definite export market aid.

Another farmer who does not belong to any of the general farm organizations expressed his opinion that they have "done little real good." He believes that the general organizations tend to exaggerate the farmer's plight. "They aim toward the small and the inefficient operator, but if they could help the little farmer, the benefits to the larger farmers would be even greater."

A socially minded farmer who did not subscribe to the policies of any farm organization felt socially pressured and joined only as a nominal member. "I know of no benefit this farm has derived from any farm organization. Nationwide, I believe some of the or-ganizations have basically harmed agriculture because they have gotten the government involved in our business. I don't think they have done a thing to improve the consumer's attitude." He has fought the farm organizations quietly, yet stubbornly, whenever he could. He survived the late 1920's and 1930's and had built a very solid economic base of operation by the time World War II prosperity arrived. He made it, and he believes others should be able to do likewise.

A very tolerant-minded individual said, "The organizations have done nothing. We belong to the Farm Bureau for two reasons—to get a friend off the place and to use their computer program. I could get the computer program at several other places, so that's nothing great. I really don't see how they can help us. We do get a few little goodies from the cattlemen's association."

A young farmer felt that it was difficult to cite any concrete contribution of a farm organization to his farm except the "Wheat Producers," which helped to pass some helpful legislation. "Farmers Union has had a strong negative impact because it really does not try to promote the best interest of the farmer. I think the local cooperatives have set back more small towns than any other single factor I know of."

This young man is a widely traveled and well-read person. His outlook was generally very optimistic. His comment on farm organizations was the only sharp critical position he took. He was able to cite examples from several states that supported his feelings.

A very active and energetic farmer did not belong to any of the general farm organizations because he felt they dissipated their energies with "Mickey Mouse services and public propaganda." He did belong to the National Corn Growers Association because it concentrated on informing its members on how to do a better job. He felt its members were much more positive in their attitude than those in the general organizations.

On the other hand, there were some farmers who had good reasons why they belonged to the general farm organizations. A politically inclined person said that he belonged to all three—Farm Bureau, Farmers Union, and NFO—for business and social reasons. Although he was not sure his farm had received any direct benefits; nevertheless, he felt that the NFO had brought the farmer's problem to the public and had helped change the Farm Bureau and the Farmers Union. He named three specific commodity organizations that he had looked at but did not join because he saw no tangible benefits coming from them. He did add, however, that he belonged to the local Chamber of Commerce.

Another believer is extremely active in his commodity organization and holds a position in it that takes more than 50 per cent of his time. At one time he belonged to all three of the general organizations, but he quit because he thought they were a waste of effort and time. He thinks some of the local independent cooperatives have made a real contribution to their farmer members and communities. As an afterthought he injected the idea that two of the general organizations were responsible for "peddling a negative attitude" to the general public.

Farm organizations have used various tactics to entice farmers and others to take out memberships. The Farm Bureau has various services and group insurance plans, but unless one becomes a member, he cannot secure their goods. Non-farmers can become associate members of the Farm Bureau, but they have no voting or decision-making privileges. The insurance agent is, in a sense, a Farm Bureau recruiter, but the majority of its members are secured and maintained through annual volunteer membership drives.

The Farmers Union, with its numerous service stations, farm supply stores, and elevators, uses the check-off system of membership. Anyone who does business at any of the Farmers Union firms becomes a member, whether or not he is a farmer. The check-off system automatically swells the membership of the Farmers Union. This is particularly true in small communities where it has the only service station, supply store, or elevator. Through this system, many individuals who have little or no ideological relationship to the organization or interest in it are counted as members.

The NFO has limited its services to the selling and buying of grains and livestock. There is little reason for non-farm individuals to join that organization unless they endorse its principles and want to join. In this respect the NFO is the "most pure" of the three general organizations in the Midwest covered by this study. The NFO pays a commission to farmer solicitors who have been considerably more energetic in getting new members than have the volunteers of the other organizations.

The NFO has a three-year membership contract with a very limited release clause. This release clause has discouraged some farmers from joining. Others, who were members but later wanted to discontinue their association, have become somewhat disillusioned by the organization's position over that clause. Generally, these members have simply refused to pay their dues or to participate in the organization.

In general, psychology plays an important part in getting members to join any organization. A. C. Townley, the moving force behind the Non-Partisan League in the 1915–1920 period, urged his organizers to find out the farmers' interests and to exploit their emotions to get memberships. His charge was:

Find out the damn fool's hobby and talk it. If he likes religion, talk Jesus Christ; if he is against the government, damn the Democrats; if he is afraid of whiskey, preach prohibition; if he wants to talk hogs, talk hogs—

talk anything he'll listen to, but talk, talk, until you get his . . . damn John Hancock to a check for six dollars.

The speakers used few facts, "relying on 'self-evident conditions'; the 'facts' used, . . . were sensational and repeated often. No qualitative descriptions of economic problems were offered." The League spokesmen informed the farmers that their problems were caused by economic-political conspiracy, and that through League political action the conspiracy would be broken. Anyone who has been around the morning, afternoon, or evening coffee counter, at the local tavern, or the country elevator, or has attended organizational meetings has heard all the "sure cures" to the farmers' problems that were promised by the organizations. The discussion appears to be no different today than it was in the past.

A farmer who is a Farmers Union check-off member has been active in the past and served as a county president, as well as a board member, of the cooperative oil station. Now he is no longer active and has basically lost interest in the organization. He has contracted a considerable volume of grain and sunflowers through the NFO, but he has no deep ideological feelings about that organization. He had been a direct marketer who sold through the NFO as well as through the terminal. He believes that some legislative help has been obtained through the combined efforts of the farm organizations, but he admitted that he could not specifically name any such legislation.

An individual who considers himself a realist explained that he once had been an NFO member but that he had not paid dues for three years. He also was a check-off member of the Farmers Union. He belonged to a commodity group, but he felt it was too weak to have any real impact. He emphatically said, "I don't believe that any of the big three have helped me a bit. I believe the fact that they are pulling in different directions hurts us. It appears that they are more interested in their administrators than the issues." It is his opinion that when farm numbers have been greatly reduced, there "could be a chance" that farmers will be unified and strong.

One farmer, who buys his auto insurance from the Farm Bureau, added, "The Farmers Union I cannot stand, and the NFO taught me to bargain." He cooperates with the NFO in buying and selling certain commodities because he feels farmers should support a cause. However, according to his experience, the financial transactions "were no better than elsewhere." He believes that nationally the organizations may have accomplished some good, but in his area they have caused "nothing but trouble" because of personality clashes.

A precise and well-informed man, who has been farming several decades and has been very active in his state, knows politics and farmers. He had a quick reply about farm organizations. "I really wonder what they have done. I think the organizations are lousy; they are too concerned with pennies. I belong to the Farm Bureau because of marketing, but I don't think they are thinking big enough. I am a check-off at the Farmers Union because I buy from them, but I disagree with them. I would really like to see men get together on valid principles alone, and then it might be possible to get things done. But I doubt that enough farmers could really be sold on ideas only in order to get them together."

The ideology of farm organizations, like religion and politics, tends to stir the emotions of many people. Much has been written pro and con about the basic ideas and concepts of the major organizations, particularly those discussed in this chapter. Some material has been highly biased in favor of the organizations while other materials have been very critical. In recent years most of the writings have been centered on the NFO because it is the latest in appearance and the most sensational in activities.

Several major scholarly works, as distinguished from pure propaganda publications, have been written about this subject in recent years. A doctoral thesis by Clara B. Riveland deals with the internal conflict within the NFO. Mrs. Riveland is very much in favor of the objectives of the NFO and approves its goals. In preparation for her thesis she found that the organization contained two factions. One group never listens to any negative facts about the NFO and refuses to look at the data critical of NFO administration, business practices, or operational procedures. The other group she worked with were ex-NFO members who were disillusioned with what they believed to be questionable ethical standards used within the organization's administration.

Mrs. Riveland expressed the personal opinion that she did not think the NFO could achieve its goals unless it could cope with the conflicts within the organization. It was her impression that every possible attempt was made "to suppress conflict and thus stifle creative thinking" within the NFO. The greatest danger arose from the conflict between the president and a large portion of dissatisfied members.

Those who have lived in rural America during the turmoil encountered in recent years have not always been comfortable with the potentially dangerous disturbances present at some of the protests. Some farmers have refused to belong to any organization because they are sensitive and do not want to be caught in a conflict. On the other hand, some farmers have belonged to all organizations as a matter of good will.

A farmer not too concerned about sensitivity belonged to one of the general organizations and to two commodity groups. But he was highly critical of the organizations because, in his opinion, they had done much to create a feeling of second class citizenship among farmers. He personally felt the reaction from such an attitude, and he sensed resentment against him by farmers who possessed the "underdog" philosophy.

A thoughtful farmer was once very active in a farm organization but he gradually became "very disillusioned." He felt that even the commodity organizations were not what he had hoped for. He could not cite a single direct benefit to his farm derived from the organizations; thus, he still had reservations. "If I thought that farmers could really cooperate, I would be active again."

Several farmers, politically very active, felt that farm organizations often make a big noise about minor issues in order to make their members think they are doing a good job.

It appears to be difficult for farmers to express in a direct manner what benefits are derived from their farm organizations. Like many people, they are inclined to point out the negative rather than the positive side of any issue or institution. But some farmers believe that there are some direct and indirect benefits gained from farm organizations.

A farmer who is very active in foreign trade made it a business to study farm exporting organizations. He felt two such organizations had helped him in that respect. The annual cost to belong to one of the organizations was $35,000. He felt that he was well repaid for his dues. He believed that some of the commodity groups were also quite good until they succeeded in establishing the check-off system. It was his opinion that funds from check-offs made leeches out of the organizations. "Once the funds flow in, they perpetuate themselves rather than develop new ideas."

An innovative and learned man has been very active in his commodity organization that has as its chief purpose the creation of a better image of the farmer with the public and encouragement in the expansion of markets. He has also been on the boards of other organizations with which he was in agreement. His faith in his organization is indicated by his payment of $30,000 annually in dues based on a fixed fee per commodity unit sold. He does not question the benefits received for that subscription fee. "My products keep selling."

Many farmers interviewed were involved in direct selling of grain and livestock through their organization, either the Farm Bureau with its marketing corporation or the Beef Improvement Council (BIC) program (for livestock), or the NFO for either grain or livestock. These farmers experienced about the same gains as the farmers attained who bypassed their local elevators and went directly to the terminals.

A young successful farmer helped the NFO assemble grain for direct sales to feedlots and over a two-year period he profited seven cents a bushel over local elevator prices. He felt that the experience gained in marketing, in addition to the extra income, was very profitable. He felt that working with the organization had given him a greater sense of pride in farming and a better sense of direction than he formerly had. He is a college graduate and a reliable and successful farmer with a conservative philosophical approach to daily and long-range social problems.

Another farmer, organizationally oriented, belongs to the Farmers Union, the NFO, and his local sugar beet growers association. It was his impression that the Farmers Union did a good job with its services, the beet association helped its members especially with daily and annual routine problems, and the NFO helped him in marketing. Formerly, he was very active in the NFO for about a decade. After he learned its method of direct marketing, he followed that practice on his own, which has proven to be very profitable because of his large volume. He actually changed his farming program because of the knowledge gained through the marketing practices of the NFO.

Cooperative elevators and service stores affiliated with the Farmers Union and Farmland Industries were cited as being fringe benefits of the organizations and the cooperative movement. Many farmers felt that the competition tended to help keep the prices of purchased products down and that elevator competition helped to keep the grain market just a bit higher.

Some farmers expressed doubt that from a competitive standpoint cooperatives were different from independents. One farmer, for example, belonged to both the Farmers Union and the NFO. He recalled selling 6,000 bushels of wheat on an NFO contract that was shipped through the Farmers Union elevator. He could not persuade the local elevator to increase its bid until it discovered that he had contracted with the NFO. Then the local elevator jumped its bid to him by four cents per bushel to match the NFO bid. From the same terminal that his elevator uses, he receives daily card quotations, and he notes that during that entire time the price of wheat had remained the same.

Surprisingly, a large portion of the farmers attributed the farm organizations with a good amount of personal benefit that they had received by attendance at informational programs and annual county, state, and national meetings sponsored by the organizations. An elderly, well-versed farmer said that the exchange of ideas he had gained through visiting with other farmers was of far greater value than the "things" that the organization was trying to sell. In this regard he was supported by a former high-ranking organization member who admitted that the idea exchange in the halls at the conventions was far more profitable than any other service he could name. "A forum for the meeting of people and the sharing of goals has long-range social and economic impact that cannot be measured in a single year's time. Exposure and education have a far greater value than pennies and nickels because they tend to enrich the mind and educate the man." He had been active in his farm organization for many years and had attended many meetings where less than a handful of people were present. His observation was that probably the organizations were well-intended, but "most people just did not become sufficiently involved."

Unquestionably, farmers put many hours of volunteer work into their farm organizations because they believe that this is the best way to help themselves achieve their goals. As one of them remarked:

I think the sales tax which we worked hard for will be the last good break the farmers of Minnesota will get for quite a while. But the 1963 crop (wheat) referendum defeat was the greatest victory I have ever personally received from working with a farm organization. That setback for a more controlled agriculture was worth all the dues I will ever have to pay.*

Organizations will continue to rise and fall in their battle to bring farmers under their banner, but the farmer still longs for that freedom and independence which are in part his reasons for being

---

*This farmer was joyous over the defeat of an issue that other farm organizations and farmers fought hard to win—positive proof that farmers are far from united and even farther from a common goal.

a farmer. The businessman–farmer who sees the need for a strong viable organization to protect his interests against other factions of our society does not yet appear to be ready to make the final commitment.[1]

NOTE

[1]"Sound Off Survey Results," *The Dakota Farmer*, XCII, No. 5, (May, 1972), pp. 10–11; interview of William Kuhfuss, Fargo, North Dakota, July 9, 1973; Louis B. Schmidt, "The Agricultural Revolution in the Prairies and Great Plains of the United States," *Agricultural History*, VIII, No. 8 (October, 1934), pp. 182, 186–188, 194; interview of Oscar M. Sabe, Gascoyne, North Dakota, April 8, 1972; Paul Dovre, "The Non-Partisan League: An Expression of Agrarian Protest," *Discourse*, VIII, No. 4 (Autumn, 1965), pp. 320–321; Clara B. Riveland, "An Analysis of the National Farmers Organization's Attempt to Reduce Rhetorical Distance," Unpublished Ph.D. Thesis, University of Minnesota, St. Paul (1974); anonymous interviews (see footnote on first page of chapter).

CHAPTER XI

The Cheap Food Policy and Pressure from the ASCS Committees*

Bringing up the topic of government programs is one of the quickest ways of getting a good discussion going in rural America. This was not always true, for in the early 1900's, when Theodore Roosevelt attempted to call attention to some adverse features of rural America through the Country Life Commission, he was unable to persuade Congress to appropriate $25,000 for the publication of the proceedings. Politicians probably were not as vote-conscious in those days or felt the farmers were no worse off than many other segments of society and, therefore, did not merit special treatment.

The parity ratio of farm prices exceeded the 100 level 17 times between 1910 and 1975. Fortunately, for the farmers, six of those parity years occurred between 1910 and 1919. Those years were a golden era for farmers, and Congress did not have to face up to the problem of an overexpanded agriculture. During 1920, farm prosperity turned downward and the 100 per cent parity ratio did not return until the wartime year of 1944.

As in the past, American farmers rose to the challenge of wartime demands during World War I and greatly expanded their production, only to be penalized with declining markets after the war. The nation, including Congress, knew that the farmers were in trouble, and many politicians presented solutions. Liberty

---

*Because of the sensitive nature of the material in this chapter, the names of farmers, their wives, or employees are not used. This was the agreement with these individuals at the time of interview. However, all documentation is on file with the author.

Hyde Bailey, a great figure in American agriculture for several decades, observed that because of the agricultural depression the farmer in his desperation was turning to the government for help. Bailey warned that ". . . solutions do not lie in promises or programs of expediency. . . ." He was well aware of the technological revolution that was adding to the farmer's plight, but greatly benefiting the consumer with cheap food and fiber. He was disturbed that the farmer was forced to produce cheap food so that Americans could buy expensive luxuries. Bailey wrote of politics and the farmer: "He takes the fairest promise and program for his vote. . . . Partisanship is not competent to solve the ills, . . . it is interested in [political] success rather than in solutions." In an address in 1920, he pointed out that there was little to fear from the "political class solidarity of farmers" because farmers had too many diverse interests. He added that farming was in for great changes for the betterment of everyone, particularly the farmer.

One difficulty in finding any solution for agriculture's ills was the great lack of data related to production costs. Hip-pocket bookkeeping was the standard for most farmers in the early twentieth century prior to the internal revenue era, and family life styles rose and fell with income. In the late 1800's, only a few farm production costs were being gathered through farm management research. There was some concern from farmers that farm cost records in the management studies might be used as the basis for government fixing of farm prices.

Farmers were not at ease having the government involved in their business, although they were distressed. In the spring of 1934, dairy farmers were decisively against government programs, and their protest caused the Agricultural Adjustment Administration (A.A.A.) to free dairying from its grips. To avoid further loss of control over the farmers, government payments were timed to coincide with elections. This was done to gain participation in the corn-hog signup that was planned in an effort to curtail production of those commodities. But consumer resistance, which included a housewives' strike against meat prices in New York in 1935, helped to bring about a reaction that led to the Supreme Court decision outlawing the A.A.A. The A.A.A. was repealed, but by 1936, it was clear that farm programs "constituted an important part of the relief picture" and had to remain a permanent plan for American agriculture.

The government has a long history in the financial and economical development of American agriculture, particularly in the area of credit. This includes such legislation as the Homestead Act, Railroad Land Grants, Indian Scrip, Soldiers Land Grants, Rural Electrification and Telephone Administrations, and a complex of lending agencies up to and including the Farm Credit Act of 1971. All programs appear to trend in the direction of aiding production for the long-range benefit of consumers and of helping make American agriculture predominant in world trade. At the same time, farmers had to be protected from the tendency to constantly overproduce. The economic and social security farmers experienced in the days of independent self-sufficient agriculture before the turn of the century was no longer adequate. In the era of industrialized, commercialized agriculture, the farmer also needed technological security to enable him to use the tools of full production.

Government programs seemed to provide a form of security for some of the farmers, while other farmers looked at the programs as an opportunity to expand, which they quickly grasped. The programs provided warehousing and a primary market. A rural banker explained: "This provided for a high degree of price stability at near poverty levels for some of the producers . . . [while] the processors of agricultural products had stocks available at reasonable and fixed prices whenever they needed them. Inventories were carried at government expense."

Such was the picture of the farm price program in the 1930's and 1940's. From 1951, farmers experienced relatively steady prices, but a decline in purchasing power caused by inflation. Not until the foreign sales of 1972 emptied the price-depressing bins of their stocks did the price of farm products rise, benefiting the farmers. At that time market forces, not legislation, determined the prices.*

A leading national farm magazine, *Successful Farming*, reminded farmers in 1972 of the impact of government influence on prices:

No politician will admit to it, but farm policy remains basically a cheap food policy. . . . Both parties practice it. So do most other nations. It's part of the formula for national economic growth. The theory is that low food costs leave more wealth to develop industry. Cheap food laws have a long history.

---

*For a good survey of the impact of government programs, see *Rural Poverty and Regional Progress in an Urban Society*, Task Force on Economic Growth and Opportunity, Fourth Report, Chamber of Commerce of the United States of America, Washington (1969).

Former Secretary of Agriculture Orville Freeman told the House Agriculture Committee why the government dumped corn on the market in 1961 and 1962. He said: "We purposely sold [corn] in order to move our prices down far enough so that they would be way below the support level, . . . so that we would thereby get compliance. That was the whole intent and purpose and thrust of the program."

It was Freeman's obvious intent to drive prices low enough to force farmers to sign up for the 1963 feed grains program. That year the farmers defeated a referendum calling for more government controls on production, which proved a decisive blow to the advocates of controlling production. In 1966, the department again used corn dumping in an attempt to secure greater participation in the programs.

Today's successful farmers are not unaware of the government's "cheap food policy" nor are they immune from pressures that the Agricultural Stabilization and Conservation Service (ASCS), as the local arm of the United States Department of Agriculture, can exert upon them to secure their participation. In the future some historian will probably record that the sub-level bureaucrats in the ASCS may have even worked contrary to the top-level U.S.D.A. administrators in seeing the programs perpetuated.*

During the interviewing there appeared to be no correlation of political philosophy, size of operation, use of the programs, type of enterprise, and the farmer's attitude toward the government programs. Some of the strongest outspoken, free-enterprising Republicans were the top financial beneficiaries of the programs. Others were liberal pro-government Democrats who disliked the programs intensely and participated only when absolutely necessary. The big farmers were generally very much big-farm oriented and that philosophy dominated their thinking.

The old axiom that the only thing that is consistent about politics is that it is consistently inconsistent certainly applies to the farmer's attitude toward the government programs. The great majority of these farmers would prefer to operate on the free market with supply and demand in control. Most had no doubt about their ability to survive the initial years without farm programs be-

---

*See Edward L. Schapsmeier and Frederick H. Schapsmeier, *Ezra Taft Benson and the Politics of Agriculture*, The Interstate Printers & Publishers, Inc., Danville, Illinois (1975) for an account of Benson's experiences with the bureaucrats of the ASCS and with politicians who wanted to use the programs for vote-getting purposes.

cause they were sure they were more efficient than the rest of the farmers. Others expressed some concern about turning completely to the free market because they were convinced that in recent decades farmers as a minority had been used as a pawn in a political chess game; therefore, they deserved some form of governmental protection. Probably each side does have a point which does not necessarily conflict with that of the other.

The large-scale commercial farmers who were interviewed realized that they represented a minority of a minority group and knew that they had no political power to overcome the long-range cheap food policy of our nation.* This fact cannot be overcome because the non-farm consumers number more than 95 per cent of the nation's political power and few politicians would want to legislate anything contrary to the wish of the majority. The repeal of the Corn Laws in England in 1847 is an outstanding early example of the cheap food policy. Sweden's legislation in the 1960's, declaring that the country was reducing its agricultural self-sufficiency and turning to the world market for cheaper foods, is a more current example of a cheap food policy. The Swedish government made provisions in the same legislation to consolidate farms and to provide relief for the dispossessed small farmers.

In order to determine the acceptance or the rejection of government help to farmers, those who were interviewed were asked the following questions: How important have government programs been to this farm operation? What is your personal feeling about the programs? What do you think is the future of government programs?

It was the opinion of one farmer that farming was so essential to the economy and the welfare of the nation that it should be treated much like a public utility. He wanted to see agriculture free of basic regulation. He was a firm believer in the soil bank principle and used that program to the maximum. He, as well as most farmers, realized that loaded government bins are a price depressant and that any large amount of storage should be avoided. He wanted to determine each future year's needs and then arbitrarily have all farmers, regardless of size, reduce their acres by the same percentage. By restricting acreage each year in this manner, he

---

*The farmers who were interviewed are included in Class I census figures of farming. This class represents 6 per cent of all farmers, but produces 60 per cent of all food and fiber in the nation.

hoped that the free market would control the prices so that they would not be too high for the consumer nor too low for the farmer.

Another farmer has used the government storage programs to the maximum. Each year he stored his own corn, took a loan on it, and used the money to buy corn on the open market for his livestock enterprise. It was his easiest way to expand. It worked so well that he became one of the largest livestock producers in his state. He did not like the programs because he was free-market oriented, and he was sure the programs were designed more for the consumer than for the farmer. He felt that the full storage bins were always used against the farmer.

He freely admits that he likes the cheap food idea because all of society profits from it, and he is convinced that he could make money if he were allowed to operate at full-scale to satisfy the domestic and foreign markets. He added that because of his farm size he has always received considerable pressure to cooperate with the programs. "When we were in the programs, the resentment and talk in the community were always less than when we stayed out, so it didn't take us long to figure out who was fostering that attitude. None of that gossip was too flattering."

A farmer with an extensive multi-enterprise operation has both free and controlled commodities. His first response to the question about the validity of government help was to point out that there was greater risk in the free commodities, but over the years those enterprises had the best average net profit. He did not alter his farming operations to comply with the programs. He used only the parts which fit his operations, but that was enough to put him consistently in the top half-dozen payment beneficiaries in his state. He wanted to get out from under the programs and take his chances on the free market because that is his philosophy. "It is best not to count on the programs because you know they are pointed towards cheap food. But because of our size, we always received intense pressure to sign up. In that manner the local committee could use us as an example."

A farmer, who has among his friends Chicago bankers and Washington lawyers and politicians, gave the impression that, good or bad, we cannot get the government out of agriculture because of the industry's capacity to over-produce. The government has to guarantee a reliable low-cost food supply to the consumers, yet at the same time encourage production so that the nation can export enough to keep its foreign trade balanced. This farmer realizes that he can undersell the world's farmers, but he also knows that they are protected by unpredictable governments, which causes wild fluctuations in foreign demands. It is his opinion that the solid base of his large operation and of farmers like him is in part due to the governmental programs.

A farmer who started in the depths of the depression of the 1930's refused to take part in the government programs because he "hated them like sin." In more recent years he has changed his mind and has taken part in them because he realized that unless something drastic happened the politicians would never get rid of the programs. He also came to see the cheap food aspect of the programs and realized that if consumers wanted cheap food and wanted to restrict his operation he could accept the subsidy like everyone else. In later years he built extensive storage "just to take advantage of the programs." He felt that on the controlled crops the payments were the profits. He also had non-controlled commodities that he considered to be his major business.

A very outspoken advocate of free enterprise bitterly complained, "If the American people insist on cheap food, they must be willing to subsidize my income." His records proved that the profits of his operation were the government payments, which he used as leverage to expand because they were far more than he needed for family living. The most recent flexible programs (up to 1972) were acceptable to him:

Something was necessary to keep overall production in line with demand, and if the consumer did not want to risk shortage, he had to pay the price of surplus. I have been on the ASCS committee for many years, and I made a practice of farming the government to the maximum. We actually planned our farm operation around the government programs. Much land around here was farmed for the programs, not the market. Yet I knew all along that cheap food was the goal of the programs. A strategic reserve for a cheap food policy is necessary, but how do you keep it from affecting the market place?

A farmer who received the top farm program payment in his state was probably also the best-known opponent of those programs. Initially, he had fought them as hard as he could, but, like many others, he saw that the competition was being subsidized, so he felt that he might as well join them. He admitted that he did not need the funds, but as long as the politicians could keep the programs in force, they would do so, and he would accept the payments. He, like several others, cited his records, showing that the non-controlled enterprises on his farm had a better long-run profit record than the controlled enterprises. That gave him a deep sense of satisfaction.

Several farmers believed that the $55,000 limitation on payments would help to ease them away from the government programs. In every case the payment restriction had caused a reduction of their compliance with the program and, as one farmer implied, it gave him courage to break away from it. One of the interviewees had his payment reduced by nearly $100,000 because it was above the legal limit. He feared that consumerism would exert its power on Congress and that farmers, especially the commercial food producers like himself, would in some manner be forced to subsidize the economy more than they already had.

Another farmer saw an obvious conflict ahead because he was locked in at the top by government programs. At the same time, his costs, many of which were caused by inflationary government programs, were rising steadily. He said, "It appears that a large segment of our society thinks that the farmers are supposed to subsidize them."

James C. Malin, a western and agricultural historian, published some reflections on agricultural policies in 1943. He pointed out to his readers that as early as 1912, employees in the United States Department of Agriculture became involved in investigative and regulatory economic activities and developed their own powerful vested interests. Malin wrote, "Instead of limiting themselves as civil servants to the administrative policies formulated by the policy-making branches of government, the politically minded bureaucrats undertook to determine policies for themselves. . . ." This position caused an unfavorable outcome to the attempted programs during the decade of the 1920's. In the 1930's, the bureaucrats saw their opportunity and extended their system nationwide, even by taking an active part in political campaigns and referendums.

Malin correctly predicted what power they would have in the future and how it would be gained. He wrote, "With the support of this vested interest, opposition to prevailing agricultural policies has little chance of becoming effective, and, on the other hand, with its determined opposition, it is doubtful whether the policy of any administration could survive."

Anyone with interest in the farm programs, either pro or con, who would attempt to go against the organization, knows exactly what Malin meant. The ASCS bureaucracy generally assumed the position of being omnipotent, and anyone who tried to oppose them soon discovered it. Threatening to take that body or any of its members to court proved to be impossible. They have the status of an administrative governmental body and cannot be sued.

But the programs were serious business to the bureaucrats who depended upon them for jobs, or for the politicians who used them to secure votes. Probably no other former Secretary of Agriculture discovered that truism more than Ezra Taft Benson. His biographers made this comment about the programs:

Federal controls became tantamount to a form of national management for agriculture. Whereas the original economic mechanism for aiding farmers had great merit, later models became increasingly corrupted by politics. Members of Congress so tampered with the federal machinery that ultimately programs designed to help farmers were in actuality detrimental to their long-range welfare.

The biography of Ezra Taft Benson, with its story of the political pressures brought against him by those outside farming who had a hand in the ASCS bureaucracy, gives credence to the question: Who really benefited most from the programs?

One farmer commented that he thought the programs were necessary when they were started. His father was an excellent manager on a sizeable farm, but he was making a small profit. It was obvious that the average, or smaller than average, farmer had no chance for any profit. This farmer had used the programs up to the time of the $55,000 limitation and then had refused to participate. He had lost all hope that the programs would be reduced or eliminated because he knew several political figures and bureaucrats, and none of them appeared willing to see it phased out.

"Too many farmers are farming for the programs, not for the market," said another farmer, and he confessed that his father hated all forms of subsidization and refused to take part in any program. Having adopted his father's ideas, he felt that the programs handicapped his progress because they enabled many inefficient farmers to "hang on" for much longer than they would have without the subsidy. Eventually, he gave in and took part in the programs, but it was not without complications. He said, "Oh, how we feel the pressures because we are big farmers and not willing cooperators! . . . We actually had the ASCS committee cut our quota out of spite. One member resigned from the board because of this issue. The chairman has publicly stated that he dislikes big farmers and will do everything he can to fight us. This really caused resentment in the community." He believes that by necessity there must be some kind of restriction on overall production. The two-price system for foreign and domestic consumption would be to his liking because he feels sure that the quality of his product would give him a foreign market. He also knows that he can compete with anyone on the world market.

A farmer of more moderate views had hoped to see the programs come to an end and had felt there was a good opportunity for such action at the end of World War II. When that did not happen, he understood that they probably never would terminate the programs. Because he was sensitive to community reaction and because his farming operation was very visible, he complied with the programs but only at the "very minimum." "I went along only because of the attitude of the people from the ASCS office. They got downright nasty with me, so I felt I had to give in. Somehow those ASCS committees manage to get really sour people as far as I am concerned. I wish that they could see the bright side of things."

Many farmers were ideologically opposed to the idea of government subsidy in any form. They wanted to remain totally free to farm as they wished. Some of them were farmers who had taken over going units from their fathers and had reasonably sound economic footings; others were farmers who had started from scratch and preferred the challenge of doing it their own way. One farmer made the following comment about the programs:

They have been a thorn in my side. When I realized how involved they were becoming, I decided to shift to potatoes after the programs were thrown out. The ASCS took grain-acre bases away from me and gave them to other farmers. What did that do to reduce production? It seems like the programs handicapped the good farmers and helped the inefficient ones to hang on. Once we got free of the government in potatoes, we did much better with them. There was more risk, but the profits were greater. The flexible program of the last two years [1972] has been a little better, but the sooner the government gets out of agriculture, the better I will like it. We might be hurt for a few years, but the adjustment would come, and we would be better off.

The programs were in full swing when one farmer started "from scratch." He used them to get some cash flow, but he quickly broke away as much as possible because he realized there were "penalties to be paid for the rewards," and the government price floor soon became the top price. He switched to several specialty crops. "Because I wanted freedom. Anyone can handle the simple commonplace crops with a fixed return. All he has to do is keep his cost of production lower than the pegged market price, so why not go into crops that require better management, have higher risk, but give a better profit potential?"

In 20 years of farming, he built a net worth at the rate of $50,000 a year, including several years of heavy crop losses to natural causes. He used the programs where they fit into his operation, but he never let the programs determine what his basic farming system was to be. He had nothing when he started farming and was not afraid of risk, so he felt he had everything to gain by going to free-market specialty crops.

One of the most anti-government-program farmers was a gentleman who flatly stated that he intensely disliked any type of program. He started farming in the 1930's and never applied for any seed, crop, or livestock loans or payments. He resisted having anything to do with the programs until he was taken to court and forced to comply. He said:

I resisted the government programs as long as I could, but now accept them because I realize we are stuck with them. They subsidize my competition. In a poor year the programs are the net profits and in a good year the income tax payments take it back because there is plenty to spare. The point that bothers me most—now that we are stuck with the programs—is that the American consumer still thinks food prices are too high. Because of that, the programs are really aimed at subsidizing the consumer.

He was intensely involved in his farming. He was a hard worker and had his costs pinned down to the penny. Although his ancestors were pioneer settlers, his success and his opposition to government programs brought him dislike from the community. He spoke against the programs, wrote articles against them, and paid $3,000 to fight the ASCS in court.

Another very outspoken individual maintained that the basic ASCS philosophy was against the free enterprise system. Feeling that way caused him to "farm outside" the programs. One year 176,000 bushels of his total wheat production of 200,000 bushels were so-called "hot wheat." It was his impression, without checking exact records, that he had paid more penalties than he had received in any form of payments until recent years when his annual payments were high in the five-digit figure. It was also his feeling that the government should have left farming alone after World War II. At the most, it should have kept a certificate system on domestic needs and should have let the farmer take his chances on the world market. He is a speculator at heart and freely admits that he is challenged most by risk. He felt that if he were trying to squeeze out a family living on 160 acres he might have a different attitude.

A young farmer refused a straight answer to the question about government programs because in no way was he willing to risk having the local ASCS committee find out how he really felt. He took advantage of the programs when they did not conflict with his farming and when they were profitable. It was his belief that the programs prolonged the agony for many marginal farmers and at the same time handicapped the successful farmers from consolidating their operations. He believed that without the programs there would be a short, sharp collapse of the farm economy, and then things would improve for the better.

Many historians have written about governmental responsibility to farmers' needs. In an article written in 1937 relating to agricultural pressure and political reaction, Alice M. Christensen summarized some of the legislative action. The "Farm Bloc" helped to break the farmers' determination to solve their problems without government aid. This was particularly true prior to 1910 in the era of free land. Christensen added that moralists, politicians, and farm leaders deplored the off-the-farm migration, but up to 1937 had offered no practical solutions as to how the movement could be stopped.

Another writer on the farm movement, stressing farming in the changing society of the 1960's, wrote words in agreement to Alexis de Tocqueville's prophecy of the 1830's about American democracy and the public treasury. Edward Higbee wrote:

In 1929, under . . . Herbert Hoover, farm leaders got their way, and the government began to tap the treasury in an effort to boost prices. From that time on, regardless of which political party has been in power, the taxpayer has become increasingly committed to paying bigger farm subsidies. Plowmen in business suits have learned that no seed yields a better harvest than that planted in the fertile minds of Congress.

At the time Higbee wrote his book, the top 1,200 farms produced as much as the bottom 1,600,000 farms. The top 102,000 farms were producing as much as the bottom 78 per cent. This is truly a reflection that mass production in agriculture had reached some farms that were responding to the needs of a massive urban society.

A farmer who sells to both the domestic and foreign markets is convinced that farm programs have hurt his sales in both markets. He believes the artificial pricing in the domestic markets makes the consumer overconscious of price, whether it is high or low, and causes him to resist. In the foreign market he feels that American farmers could have gained a bigger share of world trade if they had been actively promoting it instead of filling the government bins. He said:

The programs have been a two-edged sword. No one wants to be on a dole, but it takes guts to stay out of the programs, especially when they have become so attractive. They are two-edged in that idle acres have made the small farmer lose even more of his efficiency, while they have influenced the big farmer to get bigger equipment and to expand to do a better job. Then, they put on the $55,000 limitation, which is wrong, because they want the big farmer to idle his capital investment, but if he cannot get more than $55,000, it becomes impossible for him to reduce his production. The government defeats the purpose of the program for purely political reasons.

A leading farmer in his area, who sits on an ASCS committee, definitely feels that some of the programs "have been as logical as subsidizing work horses." It is his impression that since 1948 the programs have hurt as much as they have helped. He saw no hope for the small farmer who did not have a full-time, off-the-farm job. He could not understand why the programs were not either dropped or aimed solely at commercial agriculture. Then he added, "I think the programs will have to go in the long run. But as a committeeman I have seen the inner workings. It is amusing to see the system work for politics. This is a politician's delight."

He admitted that prior to World War II he had received some definite aid from the programs, and that they had been responsible for his farm expansion. His personal choice would be not to have them. He recalled that much resentment toward him as a large-scale farmer lessened after he became a committeeman. He did not understand why because he had "used the programs" to the peak. Although he submitted an idea about a possible workable program in the 1930's, he was disturbed that in times of prosperity the programs still continued. He was unhappy because it appeared to him that the latest generation of farmers assumed government payments as if they were a "birthright."

This same thought was elaborated on by another farmer who possesses a thorough knowledge of agriculture. He reflected that if farmers realized how little they received in contrast to how much was actually charged against the programs they would demand that the programs be thrown out.

The sentiment of many farmers in regard to these programs indicated that the programs were the net profits of their farming business. If this is really true, then some farmers live well while others cannot even buy enough food for their families. A government study in 1966 showed that 68 per cent of all farmers produced 14 per cent of all farm sales, and the lower 80 per cent of that group had a net average income of less than $1,100 from farming. Fortunately, for the survival of their families, the largest portion of those farmers had full-time, off-the-farm jobs, or were dependent on retirement income.

Arthur Mauch, agricultural economist from Michigan State University, wrote of that group:

> We must face the fact that most of our so-called farmers have farms that are just too small to provide an adequate volume of business to make it possible to get an income comparable to that obtained by those employed in non-farm activities. They make very little contribution to our economy. Hence, while they are poor, we cannot say that they are necessarily underpaid.

On the basis of 1966 sales, the lower 54 per cent (1,769,000 farmers) would have needed an increase in prices of 170 per cent to give them parity. At the same time the upper 16 per cent (527,000 farmers) were experiencing a net income per farm of $17,539, or 129 per cent of parity. Are the government programs to be a commercial farm program to help the efficient low cost food producer, or are they to be a pure and simple poverty relief program?*

Program payments to farmers reached their highest point in the late 1960's and early 1970's. In 1968, payments averaged $1,139 per farm or 29.7 per cent of net farm income, not including the amount of the payments. In the five states covered in this study, the average payments per state varied from $1,011, or 33 per cent of net farm income in Minnesota, to a high of $3,116, or 113 per cent of net farm income in North Dakota. Average government payments per farm to North Dakotans were exceeded by only one state. In the early 1970's, the top 785,242 farmers in the nation received an average of $3,620 in government payments, while the bottom 1,585,392 farmers averaged $410 and about 700,000 farmers received no payments.

---

*Much has been written about the value or lack of value of the farm programs to large- and small-sized farms. Among them see Dick Hanson, "Farm Prices Mean Little for 40% of U.S. Farmers," *Successful Farming*, Crop Planting Issue (March, 1972), p. C–6. The trend has continued, so by 1976 the lower 61 per cent of all farmers produced 5 per cent of the farm produce, while the top 6 per cent of the farmers produced 60 per cent of the goods.

What do successful farmers have to say about the farm payments? It is quite obvious that most of the farmers interviewed basically favored the free enterprise system, and regardless of their association with a political party would have preferred to operate without the government programs. But as anyone who has studied agriculture has discovered, the successful farmer is a sharp businessman. He long ago learned to forget about his political principles, and if the government program is of economic value to him, he will take part in it. In this respect, the progressive farmer has proportionately profited more from the programs than most of the farmers who have continued to practice in their traditional ways.

One farmer said candidly, "The government payments are my net profit on small grain. I hate to admit this because I am an anti-government man. We are exceedingly efficient, but with those filled government storage bins, the market price is forced down to the cost of production." He felt that some of the higher capital costs in farming were due directly to the government payments. His feeling was ably seconded by another farmer who had worked in town and had decided to enter farming even if the government was in his business. In his opinion, working in town was too much like being in jail. He used the government payments, which averaged from $40,000 to $50,000 per year, as a security base for his operation. He rented considerable land on a cash basis, and since he was undercapitalized, he felt he had to use the government payments in lieu of a banker. He has done quite well with his "banker," for at the time of interview he was farming land that once made up nearly 50 farms.

Lack of financial strength was not a problem for another farmer of many years' experience because he could borrow all the money he needed and more besides. He would have preferred to farm for the free market, but after many calculations, he determined that there were advantages in using the programs and collecting the government payments. "It boiled down to the fact that if my competition was going to use the programs, I had to keep ahead of them."

Because he had a multi-enterprise farm, another farmer of the third generation did not lack finances, nor did he need the help of the programs. He personally disliked all programs, but he used economic judgment to determine what to do. "Farming is a business and the programs are a part of the business. This year our payments are about $50,000. I can collect $47.00 an acre for idling land, and then when fall comes, I can use that for grazing. That is profitable business. The $55,000 limitation is contrary to the purposes of the program, but that was political and not common sense."

A young farmer preferred not to have any kind of government program, but, like most of his contemporaries, he was concerned about agriculture's capacity to overproduce. He felt the programs brought security to cash-grain farming. He referred to the payments as crop insurance, with the taxpayer paying the premiums. His payments were the net to his small-grain business, which was very large. But he was also quick to point out that his non-supported enterprises, although less stable, had been far more profitable.

"I voted against the government in the potato program" was the opening remark of a farmer in his evaluation of the programs. Then he pointed out how the land diversion had helped him to get a higher level of production on the remaining acres he cropped. He had the highest proven wheat and barley yields in his county and had a net profit of about $15.00 per acre, exclusive of government payments. Those crops were in rotation with potatoes, which are very beneficial to the small grains that follow. He is an exceptionally good farmer in an excellent small-grain area.

Farming in a less fertile area, another individual was realizing a $4.50 (1971) operating profit per acre of actual land harvested, including summer fallow cost on the 50 per cent idle acres. He operates on a large enough scale that he could live well if every year produced a $4.50 operating profit, but this made no allowance to cover land costs. Government payment for him represented his return to capital investment, which must be considered as an important factor in any business if it is to succeed.

Bankers have long watched the government payments to farmers, especially those who rented land for cash. Several farmers indicated that bankers seemed willing to loan the full extent of the government payments and maybe slightly more. One farmer noted that his banker kept a close tab on all government payments and was always confident as long as operating loans were within the limits of those payments. He once told his banker that it appeared as if he (the banker) had no faith in farming as a profitable industry without the subsidies. After this remark he was able to borrow more money, and it was his impression that the banking lobby in Washington might be more concerned about keeping the farm programs than many of the farmers are. Ironically, several of the farmers interviewed had used their farming profits to buy bank stock, in some cases the entire bank.

Government Programs and Their Part in Creating Larger Farms

Edward and Frederick Schapsmeier, authors of biographies of Former Secretaries of Agriculture Henry A. Wallace and Ezra Taft Benson, made it quite clear that both men were well aware of the impact of the government programs in creating large-scale farms. Henry A. Wallace, Secretary of Agriculture in the Franklin D. Roosevelt administration, was well aware of the advantage the larger farmer, and especially the land owner, would have under the farm programs of the 1930's. Edward Schapsmeier remembered seeing the statistics in the Wallace papers that "the program of rigid price supports basically helped big farmers and did little, if anything, for the smaller operator. The whole trend is for bigness, efficiency, and large capital investments." The government's managerial role has adjusted to that concept over the years and even fostered it.

Wallace understood the advantage to the larger farmer. He also understood the plight of the sharecroppers and other tenant farmers. But he also knew what had to be done to get the political factions and the influential farmers to cooperate. Political compromise decided the fate of the small farmers, short of outright welfare payments. By the late 1960's, 3.8 per cent of the farmers were collecting about 40 per cent of the total government program payments.

One of the more dramatic cases of how the programs really worked was illustrated by an individual who started farming before World War I. He acknowledged that the payments were "quite a lift" during the 1930's, but he would have farmed without them. He quickly became one of the largest beneficiaries of the programs in his state in the early days of the programs. He was very anti-government and told of his experience with much glee: "After we got going, we just increased by buying more land each year. When the government payments got so big that I could operate and live on them [and barley, flax, or oats sales], I stopped selling wheat and put it in my own storage.... The only time I sold wheat was when I saw a big piece of land that I wanted to buy. Then I had the money to pay cash for it. I kept buying until I passed the 200-quarter mark."

A young third generation farmer started farming where his father left off and built rapidly by maximum use of the government programs. He admitted that it worked fine, because each time he purchased another piece of land, he transferred the crop acres to his existing land and put all the diverted acres on the newly purchased farm. In this manner he could clean out trees, stones, and old fence lines; remove the buildings; tile; and clean up the land to get it in condition for the following year. This enabled him to get the newly acquired land in shape so that when he put his first crop in on that land, it was generally better than any that had ever been raised on those acres. "This often caused hard feelings because people in the community often made fun of some of the land I bought until I raised the first crop. The programs really enabled me to make a business of improving run-down farms." His closing thoughts about the programs were that he would rather see supply and demand determine price than the government.

"I never used the government programs," said another farmer, "until I found a run-down farm that I could buy and use for diverted acres. Up to that time I was dollars ahead each year putting it all through livestock." After he purchased his run-down farm, he used it for diverted acres, cleaned it up, and seeded it to good hay and grazing land. Each fall, he grazed his feeder cattle or his cow herd on those acres after he had collected his diversion payment for the year. As he noted, it was all according to the regulations, but contrary to his personal likes, even if the payments were good.

A farmer who received the top government payment in his state felt that the program payments were the number-one factor in the growth of his farm. He acknowledged that his farm was "ready to grow" when the programs started, so that he was able to make a business of expanding through the use of the guaranteed payments. He used every feature of the program that was available. He purchased large-scale equipment as quickly as new machines became available to keep his cost of production low, and he was able to make a good profit on small grains in addition to the payments.

Another farmer had precise figures on what the government payments meant to him. Some of his enterprises were under programs and some were not. He received 15 per cent of his gross income from government payments, and on the average it represented about 3.5 per cent return on his investment. "Most of the time I saved my payment money to use either for internal or external expansion. Whenever I bought more land, my payments automatically expanded. I have the feeling that urban-controlled Congresses will put a stop to all this."

It was also his impression that one of the most beneficial of all programs was the soil conservation program. He felt it was generally profitable to his farming, but also necessary for the long-run good of the nation. That probably would be the most singly agreed-upon comment concerning government programs.

A straightforward individual felt that the programs put farming in stronger hands because a big farmer could not help but gain more than the small operator. He felt that the new farmers were businessmen who put their philosophical feelings aside when it came to economics. He gave an excellent example of what was taking place throughout rural America. In 1971, there were 35 farms sold in his area, and 28 sets of buildings with the yards were sold off those farms as rural residences. The land from 28 of the 35 farms was consolidated into existing farms. In another community, he knew of one farmer who had purchased nine farms in a solid block to secure the size of fields he wanted for efficiency.

But another farmer expressed regret in his parting thought: "I would have expanded even more than I did if I had felt the programs were going to last as long as they did. It was easy to buy when you could definitely project your income, but I always hoped that some day these temporary programs would come to an end." The foreign grain sales did for the American farmers what the politicians did not want to do—free the farmers to operate for the market. The stability is gone; but without programs, the progressive farmer, motivated by high prices, expands more rapidly than ever. However, it was the federal programs that helped him build his sound economic base.

During the period of the programs, American agriculture went through one of its most innovative and expansive periods. The farmer learned to substitute variable costs for fixed costs. He was forced to change his techniques, which in part defeated the intents of the programs. But the American nation benefited from it by steadily declining food costs in relation to its ability to buy. In the long run, agriculture gained from the programs, because the very programs that many thought were designed to save the small farmer hastened his removal from the land, and sound economic units of production were created by those who remained. The process is not yet complete, but in the decades since 1934 great progress has been made. The 12,309 farmers who received over

$20,000 each benefited far more from the programs in 1972 than did the other 2.4 million farmers who received an average of less than $1,500 each. Industrialized agriculture was closer to reality.*

The Problem of the Free Market

A free market is the dream of all the farmers interviewed, but some doubted its realization in the near future. Although commercial farmers are in a better economic position today than at any other period in history (except for brief wartime prosperity), in some respects they are more vulnerable than ever. Fortunately, modern agriculture is in a position to be highly capitalized, but unfortunately, the modern farmer is forced to use a substantial amount of capital for purchasing a large portion of his total inputs.

One farmer, questioned about the future of the free market, had a broad perspective of the farm programs, and it is his opinion that the politicians distort the farm programs to buy votes because that is what the farmers demand. For several years he worked with farmers throughout a wide area, and it is his impression that farmers know what their problems are but renege on their responsibility to solve them. He feels sure that if the government meant business and would withdraw from regulating agriculture, the job could be done. Then he noted that it would be a pipe dream to think that the politicians would let it happen.

A gentleman who has been farming since the 1930's came to the same conclusion. He would like to see a free market. He believes that through self-regulation, farmers would keep production at a point where prices would be similar to those of the late 1960's and early 1970's. He was being realistic about prices, but he felt that a massive education program would have to be conducted to free the farmers from their past orientation of producing for the government bins. A serious readjustment in agriculture would take place caused by the psychological impact that the removal of supports would have. Nevertheless, he was willing to take that chance.

A farmer with a college degree and 18 years of farming experience had never known farming without the programs and had mixed feelings about a free market. He wanted to have a chance to

---

*It was with encouragement from Ed Smith, past president of the North Dakota Farmers Union, that this writer made a careful examination of the farm subsidy payments listed in the 1973 *Congressional Record* to determine who the largest farmers in the five states were.

produce for the world market because he knew that without political tampering he had an advantage. He was disgusted with the constant attempts by politicians to make the programs attractive to get more farmers involved. He particularly cited the provision to rent back diverted land for the purpose of planting a non-controlled crop. He saw such programs as pure attempts to ruin the attractiveness of the free crops involved. His greatest concern was that programs would hamper the American farmer in producing as efficiently as he could for the world market. "Maybe," he said, "supports for the domestic market would be as far as we should go, and then let us hustle for the world market."

The consensus of a large portion of these men was that if the government offered fewer and firmer programs, the costs would be less and the farmers would produce for the market instead of for the bins. It was the opinion of many that if the consumer feels that he must have cheap food the producer of cheap food must be protected from financial ruin caused by his tremendous capacity to produce.

Another farmer expressed the fear that the government will not only fail to get out of agriculture, but it may discriminate in the future against the larger, efficient commercial farms that the first 40 years of programs helped create. He believes that both the environmentalist and the vote-seeking politician will lead the campaign against larger economic units. He believes farm organizations are likely to join that group in order to stimulate membership subscriptions. It is also his opinion that such a campaign will stop only after the American consumer realizes that he is destroying the very institution that is providing him with low-cost food and fiber. He believes that legislation against the larger more efficient family farm will go too far before it is stopped. He pointed out that one goal of the programs of the 1930's was to maintain small farms, and although they were a complete failure in that respect, the programs were not stopped.

An editorial in a leading Canadian farm magazine reminded Canadians of a similar fact. In 1931, when the first farm programs were introduced in that nation, there were 728,664 farmers. Just 30 years later, there were 480,903 farmers remaining, but 180,000 of them were producing 80 per cent of the total Canadian production. The editorial reminded Canadians that every time the farmers called for more help the Minister of Agriculture responded by building a bigger bureaucracy.

In conclusion, one farmer questioned had almost completely

broken away from the farm programs after being totally involved in them earlier. He had deliberately made changes in his farm enterprises over a period of years because he disliked the idea of the programs, but he could well afford the risk of being outside them. He was convinced that not all farmers could afford the risk involved. He was sure that the few completely self-supporting small farmers (i.e., those not relying on off-the-farm income) would be bankrupt at once because of the collapse of prices caused by the psychological letdown of the absence of government supports. Then he added, "After that happens, there might be some real professional farmers left who not only know how to farm but would then soon learn how to keep supply in line with demand."[1]

NOTE

[1]Kenyon Leech Butterfield, *The Farmer and the New Day*, Macmillan, New York (1919), p. 85; "Prices Received by Farmers, Parity Index and Parity Ratio, 1910–1970," *1970 Handbook of Agricultural Charts*, U.S. Department of Agriculture, Washington (1970), p. 7; *1977 Handbook of Agricultural Charts*, Agricultural Handbook No. 524, U.S. Department of Agriculture, Washington (November, 1977), p. 6; Liberty Hyde Bailey, *The Harvest of the Year to the Tiller of the Soil*, Macmillan, New York (1927); G. A. Pond, et al., "The First Sixty Years, . . ." Report 283, pp. 12–13; A. B. Genung, *A Brief Survey of 35 Years of Government Aid to Agriculture Beginning in 1920*, Northeast Farm Foundation, Ithaca, New York, (1959), pp. 8–19; "Financial Development in 1971," *Gopher State Review*, Minnesota Crop and Livestock Reporting Service Bulletin 292 (March, 1972); Sir John R. Hicks, *A Theory of Economic History*, Oxford University Press, London (1969), p. 109; Leslie W. Peterson, address to the Minnesota Bankers Association Lending Conference (April 17, 1974); "What's New in Washington?" *Successful Farming*, LXV, No. 5, (May, 1967), p. 7; Paul Findley, "The Fork in the Road," a guest editorial, Chicago, *National Livestock Producer* (July, 1966), p. 30; Harold Johnson, "Meet Modern Sweden's Average Farmer," *The Farmer*, XXCIV, No. 17 (September 3, 1966), p. 38; James C. Malin, "Mobility and History: Reflections on the Agricultural Policies of the United States in Relation to a Mechanical World," *Agricultural History*, XVII, No. 4 (October, 1943), pp. 187–188; Edward L. Schapsmeier and Frederick H. Schapsmeier, *Ezra Taft Benson and the Politics of Agriculture: The Eisenhower Years, 1953–1961*, The Interstate Printers & Publishers, Inc., Danville, Illinois (1975), p. 16; Alice M. Christenson, "Agricultural Pressure and Governmental Response in the United States, 1919–1929," *Agricultural History*, XI, No. 1 (January, 1937), pp. 41–42; Edward Higbee, *Farms and Farmers in an Urban Age*, Twentieth Century Fund, New York (1963), pp. 49–50, 139; James P. Houck, "Can We Cure Farm Poverty with Commercial Farm Poverty?" *Minnesota Agricultural Economist*, No. 532 (July, 1970), pp. 2–3; Eugene H. Methvin, "Time to Say No to Big Farm Subsidies," *Reader's Digest*, XCVI, No. 577 (May, 1970), p. 79; Edward L. Schapsmeier, a letter to the author (May 25, 1974); "Farm Subsidies," *Congressional Record* (March 29, 1973), p. H2265, and "Extension of Remarks" (May 3, 1973), pp. E2832–E2870; "ASCS Payments," *The Forum* (May 15, 1973); "Time for Frankness," *Country Guide, The Farm Magazine*, an editorial, XCII, No. 2, Winnipeg, p. 8; *Changes in Farm Production and Efficiency*, a special issue featuring historical series, U.S. Department of Agriculture, E.R.S., Statistical Bulletin No. 561, Washington (September, 1976); for a detailed study on

the impact of government programs, see Charles L. Schultze, *The Distribution of Farm Subsidies: Who Gets the Benefits?*, The Brookings Institution, Washington (1971); anonymous interviews (see footnote on first page of chapter).

CHAPTER XII

Where Is the Peasant?

or

European Agriculture in the Era of Industrialization

THE UNITED STATES is historically looked upon as an appendage of Europe. Europe has led the way, and America has often followed politically, economically, culturally, and socially. At least one segment of the American social structure, however, has outpaced its European parent—agriculture. For the last century, American agriculture generally has outpaced not only Europe but also, with limited exceptions, most of the world.

Many Americans dislike the ever growing and expanding industrialization of America's agriculture and, with it, the changing structure of family-oriented farming. In their rejection of these changes, they point to other societies and areas where the peasant-oriented farm units are still functioning. Until World War II, these individuals could cite the peasant-oriented agriculture of Western Europe as an example of what they believed to be the basis of a more satisfactory socio-economic–political structure. To them the almost ageless, stubborn, peasant-oriented agriculture seemed particularly indestructible. World War I and later World War II, with their explosive impact on society throughout the world and the ensuing cry for independence, the acceleration of industry and technology, and the ever expanding overpopulation, caused a slow erosion of the antiquated basis of peasant agriculture. Finally, about 1950, the flood gates broke wide open and Western European agriculture experienced a virtual revolution in agricultural production and productivity.

The Changing European Scene

As early as the 1870's, Europeans had been feeling the effects of several aspects of the growing American and other New World agricultural economies. Each year the Americas, with their free, traditionless, innovative form of agriculture, poured ever lower-cost farm products onto the world markets. European farmers could not compete with them, and European consumers demanded and experienced improvements in their level of living. As a result of the opening of foreign markets, American farmers increased in numbers rapidly and, at the same time, improved their productivity so dramatically that even with growing domestic and foreign demands they were able to outpace the demand for their products. Those European economies which were interested in urban industrialization were quick to capitalize on the low-cost abundant food supply.

After World War I, many of the former large agricultural estates on the European scene were greatly reduced in number and size, and, in a democratic sense, a peasant-oriented agriculture was encouraged. In Eastern Europe, specifically in Russia, as a result of the Communist Revolution, the estates of the nobility were replaced by state-operated large-scale farms. Although these farms were not exactly outstanding examples of efficiency and productivity, quantitatively they eventually exceeded the total volume of output that formerly came from the combination of large estates and peasant farms. Russian society as a whole benefited from the Communist Revolution, although people of the Western World, especially those who were democratically oriented, questioned and basically disliked the methods used by the Russians and their affiliates. Industrialization of agriculture was being imposed on people who were far behind western society in their methods, and new problems arose from it.

By contrast, in the more democratic part of Western Europe, the peasants continued their casual method of farming as a way of life, and most nations accepted their position as deficit food producers as something that they had to live with.

In spite of the fact that European society had made great strides in other economic segments, its agricultural development lagged in rate of growth by comparison. The Europeans were well aware of the American agricultural problem of surpluses, as contrasted to their continued lassitude which led to food deficits. Henry A. Wallace, then American Secretary of Agriculture, expressed it in a challenge to the American county extension agents in 1933 when he said: "Having conquered the fear of famine with the aid of science, having been brought into an age of abundance, we have now to learn how to live with abundance."[1]

Industrialization of agriculture in Europe made slow inroads until the tractor appeared in limited numbers on farms in western parts of the continent by the mid-1930's. Most farms were too limited in size to justify using even small tractors as long as a relatively low-cost and surplus-captive labor supply was available.

During World War II, Western European agriculture was forced to make major increases in production while its surplus labor resources were being drained off into other industries. After the war, much of the continent experienced a rapid growth in industrial and consumer production, and surplus agricultural labor continued to find more profitable alternatives for making a living in industry and commerce.

The wartime experience with urban life had reduced the resistance of rural people to urban living, and rural-urban barriers were greatly diminished. It was no longer possible for agriculture to depend on human and animal power and to compete with mechanically powered industry to provide a satisfactory level of living.

In the 1950's, the European Economic Community and several other quasi-political–economic unions were formed to create a unified Europe so that Europeans could more effectively compete with the rest of the world and maintain their position of eminence in that world. Coal and iron were the first commodities to be freely exchanged in the "new union." Military and political cooperation advanced at an almost surprising rate. Agricultural unity and cooperation came slower than that of any other sector, partly because Europeans had been too sentimental and traditional toward their peasant-oriented agriculture. The problem of dealing with a highly fragmented and extremely politically and socially sensitive form of agriculture was difficult. But for the European Community to be a total success, it required agriculture to be fully integrated into the totality of economy.

After World War II, Europeans by necessity had to make an assessment of their future. Food was a deficit commodity for most of their countries. Somehow they would have to improve their ability to produce more of their own food needs, for it was becoming increasingly difficult to establish a balance between exports and imports, especially in light of rapidly rising imported energy costs. European leaders knew that in 1945 only 16 per cent of the population of the United States was producing a surplus of food, while at the same time large acreages were being diverted from production. Whereas, in Europe, some of the most advanced countries still had up to 52 per cent of their population in farming. On the average about 28 per cent of the population of the nations involved in this study were involved with farming. In the era of industrial growth, European nations needed workers in other segments of their economy, but the governments found it very difficult, if not impossible, to move their peasants off the farm as recruits for industry. To meet the demand for industrial workers, several European nations were forced to rely on immigration of foreign peoples. Therefore, the time had come for action, for, as one Irish political official said, "The nations could no longer afford the luxury of the leisurely life of the peasant."[2]

In 1950, Western Europeans were basically agriculturally self-sufficient in potatoes, vegetables, milk, and eggs, but they needed about 30 per cent more cereal grains than they could produce. Besides having large deficits in sugar, meat, oils, and fats, they had lesser deficits in fruits, cheese, and butter.

The European Community (E.C.)

Europeans, in 1950, were still spending about twice as much of their net income for food as were Americans at the same time. And, generally, there was a far greater portion of the work force involved in agriculture, because productivity per worker on the farm was considerably less than in America. But even a more critical situation arose when, in order to meet the balance of payments, the Europeans had to reduce their food imports wherever possible. Then a great change created an entirely different outlook for Europe: The Mansholt Plan which sought to industrialize European agriculture became a reality in the new European Community.

To determine where Western European agriculture might be headed under the European Community, and how far agricultural industrialization had progressed, the author undertook a trip in the spring of 1977 to some European countries to visit with progressive farmers. The countries visited were Austria, Denmark, England, France, Hungary, the Netherlands, Spain, and Sweden. Previous contacts had been made in West Germany and Ireland. The same questions used in interviews with progressive American and Canadian farmers were asked of these innovative Europeans. It quickly became obvious that progressive, innovative farmers are a universal breed, and regardless of their geographical location, their mental processes and their innovative and progressive ideas are very similar. Their attitudes and outlook appear to be modified more by the political climate than by any other single factor.

Without a doubt, most of these farmers could be transplanted to another country and it would be only a matter of time before they would develop into farm leaders in their new location.* Their philosophies and attitudes toward farming and society were nearly identical to those of their American and Canadian counterparts.

Limiting this discussion to one chapter means that only generalizations can be made. Therefore, this chapter will be a miniature picture of the first 11 chapters of this volume. In nearly every case, as experienced in mid-America, the women participated in the interview process. It did not take long to determine that, like their American counterparts, the farm wives of Europe are a vital part of progressive family farming. Like their husbands, they are proud to be farmers and are also determined to make the farm an even better business than it already is and an even better place to live. Many of the European farmers gave considerable credit to their wives, just as the Midwestern farmers had done. The Five M's of successful farming, plus the sixth M, marketing, were every bit as obvious to progressive farmers in Europe as they were in North America. These farmers are not of the old-fashioned, peasant-oriented mentality. They look on farming as a good business and are interested in more than making a subsistence living; they want to make progress.

First of all, the European farmers were asked if they felt that they could be competitive on the world market. In general, their answers were yes, but they were not quite as confident of it as the North American farmers had been because they realized that their toughest foreign competitors were the Americans. The only absolutely no answers came from farmers in Austria and Spain. Their negative answers were based on awareness of the fact that their average farm was too small to be an economically efficient unit to be competitive. However, Spanish farmers personally felt that they could compete because they had sizeable, automated industrialized farms.[3]

A Dutch dairy farmer, who had traveled widely in Europe, was not sure that he could compete with the North Americans or New Zealanders, but with his 139 milk cows, he felt he was as good as

---

*This writer has become well acquainted with many Europeans who have migrated to Canada and to the United States since the Suez Crisis in 1956. These people are pioneers of the twentieth century, and they have been very successful, progressive, innovative farmers. They are very excited about making a case for the success of farming in North America, as contrasted to defeats by the political and traditional obstacles of Europe.

any of his European competitors. He added, "But in any case, leave me here; I like Holland best."[4] The Europeans were all well aware of the high level of protection they were receiving from the tariff barriers, and generally thought such protection was being overdone. On the other hand, they admitted that as long as they could profit from that protection they would eagerly participate. Generally, however, they felt that the days of high governmental protection were numbered.

Dr. Robert Burgert, director of the largest collective farm in Hungary (Babolna), farms in a far different political climate than that of farmers who live in the more democratic states of Europe. In regard to the future of agriculture in general, he believes it is an industry that is being increasingly involved in world trade. Dr. Burgert said:

We take part in international trade and we are very active in that trade. [Over 600 plane loads of chickens annually leave his farm.] In regard to competitiveness, we are not subsidized by our government so we must compete independently in world trade. We have to fight for our own trade. But we will succeed because we are truly convinced that we are running the type of farm of the future. No more needs to be said on that subject.[5]

Basically, the farmers of Western Europe were well aware that they had one very significant advantage in the international competition and that was their nearness to over 300 million well-paid consumers. As Sam Moreton of England expressed it: "Transportation from 1936 on is one of the most unbelievable changes in agriculture. Even in England we have changed from parish-oriented to an internationally oriented farming."[6]

Moreton, a very progressive farmer, was happy for the change because it forced each area to make use of its comparative advantage. This he knew would hasten internationalization of agriculture which he felt was best for the consumer and in the long run also best for the producer. He believed that he had advantages in potatoes because of transportation cost and also in livestock because he farms in some of England's best grass producing country. This was why he can compete on the international level.

K. G. Insulander, a member of the Royal Society of Agriculture of Sweden, and his son, Alf, were both convinced that in their specialty, hogs, they could compete with most of the world. The Insulanders commented that their Yorkshire–Swedish Landrace pigs were of unmatched quality except in the Netherlands and in Denmark. Although they had toured American Midwest hog units, they were not concerned about Sweden being overrun with American pork.

The Insulanders' 1975 production records, with 300 sows that averaged 2.2 litters each, would make the majority of American hog farmers envious. They averaged 10.6 pigs born and 9.7 pigs weaned per litter that year. The feed conversion ratio on Swedish-produced barley and imported American soybean meal was 2.92 kilograms of feed to each kilogram of animal gain.[7] It quickly became clear that the top farmers, regardless of where they live, make farming difficult for the less efficient. Because of certain traditional, economic, geographical, and technological advantages which the North American farmers had in the past, they might have a superiority in competitive agriculture. The future, however, will not be like the past, and it is apparent that the free, innovative farmer of Western Europe, and the progressive collective farm of the Eastern sector, eventually might become greater competitors. This might not be true of the many existing small units in Europe where the farmer is only partially employed or where he supports his farm with factory earnings, but as land is consolidated into more efficient businesses, European agricultural competition will be felt on the world market.

Like their American counterparts, the European farmers were asked about their views on the economy of size of operations necessary to make a farm efficient and at the same time provide at least a satisfactory living for the farm family. The European nations have wrestled with the farm size problem for many decades but politically have never been able to face up to the need for a change until relatively recent times. In 1967, over 80 per cent of all farms in the European Economic Community countries were under 10 hectares* and generally had farms too small to keep one man fully employed. At the same time, these farms failed to provide enough income to secure weekend or holiday help. This, then, virtually made the peasant operator a slave to his occupation, although he was not fully employed on his farm.[8]

After World War II, the governments of Europe faced the fact that to achieve true efficiency in agriculture they would have to increase farm size and find alternative employment for a major portion of their farm population. The government of the Netherlands was one of the first of the Western European nations to become active in reducing both the number of farms and the number

---

*One hectare equals 2.47 acres.

of people working on the land. The occasion came about quite naturally after the major flooding of 1953 when many farmers were forced to vacate their farms. The Dutch government, with the agreement of the Dutch Farmers Union, declared the "times were changing. Not everyone would be allowed to return to his farm. Rationalization must come. It's not possible for all farmers to start again. . . . Planners are recognizing the agricultural revolution."

The Director General of Food Supply for the Netherlands, A. P. Franke, who is also a member of the European Community Agricultural Council, declared that the best farm of the future will be a fully mechanized two-man farm. He suggested that before Europe's agricultural income problem can be even partially solved, "Some European countries will have to move 89 per cent of their farmers out of agriculture."[9]

From year to year the Western European democracies have taken steps to ease the farm income problem by various methods of aiding the farmer in search of alternative forms of income so that farm land can be merged into larger units. The movement, however, having to work against a sentimental and political opposition to farm consolidation, has been great although slow. Some sociological pains have been felt, but in the long run total society has gained, for even the remaining farmers have improved their income and the consumers have profited from relatively lower food costs.

The Communistically inclined nations east of the Iron Curtain face the same problem as the Western democracies. Dr. Burgert said of the long-range trend:

It is worthwhile to face the sentimentalist, for in the case of peasant agriculture it is pride of ownership by the families and this has nothing to do with economics. The small farms have hung on too long . . . but Europe still suffers from the peasant's political power. There is a surplus of those people, and they survive because they ignore the economic facts. . . . The size of concentration of land must be decided by scientific results, not by sentiment. Those who ignore the facts of economics must pay the price. . . . Science now determines all over the world; it penetrates into agriculture and determines the future.

Dr. Burgert specifically stated that a basic corn unit in Hungary would have to be at least 500 hectares (1,235 acres) to keep a complete line of machinery busy. On the farm he directs, however, 1,660 hectares is a basic corn machine unit: ". . . but that is not the end yet. Some say that we think only about machines, but labor is more expensive than machines and forces us to go to large units, because we must have profit."[10]

These words may seem strange coming from a director of a Communist-controlled state farm, but they help to prove that economic facts cannot be ignored in the long-run by any society if it is to succeed. Many farmers of Western Europe are quite in agreement with this thought. Although the farmers interviewed are among the innovators of their areas, and their agricultural enterprises are far larger than the average for their respective countries, they agreed unanimously that they still had to strive for additional expansion in order to achieve greater economy.

Ade Brouwer of the Netherlands, who milks 139 cows, was of the opinion that the smallest economic unit for a family-operated dairy farm would be 50 cows. But unless the owner had at least 40 per cent of the necessary capital, he would be unable to make such a unit pay. Ironically, the average-sized milking cow operation in the Netherlands is only 19 head.

Another Dutch farmer, H. Thielen, who milks 80 cows, has won nine plaques for having been named the outstanding farmer of his district for as many years. Thielen believes that the smallest possible economic dairy operation would be 50 cows if the farmer had good control of the necessary land to raise all the feed required. He personally would not feel comfortable with an operation of that size because there would be no margin for "comforts," nor would it be large enough to support a helper to rotate the work schedule.[11]

Gilbert Moeyaert, a French corn farmer who operates a continuous corn farm of nearly 1,000 hectares, believes that the smallest economic continuous corn farm in Southwestern France would have to be at least 100 hectares. However, the average in his area is at least 150 hectares for full-time farmers. Those with less are usually not doing well unless they have the support of family members with non-farm jobs. This size contrasts to the average-sized farm in France in 1975 of only 24 hectares, which is nearly double the average prewar size.

Between 1964 and 1975, France pensioned off over 503,000 small farmers so that their farms could be merged into larger and more efficient units. By 1975, one-fourth of all the land used in agriculture in France had already been amalgamated into larger units through the government program. At that time, the consolidation program was moving effectively in spite of a strong sentiment in that nation in favor of peasant agriculture. This consolidation was made possible because of the economic alternatives provided by the government to ease excess population out of agriculture "to achieve a fairer redistribution of wealth in favour of farmers whose branch, essential to the life of the nation, has been affected more than any other by the need to transform and adapt to the modern economic world."[12]

Sam Moreton, who is reputed to be the fifth largest potato farmer in England, farms about 2,400 acres.* Moreton remembered that when his grandfather retired in 1920 he owned and farmed 46 acres. When Sam Moreton's father, George F. Moreton, started farming that year, he rented those 46 acres plus an additional 10 acres. Those 56 acres were divided into 27 fields. George Moreton had two full-time employees to help with the crops in addition to milking 20 cows and farrowing 5 sows twice a year. Two horses were used as power to work the 8 acres of potatoes, 10 acres of oats, and 8 acres of wheat. The remainder of the farm contained some pasture, but chiefly hay land. All the hay was hand-forked.

Sam Moreton said that prior to 1939, when the first tractor was purchased, the only engine on the farm was in his motor bike. With the purchase of that tractor and then one of the very first combines in Warwickshire in 1942, the farm expanded rapidly. When George Moreton retired in the mid-1940's, he was farming 415 acres with the help of one son and four full-time employees. George Moreton had never owned land because he did not want to accumulate debts.

Sam Moreton, the third generation member of the family, started in 1942 with 192 acres of rented land and £3,000 of borrowed money. By 1947, he had expanded to 380 acres and 85 milk cows and was hiring 27 workers to work with potatoes, carrots, and garden beets. Once farm machinery became available after the war, he mechanized and expanded his enterprise as fast as he could buy or rent land, building up to 1,192 acres and 170 milk cows, but reducing his permanent work force to 13. Today, Sam Moreton's four sons operate more than 52 times as much land as their great-grandfather did only 57 years earlier, using 15 tractors with a combined total of 1,420 horsepower. In addition, they are involved in several other enterprises not directly related to the farm.

The Moretons are well aware of the fact that the average-sized farm in England is only 160 acres (65 hectares) if all farms are considered, or 249 acres (101 hectares) if only full-time farmers are

---

*The English use the land unit term "acre" rather than "hectare" (2.47 acres), which is standard for the continental countries.

involved. But they do not believe that any farm under 500 acres can be economically profitable nor can it provide a satisfactory living. Neither Sam Moreton nor his son Fred would be satisfied to operate a farm of that limited size. It is their opinion that a farm with 100 acres of potatoes rotated with 400 acres of grain can provide a farmer and his wife with only an average independence and a very low standard of living.[13]

Trevor Ensor, who farms in the English Midlands, believes that a farm of under 500 acres can provide only a modest family living. Ensor said, "That is if the land is rented, for it would not be economically possible to purchase land at current prices and have anything left to live on." Land rental rates were less than 3 per cent of market value of the land in his area. Travel between fields caused some disadvantages to larger-scale farming, but, according to Ensor, these problems were more than offset by the gains in purchasing and marketing, as well as by the use of better large-scale equipment.[14]

Geoffrey H. Ballard studied American agriculture in his student days in the United States before returning to England to farm. He felt that if he had to make a living from straight grain farming, he would want a thousand acres to gain the necessary economies to provide an adequate living. Ballard realized that if sugar beets or potatoes were included in the rotation a 500-acre farm with at least 100 acres of either beets or potatoes would be adequate. His farm is larger than his prescribed minimums and also includes a milking herd of over 90 cows, a hog operation that farrows 170 litters of pigs, and a beef fattening enterprise. Each of these individual enterprises exceeds the average for the farms in his area and in the nation.[15]

Fred Harper, who is a member of the English County Council Agricultural Board, stated that the governing body was steadily creating larger farms through the process of consolidation of farms that became vacant. The current policy in his county is that a dairy farmer should have at least 75 cows and enough acreage to support that herd and the young stock. Harper, who has been farming since the late 1930's, said that he has observed that many farmers have failed in his area during his lifetime because they were too small. "But," he added, "I have seen no well-managed farm fail, and I know of no farm in our area that is too large to be economically efficient." Harper is encouraging his son, David, to expand as rapidly as he can generate and borrow capital.[16]

Similar reactions to economy of scale were gathered from the farmers of the other nations. Again, it must be remembered that these are not average farmers, for they are the agricultural pacesetters in their respective areas. Their attitudes and their management processes and abilities exceed those of the average. Those attitudes are affected by personal traits as well as by the way they look upon farming as a successful and changing business.

Limitations on Progress

When asked what is the greatest limitation to future expansion in farming, they had a variety of answers, but basically they were similar to those of their North American contemporaries. The three most frequent replies to the question about limitations to growth pointed out governmental regulations, lack of land, and lack of quality labor, with availability of capital being a very weak fourth problem.

The govermental regulation factor is not intended to appear as a contradiction to what has been mentioned previously relative to programs of farm consolidation which strive to create economic units and greater overall efficiency in European agriculture. All the farmers interviewed are already operating considerably in excess of the established minimum goals for farm size. However, there are discriminatory laws generally against larger farms in several of the countries visited. These laws were passed, not because of their economic logic, but chiefly because it is politically popular in those countries to be opposed to larger farms.

Flemming Juncker of Denmark, who is very opposed to governmental policies of any nature, said, "The government dreams of small farms, but its image of what a small farm is is constantly changing. The size increases naturally, because technology gives us cheap food, and it is ridiculous to fight technology in a welfare state because it is the only way you can afford the high standards."

Mr. Juncker used his farm as an example of what technology had done to reduce production costs. During World War II, he employed more than 40 workers, 48 horses, and 2 tractors. By 1977, he had more than doubled his acres, but was using 18 workers and 8 tractors. Juncker's parting comment: "Foolhardy legislation will try to restrict farm size, but it will fail because you cannot restrict technology."[17]

K. G. Insulander of Sweden brought to our attention the fact that the operators of average-sized farms that were solely family-run were provided with state-paid laborers to enable the family to take a vacation. Larger than family farms received no such benefits. He also stressed that in times of surplus of some commodities in some of the countries the prices are maintained for the products of the small farmer; whereas, the larger farmer must accept open market prices. Swedish farmer Douglas Kennedy, who produces pork and milk, added: "In this manner the larger farmer is made to bear the losses while the small farmer is shielded from the reality of the open market."[18]

Three Danish farmers commented that they could not purchase additional land unless such land were adjacent to their existing farms (or not more than a half mile from the building site) because a farmer cannot own more than two farms. But at the same time, they were restricted by law from renting land within 10 miles of their existing farms. This created extremely difficult bargaining positions for these farmers who were young, and, although larger than average, still wanted to expand. They were all taking the unrestricted alternative route by developing highly automated livestock enterprises.[19]

Regardless of the degree of governmental restrictions on the size of farms, it appeared that they were more of a challenge for the innovator to overcome than they were a solid obstacle to expansion. Probably Flemming Juncker was correct in his statement that such limitations are quickly made obsolete by technology as well as by the demands of the consumer. Therefore, in the long run, they are circumvented unless society chooses to pay the additional cost. In any case, the long-range program of the European Community clearly pointed to the direction of continued consolidation of farms in an effort to make farms more economically efficient, to improve the income of farmers, to free labor for other industries, to increase total agricultural production, thereby reducing the amount of imports, and, above all, to reduce the relative cost of food to society.*

The inability to rent or purchase land was the second most frequently given reason why the European farmers interviewed

---

*One of the most unique restrictions on farm size is imposed on the farmers of Austria where the government requires very precise record keeping once gross sales equal 3,000,000 Austrian schillings ($205,000 to $208,000). The farmers must submit projections on all purchases and sales, in addition to having other governmental interference in their operations, which rapidly increases the cost of doing business. The average gross income per farm in Austria is 236,000 Austrian schillings ($16,300) by contrast to 193,060 Austrian schillings per employed person. It is obvious that the average Austrian farm cannot support one fully employed person irrespective of family responsibilities because the net profits would only be about one-fourth of what the average worker makes.[20]

found it difficult to expand farms. This was in spite of the fact that nearly all the governments were directing a deliberate policy of land consolidation. In some respects the government policy hurt individual farmers because governmental committees closely controlled those who were permitted to increase the size of their farms.

In England, a Land Tenure Act, passed in the 1970's, enables a tenant to hold lease to the farm that he operates for his life and the lifetime of his heir if he succeeds his father as a farmer. In effect it is a two generation lease. This law aims at breaking down some of the older privately held estates. It basically takes most rights away from the landlord except the right to bargain rental rates, which must be done through a county agricultural committee. About the only basis it provides for removing a tenant is his failure to practice good husbandry.

The Land Tenure Act has discouraged private individuals from purchasing land for investment purposes. It has created a strong desire, however, to buy for farm enlargement. On the other hand, institutional buyers have stepped up the purchase of land because they look favorably upon long-range rental situations. The more innovative farmers believe that the Land Tenure Act will straightjacket farming unless the county land review committees periodically upgrade their estimates of what constitutes good husbandry, thereby forcing the tenants to improve constantly or face the threat of removal. Forceful removal of either tenant or landlord as practiced in the post World War II decades proved to be a very unpopular task. Although the British Farmers Union, which is the dominant farm organization of England, encouraged passage of the Land Tenure Act, it is not popular among the more innovative farmers of that nation.[21]

Compounding the pressure on the availability of land is the fact that inflation in most of the countries (West Germany being the major exception) is even more rampant than in the United States. This is causing some farmers and even speculators, on the continent in particular, to purchase land although sound economic judgment dictates otherwise. One young Austrian farmer commented, "There just is no land to rent or buy, but if I had a chance to secure a sizeable block under either method I would plunge." One farmer acknowledged that he purchased a large block of land on the hunch that his country would join the European Community and he would experience higher prices for his goods. He guessed correctly and profited by his good judgment.

Inflationary speculative pressures have affected both the price of land and rental rates. Many farmers felt that rental rates had increased 25 to 50 per cent purely out of inflationary pressures, although profits did not justify higher rates. All the farms, except Babolna State Farm, have a considerable portion of their land leased. The rental rates vary from 1 per cent to 3 per cent of the market value of the land. Most rates tend to be less than 2 per cent, which is a clear indication that the landlord is willing to accept the fact that his long-term profits are in growth and not in direct return on investment. Loans secured by mortgages on the land have, to a degree, been motivated with the idea that if the borrower should default, the lender would have a high priority of being able to claim ownership.*

Liberal government policies toward financing agricultural expansion, especially for mechanization and facilities, have also encouraged farmers to use all the credit they can secure and manage. The purpose of the credit for agriculture is in part to relieve farmers of many manual tasks so they can increase their production, release labor, and improve their income. The trend is similar in all countries. Probably the most obvious growth in that direction has come in West Germany where the investment per worker stands at 157,000 DM's ($78,500). That is in contrast to the entertainment industry or the highly mechanized foundation garment and mining industries in which investments are 135,000, 130,000, and 106,000 DM's respectively.

An agricultural specialist of Denmark summed up government policies and influence on agriculture as follows:

We would like to know just what the long-range governmental policies will be. Farming and labor provide our nation with its major source of income. Agriculture represents 50 per cent of our foreign trade. When things are going well, the leaders look at other industries, but as soon as the nation gets in trouble, it listens to agriculture, otherwise not. But in any case, the problem for the average farmer is still the shortage of income because the farms are too small. Presently, the government wants to increase farm size, but the unemployment rate is disturbing the politician, and the political winds could change.

Gilbert Moeyaert of France agrees as to the unpredictability of

---

*In some of the nations the laws prohibit non-farmers from purchasing land to prevent land speculation by non-farm capital. But land can be secured by default of a mortgage, so the lending route is the only remaining loophole for urbanities desiring to secure land. In any case, the new purchaser must agree to live on and operate the farm.

the government decisions for agriculture. In the late 1950's, the French government encouraged farmers to move into the forested area of Southwest France to clear and develop 50 hectares (123 acres) of land for farming. After a few years, a large portion of these farmers failed, and their land was consolidated into larger, successful units. The current policy in Mr. Moeyaert's department is that forest land cannot now be cleared for crop production; consequently, it is extremely difficult to get a permit to improve and develop more land for agriculture. The decisions to clear land and then to stop clearing it were political, resulting in personal disaster for many of those who were affected by the laws.[22]

Land policies are clearly tied to governmental policies, either directly or indirectly, as is the third most often mentioned reason—the difficulty in acquiring quality labor. It does not take long to realize that the productivity of farm labor generally in Europe is not equal to that of the American farm worker. Over the decades, Europe's population grew more rapidly than industry could absorb it. The surplus population had two choices— emigrate to foreign lands or go back to the land. As the surplus labor accumulated on the land, the congestion caused a strong demand for land. The small farms of peasant-oriented agriculture were the result. Only England and Denmark avoided that rather unpleasant era: England, because industrialization at an early date absorbed many workers; and Denmark, because it passed laws preventing farms from becoming too small.

Farms in Europe became so small that without governmental aid they could not contribute much toward feeding the European people. Government programs, which often perpetuated the misuse of capital and labor in agriculture, soon built up strong vested interests with great political power. It was not until the declining birth rates of the 1920's and 1930's and the rising industrial demands for labor since the 1950's that there has been a migration off the farm. The trend is being encouraged by most governments so that living standards can rise and food costs can be lowered as farm sizes increase. If the current trend continues, the European nations may be able to provide nearly all their temperate zone food products, something not thought possible a few decades ago.[23]

It is apparent that probably labor is not in as short a supply on the farms as some farmers believe; instead, it is the fact that the governments regulate conditions for farm laborers to such a degree that the farmers resent or cannot justify the economics of hired labor. One farmer simply said, "I will expand as far as I can without having to become involved with full-time hired employees. I would reduce the size of my farm if my boys did not want to stay home and farm because I would not want to be forced to rely on hired help."

A Danish farmer pointed out that unionized labor was not really competitive if it was employed under traditional methods of farming. He felt that it caused farmers to mechanize and automate in every way possible. This made it possible to hire better qualified workers, to pay better wages, to be more productive, and to make a profit. This farmer felt that a farm had to be large enough to hire at least one full-time man so the work load could be rotated. This enabled both the farmer and the employee to have some free time available. This farmer's family also felt much more relaxed because it was not under the pressure of having to do livestock chores seven days a week.

A Dutch farmer, who milks 90 cows and feeds beef cattle and hogs, all with family labor, asserted that he will expand as large as technology will enable him to do so without hiring outside full-time labor. He does, however, hire efficient part-time help from neighboring farmers. This Dutch farmer, who felt that labor was too powerful and dictatorial, commented that farmers in his area had the following saying about labor: "A farmer is the boss who hires a worker and tells him what to do and from then on the worker bosses the farmer."*

A Dutch farmer, who employs more than 20 workers, felt that the success of his farm depended upon the good teamwork he got from his workers, most of whom were sons of farmers or small farmers who needed additional income. This farm has 400 milk cows, beef cattle, an orchard, and forest land. Labor cost amounts to 25 per cent of the gross income of the farm, which is a labor-intense operation. This farmer screens his prospective employees very thoroughly before hiring them, and he gave three reasons for his critical selectivity: (1) the negative attitude of many workers toward profit and lack of motivation in any manner to do a better job; (2) governmental regulations and red tape relative to working hours and fringe benefits; and (3) the inability to get rid of unsatisfactory labor or to discontinue employment if the worker is no longer needed. The

---

*This Dutch farmer cited another popular old saying in his area which gave some insight on peasant-oriented agriculture: "In Holland a farmer could succeed in the old days with a Belgian horse and a good strong wife."

high cost of unemployment taxes also makes this farmer very cautious about the kind of individuals he employs.

Sweden is probably the nation where the farmers feel the greatest actual pressure exerted by labor costs because it appears to have the highest labor rates and the highest rate of fringe benefit costs attached to wages. Social costs amount to 43 per cent above the actual pay the worker receives who then is also taxed 43 per cent of his wages. All workers receive four weeks paid vacation as prescribed by law. They are limited to a 40-hour work week with a provision that limits overtime to 150 hours per year. Only with very special permission are farmers allowed to go over the 150-hour overtime limit.

Field work is discouraged on Saturdays, and only the essential livestock chores are conducted on Saturdays and Sundays. To overcome the escalating labor cost, farms that must employ outside labor have rapidly adopted automation. A good example of this is presented in the way in which one large pork-producing farm has handled the situation. In 1972, 37.9 hours were required to handle a sow and her 2.2 litters of pigs to the time of market for pork. In 1975, the total time required was reduced to 20.2 hours, but wages for the same work unit were 663 kronor in 1972 and 652 kronor in 1975 in spite of a 47 per cent reduction in time.* Thus, the farmers with the larger farms were paying nearly double of what appeared to be the standard wages for farm workers in Sweden. On their labor-intense pork and milk producing farms, these farmers were paying just over 20 per cent of their gross income for direct wages and taxes, paid in addition to housing costs. Interestingly, there seemed to be an adequate supply of qualified farm labor available in Sweden, as was generally true in the other European countries.

In some respects the most unique comment relative to labor in agriculture came from the Farm Director in Communist Hungary. He said, "Profitability must determine the end results in all societies. There is one point of concentration. I am thoroughly convinced that only the big farm can go forward when all the personalities are considered by the management. The computer cannot handle the problems of personalities."**[24]

---

*A Swedish krona was about 22 cents in United States money in April, 1978.

**The Babolna State Farm in Hungary employs 4,306 workers. Using average figures of American agricultural productivity, about 515 American farm workers could do the work of the 4,306 Hungarians. Such comparisons help to explain why those governments can boast about full employment.

The Psychology of Growth

After the first interviews in Europe, it quickly became apparent that European progressive, innovative farmers have viewpoints similar to their North American contemporaries. The small percentage of top-level farmers of Europe and North America have more in common with each other than they do with their neighbors who make up the great majority of average farm operators. Their responses to questions of a philosophical nature were so universally similar that it was obvious that international boundaries are no hindrance to the world of ideas. It was only with questions dealing with mechanical matters that the local geographical, political, market, or labor problems reflected any noticeable differences and showed variances in the method with which problems were solved.

When they were asked the basic questions of why they expanded their farms, what caused them to be successful, and what were their future plans, their answers clearly indicated that mental attitude was the ingredient basic to all considerations. These farmers, like their North American counterparts, were proud to be in the business of farming. They were challenge- and risk-oriented as were their wives; often they were ably backed or led by their wives and were quick to acknowledge that fact. They liked being leaders, and they had a wide range of interests.

Nearly all these farmers expressed having difficulties at one time or another in their career in getting financed. The one single answer that best explains how most of them felt about the risk of borrowed money and expansion came from a Dutch farmer:

We were married in 1957, and to get started we had to borrow 50,000 guilders [a guilder is 46¢], and I couldn't sleep. Shortly after that, I decided that to get ahead we needed to expand, and I borrowed 100,000 guilders, and then my wife couldn't sleep. In a few years we both decided we had to expand again and we borrowed 250,000 guilders, and now our banker can't sleep.

Such are the problems of a Dutch farmer who farms 150 acres of land of which 110 are owned, milks 90 cows, and feeds out his male stock as beef. His gross income is large enough to place him among the top 10 per cent of American farmers. Both he and his wife credit the initial struggle with borrowed money as a motivating factor in their success. They admitted that as their milking herd grew they were quick to see the advantages of mechanization as a way of expansion; thus they overcame the fear of debt. Both acknowledged, "We really hated to sell good cows so we expanded."

A Danish farmer, who prefers to farm big enough so that he and his family can travel and otherwise enjoy life, explained why he expanded as soon as he could: "A man has a feeling that he wants to test himself. It keeps him in harmony with his education, ability, and experience. We cannot spend more on personal living than we do today, because we have more than we know we can use. But too many farmers restrict themselves to their physical capacity and not their mental ability. They are not getting the best out of life."

A young English farmer whose parents were very risk-oriented people admitted that he grew up in a home where the motto was: "One is a fool not to use all the capital he can manage, for I know of no farm that is so large that it is uneconomical." The parents traveled extensively and encouraged their children to do so. Two of the sons were on an international exchange program for farmers.

This young farmer remarked of another lasting impression from his earlier years:

The folks always came home from travels with new ideas and gave us lots of encouragement about what a good business farming was. I realized early in life that an adherence to tradition really was a major restriction to agriculture. I saw that in America and also in Africa. I also saw that most people resented large farmers, but at the same time they wanted cheap food and the old-fashioned peasant could not supply that. Today, my workers live far better and get more out of life than even the very best that general English peasant agriculture could afford.

Another English farmer, Geoffrey H. Ballard, who has an extensive pork, dairy, and orchard operation, besides being actively involved in several cooperative marketing and processing enterprises, knew exactly why he was a large-scale farmer. He said, with great emphasis:

A good marriage. Sheila and I started with nothing, so we never felt we were denying ourselves personal comforts for the sake of getting ahead. We have always done everything together or we don't do it. We decided to work like fools to get what we needed. In our first 10 years, all we did was plan and grow. We were not afraid because we knew that my grandfather had gone broke when the cheap grain from the American bonanza farms arrived in England, and he started over again with new methods and became successful.

Our initial hardships were a great educator, but more important was the motivation that came from overcoming the obstacles. Then came the big boost. I won a Nuffield Award* which enabled me to travel and work with farmers of other countries. This not only gave Sheila and me great confidence in ourselves, but also it opened our eyes as to what could really be done in farming. I learned on that trip that the reason there are many small farms is that there are many small-minded farmers. Realizing that really opened my eyes.

An English farmer, who started farming in 1942 and has expanded nearly every year since, knew precisely why he had made the progress that he did:

When you have a wife like Kathleen, who will feed 12 men at 3 A.M. after the harvester stops, you know why you are a success. She was not only doing a bit extra, but always encouraging me. Then in 1953 at the age of 35 I got a setback that really put me on the right track. I was hospitalized with heart trouble and realized that I could no longer do all the physical work I wanted to do. While in the hospital, I learned that what I really had to do was to see my operation from a distance and get better organized. This really made it easier for me and made the farm more profitable.

By the time I reached 50, I wanted to sit back and quit expanding because the income tax people were getting too expensive, and I was really enjoying all the committee work I was involved in. This was not doing the farm much good, but the boys were ready to become involved. Since then there have been all kinds of motives for growing, and it comes so easy.

When asked what his motives were for expanding his farm, a Swedish farmer replied, "I spend two days each week helping to manage 37,000 hectares for the State Church. If I didn't have a large operation that is well-managed, I could not afford either the time or the money to do that work. My wife and I are happiest when we are busiest."[25]

The above is a good cross section of the major motives why these progessive European farmers chose not to stand still in their farming operations. Some of these farmers realized that they were not as popular with the average European as were the traditional small farmers and the peasant-oriented unit. But they were well aware that times and attitudes were changing and resentment against them was diminishing. This new attitude is also being reflected in the changing governmental regulations that are now en-

---

*The Nuffield Award is given each year to 6 to 10 practical English farmers who have made positive contributions to agriculture. Its purpose is to enable the recipients to be exposed to new ideas in agriculture in England and in other nations. Mr. Ballard visited the author's farm on his stay in the Red River Valley in the mid-1960's. Mrs. Ballard spends half of her time keeping farm records, which has been a real key to their farm management success.

couraging consolidation of land and the development of more viable livable farm units. Parity of income for farmers cannot come until the surplus of rural labor is moved off the farms and the remaining units are large enough to generate the necessary income.

Buying and Marketing Practices

One of the greatest differences between North American and European agriculture is the degree to which Europeans are involved in cooperative buying and selling. There is no special reason to discuss in general the history of either the producer or the consumer cooperatives in these pages. But it must be pointed out that the inability of most European farmers to develop any buying or marketing power because of their very small volume made them receptive to cooperative types of organizations. The cooperatives have become very powerful in several of the European countries because they have, with strong governmental backing, been able to persuade most farmers to join them. They have been able to develop a degree of orderly marketing and to establish better quality production to ease marketing problems.

Neither the cooperatives nor the government programs, however, have proven to be a panacea for the farmer's problems. His problems are basically caused because of his small unit business, hence low income, or by the law of supply and demand which rules in the long run, even in the more social-oriented countries. Most farmers realized these facts; therefore, they expressed a desire to attempt new avenues of business. This was especially true as they developed larger farms because the larger farmers have the power of volume that is recognized in the free market but is ignored by the traditional cooperatives which base their buying and marketing methods on an egalitarian philosophy.

Purchasing and selling are important to the progressive European farmers, and like the innovative American farmers, they spend a greater portion of their time in those phases of management than the average farmers of either continent. It must not be overlooked that even on the Babolna State Farm a great deal of emphasis was placed on purchasing and selling, and specialists were employed for those jobs.

Austrian chicken farmer Karl Latschenberger sells a half-million dozen eggs each year. He acknowledged that each time he has expanded his operation he has become more efficient and has reduced his cost of production. He has always contracted his total production, which has netted him two Austrian schillings per kilogram of eggs (a schilling is 7 cents) above the nationally established price. Latschenberger had a clear-cut answer to his buying and selling practices: "Production is no problem, but selling is, and I will expand my operation only if I can contract what I produce." This Austrian farmer is engaged professionally in agricultural marketing in Austria and other countries and is well aware of the chronic surplus production problems in agriculture.

Hans Fehringer, an Austrian egg, milk, beef, and mutton producer, buys concentrate feeds and protein in semi-trailer lots jointly with a neighbor to get volume discount. He has attempted to form pools with other neighbors to purchase seed, chemicals, and fertilizers, but has had only limited success because his neighbors say their farms are "too small to make a difference." But two other young, aggressive, large-scale farmers do buy jointly with him, and they have realized significant savings. Fehringer eggs are sold on a quality contract basis which requires extra work, but "pays well." His milk is sold to a local cooperative creamery that his father helped to organize. "But," he says, "selling to the co-op makes no difference because we have a uniform price established by the government." All beef is produced especially for an export market that brings a premium if specific standards are met. His packer supplies him with replacement cattle each time he sells finished animals.

These Austrian farmers are active in several cooperatives; but, they have noticed that as they have increased their volume of business they have been able to buy and sell to their advantage outside the cooperatives. It is their opinion that the cooperatives are beneficial chiefly because they "serve as competition to the other merchants."[26]

A French farmer, whose farm is many times the average-sized farm in his nation, does all his buying direct because he secures volume discounts that nearly always enable him to buy at considerably less than cooperative prices. The cooperatives do about half of the total supplying of farmer needs in his region. This farmer sells half of his estimated total production prior to harvest on contract sales by private treaty. His overage, which can amount to as much as 50 per cent of his crop, is sold to a local cooperative on a calendarized schedule in an attempt to get a good average price. This farmer did not feel that there was much to gain from the cooperatives other than the element of an additional competitor.

Sweden, which was an early leader in the farmer cooperative movement, has one central organization for buying and selling for farmers. This organization wields considerable power economically and politically in that nation. The government is quite responsive to the requests of that organization, and at the same time, it dictates levels of production chiefly as a "food safety factor to guarantee the consumers an adequate supply at stable prices."

One Swedish farmer replied that formerly he bought and sold all his needs and produce through cooperatives, but as his farm grew, he tended to do more business with private firms. He said, "In the future I will do even more with private merchants because our cooperatives are going to sleep." Another Swede felt that the cooperatives were "extremely conservative" and were not as alert to the real needs of farmers or as efficient as they might be. A third Swedish farmer, who is involved in 10 cooperatives and is on the board of directors of 2 of the larger ones, had doubts about the real value of those organizations. He said, "In 1976, we paid 120,000 crowns [about $26,620] to our cooperatives on the check-off basis of sales or purchases, and I'm not sure we profit nearly as much as the small farmers do. I sometimes doubt the profitability of the cooperative system."

A Dutch farmer explained why he felt the cooperatives were able to maintain their position: "In 1960, we had 70 farmers in our local district and in 1976, we had only 20, but many of them had factory jobs. Farming is no longer their major interest, and because they have always bought and sold through the co-ops in the past, it is easier for them to continue doing so."[27]

Danish pork producer Jorgen Braad buys many of his inputs on a volume basis and realizes good discounts. He belongs to a small group of large-sized hog farmers who have pooled their buying power to buy grain, medicine, and consulting services, in addition to buying special breeding pigs on the international market. Other farmers have been invited to join, but they have declined because of the size of operation of the initial members of the group. Braad sells all his hogs to a cooperative packing plant owned by 1,000 farmers. The plant makes 40 per cent of its sales to England, 40 per cent to other international markets, and 20 per cent to the domestic Danish retail market. Cooperative packers of this nature control 92 per cent of the Danish pork production.

Otto B. Kjeldsen of Denmark produces specialty seed crops on a contract basis for about one-third of his income and raises pork for the remainder of his business. He likes the specialty seed crop business because it pays a good premium for good management.

He is in the pork production business because it offers a better opportunity to expand his volume than attempting to secure more land. Kjeldsen said of his buying practices:

I enjoy bargaining, but I do not want to be a hard bargainer because there is too much tension and loss of faith involved. Every business must have a profit, and I don't think hard bargaining pays in the long run. There are basic prices for all commodities and not much can be done to influence them. I sell all my bacon hogs to a cooperative packing plant, but their price is set in Copenhagen and does not vary much from the price of the private trade. I think maybe farmers should be tougher and act more like the labor union people do, but farmers try too hard to please too many people.[28]

The greatest deviation from what might be considered a national pattern of buying or selling was found in England where a free market for most commodities, along with cooperative and government programs, offered what appeared to be the most competitive situation. One English farmer flatly stated:

I am too independent to be involved in any cooperative or anything of that nature. I directly market my grain, flowers, potatoes, and berries. I even own my own potato processing plant. I am in an excellent cash position. I use no futures, no contracts, and am not on the commodity market, but I find my buyers, and because I have specialty crops and volume, I get their attention. In our society we must recognize that the cheap food policy is the great long-run profit for the nation; therefore, we have to learn how to produce efficiently. The democratic system seems to depend upon the bribery of the electorate, but in the long run the market forces must dictate.

David Harper and Geof Ballard are both very active in cooperatives that they or their fathers helped to organize. It is their opinion that the market forces must dictate, so not much can be done about prices. Their interest in the cooperatives rests on the ease of marketing because pooled activity and greater stability of prices through the cooperatives seem to exert a better control on the volume of goods that reach the market.

Another English farmer, who has been active in many organizations for buying and selling and for political help so that his farm and others might gain, closed his interview with this thought: "You can organize all you want, but basically each man must do his own buying, selling, and managing. The government can issue all the White Papers it wants, but its basic goal is cheap food. Except for the social aspects of all my organizational work, I frankly think gold would do me more good."[29]

European agriculture will continue its rapid transition to mechanization and automation in the decades ahead. Peasant agriculture as we now know it will disappear rapidly except for the more remote areas. Farms will continue to grow in size, but their acreages, in comparison, will not equal those of the United States or Canada, for Europe just does not have the space. On the other hand, the average European farm need not be as large in acreage as in North America, for European farming tends to be more intensive. Therefore, relatively higher income can be derived from smaller farms.

The four-wheel-drive tractor, which is associated with very large farms in North America, will become quite popular on much smaller-sized farms in Europe. To date, European farm workers are not as productive as the North American laborers, and the need to reduce labor costs is even greater in Europe than in North America. As in North America, the European farmers want to keep their farms family-oriented if possible, and technology can offer them that opportunity.

In general, the progressive farmers in Europe appear to be ahead of North American farmers in the use of automation and confinement in poultry and livestock enterprises. Confinement facilities, which are almost novel on the agricultural scene of North America, have a long history in Europe. Basically, most of the European governments are very progressive in helping to finance facilities for the intensification of agriculture. Where land is a limiting factor, technology is the obvious substitute. Technology must also replace labor which will continue to leave the farms if parity of income for farmers is to be gained. The proper level of income must come from the volume of production per person, not from the price per unit. This must happen if society as a whole is to obtain the maximum benefits. Industrialization of agriculture, to be sure, will soon present a new problem to Europe's agriculture and economy. There will be a problem of surplus food rather than the historic deficit. This may be disturbing to the North American food exporters, but it is a good omen for mankind world-wide.

This survey was in no way intended to be a full picture of the cross section of European agriculture. Only a select group of very progressive farmers were interviewed, but it quickly became apparent that, like their North American contemporaries, they are not conformists in regard to opinions on how to solve agriculture's ills. But, like the American innovators, they are positive in their opinions about the long-range success of modern mechanized agriculture.*

---

*One Dutch farmer belongs to a Dairy Herd Improvement Association that has 6,300 cows on record. This farmer has a herd of 80 milk cows, 35 of which are in the top 153 of the Association's program. He would like to challenge the international market to prove to the world how competitive the Dutch dairymen are.

NOTES

[1]Henry A. Wallace, Foreword, Koochiching County (Minnesota) Agents' Report, (1933).

[2]Jean Rylands, Irish staff member, American Embassy, Dublin, Ireland; interviewed at Moorhead, Minnesota, May 28, 1977.

[3]Interview with Hans Fehringer, Schramelhof, Aschbach, Austria, April 2, 1977; interview with Louis Rosenaur, Loeches, Spain, April 6, 1977.

[4]Interview with Ade Brouwer, Abcovensedyk, Goirle, Netherlands, March 22, 1977.

[5]Interview with Dr. Robert Burgert, Director, Babolna State Farm, Babolna, Hungary, March 30, 1977.

[6]Interview with Sam Moreton, Offchurch, Burnt Heath Farm, Leamington Spa, Warwickshire, England, March 16, 1977.

[7]Interviews with Alf Insulander and K. G. Insulander, Wappa Säteri, Enköping, Sweden, in Fargo, North Dakota, November 29, 1976, and in Sweden, March 28, 1977.

[8]"Selected Agri-figures of the E.E.C.," Statistics and Documentation—Ministry of Agriculture and Fisheries, The Hague (February, 1974), p. 11.

[9]Don Baron, Editor of *Country Guide, Holland: The Miracle of Dutch Agriculture*, Holland Foreign Agricultural Service, The Hague, (August, 1970), pp. 15, 18, 22.

[10]Burgert interview.

[11]Brouwer interview; interview with H. Thielen, Alphensebaan 2, Gilze, Netherlands, March 21, 1977; *Aspects of Dutch Agriculture*, Ministry of Agriculture and Fisheries, The Hague (October, 1976), p. 13.

[12]Interview with Gilbert Moeyaert, Lugos, 33830, Belin, France, April 4, 1977; *Agriculture in France*, Press Information Service, Embassy of France, New York 1977, p. 7; "A Survey of Agricultural France," France Information No. 43, Ministry of Agriculture, Paris (April–May, 1972), p. 8.

[13]Sam Moreton interview; interview with Fred S. Moreton, Offchurch, Burnt Heath Farm, Leamington Spa, Warwickshire, England, March 18, 1977.

[14]Interview with Trevor Ensor, Nuneaton, Warwickshire, England, March 17, 1977.

[15]Interview with Geoffrey H. Ballard, Old Yates Farm, Abberley, England, March 18, 1977.

[16]Interview with Fred Harper, Holt Heath Castle, Holt Heath, Warwickshire, England, March 19, 1977.

[17]Interview with Flemming Juncker, Overgaard, Havandal, Denmark, March 25, 1977.

[18]K. G. Insulander interview; interview with Douglas Kennedy, Rábelöf Farm, Kristianstad, Sweden, March 26, 1977.

[19]Interview with Jorgen Braad, Hogholt, 9560 Hadsund, Denmark, March 23, 1977; interview with Torben Lindegaard, Hadsund, Denmark, March 25, 1977; interview with Otto B. Kjeldsen, Tvedevej 17-Hald, 8983 Gjerlev J., Denmark, March 24, 1977.

[20]Interview with Johann Fehringer, Schramelhof, Aschbach, Austria, April 2, 1977; interview with Karl Latschenberger, Biberbach, Austria, April 3, 1977; *Austria Facts and Figures*, Federal Press Service, Vienna (1976), pp. 63, 67.

[21]Fred S. Moreton interview; Fred Harper interview; Trevor Ensor interview.

[22]Hans Fehringer interview; Torben Lindegaard interview; interview with David Harper, Holt Heath Castle, Holt Heath, Warwickshire, England, March 17, 1977; Otto B. Kjeldsen interview; interview with Curt Roos, 24500 Staffanstorp, Sweden, March 26, 1977; "Landwirtschaft: Hähne Auf und Zu," *Der Spiegel*, No. 48/77, (November 22), pp. 81, 84, 86; interview with Kaj Skriver, Senior Agricultural Advisor of Denmark, Arhus, Denmark, March 23, 1977; Gilbert Moeyaert interview.

[23]P. Lamartine Yates, *Food, Land and Manpower in Western Europe*, St. Martin's Press, New York (1960), pp. 7–9.

[24]Ade Brouwer interview; Otto B. Kjeldsen interview; interview with P. F. G. von Happen, Waalre, North Brabant, Netherlands, March 21, 1977; interview with Peter C. Heemskerk, Veldhoven, North Brabant, Netherlands, March 21, 1977; interview with Ingemar Oredsson, Rábelöf Farm, Kristianstad, Sweden, March 26, 1977; Alf Insulander interview; Dr. Robert Burgert interview.

[25]P. F. C. von Happen interview; Otto B. Kjeldsen interview; Fred Harper interview; David Harper interview; Geoffrey H. Ballard interview; Sam Moreton interview; K. G. Insulander interview.

[26]Karl Latschenberger interview; Hans Fehringer interview.

[27]Gilbert Moeyaert interview; interview with Henning Clemedtson, 29073 Trensum, Sweden, at Moorhead, Minnesota, April 6, 1978; Alf Insulander interview; K. G. Insulander interview; Ingemar Oredson interview; Curt Roos interview; Douglas Kennedy interview; Ade Brouwer interview.

[28]Jorgen Braad interview; Otto B. Kjeldsen interview.

[29]Trevor Ensor interview; David Harper interview; Geoffrey H. Ballard interview; Sam Moreton interview; H. Thielen interview.

Small land parcels and farms in the Netherlands, where a 10-acre farm could be subdivided into several fields, and farmers could not make their business efficient. In the 1950's, consolidation was started by law. (Photo, *Aspects of Dutch Agriculture*)

The same area after consolidation, showing new innovative farmsteads that replace outmoded facilities as part of the consolidation program. Farms are made into ever-increasing size units to get economy of operation, with the Dutch government paying 65 percent of the cost in the form of a grant. (Photo, *Aspects of Dutch Agriculture*)

When it comes milking time, cows still have the right-of-way in Belgium, as they do on most smaller highways of Europe. Note cement fence posts and steel electricity poles. (Photo, Larry Larson)

Straw being fed to 300 dry and replacement cows in a barn with a full manure pit measuring 11 by 75 meters (36 by 244 feet). The 10,374-acre Råbelöf farm, Kristianstad, Sweden. Owned by Douglas Kennedy. Note wooden stave silo. This farm also has cement silos and two oxygen-limiting Harvestores. March, 1977.

Part of a herd of 300 milk cows at Råbelöf farm, Kristianstad, Sweden, owned by Douglas Kennedy. Some buildings on this farm date back to 1637, but most are ultra-modern. Cows in this slatted-floor barn averaged 15,479 pounds of milk and 666 pounds of butterfat in 1976. March, 1977.

A 12- by 30-meter two-story confined barn with manure pit on the Hans Fehringer farm, Aschbach, Austria. Lower floor has 120 beef bulls; top floor, 2,000 layer chickens producing special heavy broiler hatching eggs. April, 1977.

K. G. Insulander hog unit, Enköping, Sweden, where 660 litters are farrowed and finished annually. Three of six hog barns, 20 by 111 meters (65 by 360 feet) each with 1,000 to 1,500 hogs or sow farrowing units. Total feed processing and air-flow feed system. Offices and sick bays in left building. Three partially submerged manure pits in foreground. March, 1977.

Confined hog barn on Råbelöf farm, Kristianstad, Sweden, owned by Douglas Kennedy. Measures 18 by 80 meters (58 by 260 feet), capacity of 1,000 feeder pigs, and has feed processing and piped air-flow feed system. Environment controlled. Farm farrows 600 litters annually. March, 1977.

A Fiat 1300 four-wheel-drive, 150-H.P. with nitrogen tank and field cultivator on the 6,000-acre Flemming Juncker farm near Havandal, Denmark. This land is reclaimed from the North Sea. March, 1977.

Fred Moreton with Mercedes-Benz 800, 80-H.P., four-wheel-drive with differential lock/40-foot pneumatic fertilizer spreader. Spreads 200 acres in a 10-hour day at 400 pounds an acre. Tractor cost £11,500; spreader, £1,500 ($1.70 to a £). Offchurch, Burnt Heath Farm, Leamington Spa, Warwickshire, England. March, 1977.

Hand-spreading manure on a farm in central Belgium. Most farmers have liquid manure from pits and cannot afford a second or any spreader, so hand-spreading is common. Tractor is an International. (Photo, Larry Larson)

A Russian-built four-wheel-drive with P.T.O., pulling a soil mulcher after corn harvest. This state farm used the consulting services of Chicago-based Corn Production Systems. Baja, Hungary. September 29, 1972. (Photo, Tom Kiss)

A 1972, 126-H.P. four-wheel-drive Volvo diesel on K. G. Insulander farm, Enköping, Sweden, 1,200 hectares (2,964 acres). This farm has 20 tractors. First tractor, a 1920 Avancs. In 1964, two 70-H.P. Volvos were put in tandem and proved to be superior to small front-wheel-drives. Alf Insulander (26) on left with farm manager.

Used tractors traded in on four-wheel-drive tractors in Hadsund, Denmark, showing the power trend in that nation. Neils Lubeck, dealer. Left to right: Italian 70-H.P. Fiat; two English/American 75-H.P. Ford 7000's; Russian 70-H.P. Belarus; Canadian/American 105-H.P. Massey-Ferguson 1100. March, 1977.

Horseshoeing at a blacksmith at Ebene Reichenau, Austria (southern border), 1976. A worldwide practice, but seldom-pictured task. Except for sport, it is no longer part of American agriculture. (Photo, Larry Larson)

A one-horse produce-and-manure cart at Manzanares, Spain, about 30 miles from Madrid. Spain is still suffering from a static primitive agriculture which will soon experience rapid changes. April, 1977.

Farmer with grain drill and harrow on the way to his field. About one-fourth of the farmers still use horses in rapidly changing Belgian agriculture. Big door enters into a farmstead yard. All farmers in this area live in villages and travel to their fields. About 5 acres a day can be seeded with this rig. (Photo, Larry Larson)

A two-way, one-bottom, 12-inch plow on a 20-acre farm in Northeast Belgium. At the most 1½ acres can be plowed in one day. This is evidence of the low productivity of European agriculture and explains the reason for low labor returns and why farm consolidation is taking place. (Photo, Larry Larson)

Fred Moreton with Steiger Cougar 250-H.P. with 9-bottom, 14-inch reversible Dowdswell plow, effectively used in fields as small as 6 acres. This is one of the larger potato farms in England, where farms are growing to enable labor income improvement. Sam Moreton farm, Offchurch, Burnt Heath Farm, Leamington Spa, Warwickshire, England. March, 1977.

A four-wheel-drive truck with "pup" hauling shell corn from a German-made combine on a state farm at Baja, Hungary, managed by Corn Production Systems, headed by Hungarian-born Tom Kiss, now of Chicago. (Photo, Tom Kiss)

K. G. Insulander's main farm place, feed mill, and grain storage unit built in 1870, Enköping, Sweden. The 3,000-acre farm has 250 milk cows, 250 young stock, 300 sows, and 6,000 to 8,000 finished pigs each year besides 1,500 acres of cash crop. March, 1977.

Part of 235,000-bushel grain cleaning and storage facility on one of K. G. Insulander's farms, Enköping, Sweden. Alf Insulander facing camera. Lower floor of building on left contains young stock replacement cattle. March, 1977.

Grain drying and storage 40 by 50 feet (approx. 60,000 bushels each). Floor contains air flues for continuous drying of major crops—rape, barley, and wheat. Flemming Juncker's "Overgaard Farm," Havandal, Denmark. March, 1977.

A farm of less than 1 hectare (2.47 acres) at Ebene Reichenau, Austria. The farmer scythed the hay and hauled it to storage in this manner for his herd of goats and rabbits. Proof of the poetically beautiful but economically poor peasant agriculture. (Photo, Larry Larson)

A German farmer's wife unbinding hay on a tripod in preparation for baling. The hay was tractor-cut by a custom operator and then hand-forked by the women onto the tripod for drying. (Photo, Larry Larson)

A custom baler at same German farm. One man operates the tractor while the farmer handles the bales and his wife (right) and elderly lady pitch hay from tripods into the American baler. (Photo, Larry Larson)

Two 60-cubic meter (13- by 14-foot) silos on Hans Fehringer farm, Aschbach, Austria. Each holds about 2½ acres of corn silage. Farm name dates to 1200's. Hans is a tenth generation owner. April, 1977.

A bunker silo, 40 by 6 by 3.5 meters (130 by 20 by 11 feet), that holds about 30 acres of corn silage grown on the 111-acre Hans Fehringer (pictured) farm, Aschbach, Austria. Filled by dumping over the open side. Most bunkers in this area have roofs, some are completely enclosed. April, 1977.

A potato field and hay field with hay stacked for drying, showing two styles of modern Belgian farm homes. (Photo, Larry Larson)

The farm home of Fred and Kathleen Harper, Holt Heath Castle, Holt Heath, Warwickshire, England. Four other families lease apartments in this 30-large-room structure because of the great cost of maintaining it. This castle was purchased along with 100 acres of land in 1947 for £100 an acre (estimated $275 in 1947). The Harpers operate 780 acres in an intense crop-livestock program. March, 1977.

Home of Gilbert Moeyaert, farm manager on 1,800 acres of irrigated corn land, Belin, France. This land has been reclaimed from forest since 1956. Southwest France is a rapidly expanding corn area. April, 1977.

Main courtyard, viewed from visitors' quarters of Babolna State Farm, Babolna, Hungary, managed by Dr. Robert Burgert. Entire yard is walled by a farm building. The building to right is a horse-show ring. Racing and riding horses are raised as part of the program on this 55,000-acre farm. The wagon of manure was hand-loaded and unloaded in the same field where 325-H.P. four-wheel-drive American tractors were working. Jeep is Russian. March, 1977.

Geoffrey and Sheila Ballard, Old Yates Farm, Abberley, England, operate 700 acres on which they raise sugar beets, potatoes, onions, and fruit; milk 90 cows; feed 200 beef cattle; farrow 170 sows at 2.2 litters per year; and wean 18.9 pigs per sow per year. Ballard is a recipient of one of England's Top Farmer awards. March, 1977.

Left to right: Fred and Kathleen Harper and son David, who aids in managing the 780-acre farm of his parents besides the 340-acre farm of his own. The farms include potatoes, sugar beets, onions, strawberries (6 acres), 200 ewes with 340 fattening lambs, and 80 beef cattle. David employs two year-round men, two students, and four women at potato and onion harvest. Holt Heath Castle, Holt Heath, England. March, 1977.

P. F. G. von Happen family, Waalre, North Brabant, Netherlands, owns 30 and rents 26 hectares (138 acres) of land, which is in grass, maize, or wheat silage (no hay or grain grown). Feeds 90 milk cows and 45 head of replacement cattle with 2,463 U.S. tons of forage at 68 percent moisture. Buys 77 U.S. tons of concentrate feed. After deducting purchased feed, returns $900 per acre on $7,200-land.

Left to right: Janice, David, Janet, Iver, Sally, and Fred Moreton (Les and Fiona missing). Four sons who aid their father in producing 700 acres of potatoes, 900 of wheat, and 750 of rape. They retail or direct-sell bagged potatoes to stores and employ 24 full-time workers because they are involved with machinery manufacturing of a specialty nature and a land-drainage business. Offchurch, Burnt Heath Farm, Leamington Spa, Warwickshire, England. March, 1977.

Left to right: Gilbert Moeyaert, farm manager; Martine Prores, secretary accountant for a farm implement firm; and Stephanie, also a farm manager. All were interviewed in Southern France on Moeyaert's 1,800-acre irrigated corn farm and Stephanie's grape-growing/wine-processing farm. April, 1977.

Left to right: Hans, Ernestine (Han's wife), Leopoldine (Mrs. Johann), Hansi, Aunt Pol, Johann, and Aunt Marin Fehringer, Aschbach, Austria. Three generations and two aunts at Schramelhof Farm, which has been in the family since the 1600's. Hans is the tenth generation to be farming the 111 acres of crop and 74 acres of pasture (in mountains). The $5,345-an-acre crop land supports 200 feeder bulls, 20 milk cows, 15 replacements, 100 sheep, and 2,000 heavy-layer hens, and buys concentrate and grain. April, 1977.

Sam and Kathleen Moreton, Offchurch, Burnt Heath Farm, Leamington Spa, Warwickshire, England. He is one of the largest potato farmers in England, who started farming in 1942 on 192 rented acres with all borrowed money. By 1955, he was renting 1,192 acres, concentrating on potatoes and milk cows, which he built to 170 head. Has 15 tractors totaling 1,420 H.P. March, 1977.

Left to right: Dr. Istvan Szuror, Director of Veterinary Medicine in charge of 18 veterinarians; Jeno Soltesz, Head of Department for Feedstuffs Control, mixing 310,000 tons of concentrate yearly; Palfi Sandor, Interpreter and Foreign Trade Council, selling 600 plane loads of chickens to the Near East each year. State Farm of Babolna, Hungary. Consists of 49,400 acres plus pasture land and employs 4,306 workers. March, 1977.

Left to right: Alf, Mrs. K. G., and K. G. Insulander, Wappa Säteri, Enköping, Sweden. Operate 2,964 acres, milk 250 cows, have 300 sows, farrow 2.2 times a year, and sell 5,500+ finished hogs a year. The two brothers started in 1941 on a farm of 350 hectares, which was split in 1949. They have 20 tractors totaling 1,425 H.P. and 5 combines. Labor is limited to a maximum of 150 hours overtime annually in Sweden. March, 1977.

The Torben Lindegaards, Hadsund, Denmark, purchased 250 acres in 1956. Now own 2,300 acres and rent 1,900 acres, including 800 acres of forest land, 2,300 of grain, 700 of rape, and 240 of seed specialties. Operate with 12 tractors totaling 1,600 H.P., and four combines. Have six full-time men, including three who work in the woods. Lindegaard is an extremely efficient crop farmer. March, 1977.

CHAPTER XIII

Looking Beyond the Furrow*

In the past, many Americans have lived under the illusion that the best society is an agrarian society, in which a large portion of the people are involved in tilling the soil for the benefit of mankind. This is a strong but rather sentimental illusion for which there is very little proof. But still this strange "Jeffersonian agrarian myth" lingers on.

When our country's first census was taken in 1789, over 96 per cent of all our people were considered rural in character and most of them were actually living on farms. Today, only about one-fourth of the nation's population is considered rural, but only approximately 3.2 million people are involved in farming. If the nation's usable farm land were equally divided among the nation's families, the average farm would be 24 acres and the "farm for everybody" would have about 7½ acres of cropland available, one-fifth of a cow, one-third of a sheep, and just over five hens. More importantly, the net annual income from such a farm "for everybody" would be $486.

If dreams, sentiment, and poetry are significant, a small farm for everybody would be the ideal. However, what dreamers and poets in their praise of the small farm neglect to mention is the hardships and failures associated with those "poetically beautiful small farms" that seldom could produce an adequate net income and are in no position to feed our nation or mankind.

Today, the average size of all American farms is nearly 400 acres. Even with this average size, most farms are not large enough to provide a modest living. The United States Department

---

*Because of the sensitive nature of the material in this chapter, the names of farmers, their wives, or employees are not used. This was the agreement with these individuals at the time of interview. However, all documentation is on file with the author.

of Agriculture pointed out in a 1973 survey that an efficiently operated one-man wheat farm needs 1,950 acres with capital assets of $321,000, and a one-man, corn-soybean farm needs 800 acres requiring $769,000. There is little that is poetic or sentimental about a one-man farming operation of this size, but it does provide a livable income for the farmer and his family and cheap food for the American consumer.

But such a farm operation is far beyond the size of an average American farm. Sixty-one per cent of our farms have a gross income of less than $10,000 a year and produce 5 per cent of the gross farm sales. The next 11 per cent of our farms, which gross $10,000 to $20,000, produce another 5 per cent of all farm sales. This means that 72 per cent of America's farmers produce a combined total of only 10 per cent of all our total production. It becomes obvious that these farmers cannot exist on farming alone. They must rely on a full-time, off-the-farm job which pays them considerably more than they earn from farming. On the other hand, the top 28 per cent of our farmers are operating on a larger scale and provide 90 per cent of all our food and fiber. They are the commercial food producers of the nation.

If we are concerned about the welfare of the nation, about the American consumer, and even about the starving people of other lands, then we must emphasize the importance of that part of our farm population which most efficiently produces the major portion of our food and fiber at ever-decreasing relative costs. Then the 782,000 farmers, who produce 90 per cent of our agricultural products, will have to accept an ever-increasing share in the picture of America's agricultural economy and policy. It is from these 782,000 farmers, who have $20,000 or more in gross sales, that the farmers of tomorrow will emerge. Their productive capacity per man might help to revolutionize the status of agriculture and its accomplishments in America and in the world around us. They are the ones who are already looking beyond the furrow.

Rural America has experienced drastic changes in our century and many of them have to be credited to the adoption of new technology. Liberty Hyde Bailey, one of the great spokesmen for agriculture, wrote in 1900: "Never were there so many opportunities in farming as now. Neither economically nor socially is agriculture on the decline. It is only changing. Old methods are going out, and many farmers are going with them." If he returned to life today, he could see how true his prediction was. The biggest change is that the farmer of today has shed his overalls and has become a full-fledged member of the business community. With this association the opportunities in agriculture have changed direction, for today's agriculture depends to a great degree on the agri-business segment to satisfy input needs. The farm-reared boy with a college degree or vocational training is in great demand by the growing industrial agri-business complex. When Bailey was writing about the traditional 160-acre homestead in 1900, that institution was already in trouble. Its successor, the mechanically powered, commercial farm, was just coming into being, but it was not yet recognized. Not until the World War I era would mechanically powered, professionally managed farms such as Tom Campbell's gain any great fanfare from the agricultural journals.

A report by the Country Life Commission of 1901–1910 identified some of the disadvantages of rural life as the lack of education, the lack of interest in social problems, and the lack of progressiveness. Theodore Roosevelt and members of the Commission recognized these facts, while Congress refused to listen. But agricultural movements were started to help the farmer. Extension services, farmers' clubs, and consolidation of schools brought the farmers into the new age.

In former times it was generally felt that the most aggressive and alert farm youth left the farm and went to town in order to improve their style of living. This is still partially true today, because not all can farm, and some must seek opportunities elsewhere. Others, after years of education, return to the farm or become engaged in agri-business. The records of the land grant colleges that educate and graduate many of those interested in vocational agriculture are proof of that trend.

The well-known hardships of the hired girl and hired man who worked long hours on pioneer farms were a part of the costly experience of opening the frontier. The modern farmer knows that output per worker determines the standard of living of any society. Out of necessity, he cannot afford the "cheap hired help" of the past, but he must look to a qualified, alert employee capable of handling a number of jobs. To be able to pay these employees the wages they need and deserve, the farmer of today and tomorrow has made one of the largest capital investments per employee of any of the nation's industries. In the last decade, the capacity of a farm laborer has increased from being able to provide for 26 people in 1960 to being able to provide for 56 in 1976.

A word must be said about the decline of the farm population which dropped from 32 million in 1910 to 8 million by 1976. Not all land was settled in the Dakotas and Montana by 1910, and their farm population actually increased until the 1930's. Despite the serious economic situation on the farms during the 1920's and 1930's, the most rapid decline in farm numbers and population did not come until the prosperity of the World War II era and after. The alternative opportunities of the industrial society that took people away from the farm were probably more significant in the out-migration than was the depressed state of the agricultural sector. Despite the loss of 24 million people from farming since 1910, agriculture still suffers the chronic problem of underemployment. As recently as 1950, underemployment was serious enough that if all farmers had been fully employed an equivalent of 1,600,000 workers could have been added to the labor force.

While many farmers were underemployed, the farmer expanding the size of his operation was substituting capital for labor as rapidly as he could generate or borrow money. Overcapitalization continued to plague the industry as well. It appears that generally the same farmer who suffered from underemployment also experienced the burden of overcapitalization. His alternatives were to expand, take an off-the-farm job, sell out, or ignore his opportunities until he was sold out. The problem has been slowly solving itself since 1910, but is not yet complete. When it is finally solved through farm consolidation, society will adjust itself as it always has. The final stabilization is not yet in sight, for there is no evidence as to how large a farm can become before it is uneconomical. However, income and estate taxation have become major obstacles in modern agriculture. As farms grow and profits increase, the tax rate also grows, giving the large, well-to-do farmer a definite disadvantage in contrast to an expanding but less liquid farmer.

Most of the farmers questioned for this survey were challenge-oriented and expected the next generation to think likewise. However, some of the interviewees had stopped expansion because they either had no successor or none of them were interested in farming. Nearly all the interviewees felt that their farms had as much to gain from integrated expansion as from external growth. One farmer noted that his volume in dollars had increased ten-fold from 1952 to 1973, and he expected growth to continue at about the same amount per year. This would not be out of line with what has happened to the growth of large-scale farms in general. In 1929 there were 2,420 farms that exceeded

$100,000 in gross sales; in 1959 there were 19,979 such farms; in 1964 there were 31,401; and by 1976 there were 155,000 with a $100,000 volume.

A question related to the size of farms sheds considerable light on the traditional belief about the virtue of small-scale agriculture. All interviewees were asked if they were socially satisfied with being farmers. Then they were asked if their community was socially satisfied with them. These farmers expressed full satisfaction with their lives as farmers. Most added that they would not want to do things differently if they could live their lives all over again.

Of course, in some communities there was strong resentment against the large-scale farmer. Resentment was strongest against farmers who had moved into communities and had become very successful in a period of 10 to 15 years. Generally, the newcomers succeeded because they saw and made use of opportunities that the natives were failing to take advantage of. However, the majority of these farmers were second and third generation farmers in the area, and antagonisms against them were found chiefly among the older generation. Apparently, the youth had grown up knowing enough about the "big farmer" to accept the fact. In areas where there were several very large farms the local resentment against any single farm was much less than in an area where there was only one sizeable operation. Many farmers expressed the opinion that a fair amount of pressure was exerted against their children at school by both the teachers and other children. Because of this antagonism, several of these farmers had actually stopped buying land in their immediate community and had gone to other states and to Canada to start new operations. Others expanded into non-farm enterprises.

Certain personal traits can be observed in these successful farmers. These traits, more than any other single factor, have been their reasons for success. True, some of these farmers had started with a good operation because of inheritance or marriage; but many, especially among the Outstanding Young Farmers, started with nothing but determination.

Five traits and one outside factor stand out as probably being the most significant in the growth of large farmers:

(1) These men had *positive mental attitudes* toward farming. Farming was a money-making business and offered just as much opportunity as in any other business or profession in which they

could have been involved. They came from homes that had a positive attitude toward farming.

(2) *Innovative ability* caused them to be ahead of a large portion of the farmers in the entire region. This made them extremely conspicuous in their home community. They often succeeded by virtue of what they learned from their mistakes. These successful farmers were people with new ideas—people who enjoyed talking about what they were going to do next.

(3) These men were *challenge seekers*, whether in regard to expansion or new innovations. They were the kind of men who could not stand still. Several had worked at industrial and professional jobs, but quit to start farming because they could not find the excitement they wanted in their former vocation. One thing they could not do was to work at a restricted pace. With them, it was work at full speed.

(4) *A solid family backing*, particularly that of the *wife*, was a factor in the success of these men. Even some very dominant men frankly admitted that their wives were the key to success. As stated earlier, the wives frequently answered a large share of the questions or at least added to their husbands' answers. It was clear in some cases that the wife was the strong force in the family and probably was more aggressive than the husband. This appeared to be more true of the younger couples. In some cases, the husband sometimes held back on expansion or restrained his innovation because of the possible risk it involved for the family. In other cases, it was with the urging of the wife that the next move toward success was made.

(5) These large farmers were *willing and able to borrow considerable sums of money* to operate and expand their farms. Farming historically has generated a large portion of its expansion capital. Modern farmers want to enjoy life and live as well as their city counterparts. These families lived well, traveled widely, and in general did whatever they wanted along personal lines. Many of the second and third generation farmers admitted that they had a generous backlog of unmortgaged assets and did not have to borrow money. Many did not have to borrow for machinery or livestock, or for operating expenses. Some would have been able to buy very sizeable pieces of land without outside financing. On the other hand, many borrowed extensively and used leverage to such a degree that they were their bankers' "nightmare." Outsiders were very critical of these farmers and were sure that they would

soon be broke. What the critical neighbor did not understand is that the successful farmer was the one who understood that borrowed capital was probably his cheapest input and the one that gave him the greatest profit potential.

(6) The outside factor significant in the growth of large-scale farms was the impact of *government programs*. Despite the fact that the Agricultural Acts of 1948 and 1949 were definitely cheap food acts, they were a positive factor in the success of many farmers. The cost-oriented and cash-flow-conscious farmer saw the value of the guaranteed income of the government programs. Each time he expanded his farm, his guaranteed payments increased. Most of these farmers did not like the programs, but used them to the fullest extent to build their farming enterprises.

Today, the large farmer would probably like to stand on his own, but times have changed. The American consumer, although living at the lowest relative cost of any nation's consumers, is often unreasonable about the price of food. The consumer has the votes and few politicians have the courage to defend the farmer.* If they attempted to do so, the consumer probably would not approve. It appears that as much as the farmer of tomorrow would like to go to the free market both at home and abroad, he may not have that ópportunity. Quite likely, politics might find a way to control the farmer.

Farmers generally receive 30 to 40 per cent of the ultimate cost of food. The remainder goes to labor and to the middlemen. It is ironic that labor frequently opposes the farmer because of the price of food, when labor's wages are equal to or larger than the farmer's share of the consumer costs. Even more serious to the farmer's and to the nation's long-range goals are embargoes and strikes often imposed by labor to hinder foreign export sales. The farmer needs these sales to stay financially sound; the nation needs these sales for its long-range business; and labor needs the jobs that the sales are providing and will continue to provide.

Neither the American nation nor its farmers can tolerate restriction to international trade. The long-range good of both must come through greater free trade. Our farmers, and particularly the farmers of tomorrow, realize that they are competitive or equal to all other food producers of the world.

The day of the antiquated homestead farm is gone, and the

*In the most recent Congress only 35 Congressmen had districts with 20 per cent or more farm voters.

farmer of tomorrow looks beyond the furrow. For this purpose, he has to use every business technique that is at his disposal. Dr. Don Paarlberg, former Director of Agricultural Economics for the United States Department of Agriculture, cautions our leaders to use common sense in attempting any kind of legislation that would prohibit agriculture from finding its rightful place in society. He feels that this country can have any kind of farm it wants, but the taxpayer will have to ask himself if he wants to subsidize the inefficient little farmer so he can afford to farm. Or, does the taxpayer want larger farmers who can stand on their own feet and produce the cheapest possible food and fiber?

Myron Just, Commissioner of Agriculture for North Dakota, wrote in 1968: "In the Dakotas, 75 to 90 per cent of the farms sold were going to enlargement. Gradually, this eliminates the uneconomical units except near the cities where they are supplemented by off-the-farm jobs." This movement that Commissioner Just pointed out has not stopped and will not stop if the natural laws are left alone. Vernon W. Ruttan, Chairman of the Department of Agricultural Economics, University of Minnesota, in 1965, pointed out that if the techniques used on all farms producing over $40,000 gross sales were applied to all agriculture, only 400,000 farms could meet the nation's needs.

The technology is obviously here; the capital is available for the proven manager; the skilled labor force is available; the management is available; the forces of agri-business are available. The farmers interviewed have proven that under a free enterprise system men who are willing to take risks, who are innovative and challenge-oriented, are here to lead the way. The agricultural evolution they have started is on its way and is ready for tomorrow!

The farmer of today has but three choices: (1) to adapt, expand, and succeed; (2) to survive by taking a non-farm job; or (3) to insulate himself from a practical and profitable way of life by ignoring change. The first two choices are productive and progressive; the third choice leads to stagnation and eventual extinction.

Unless the American consumers are willing to pay a much higher proportion of their incomes for food and fiber, and unless the American nation wants to sacrifice its position as the low-cost food provider for 25 per cent of the world's population, industrialized agriculture with its effective agri-business must become a reality. The outcome of this agricultural evolution appears inevitable.[1]

NOTE

[1]"Everybody's Farm," *Gopher State Review*, Minnesota Crop and Livestock Reporting Service Bulletin 318 (May, 1974); "The Farmer and His Farm," *Gopher State Review*, Minnesota Crop and Livestock Reporting Service Bulletin 331 (June, 1975); Carl F. Reuss, "Economic Problems of Rural America," A Report of the Commission on Research and Social Action of the American Lutheran Church (March 15, 1970); Liberty Hyde Bailey, "Can I Make a Farm Pay? Yes, If You Like It," *World's Work*, I, No. 5 (March, 1901), p. 550; Lewis E. Atherton, "The Midwestern Country Town—Myth and Reality," *Agricultural History*, XXVI, No. 3 (July, 1952), pp. 73, 76, 79; W. C. Collins, Economic Research Manager, Massey-Ferguson, Inc., "Farming in the Future," A speech given at Jefferson, Iowa (January 26, 1974); Louis B. Schmidt, "The Agricultural Revolution in the Prairies and the Great Plains of The United States," *Agricultural History*, VIII, No. 8 (October, 1934), pp. 190–193; Quentin W. Lindsey, "The Problem of Periodic Reorganization in American Agriculture," *American Journal of Agricultural Economics*, XIV (May, 1961), p. 362; Russell L. Berry, "Higher Prices Not Enough," *The Farmer*, XXXIII, No. 11, (June 5, 1971), p. 18; Kenneth L. Bachman, "Changes in Scale in Commercial Farming and Their Implications," *Journal of Farm Economics*, XXIV, No. 2 (May, 1952), p. 169; Leon E. Truesdell, "Farm Population in the United States," *Census Monographs*, VI, Bureau of the Census, U.S. Department of Commerce, Washington (1926), pp. 5, 8, 12, 45; Kenneth R. Krause and Leonard R. Kyle, "Midwestern Corn Farms . . . ," U.S. Department of Agriculture, Agricultural Economic Report No. 216, Washington (1971), III, pp. 25-28; Leonard R. Kyle, "The Economics of Large-Scale Crop Farming," Staff Paper P70–77, Michigan State University (May, 1970), pp. 16–20; Radaje Nikolitch, "Our 100,000 Biggest Farms: Their Relative Position in American Agriculture," U.S. Department of Agriculture, E.R.S. Report No. 49 (February, 1964), p. 4; "Can Your Kind of Farming Survive?" an editorial, *Big Farmer*, XLIV, No. 5 (August, 1972); Myron Just, "The Land Price Spiral . . . What's Behind It? What's Ahead?" *The Dakota Farmer*, LXXXVIII, No. 1 (January 6, 1968); conversations with Dr. Vernon W. Ruttan, University of Minnesota, St. Paul (April, 1970); *The Forum*, Fargo-Moorhead (May 9, 1974); *1977 Handbook of Agricultural Charts*, Agricultural Handbook No. 524, U.S. Department of Agriculture, Washington (November, 1977), p. 6; anonymous interviews (see footnote on first page of chapter).

Appendix

TABLE I

Farm Population in the United States and in Selected States[1]

Year	National	Iowa	Minnesota	Montana	North Dakota	South Dakota
1900	29,875,000	1,139,000	856,000	67,000	239,000	274,000
1910	32,077,000	1,053,000	833,000	111,000	369,000	371,000
1920	31,974,000	991,000	903,000	228,000	398,000	364,000
1930	30,529,000	981,000	898,000	205,000	398,000	391,000
1940	30,547,000	931,000	915,000	176,000	328,000	307,000
1950	23,048,000	783,000	740,000	136,000	254,000	254,000
1960	15,635,000	755,000	671,000	123,000	220,000	228,000
1970	9,712,000	565,000	502,000	94,000	161,000	178,000
1977	7,800,000	—	—	—	—	—

[1]Historical Statistics of the United States from Colonial Times to 1970, Series K 1-16, U.S. Department of Commerce, Washington (1972), pp. 457-459; 1977 Handbook of Agricultural Charts, Agricultural Handbook No. 524, U.S. Department of Agriculture, Washington (November, 1977), p. 31.

TABLE II

Number of Farms and Average Size of Farms in the United States and Selected States[1]

Year	National	Iowa	Minnesota	Montana	North Dakota	South Dakota
			NUMBER			
1900	5,740,000	229,000	155,000	13,000	45,000	53,000
1910	6,366,000	217,000	156,000	26,000	74,000	78,000
1920	6,454,000	213,000	178,000	58,000	78,000	75,000
1930	6,295,000	215,000	185,000	47,000	78,000	83,000
1940	6,102,000	213,000	197,000	42,000	74,000	72,000
1950	5,388,000	203,000	179,000	35,000	65,000	66,000
1960	3,962,000	175,000	146,000	29,000	55,000	56,000
1970	2,954,000	140,000	111,000	25,000	46,000	46,000
1974	2,752,080	131,000	110,000	23,300	40,000	42,000
			AVERAGE SIZE (IN ACRES)			
1900	147	151	170	866	343	362
1910	139	156	177	517	382	335
1920	149	157	169	608	466	464
1930	157	158	167	940	496	439
1940	175	160	165	1,111	513	545
1950	216	169	184	1,689	630	674
1960	297	194	211	2,213	755	805
1970	373	239	261	2,522	930	997
1974	393	261	262	2,678	1,040	1,083

[1]*Historical Statistics of the United States from Colonial Times to 1970*, Series K 1-16, U.S. Department of Commerce, Washington (1972), pp. 457-459; *Census of Agriculture* (1974), AG 74-P-00-001.

TABLE III

Select Data to Indicate the Productivity Increase per American Farm Worker in Relation to Use of Two Major Technological Inputs—Tractors and Primary Fertilizer[1]

Year	Tractors*	Tractor Horsepower*	Tons of Nitrogen Phosphate Potash*	Total Hours All Farmwork*	Per Cent of Farm Labor in Nation's Labor Force	Agricultural Exports as Per Cent of Total Exports**	Acres Produced for Exports*	Persons Supplied per Farm Worker
1900	—	—	—	—	38.0	58	—	6.9
1910	1	—	856	22,547	31.0	45	37,000	7.1
1920	246	10,000	1,145	23,995	27.0	42	60,000	8.3
1930	920	25,000	1,526	22,921	21.0	32	39,000	9.8
1940	1,567	42,000	1,766	20,472	18.0	22	8,000	10.7
1950	3,394	93,000	4,058	15,137	12.0	22	50,000	15.5
1960	4,688	153,000	7,463	9,795	8.0	23	64,000	25.8
1970	4,619	203,000	16,068	5,981	4.6	21	72,000	54.0
1975	4,263	222,000	17,571	5,283	3.5	21	100,000	62.0

*In thousands.

**During most of the 1800's, agriculture provided over 70 per cent of the total American exports.

[1]Changes in Farm Production and Efficiency: A Special Issue Featuring Historical Series, Statistical Bulletin No. 56, Economic Research Service, U.S. Department of Agriculture (September, 1976), pp. 16, 25, 29, 31; A Chronology of American Agriculture, 1776-1976, Economic Research Service, U.S. Department of Agriculture (March, 1977); 1969 Handbook of Agricultural Charts, Agricultural Handbook No. 373, U.S. Department of Agriculture, Washington (November, 1969), p. 20; Statistical Abstract of the United States, 1977, 98th Annual Edition, U.S. Department of Commerce, Washington (September, 1977), p. 696.

TABLE IV

Production Time (in Man-Hours) per Acre and per Bushel[1]

	Corn				Wheat			
	Hours per Acre	Yield per Acre	Minutes per Bushel	Bushels per Man-Year[2]	Hours per Acre	Yield per Acre	Minutes per Bushel	Bushels per Man-Year[2]
1915-19	34.2	25.9	79.2	1,502	13.6	13.9	58.7	2,043
1945-49	19.2	36.1	31.9	3,754	5.7	16.9	20.2	5,932
1960-63	7.0	61.7	6.8	17,646	2.9	25.1	6.9	17,319
1971-74	4.8[3]	88.2	3.25	23,197	1.8	31.0[4]	3.5	20,514
Farmers Interviewed[5]	1.9	116.0	0.98	87,238	0.5	40.0	0.75	92,000

[1]Luther Tweeten and Dean Schreimer, "Economic Impact of Public Policy and Technology on Marginal Farms and the Nonfarm Rural Population," *Benefits and Burdens of Rural Development: Some Public Policy Viewpoints*, ed. Earl Heady, Iowa State University–Center for Agricultural & Economic Development, Ames (1970), p. 49.

[2]Based on acres per farm assuming a one-man operation, except in the case of the nine farmers interviewed, where the actual amount of labor was used.

[3]Charles H. Bailey, "47 Seconds per Bushel of Corn," *Farm Quarterly*, Vol. 26 (November–December, 1971), pp. 46-47; "Here's 50 Bushel a Minute Corn Handling," *Successful Farming*, Vol. 70, No. 11 (October, 1972), pp. 40-41.

[4]1977 *Handbook of Agricultural Charts*, Agricultural Handbook No. 524, U.S. Department of Agriculture, Washington (November, 1977), p. 86.

[5]Four corn farmers interviewed specifically for this data were David Garst, Virgil Mellies, Frank Seitzinger, and Carroll Wilson. Five wheat farmers interviewed specifically for this data were Les Curnow, Milton Hertz, Allan Kolstad, David Miller, and the Torske brothers.

TABLE V*

Economy of Size Based on a Study of 1,200 Farms
in New York State During 1906-1910[1]

Acres Farmed	Avg. Acres per Farm	Tillable Acres	Avg. Labor Income per Farm	Acres per $100 Labor	Acres per Horse	Machinery Investment per Acre
0-30	21	18	$ 111	5	15	$7.05
31-60	46	37	275	—	21	6.37
61-100	81	62	405	18	30	5.26
101-150	125	96	514	—	37	4.12
151-200	176	129	785	26	41	4.04
Over 200	283	200	1,014	30	41	3.13

*This table demonstrates the economical advantage of the larger-than-average farm in the day of animal power. The national average-size farm in 1910 was 138 acres.
[1]G. F. Warren, Farm Management, New York (1913), pp. 243, 256, 259.

TABLE VI

Significant Facts on the Farm Operations of the 134 Farmers Interviewed from Whom All Enterprise Data Was Requested*

72.6 per cent of all land farmed was owned.

40 per cent of all land farmed or ranched by Montanans was rented.

5.9 per cent of all land farmed or ranched by South Dakotans was rented.

57.2 per cent of all land in farms was in crop or summer fallow.

88.8 per cent of all farmers had one or more major non-farm enterprises whereby they did business with the public.

11.26 tractors per farm averaging 94.82 H.P. per tractor and 1,067.7 H.P. per farm.**

938 acres per tractor and 9.9 acres per H.P.

537 crop acres per tractor and 5.66 crop acres per H.P.

Iowa farmers averaged 2.9 crop acres per H.P. Montana farmers had 10 crop and fallow acres per H.P. Montana had 1,083 crop and fallow acres per tractor. Iowa had 218 acres per tractor.

8.85 full-time workers per farm, including family members.

1,149 acres per full-time worker.

657 crop acres per full-time worker.

8.78 part-time workers per farm, whose combined total time was equal to 2.19 man-years.

907.2 total acres per man-year.

518.9 crop and fallow acres per man-year.

233.87 crop acres per man-year in Iowa.

1,422.47 crop/fallow acres per man-year in Montana.

76.1 per cent of all farms had extensive livestock, poultry, or labor-intense crop operations (sugar beets, potatoes, or specialty crops associated with seed production and processing).

75.4 per cent of all farms had at least two major farm enterprises; the others relied exclusively on cash grain, livestock, or poultry for their farm income.

*A total of 224 individuals were interviewed.
**At the time of interview 65 per cent of all farms had four-wheel-drive or track-type tractors. By 1977 only 2 per cent did not have such equipment, but 70 per cent had two or more four-wheel-drive tractors.

TABLE VII

Optimum Size Farms for Corn and Wheat (in Acres)[1]

	Optimum Size Farms (U.S.D.A. Studies)				Actual Average Size Farm	Suggested Minimum and Actual Size Enterprise for Farmers in This Study (Interviewed 1968-74)	
	1915-19	1945-49	1960-63	1973	1973	Suggested Minimum	Actual Average Production
Corn	58	104	286	800	263	972	1,646
Wheat	147	351	690	1,950	694	3,097	4,613

[1]Luther Tweeten and Dean Schreirner, "Economic Impact of Public Policy and Technology on Marginal Farms and the Nonfarm Rural Population," *Benefits and Burdens of Rural Development: Some Public Policy Viewpoints*, ed. Earl Heady, Iowa State University–Center for Agricultural & Economic Development, Ames (1970), p. 45; "Big Farm Study," U.S. Department of Agriculture, Washington (1973); interviews previously cited for 1968-74 by the author.

TABLE VIII

Expenses per Acre and Production per Man, Iowa, 1969, by Size of Farm[1]

	Acres per Farm				
	160	240	320	440	640
	EXPENSES PER ACRE				
Machinery, Power, Fuel	$ 38	$ 31	$27	$25	$21
Taxes, Ins. on Bldgs.	19	15	14	13	12
Crop Expenses	18	15	15	15	16
Hired Labor	3	3	3	4	5
Other	7	4	4	3	3
Total	$ 85	$ 68	$63	$60	$57
Non-real Estate Capital @ 8%	12	10	9	9	8
Operator and Family Labor	39	27	20	15	10
Total Expenses per Acre	$136	$105	$92	$84	$75
Machinery Investment Charge	$ 53	$ 41	$38	$35	$31
	PRODUCTION PER MAN				
Livestock Income over Feed Cost	$10,773	$12,746	$13,541	$13,905	$13,485
Crop Production	11,077	14,278	18,750	21,836	26,952
Other Income	1,112	1,189	1,320	1,845	1,743
Gross Income per Man	$22,962	$28,213	$33,611	$37,586	$42,180
Total Labor-Months per Farm	13.5	14.0	15.1	17.4	23.8

[1]H. B. Howell, *Changes in Iowa's Agricultural Present and Future—Recent Trends*, FM 1602, Iowa State University, Ames (November, 1970), p. 6.

TABLE IX

Comparative Costs of Midwestern Corn Farms[*][1]

	Acres per Farm			
	500	1,000	2,000	5,000
Machinery Investment per Acre at Full List	$90.37	$81.99	$73.12	$68.95
Actual Purchase Price of Machinery per Acre	87.12	74.65	62.66	56.74
Annual Machinery Cost per Acre	13.07	11.20	9.40	8.51
Horsepower per Farm	135	300	525	1,295
Cash Costs per Acre	$42.63	$39.55	$36.55	$34.13
Machinery Depreciation	13.07	11.20	9.40	8.51
Labor	6.37	6.82	7.73	8.19
Management	5.00	6.00	6.00	7.00
Operating Cost per Acre	$67.07	$63.57	$59.68	$57.83
Savings in Operating Cost per Acre over the 500-Acre Farm	-0-	3.50	7.39	9.24
Income Tax Cost @ 60% Equity*	$2,170	$5,728	$22,626	$82,684
Net Return 1969-70 on 60% Equity After Income Taxes	5%	5.9%	5.6%	6.1%

*According to Leonard Kyle, the greatest single disadvantage of the large-scale corn operation appears in the federal income tax cost.

[1]Kenneth R. Krause and Leonard R. Kyle, *Midwestern Corn Farms: Economic Status and the Potential for Large and Family-sized Units*, U.S. Department of Agriculture, Agricultural Economic Report No. 216, Washington (1971), pp. 19-26.

TABLE X

Index Number of Per-Capita Food from Domestic Agricultural Production, Western Europe, 1957-1974[1]

(1961-1967 = 100)

Year	Index No.	Year	Index No.	Year	Index No.
1957	88	1963	100	1969	110
1958	90	1964	100	1970	111
1959	91	1965	100	1971	115
1960	96	1966	101	1972	112
1961	95	1967	107	1973	117
1962	100	1968	111	1974	121

[1]*Statistical Yearbook*, United Nations Food and Agricultural Organization, for each year.

TABLE XI

Trends in European Agriculture[1]

	Year	Austria	Denmark	England	France	Germany	Holland	Spain	Sweden
Farms	1945	450,000	208,000	—	—	1,646,751	220,532	—	296,227
	1955	405,560	201,000	420,000	2,286,000	1,251,000	260,000*	—	262,000
	1970	367,702	176,400	210,000	1,552,200	895,400	185,000*	2,558,814	168,000
	1975	201,790	127,000	160,000	1,335,355[2]	781,600	140,000*	—	132,000[3]
Full-Time Workers on Farms	1945	1,422,802	385,000	1,257,649	7,484,000	5,580,000	747,000	4,981,000	733,000
	1955	797,000	260,000	520,000	4,500,000	4,350,000	600,000	4,900,000	541,000
	1970	462,000	160,000	390,000	2,780,000	1,775,000	340,000	3,052,000	240,000
	1975	251,090	130,000	236,000	2,256,000	1,495,000	220,000	—	—[4]
Average Size of Farms, in Hectares**[5]	1945	17	14	—	—	6.9	8	—	12
	1955	19	15	27	14	7.5	9	—	13
	1970	21	21	55	20	10.0	11	17.8	20
	1975	23	23	65[6]	24[7]	14.0	15[8]	—	23[9]
Tractors	1945	5,000	3,215	200,000***	37,000	75,142[10]	8,000	—	22,000
	1955	96,000	50,100	420,788	268,216	383,852	44,500	22,443	18,423
	1970	248,980	175,000	444,400	1,309,900	1,370,000	156,100	259,819	181,519
	1975	284,000	185,000	485,000	1,350,000	1,430,000	176,000	370,554	183,000

*Includes part-time.
**1 hectare equals 2.47 acres.
***Estimated.

Numbered Footnotes for Table XI

[1]E.E.C.—In 1967 over 80 per cent of all farms in all E.E.C. countries were less than 10 hectares. Since that date governments have taken a positive position of reducing farm numbers to increase size, decrease labor needs, and increase total production. The Dutch director general of agriculture, speaking as a member of the E.E.C. Council, stated that as many as 89 per cent of the farmers in one country would have to be removed from farming. Data in this table are taken from agricultural statistical documents provided by the agricultural information services of the respective countries or by their embassies in the United States.

[2]France—Since the government program of forcing farm consolidation was started in 1964, over 503,000 small farmers have been pensioned and their farms merged into larger units. This number is exclusive of a large number of cooperative ventures in which farmers are joining their enterprises in an effort to use large-scale equipment. Up to 10 farmers are permitted to merge into such joint farming ventures.

[3]Sweden—There are more than 180,000 farms in the country, but only 132,000 over 2 hectares. Only 43,000 are over 20 hectares and can be called commercial units.

[4]Sweden probably suffers more from extreme labor cost than any other nation listed in this study. A large portion of the agricultural labor force is involved in forestry.

[5]All forms of livestock and poultry units are increasing in size and reducing in numbers as fast as, or faster than, land units. This is done to gain economy of scale as well as to take advantage of mechanization and technology available to larger units.

[6]England—The full-time units average 101 hectares. The figure of 65 hectares includes all 160,000 farms. "In 1965 the [British] government announced a selective expansion programme for agriculture and called on the industry to make two main contributions to faster economic growth; First to increase production to meet the major part of the growth in demand for temperate food stuffs . . . and thus ease the pressure on the country's import bill; secondly, to continue releasing substantial manpower resources to other sectors of the economy." (*Agriculture in Britain*, issued by Reference Division, British Information Services, London [April, 1967], p. 18).

[7]France—The government's position since 1967 has been that a family unit should be at least 50 hectares. This is double the current average-sized farm.

[8]Holland—Labor in agriculture is to be reduced to 4 per cent of the total by 1980. It is projected that farm numbers will be reduced in half from 1970 to 1990. In 1970 half of all farmers were over 55 years of age. They will not be replaced. Dr. E. W. Hofstee, world-renowned Dutch sociologist, indicates that, except for horticulture and livestock, Dutch farms will have to become at least 150 hectares. According to Dr. F. Coolman, Director of the Institute of Agricultural Engineering and Rationalization, farmers will need at least 50 hectares per employee. Over 50 per cent of cereals, potatoes, and beets are contract harvested.

[9]Sweden—Farms over 50 hectares are increasing at over 5 per cent per year.

[10]Figure is for 1949, the earliest reliable postwar data.

TABLE XII

Index Number of Agricultural Production[1]

Year	Austria[2]	Denmark	France	Germany[3]	Netherlands	Spain	Sweden	United Kingdom
1934-38 = 100								
1946	80	94	83	65	88	88	103	113
1947	71	75	74	62	85	84	103	104
1948	80	99	91	84	101	82	106	122
1950	97	126	111	105	121	87	112	127
1951	92	122	104	112	125	108	110	128
1952	101	129	110	113	129	102	113	130
1953	108	135	117	119	127	98	114	135
1954	105	134	125	119	136	102	112	137
1955	115	132	126	118	137	97	103	130
1952-57 = 100								
1956	108	102	101	102	98	102	101	108
1957	110	110	103	105	105	109	100	108
1958	121	112	104	111	114	110	98	102
1959	113	115	109	107	115	118	95	108
1960	123	116	125	121	123	118	99	116
1961	127	125	123	112	125	120	101	120

(Continued)

TABLE XII (Continued)

Index Number of Agricultural Production[1]

Year	Austria[2]	Denmark	France	Germany[3]	Nether-lands	Spain	Sweden	United Kingdom
1963 = 100								
1962	94	107	102	96	106	87	106	99
1963	100	100	100	100	100	100	100	100
1964	99	104	101	99	100	90	107	105
1965	89	104	108	92	97	90	105	107
1966	96	103	104	99	101	100	98	110
1967	104	103	114	105	109	103	112	113
1968	104	109	121	111	110	107	114	109
1969	108	102	116	109	112	109	98	110
1970	110	94	116	116	129	125	104	116
1971	112	98	121	121	138	129	106	120
1972	109	96	122	115	133	132	108	121
1973	114	99	129	119	140	142	102	124
1974	121	108	131	122	148	152	124	131

[1]*Statistical Yearbook*, United Nations Food and Agricultural Organization, for each year.

[2]Mechanization has produced some dramatic increases in labor capacity and real wages to Austrian workers. At Abbey Seitenstetten, near Ashbach, 100 workers in 1950 received the same wages as 12 did in 1971, but the total production of the 12 workers in 1971 was three times more than that of 1950, according to the farm manager when interviewed May 16, 1971.

[3]In 1950, a labor unit in Germany could produce 8.76 units of grain. In 1974, that labor unit could produce 47.93 units of grain, as reported in *The Federal Republic of Germany Portrait of a Modern Agriculture*, German Information Service, Bonn (1975), p. 4.

North American Bibliography

Articles and Books

Bailey, Liberty H. *The Harvest of the Year to the Tiller of the Soil.* New York, Macmillan, 1927.

Butterfield, Kenyon Leech. *The Farmer and the New Day.* New York, Macmillan, 1919.

Drache, Hiram M. *Beyond the Furrow: Some Keys to Successful Farming in the Twentieth Century.* Danville, Illinois: The Interstate Printers & Publishers, Inc., 1976.

Ducoff, Louis J. "Occupations and Levels of Living." *Yearbook of Agriculture, 1963: A Place to Live.* ed. Alfred Stefferud. Washington, D.C.: U.S. Department of Agriculture, 1963, 19–25.

Genung, A. B. *A Brief Survey of 35 Years of Government Aid to Agriculture Beginning in 1920.* Northeast Farm Foundation, Ithaca, New York: Cornell University Press, 1960.

Hamilton, Carl. *In No Time at All.* Ames: Iowa State University Press, 1974.

Hansmeier, Henry F. *This Is My Life.* Webster, South Dakota: Reporter and Farmer Co., 1959.

Hecht, Reuben W., and Eugene G. McKibben. "Efficiency of Labor." *Yearbook of Agriculture, 1960: Power to Produce.* ed. Alfred Stefferud. Washington, D.C.: U.S. Department of Agriculture, 1960, 317–326.

Hicks, Sir John R. *A Theory of Economic History.* London: Oxford University Press, 1969.

Higbee, Edward. *Farms and Farmers in an Urban Age.* New York: The Twentieth Century Fund, 1963.

Schapsmeier, Edward L. and Frederick H. *Ezra Taft Benson and the Politics of Agriculture: The Eisenhower Years, 1953–1961.* Danville, Illinois: The Interstate Printers & Publishers, Inc., 1975.

Schultze, Charles L. *The Distribution of Farm Subsidies: Who Gets the Benefits?* Washington, D.C.: The Brookings Institution, 1971.

Warren, G. F. *Farm Management.* New York, Macmillan, 1913.

281

Public Documents

Changes in Farm Production and Efficiency. A special issue featuring historical series. Economic Research Service Statistical Bulletin No. 561. U.S. Department of Agriculture, Washington, D.C., September, 1976.

Congressional Record. CXVIII, No. 101, June 21, 1972, H-5905 and H-5910.

"The Daylighters." *Agricultural Situation.* U.S. Department of Agriculture, Washington, D.C., LVII, No. 6, July, 1973.

"Efficiency Winner: The One Man Farm." *Agricultural Situation.* U.S. Department of Agriculture, Washington, D.C., LXXIV, No. 58, March, 1974.

"Farmers' Efficiency: The Sky's No Limit." *Agricultural Situation.* U.S. Department of Agriculture, Washington, D.C., LVI, No. 8, September, 1972.

"Farm Subsidies." *Congressional Record.* House. March 29, 1973, H-2265. Extension of remarks, May 3, 1973, E-2832 to E-2870.

Hopkins, John A. "Changing Technology and Employment in Agriculture." Bureau of Agricultural Economics, U.S. Department of Agriculture, Washington, D.C., May, 1941, 1–182.

Jennings, R. D. "Large-Scale Farming in the United States, 1929." *Fifteenth Census of the United States: 1930 Census of Agriculture.* Bureau of the Census, U.S. Department of Commerce, Washington, D.C.

Krause, Kenneth R., and Leonard R. Kyle. *Midwestern Corn Farms: Economic Status and Potential for Large- and Family-Sized Units.* Agricultural Economic Report No. 216. U.S. Department of Agriculture, Washington, D.C., III, 1971.

Nikolitch, Radoje. "Our 100,000 Biggest Farms: Their Relative Position in American Agriculture." Agricultural Economic Report No. 49. U.S. Department of Agriculture, Washington, D.C., February, 1964.

———. "Our 31,000 Largest Farms." Agricultural Economic Report No. 175. U.S. Department of Agriculture, Washington, D.C., March, 1970.

1977 Handbook of Agricultural Charts. Agricultural Handbook No. 524. U.S. Department of Agriculture, Washington, D.C., November, 1977.

"Prices Received by Farmers, Parity Index and Parity Ratio, 1910–1970." *1970 Handbook of Agricultural Charts.* U.S. Department of Agriculture, Washington, D.C., September, 1970.

Truesdell, Leon E. "Farm Population in the United States." *Census Monographs.* VI. Bureau of the Census, U.S. Department of Commerce, Washington, D.C., 1926.

United States Census of Agriculture, "Economic Class of Farm," A3, II. Bureau of the Census, U.S. Department of Commerce, Washington, D.C., 1200.

Unpublished Material

Berry, Russell L. "Economies of Size of Farm Plants and Firms." Manuscript. South Dakota Agricultural Experiment Station, Brookings, December 28, 1970.

_____. "Factory Farms in the Corn Belt: Are They Feasible Today?" Manuscript. South Dakota State University, Brookings, December 16, 1970.

_____. "Family Farms: Will They Be Replaced by Large-Scale or Factory Farms?" Manuscript. South Dakota State University, Brookings, October 2, 1970. Dr. Berry's articles also appeared in *The Dakota Farmer* and *The Farmer*, St. Paul, Minnesota.

Collins, W. C. "Farming in the Future." An address by the economic research manager, Massey–Ferguson, Inc. Given at Jefferson, Iowa, January 26, 1974.

Finch, Lindley. "Structural Changes in the Agricultural Society." An address delivered to a seminar on Feeding The World's Hungry, A Challenge to Business. No date.

_____.Letter to author, August 16, 1974.

Peterson, Leslie W. An address to the Minnesota Bankers' Association Lending Conference, April 17, Minneapolis, 1974.

Riveland, Clara B. "An Analysis of the National Farmers Organization's Attempt to Reduce Rhetorical Distance." Ph.D. thesis. University of Minnesota, St. Paul, 1974.

Schapsmeier, Edward L. Letter to author, May 25, 1974.

Bulletins, Newspapers, and Periodicals

Atherton, Lewis E. "The Midwestern Country Town—Myth and Reality." *Agricultural History*. XXVI, No. 3, July, 1952.

Baccus, Jim. "Elevators Buying, Leasing Railroad Cars and Trucks." *The Farmers Forum* (Fargo-Moorhead). June 7, 1974.

Bachman, Kenneth L. "Changes in Scale in Commercial Farming and Their Implications." *Journal of Farm Economics*. XXIV, No. 2, May, 1952.

Bailey, Liberty H. "Can I Make a Farm Pay? Yes, If You Like It." *World's Work*. I, No. 5, March, 1901.

Ball, A. Gordon. "How Much Do Farmers Want to Expand?" *Iowa Farm Science*. XXV, No. 3, November–December, 1970, 3-687 to 4-688.

Bentley, Terry L. "Most South Dakota Land Sales Made for Expansion." *The Dakota Farmer*. XCII, No. 13, December, 1972.

Benton, A. H., Andrew Boss, and W. L. Cavert. "A Farm Management Study in Southeastern Minnesota: Factors Influencing Profits." University of Minnesota Agricultural Experiment Station Bulletin No. 172. October, 1917.

Berry, Russell L. "Higher Prices Not Enough." *The Farmer*. LXXXIX, No. 12, June 5, 1971.

Bird, John. "Farewell to Farmer Tuttle." *The Saturday Evening Post*. CCXXXVIII, No. 4, December 4, 1965.

"Birth to Beef Steak." *Gold Label News Nuggets*. XI, No. 5, May, 1974.

Black, Roe C. "Why You Need to Care About Exports." *Top Op*. IV, No. 5, May, 1972, 42.

The Britton (S.D.) Journal. May 10, 1972.

"Can Your Kind of Farming Survive?" *Big Farmer*. XLIV, No. 5, August, 1972.

Christenson, Alice M. "Agricultural Pressure and Governmental Response in the United States, 1919–1929." *Agricultural History*. XI, No. 1, January, 1937.

"A Chronology of American Agriculture, 1790–1965." Economic Research Service, U.S. Department of Agriculture, Washington, D.C., 1966. A chart.

"A Chronology of American Agriculture, 1776–1976." Economic Research Service, U.S. Department of Agriculture, Washington, D.C., 1976.

"Computer Record Keeping." *The Dakota Farmer*. XCIII, No. 9, August, 1973.

Dahl, Reynold, and Maggi Liu. "How Minnesota Farmers Market Their Grain." *Minnesota Agricultural Economist*. No. 549, September, 1973.

Dahl, Reynold, and Michael Martin. "Multiple-Car Rail Rates—Their Impact on Grain Transport." *Minnesota Agricultural Economist*. No. 563, January, 1975.

Dovre, Paul. "The Non-Partisan League: An Expression of Agrarian Protest." *Discourse*. VIII, No. 4, Autumn, 1965.

"Everybody's Farm." *Gopher State Review*. Minnesota Crop and Livestock Reporting Service Bulletin No. 318. May, 1974.

Fargo Forum. May 15, 1973; February 2, 1974; August 16, 1974; May 9, 1975.

"The Farmer and His Farm." *Gopher State Review*. Minnesota Crop and Livestock Reporting Service, Bulletin No. 331. June, 1975.

"Farm Living Expenditures Averages Nearly $11,000 in 1973." *Gopher State Review*. Minnesota Crop and Livestock Reporting Service Bulletin No. 330. May, 1975.

"Farm Suppliers: A Mighty Link in the Marketing Chain." *Gopher State Review*. Minnesota Crop and Livestock Reporting Service Bulletin No. 316. March, 1974.

"Financial Development in 1971." *Gopher State Review*. Minnesota Crop and Livestock Reporting Service Bulletin No. 292. March, 1972.

Findley, Paul. "The Fork in the Road." *National Livestock Producer*. XXXVII, July, 1966.

"Formula for World Famine." *U.S. News & World Report*. LXXVI, January 28, 1974, 52.

Gopher State Review. Minnesota Crop and Livestock Reporting Service Bulletin No. 308. July, 1973.

Gopher State Review. Minnesota Crop and Livestock Reporting Service Bulletin No. 322. September, 1974.

Gopher State Review. Minnesota Crop and Livestock Reporting Service Bulletin No. 329. April, 1975.

"Grain Elevator Costs Climb." *Gopher State Review.* Minnesota Crop and Livestock Reporting Service Bulletin No. 318. May, 1974.

Hayami, Yyjiro, and Vernon W. Ruttan. "Agricultural Productivity Differences Among Countries." *The American Economic Review.* XL, No. 5, December, 1970, 895–980.

_____."Factor Prices and Technical Change in Agricultural Development: The United States and Japan, 1880–1960." *The Journal of Political Economy.* LXXVIII, No. 5, September–October, 1970, 1120–1128.

_____."An International Comparison." Technical Bulletin No. 227. University of Minnesota, St. Paul, 1971.

_____."Resources, Technology and Agricultural Development: An International Perspective." Department of Agricultural Economics, University of Minnesota, St. Paul, January, 1970.

Hoffer, Charles R., and Dale Stangeland. "Farmers' Reactions to New Practices: Corn Growing in Michigan." *Michigan State University Agricultural Experiment Station Technical Bulletin* No. 264. February, 1958.

Houck, James P. "Can We Cure Farm Poverty with Commercial Farm Poverty?" *Minnesota Agricultural Economist.* No. 532, July, 1970.

Howell, H. B. "Present and Future: Changes in Agriculture." *Iowa Farm Science.* XXV, No. 4, January, 1971.

Huheey, Thomas. "To Begin With." *The Farm Quarterly.* XXVII, No. 3, March, 1972.

International Conference on Mechanized Dryland Farming. eds. W. C. Burrows, R. E. Reynolds, F. C. Strickler, and G. E. Van Riper. Deere & Co., Moline, Illinois, 1970.

Johnson, Harold. "Meet Modern Sweden's Average Farmer." *The Farmer.* LXXXIV, No. 17, September 3, 1966.

Johnson, Jerome E. "The 1973 Farmland Market." *North Dakota Farm Research Bulletin.* North Dakota Agricultural Experiment Station, Fargo, XXXI, No. 4, March–April, 1974.

Just, Myron. "The Land Price Spiral . . . What's Behind It? What's Ahead?" *The Dakota Farmer.* LXXXVIII, No. 1, January 6, 1968.

Kyle, Leonard R. "The Economics of Large-Scale Crop Farming." Staff paper P70-7. Michigan State University, East Lansing, May, 1970.

_____."5,000-Acre Farms in the Corn Belt." *Successful Farming.* LXVIII, No. 8, August, 1970.

_____."Size Is No Limit." *The Farm Quarterly.* XXV, Spring/Planning, 1970.

"A Letter Written by Horace Goodhue, Jr." *North Dakota History.* XVII, No. 1, January, 1950.

Lindsay, Quentin W. "The Problem of Periodic Reorganization in American Agriculture." *Journal of Agricultural Economics.* XIV, May, 1961.

Malin, James C. "Mobility and History: Reflections on the Agricultural Policies of the United States in Relation to a Mechanical World." *Agricultural History.* XVII, No. 4, October, 1943.

"Market Style of the Future." *Big Farmer Cattle Guide.* II, No. 8, September, 1972, 12–13.

McElveen, Jackson W. "Farm Numbers, Farm Size, and Farm Income." *Journal of Agricultural Economics.* XLV, February, 1963.

Methvin, Eugene H. "Time to Say No to Big Farm Subsidies." *Reader's Digest.* XCVI, No. 577, May, 1970.

"Milt Hertz Wants to Do Better Than His Dad." *The Bismarck Tribune.* April 19, 1969.

Moraczewski, Bob. "How to Turn Yourself On." *The Farmer.* LXXXIX, No. 22, November 20, 1971.

―――."Roy Keppy—A Study in Motivation." *The Farmer.* LXXXIX, No. 20, October 16, 1971.

―――."She Is More Than a Wife." *The Farmer.* LXXXIX, No. 22, November 20, 1971.

Nalewaja, John D. "The Energy Requirements of Various Weed Control Practices." Proceedings of the North-Central Weed Control Conference. North Dakota Agricultural Experiment Station, Fargo, XXIX, 1974.

Parish, Ross. "Innovation and Enterprise in Wheat Farming." *Review of Marketing and Agricultural Economics.* XXII, 1954.

"Pasture and Chaff Help Hertz Produce More Beef." *Successful Farming.* LXXI, No. 6, April, 1973.

Pond, G. A., S. A. Eugene, T. R. Nodland, S. O. Berg, and C. W. Crickman. *The First Sixty Years of Farm Management Research in Minnesota 1902–1962.* Report No. 283, Department of Agricultural Economics, University of Minnesota, St. Paul, 1963.

Raup, Philip M. "The Minnesota Rural Real Estate Market in 1973." *Minnesota Agricultural Economist.* No. 555, May, 1974.

Reuss, Carl F. "Economic Problems of Rural America." A report of the Commission on Research and Social Action of the American Lutheran Church. March 15, 1970.

Schaffner, L. W., and Richard Arntson. "North Dakota Farm Labor Projections 1975 . . . 1980 . . . 1985 . . ." North Dakota Agricultural Experiment Station Bulletin Reprint No. 720. *Farm Research.* XXVIII, No. 3, January–February, 1971.

Schmidt, Louis B. "The Agricultural Revolution in the Prairies and Great Plains of the United States." *Agricultural History.* VIII, No. 8, October, 1934, 182–196.

Seim, Dick. "They Bought a Local Elevator." *Farm Journal.* XCVI, No. 6, June, 1972, 22A–B.

"Sound Off Survey Results." *The Dakota Farmer.* XCII, No. 5, May, 1972, 10–11.

Taeuber, Conrad. "Rural-Urban Migration." *Agricultural History.* XV, No. 3, July, 1951.

"Time for Frankness." *Country Guide, The Farm Magazine* (Winnipeg, Manitoba, Canada). XCII, No. 2.

"U.S. Farm Products Exports to Reach $21 Billion." Minnesota Crop and Livestock Reporting Service Bulletin No. 319. June, 1974.

U.S. News & World Report. LXX, No. 5, July 31, 1972, 81.

"What's New in Washington." *Successful Farming.* LXV, No. 7, May, 1967, 7.

"Who Says Cows Can't Fly?" *The Dakota Farmer.* XCIII, No. 5, 1973, 51.

Personal Interviews

Allen, Merle S. Moorhead, Minnesota, July 9, 1974. Served as consultant.

Anderson, Dennis L. Rapid City, South Dakota, April 9, 1972.

Asmussen, Stanley. Agar, South Dakota, April 13, 1972.

Bleecker, Richard C. Lisbon, North Dakota, February 11, 1972.

Bogestad, John. Karlstad, Minnesota, February 26, 1972; March 22, 1972.

Boler, Gerald. Truman, Minnesota, March 29, 1972.

Bones, Walter J., Jr. Parker, South Dakota, February 24, 1972.

Bourgois, Ervin. Bismarck, North Dakota, March 10, 1972.

Bresnahan, Ellery. Casselton, North Dakota, December 28, 1969; June 21, 1973.

Buer, Martin. Atwater, Minnesota, April 1, 1972.

Burbidge, Arden. Park River, North Dakota, January 3, 1970; March 14, 1973.

Butts, Alan. Carrington, North Dakota, March 7, 1972.

Butts, Lloyd. Carrington, North Dakota, March 7, 1972.

Cannon, Charles A. Pierre, South Dakota, March 5, 1973; May 5, 1973.

Carlson, Clarence. Argyle, Minnesota, February 20, 1971; February 18, 1972.

Carlson, David. Argyle, Minnesota, February 18, 1972.

Carlson, Lauren. Chokio, Minnesota, June 17, 1975.

Carlson, Ron. Argyle, Minnesota, February 18, 1972.

Christianson, Earl. Elbow Lake, Minnesota, February 26, 1973; February 12, 1975.

Chrystal, John. Coon Rapids, Iowa, June 13, 1972.

Cox, Robert L. Baker, Montana, May 18, 1972.

Crockett, R. C. Pelican Rapids, Minnesota, February 17, 1971.

Dahl, Jack. Gackle, North Dakota, February 10, 1973.

Dalrymple, John S. III. Casselton, North Dakota, March 7, 1973.

Dann, Harvey. Winnipeg, Manitoba, February 16, 1973.

Davison, Earl. Tintah, Minnesota, December 8, 1970.

Dean, John S. Hatton, North Dakota, November 15, 1972.

Dilse, T. A. Scranton, North Dakota, April 8, 1972.

Docter, Dalton. Amherst, South Dakota, December 16, 1972; March 17, 1975.

Driscoll, Keith. East Grand Forks, Minnesota, January 17, 1972.

Driscoll, Ray. East Grand Forks, Minnesota, January 17, 1972.

Drum, David G. Billings, Montana, May 16, 1972; March 19, 1973; April 28, 1975.

Dullea, Ed J., Jr. Georgetown, Minnesota, January 5, 1972.

Dunn, Edward. Fargo, North Dakota, February 5, 1974.

Ehlers, Alfred. Presho, South Dakota, April 10, 1972.

Fisher, David. Hubbard, Iowa, January 26, 1974.

Flaat, Ole A. Grand Forks, North Dakota, January 18, February 15, 1972; April 18 and 19, 1974.

Garst, David. Coon Rapids, Iowa, June 12, 1972.

Garst Farm Management Staff—David Garst, Roswell Garst, Stephen Garst, John Chrystal, Bob Henah. Coon Rapids, Iowa, June 13, 1972.

Garst, Roswell. Coon Rapids, Iowa, June 14, 1972.

Garst, Stephen. Coon Rapids, Iowa, June 15, 1972.

Geritz, Jacob. Lakota, North Dakota, November 7, 1970.

Glidden, Earl. Hallock, Minnesota, January 17, 1972.

Glinz, David. Pingree, North Dakota, June 24, 1971.

Gordon, Arlo J. Murdock, Minnesota, March 15, 1972.

Gray, Donald. Carter, Montana, May 14, 1972.

Gray, George. Great Falls, Montana, May 14, 1972.

Grotberg, Richard H. Oakes, North Dakota, January 21, 1974.

Hagen, Vernon G. East Grand Forks, Minnesota, March 29 and 30, 1974.

Hall, Bill. Hoople, North Dakota, February 14, 1973.

Hall, Bjorn. Hoople, North Dakota, February 14, 1973.

Hall, Joe W. Hoople, North Dakota, February 14, 1973.

Hansmeier, Ralph H. Bristol, South Dakota, March 3, 1972.

Hartness, Donald (Tom). Gwinner, North Dakota, February 11, 1972.

Hawbaker, Charles. Plainview, Minnesota, March 2, 1973.

Hebel, Clem. Mason City, Iowa, February 21, 1972; June 4, 1975.

Hector, Ernest C. Crosby, North Dakota, April 5, 1972.

Heline, John. Pierson, Iowa, February 23, 1972.

Hempstead, P. D. Houston, Minnesota, March 28, 1972.

Henah, Bob. Coon Rapids, Iowa, June 14, 1972.

Hermanson, Pete A. Woodland Farms, Story City, Iowa, February 22, 1972.

Hertz, Milton. Mott, North Dakota, April 7, 1972.

Hofstrand, Harold. Leeds, North Dakota, December 12, 1970.

Hoggarth, Gerald. Courtenay, North Dakota, March 8, 1972.

Horn, Paul, Jr. Moorhead, Minnesota, December 23, 1969.

Howe, George C., Jr. Casselton, North Dakota, December 22, 1969.

Hvidsten, Earl. Stephen, Minnesota, January 17, 1972.

Hvidsten, Ralph. Stephen, Minnesota, January 17, 1972.
Irwin, James. Bagley, Iowa, January 26, 1974.
Jarrett, Donald. Britton, South Dakota, March 2, 1972.
Jarrett, Ray S. Britton, South Dakota, March 2, 1972; December 14–16, 1972.
Jensen, Ellis. Vermillion, South Dakota, February 24, 1972.
Jetvig, Loren C. Lake Park, Minnesota, January 14, 1972.
Johnson, Charles V. Jackson, Minnesota, March 28, 1972.
Johnson, Walter E. Courtenay, North Dakota, March 8, 1972.
Keil, Daniel. Ledger, Montana, May 12, 1972.
Keil, Edgar. Ledger, Montana, May 12, 1972.
Keil, Mrs. John. Ledger, Montana, May 12, 1972.
Keil, Stephen. Ledger, Montana, May 12, 1972.
Kenner, Alvin. Leeds, North Dakota, December 12, 1970.
Keogh, Brooks J. Keene, North Dakota, April 6, 1972.
Kinkler, Kenneth. Onida, South Dakota, April 11, 1972.
Kolstad, Allen C. Chester, Montana, May 11, 1972.
Kroeker, Donald. Winkler, Manitoba, February 15, 1973.
Kroeker, Walter. Winkler, Manitoba, February 15, 1973.
Krueger, Walter. McKenzie, North Dakota, March 10, 1972.
Kuhfuss, William. Fargo, North Dakota, July 9, 1973. At the time of the interview Mr. Kuhfuss was President of the American Farm Bureau Federation.
Lacey, Jack C. Wendell, Minnesota, April 1, 1972.
Lang, Jack. Malta, Montana, May 9, 1972.
Larimore, Jameson II. Larimore, North Dakota, December 12, 1970.
Larimore, Jameson III. Larimore, North Dakota, August 20, 1971.
Larson, Lyall P. Sargeant, Minnesota, March 26, 1972.
Lee, Herman H. Borup, Minnesota, February 17, 1971.
Link, John. Bismarck, North Dakota, October 20, 1974.
Lysfjord, Charles. Kennedy, Minnesota, January 8-11, 1972; March 14, 1973.
Mattson, Grant. Casselton, North Dakota, January 4, 1973.
Mellies, Virgil. Hector, Minnesota, March 16, 1972.
Mertens Brothers. Devils Lake, North Dakota, March 11, 1974.
Miller, Darrell. Wahpeton, North Dakota, April 20, 1972.
Miller, David. Wahpeton, North Dakota, February 12, 1973.
Moe, Skulason. Poplar, Montana, May 9, 1972.
Moore, Delbert. Forbes, North Dakota, November 20, 1974.
Moser, Roy R. Amana, Iowa, February 21, 1972.
Mutschler, Freddie. Wimbledon, North Dakota, June 24, 1971; June 13, 1975.
Myhro, Dean. Moorhead, Minnesota, January 8, 1970; June 11, 1975.
Natwick, Herman A. Ada, Minnesota, March 10, 1971; May 1, 1975.
Noy, Bill A., Jr., and Shirley. Vernon Center, Minnesota, February 28, 1973.

Nygaard, Peter A. Williston, North Dakota, April 4, 1972.

O'Day, R. S. Great Falls, Montana, May 14, 1972.

O'Farrell, Jack. Marvin, South Dakota, February 25, 1972.

Olson, Earl B. Willmar, Minnesota, April 24, 1972.

Olson, Stanley D. Fairmont, Minnesota, March 29, 1972.

Osterkamp, Earl. Pierre, South Dakota, October 19, 1972.

Petersen, Harold T. Murdock, Minnesota, March 30, 1972.

Peterson, Henry R. Moorhead, Minnesota, December 12 and 29, 1969; April 4, 1974.

Rauenhorst, George. Olivia, Minnesota, March 16, 1972; April 10, 1976.

Reimers, Robert F. Melville, North Dakota, January 6, 1970.

Rendahl, J. L. Moorhead, Minnesota, July 19, 1977.

Reque, John H. Redwood Falls, Minnesota, March 15, 1972.

Retz, Richard. Jefferson, Iowa, January 26, 1974.

Romain, Clarence. Chester, Montana, May 12, 1972.

Romain, John. Havre, Montana, March 11, 1972.

Ruttan, Vernon W. St. Paul, Minnesota, April 20, 1970; April 24, 1978.

Ryan, Gerald C. East Grand Forks, Minnesota, February 14, 1973.

Ryan, Thomas W. East Grand Forks, Minnesota, February 14, 1973.

Sabe, Oscar N. Gascoyne, North Dakota, April 8, 1972.

Schmitz, Herman A. Williston, North Dakota, April 5, 1972.

Schnell, Raymond. Dickinson, North Dakota, May 18, 1972.

Schuller, George C. Claremont, South Dakota, March 3, 1972; April 10, 1972.

Schulz, Donald A. Faribault, Minnesota, March 25, 1972.

Schwartz, Earl. Kenmare, North Dakota, April 4, 1972.

Scott, John W., Jr. Gilby, North Dakota, November 15, 1972; March 7, 1973.

Scott, John W., Sr. Gilby, North Dakota, January 3, 1970; June 16, 1971; February 10, 1973.

Seitzinger, Frank. Onawa, Iowa, June 16, 1972.

Selley, Roy. Odebolt, Iowa, February 23, 1972.

Severson, Allan M. Owatonna, Minnesota, June 20, 1974.

Shepherd, Ronald D. Baker, Montana, May 17, 1972.

Short, Don L. Beach, North Dakota, April 7, 1972.

Sinner, George. Casselton, North Dakota, December 28, 1969; June 21, 1973.

Sinner, William. Casselton, North Dakota, December 28, 1969; June 21, 1973.

Skolness, Art. Glyndon, Minnesota, February 17, 1971.

Smith, Eldon. Gettysburg, South Dakota, March 1, 1972.

Smith, Max. Nisland, South Dakota, April 10, 1972.

Snortland, Thomas (Buck). Sharon, North Dakota, January 8, 1972.

Spicher, Bill. Hingham, Montana, May 10, 1972.

Spicher, Daryl. Hingham, Montana, May 10, 1972.

Spicher, George. Hingham, Montana, May 10, 1972.

Spicher, Richard. Hingham, Montana, May 10, 1972.

Stegner, William A. Rhame, North Dakota, April 8, 1972.

Sutton, John, Jr. Agar, South Dakota, April 12, 1972.

Sutton, John, Sr. Onida, South Dakota, April 11, 1972.

Swenson, John W. Fergus Falls, Minnesota, January 11, 1970.

Swisher, Jay C. Groton, South Dakota, March 1, 1972.

Thompson, Joe. Grafton, North Dakota, March 13, 1973.

Tibert, J. Budd. Voss, North Dakota, March 13, 1973.

Torske, Eric. Hardin, Montana, May 17, 1972.

Torske, Larry. Hardin, Montana, May 17, 1972.

Triebold, Vernon. Oriska, North Dakota, February 13, 1973.

Trowbridge, Mrs. Hugh. Barnesville, Minnesota, April 19, 1967.

Underlee, C. H. Hendrum, Minnesota, January 19, 1972.

Underlee, Leslie. Hendrum, Minnesota, January 19, 1972.

Underlee, Nolan. Hendrum, Minnesota, January 19, 1972.

Velo, Eddie A. Rothsay, Minnesota, February 26, 1973.

Walton, James J. Breckenridge, Minnesota, April 20, 1972.

Warren, Floyd Darroll. Hardin, Montana, May 16, 1972.

Weckerly, Norman. Hurdsfield, North Dakota, March 8, 1972.

Whitman, Ward. Robinson, North Dakota, March 7, 1972; February 2, 1974.

Wilson, Carroll G. Faribault, Minnesota, February 20, 1972.

Wright, John W. Edmore, North Dakota, November 7, 1970.

European Bibliography

Articles and Books

Andrews, Stanley. *Agriculture and the Common Market*. Ames: Iowa State University Press, 1973.

Self, Peter, and Herbert J. Storing. *The State and the Farmer: British Agricultural Policies and Politics*. Los Angeles: University of California Press, 1963.

Tracy, Michael. *Agriculture in Western Europe*. New York: Frederick A. Praeger, 1964.

Yates, P. Lamartine. *Food, Land and Manpower in Western Europe*. New York: St. Martin's Press, 1960.

Government Publications

Agricultural Policies in Europe and North America. First Report of the Ministerial Committee for Agriculture and Food, Organization for European Economic Cooperation, Paris, May, 1956.

Agricultural Policies in Europe and North America. Second Report of the Ministerial Committee for Agriculture and Food, Organization for European Economic Cooperation, Paris, May, 1957.

Agricultural Policies in Europe and North America. Third Report of the Ministerial Committee for Agriculture and Food, Organization for European Economic Cooperation, Paris, May, 1958.

Agricultural Policies in Europe and North America. Fourth Report of the Ministerial Committee for Agriculture and Food, Organization for European Economic Cooperation, Paris, March, 1960.

Agricultural Policies in Europe and North America. Fifth Report of the Ministerial Committee for Agriculture and Food, Organization for European Economic Cooperation, Paris, July, 1961.

"L'Agriculture Francaise en Chiffres." Ministre de l'Agriculture, Paris, January, 1976.

Agriculture in Britain. British Information Services, Central Office on Information, London, 1967.

Agriculture in Denmark: Annotated Statistics 1976. Agricultural Council of Denmark, Federation of Danish Farmers' Unions, Department of Information, Copenhagen, 1977.

Agriculture in France. Service de Presse et d'Information, Ambassade de France, New York, 1977.

Agriculture in Great Britain. British Information Service, London, September, 1974.

Annual Review of Agriculture 1977. Ministry of Agriculture, Fisheries and Food, Her Majesty's Stationery Office, London, 1977.

Aspects of Dutch Agriculture. Ministry of Agriculture and Fisheries, The Hague, October, 1976.

Austria Facts and Figures. Federal Press Service, Vienna, 1976.

Balogh, Dr. A., and Dr. V. Kulcsar. *Agricultural Policy and Development of Agriculture in Hungary, 1945–1975.* Research Institute for Agricultural Economics and Institute of Economic Planning, Hungarian National Planning Office, Budapest, September, 1975.

Baron, Don. *Holland: The Miracle of Dutch Agriculture.* Ministry of Agriculture and Fisheries, The Hague, Foreign Agricultural Service, August, 1970.

Dutch Agriculture in Facts and Figures. Ministry of Agriculture and Fisheries, The Hague, October, 1975.

"Economical and Integration Problems of the Large-Scale Farming in Hungary." Bulletin No. 38. Research Institute for Agricultural Economics, Budapest, 1976.

Fact Sheets on Sweden: Agriculture in Sweden. The Swedish Institute, Stockholm, June, 1976.

The Federal Republic of Germany: Portrait of a Modern Agriculture. Federal Ministry of Food, Agriculture and Forestry, Bonn, 1975.

Food and Timber Economy—1974. Centre of Statistics and Economic Analysis, Ministry of Agriculture and Food, Budapest, 1975.

A Panorama of Spanish Agriculture. The Ministry of Agriculture, Madrid, 1975.

Propagating Stock from the Netherlands. Ministry of Agriculture and Fisheries, The Hague, 1975.

"Review of the Swedish Agricultural Policy—Summary of the Report of the Agricultural Government Commission of 1972." The Commission, Stockholm, March 24, 1977.

"Selected Agri-figures of the E.E.C." Statistics and Documentation— Ministry of Agriculture and Fisheries, The Hague, February, 1974.

Statistical Pocket Book of Hungary. Hungarian Central Statistical Office, Budapest, 1976.

Statistical Yearbook. United Nations Food and Agriculture Organization, Rome. For each year for which data was used.

Statistical Yearbook of People's Republic of Germany 1976. German Information Center, New York, 1976.

"A Survey of Agricultural France." *France Information 43.* Service (de Presse et) d'Information, Paris, April–May, 1972.

Swedish Agriculture. Swedish Agricultural Information Office and Ministry of Agriculture, Statens Lantbruks Information, Jönköping, 1976.

Unpublished Material

"Agricultural Combine, Babolna—Founded: 1789." A printed fact sheet of Babolna State Farm, Babolna, Hungary, showing production data from 1959 through 1976.

"Råbelöf Farm." A typed manuscript explaining in detail the operations of this Swedish farm.

Bulletins, Newspapers, and Periodicals

Agriculture: Some Basic Statistics. National Farmers Union (Great Britain) Information Division, Agricultural House, Knightsbridge, London, October, 1974.

Holmström, Sven. *Swedish Farming—Agriculture and Combined Agriculture/Forestry.* Agricultural Economics Research Institute, Stockholm, 1975.

"Råbelöf—Ett Modernt Jordbruk." ("Råbelöf—A Modern Farm.") *Traktor Journalen.* Stockholm, December, 1976.

Statistics on Danish Agriculture 1975. Federation of Danish Farmers' Unions, Copenhagen, November, 1975.

"Time to Move over Dad and Save Tax Too!" *British Farmer and Stockbreeder.* National Farmers Union, March 19, 1977, 22.

Wallace, Henry A. Foreword, Koochiching County (Minnesota) Agents' Report, 1933.

Personal Interviews

Ballard, Geoffrey H. Old Yates Farm, Abberley, England, March 18, 1977.

Braad, Jorgen. Hogholt, 9560 Hadsund, Denmark, March 23, 1977.

Brouwer, Ade. Abcovensedyk, Goirle, Netherlands, March 22, 1977.

Burgert, Dr. Robert. Director, Babolna State Farm, Babolna, Hungary, March 30, 1977.

Clemedtson, Henning. 29073 Trensum, Sweden. Interviewed at Moorhead Minnesota, April 6, 1978. Mr. Clemedtson farms in Sweden and in Minnesota.

Ensor, Trevor. Nuneaton, Warwickshire, England, March 17, 1977.

Fehringer, Hans. Schramelhof, Aschbach, Austria, April 2, 1977.

Fehringer, Johann. Schramelhof, Aschbach, Austria, April 2, 1977.

Happen, P. F. G. von. Waalre, North Brabant, Netherlands, March 21, 1977.

Harper, David. Holt Heath Castle, Holt Heath, Warwickshire, England, March 18, 1977.

Harper, Fred. Holt Heath Castle, Holt Heath, Warwickshire, England, March 19, 1977.

Heemskerk, Peter C. Manager, Veldhoven, North Brabant, Netherlands, March 21, 1977.

Hilmersen, Arne. Director of Engineering, Norwegian Institute of Agricultural Engineering, AS-NLH, Norway. Interviewed at Fargo, North Dakota, September 20, 1977.

Insulander, Alf. Wappa Säteri, Enköping, Sweden, March 28, 1977. Also interviewed at Fargo, North Dakota, November 29, 1976.

Insulander, K. G. Wappa Säteri, Enköping, Sweden, March 28, 1977. Also interviewed at Fargo, North Dakota, November 29, 1976.

Juncker, Flemming. Overgaard, 8970 Havandal, Denmark, March 25, 1977.

Kennedy, Douglas. Råbelöf Farm, Kristianstad, Sweden, March 26, 1977.

Kieft, Andrei F. Manager, Cohave, Vegel, Netherlands, March 22, 1977.

Kjeldsen, Otto B. Tvedevej 17-Hald, 8983 Gjerlev J., Denmark, March 24, 1977.

Latschenberger, Karl. Biberbach, Austria, April 3, 1977.

Leon, Dr. Manuel Muelle. Professional Agriculture Consultant, Loeches, Spain, April 6, 1977.

Lindegaard, Torben. Hadsund, Denmark, March 25, 1977.

Lubeck, Jens. Hadsund, Denmark, March 24, 1977.

Moeyaert, Gilbert. Lugos, 33830, Belin, France, April 4, 1977.

Moreton, Fred S. Offchurch, Burnt Heath Farm, Warwickshire, England, March 18, 1977.

Moreton, Sam. Offchurch, Burnt Heath Farm, Warwickshire, England, March 16, 1977.

Oredsson, Ingemar. Manager, Råbelöf Farm, Kristianstad, Sweden, March 26, 1977.

Roos, Curt. 24500 Staffanstorp, Sweden, March 26, 1977.

Rosenaur, Louis. Loeches, Spain, April 6, 1977.

Rylands, Jean. Irish staff member, American Embassy, Dublin, Ireland. Interviewed at Moorhead, Minnesota, May 28, 1977.

Sandor, Palfi. Manager, Foreign Trade, Babolna State Farm, Babolna, Hungary, March 28–30, 1977.

Seitenstetten, Abbey. Manager, Seitenstetten, Austria, May 16, 1971.

Shipway, G. P. Ministry of Agriculture, Woodthorne, Wolverhampton, England. Interviewed at Fargo, North Dakota, September 20, 1977.

Skriver, Kaj. Senior Agricultural Advisor of Denmark, Arhus, Denmark, March 23, 1977.

Soltesz, Jeno. Director of Nutrition, Manager of Feed Manufacturing, Babolna State Farm, Babolna, Hungary, March 28–30, 1977.

Szuror, Istvan. Director of Veterinary Medicine, Babolna State Farm, Babolna, Hungary, March 28–30, 1977.

Thielen, H. Alphensebaan 2, Gilze, Netherlands, March 21, 1977.

Vermer, Albert. Rivierduinwej 14, Swifterbant, Southeast Flevoland, Netherlands, May 6, 1970. Mr. Vermer, in addition to farming, was also National President of the Seed Potato Growers Association and National President of the Potato Chip Association.

Index

297

Feed, availability of, 55; contracted production, 58; conversion of, 235; free, 144; grains program, 209; loss of, 131; manufacturing firms, 168; pelleted, 80; processed, 59
Feeder cattle, 53-54, 198
Feeder hogs, 189
Feedlots, 38, 54, 57, 180; purchase of grain, 186; size of, 54
Fehringer, Hans, 251
Fergus Falls, Minnesota, 42, 115
Fertilizer, 71, 134; business, 175; dealerships, 60; plants, 60; pools, 170; spreading equipment for, 171
Field cultivators, capacity of, 48
Field size, 40n, 238
Fillmore, North Dakota, 17
Financial, leverage, 79, 166; losses, 82-83; policies, 243; problems, 79, 81; returns, 156ff; reverses, 156-157; rewards, 160, 164; stability, 81
Financial Limitations, 119-121
Financial Management—Another Key to Success, 79-82
Financing, 42, 107, 254; availability of, 115; burdens of, 17; need of, 42
Finch, Lindley, 42
Finley Farmers Elevator Company, 184
Fisher brothers, 59
Fisher, David, 59
Fisher, Minnesota, 14
Five *M*'s, 4-8, 233
Fixed costs, 224
Fixed prices, 207
Flaat, Ole A., 14, 37
Flame thrower, 70
Flying Farmers, 101
Food, 33, 231; abundance of, ix, 22; cost increase in, x; cost of, 4, 232; cost reduction of, x, 224, 241; deficient nations, 21; dollar, 168, 263; exchanged for oil, 21; size of industry, 168; supply of, 19, 22
Forage, 58-59
Fordson tractors, 80
Foreign markets, 192, 212, 217, 230
Foreign sales, 208, 224; of cattle, 26; of grain, 26; of potatoes, 26
Foreign trade, 27, 202, 243
Foundation seed, 82, 158-159
Four-wheel-drives, 10, 15-16, 34, 37, 38, 40, 48, 61, 89, 91, 126, 129, 130, 140, 142, 143, 147, 151, 152, 254
Four-Wheel-Drive Tractor, The, 15-16
France, 232ff; government of, 243-244

Franke, A. P., 236
Free enterprise, 87, 145; nature of, 4; risk of, 167
"Free homesteads," cost of, 17
Freeman, Orville, 102, 209
Free market, 209, 211; expresses false values, 27; unknown, 225-226; world, 22
Free stall barn, 81
Free trade, a goal, 25
Freight costs, 24, 183-184
Frontier, cost of opening, 3
Frost, 78
Fuel, 175; cost of, 174; purchase program, 175
Future Farmers of America (F.F.A.), 39

Garnaas, L. B., 9
Garst, David, 42, 77-78, 119; need for maximum production, 33
Garst, Elizabeth (Mrs. Roswell "Bob"), 13
Garst Farms, 119
Garst, Roswell "Bob," 71, 78; innovations of, 13
Garvey Elevator Company, 184
Geography affects farm size, 41, 49
Geritz, Jacob, 36, 43-44, 79
Germany, 232ff
Gilby, North Dakota, 77
Glidden, Earl, 34, 43
Glinz, David, 47, 91, 126
Glinz, Orville, 91
Goals, 109, 120, 161, 204; boyhood, 165; common, 204, 204n; of agriculture, ix
Gordon, Arlo J., 52, 120
Gordon, Arthur, 120
Government payments, 44, 207, 212-213, 215, 217, 219, 222-225, 225n
Government programs, 35, 112, 206ff, 263; abandoned, 227; advantages of, 222; Agricultural Stabilization and Conservation Service, 209, 209n, 214-216; aiding production, 208; American Agricultural Administration, 207; anti small farms, 224, 226, 227; artificial pricing, 217; benefits of, 208, 209, 211, 220, 222, 224; bins, 208, 210, 217, 225, 226; bureaucracy, 213-214, 226; cause of success, 212; cheap food, 208-212, 226; Class I farmers, 210n; consumer resistance, 207, 217, 218; corn dumping, 209;

ABOUT THE AUTHOR

Hiram M. Drache was born at Meriden, Minnesota, where, at an early age, he became acquainted with agri-business–first, by watching his father buy grain and hides, test cream, and candle eggs; then by helping in loading cattle and riding along to the stockyards or packing plant. As soon as he was old enough he worked on farms, doing every job from gathering eggs among the willows, to slopping hogs with ground oats soaked in skim milk, to eventually handling "his own" bundle team. He also milked cows and delivered milk in the community with a bicycle and "side car." He has done most jobs required of any farm worker in the horse-powered not such "good ol' days."

Dr. Drache purchased his first farm while still in college and, since then, has regularly added to his operations. Currently, at the family's home farm, the Draches are involved in an automated and confined feedlot in partnership with Ronald D. Offutt, Jr., a former student who has extensive potato operations of his own. Drache's son Paul manages the cattle-feeding business. Many articles have been written in regional and national agricultural publications about Drache's farming activities. He travels the speaking circuit throughout the United States and Canada several months each year.

This is the fourth book Drache has published on farming, in addition to contributing to three other books. He has written numerous articles for various historical or agricultural periodicals. Besides his writing, speaking, and farming he has been a Professor of History at Concordia College, Moorhead, Minnesota, since 1952.

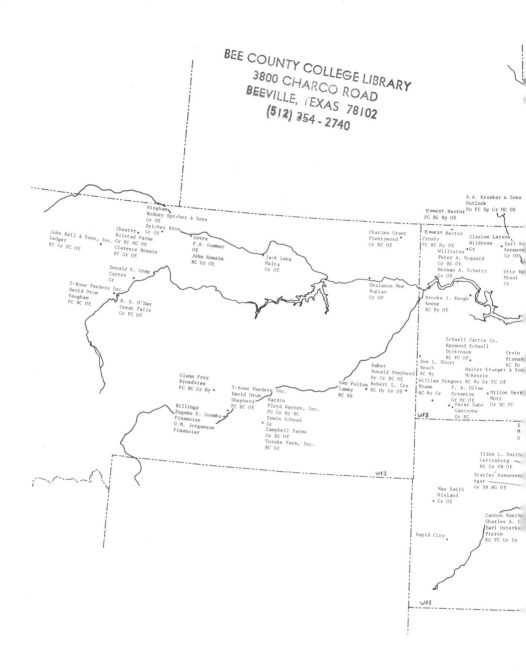

A.A. Kroeker & Sons
Outlook
Po FC Sp Gr HG OE

ERNEST Hector
FC HG Hy OE

Hingham
Rodney Spicher & Sons
Gr OE
Spicher Bros.

Chester
Kolstad Farms
Gr OE

Charles Grant
Plentywood
Gr BC OE

ERNEST Hector
Crosby
FC HG Hy OE

Clarion Larson
Wildrose
Gr

John Keil & Sons, Inc.
Ledger
BC Gr FC OE

Kolstad Farms
Gr BC HG OE
Clarence Romain
BC Gr OE

Havre
F.A. Gummer
OE
John Romain
BC Gr OE

Jack Lang
Malta
Gr OE

Earl Se
Kenmare
Gr OE

Williston
Peter A. Nygaard
Gr BC OE

Donald S. Gray
Carter
Gr

Herman A. Schmitz
Gr OE

Otto Ec
Minot
Gr

T-Bone Feeders Inc.
David Drum
Vaugham
FC BC OE

R. S. O'Day
Great Falls
Gr FC OE

Skulason Moe
Poplar
Gr OE

Brooks J. Keogh
Keene
BC Hy OE

Schnell Cattle Co.
Raymond Schnell
Dickinson
BC FC OF

Ervin
Bismar
BC Po

Don L. Short
Beach
BC Hy

Walter Krueger & Son
McKenzie

Glenn Frey
Broadview
FC BC Gr Hy

Baker
Ronald Shepherd
Hy Gr BC OE

William Stegner BC Hy Gr FC OE
Rhame

T. A. Dilse
Scranton
Gr BC OE

Milton Hert
Mott
Gr BC FC

T-Bone Feeders Inc.
David Drum
Shepherd
FC BC OE

Dan Fulton
Ismay
BC SH

Robert L. Cox
BC Hy Gr OE

BC Hy Gr

Oscar Sabe
Gascoyne
Gr BC

Billings
Eugene E. Coombs
Financier
O.M. Jorgenson
Financier

Hardin
Floyd Warren, Inc.
FC Gr Hy BC
Erwin Schnad
Gr
Campbell Farms
Gr BC OE
Torske Farm, Inc.
BC Gr

WFS

E
M
G

Eldon L. Smith
Gettysburg
HG Gr SH OE

Stanley Asmussen
Agar
Gr SH HG OE

WFS

Max Smith
Nisland
Gr OE

Cannon Ranch
Charles A. C
Earl Osterka
Pierre
BC FC Gr Co

Rapid City

WFS

IOWA, MINNESOTA, MONTANA, NORTH DAKOTA,
SOUTH DAKOTA, AND SOUTHERN CANADA